# In touch with
# GOD

# In touch with

# GOD

## Edward Heppenstall

This book is published in collaboration with
the Youth Department as an enrichment
of the Morning Watch devotional plan.
Review and Herald Publishing Association
Washington, D.C. 20012

Editor: Raymond H. Woolsey
Cover design: Helcio Deslandes

## DEDICATED TO:

My wife, Margit, a true Christian,
who for almost forty years has
inspired and challenged me by heart,
mind, and a life of self-forgetting
devotion, to keep this faith by which
we have lived together.

# HOW TO USE THIS BOOK

*My voice shalt thou hear in the morning, O Lord; in the morning will I direct my prayer unto thee, and will look up. Ps. 5:3.*

From texts such as this, and from others that tell of Jesus' early-morning devotions (e.g., Mark 1:35), many Christians have found the inspiration to begin the day with God. The Morning Watch devotional books have been designed to aid in such a practice. Differing personalities, under differing circumstances, have found different ways to use the books. We include a few suggestions here, as an encouragement to make a devotional period a regular part of your daily schedule:

1. Keep the book by your bedside, to be read first thing in the morning.

2. Place it on the breakfast table, and read to all the family when they have assembled for breakfast. The prayer following the reading can include thanks for the food.

3. Assemble the family in the living room for a short devotional period, where all can kneel in prayer. This may be upon rising, just before breakfast, or just after.

4. Let members of the family take turns reading, changing readers daily or weekly. Similarly, let them take turns in praying aloud.

5. Memorize the daily text, and repeat occasionally during the day.

6. Have the family repeat the text after you, phrase by phrase.

7. Discuss the lesson of the reading; volunteer your own thoughts on the subject.

8. Sing a short song that all know by heart, such as "Lord, in the Morning" (No. 39, *Church Hymnal).*

9. Vary the songs, perhaps using one of the popular gospel choruses.

10. Ask the family for suggestions on how to make the devotional period more meaningful.

# GOD'S ACCEPTABLE YEAR

*But as for me, my prayer is unto thee, O Lord, in an acceptable time: O God, in the multitude of thy mercy hear me, in the truth of thy salvation. Ps. 69:13.*

The first morning of the new year we meet together with God to begin life anew. The beauty of the living Christ, coming to us with gifts of faith, hope, and love, reminds us of the glory of the God we serve, the life communicated to us by Christ. Above the kingdoms of the world there rises the kingdom of Christ, with its moral and spiritual power that fills the life with sunshine and the perfumed breezes from the courts of heaven. We are called to enjoy the unsearchable and inexhaustible riches of Christ. We serve the King of kings. In us and through us He is marching to victory.

Our faith is well founded. "These all died in faith, not having received the promises, but having seen them afar off, and were persuaded of them, and embraced them, and confessed that they were strangers and pilgrims on the earth" (Heb. 11: 13). We are like travelers coming suddenly to the brow of a hill. We see far away on the horizon, distant but visible, the city to which we are going. Or like sailors upon some stormy sea, coming on deck in the morning, we see lying across the waves a faint outline of what we know to be the land where our haven lies. Throughout this new year let us reach out with sure hope of the soon return of our Lord. Let us keep clear before us the vision of the kingdom of God. Decay is written upon the portals of the world we live in, but not upon the cause of Christ. We are not stumbling sheep making our way in the gathering darkness toward the fold. Christ is everything to us. We are sure that we are in Christ.

We are to live more like Christ, to excel in all that elevates us. We covet earnestly the best gifts. With Christ we seek to acquire the full stature that He has promised. All are yours, and ye are Christ's, and Christ is God's. We do not isolate life. We enrich life. We are more than ever devoted to the service of God and humanity. Every power and every gift that God has given to us is awakened by the power of His love. We have an anchor within the veil, secure by no finite will, but by the power of the Holy Spirit within us.

# MANNA AT DAYBREAK

*Then said the Lord unto Moses, Behold, I will rain bread from heaven for*
*you. . . . And in the morning, then ye shall see the glory of the Lord.*
**Ex. 16:4-7.**

Let us take these words of promise out of their historic setting and framework in the record of God's daily provision for
Israel in the wilderness. Let us consider this spiritually to be
God's approach to us. Christmas is over, and the new year is
here. We have wished our friends and loved ones a happy
Christmas and a happy new year. Let us put our wishes into
action.

With the dawn of every new day for this coming year there
waits to speak to us a voice from God: "Behold I make all
things new." Consecrate yourself to Him anew every morning.
Do it as definitely as if you have never done it before. Pray
every morning before you do anything else. God will make all
things new and fresh and fair. We need God. We need the resources of the Holy Spirit. Every time we pray and read the
Word of God we wait for God to speak to us. God waits to respond to us.

The princes of Babylon conspired against Daniel. As Daniel
talked with God, communed with God, the Lord inspired in
him the ability to rely entirely on divine power, so that when he
was cast into the den of lions he had no fear and no anxiety.
Each day we are to get ready for the temptations and the crises
of life before they get ready for us.

Are you thirsty each morning for one cool draught of God's
presence and power to clear the heart and mind? Our minds
can be trained to feel our daily need of God. We can accustom
our lungs to pure air. We can so habituate ourselves to God's
love and presence that we are ready each day for everything
that comes our way.

We can be sure of God. Each morning we discover simple
courage because God is there. He makes us faithful and true.
He inspires us to steadfastness.

We are to glory in His truth, righteousness, and love; in His
grace, His kingdom, and His soon return. This is the atmosphere we are meant to breathe, the spiritual food we are to eat.

# FAMILY WORSHIP

*"But if it does not please you to worship the Lord, choose here and now whom you will worship. . . . But I and my family, we will worship the Lord."* Joshua 24:15, N.E.B.

Family worship is the most ancient of all religious practices. That is all the worship Adam and Eve practiced, since they constituted the only family on the earth. Says the Scripture: "Then began men to call upon the name of the Lord" (Gen. 4:26). Family worship must have been the only form of worship addressed to God for a long time, since the earth still remained to be occupied. Only when the number of men and families multiplied did public worship begin. Abraham was a prime example of leading his family in worship. "For I know him, that he will command his children . . . after him, and they shall keep the way of the Lord, to do justice and judgment" (chap. 18:19).

Under the leadership of Moses public worship was established in the wilderness. Nevertheless, the children of Israel were counseled to hold family worship.

What real security and happiness a Christian family will find in erecting the family altar, in being united to offer up living sacrifices unto the Lord. In a house where God is forgotten, there exists greater temptations to ill-humor, to impatience, to lack of respect for and honor of parents. How many troubles and tragedies exist in families where God is left out. Domestic piety is a safeguard against so many evils. It encourages confidence and trust in God. When the hour of trial comes, which sooner or later comes to us all, divine strength is ours. We have assurance of God's guidance through every day.

Establish such a worship hour in accordance with your needs as a family. Let there be liberty, not dry routine. Let the Word of God be studied, so that each family member will find divine guidance in his life. You know how to speak to a friend. Why should you not speak to God? He is your greatest and best Friend. Everyone is important to God. Let Christ set the spiritual and moral tone for the day.

Worship is creative. Before God we are not pawns to be pushed about by circumstances or fate. Worship shapes our lives in accordance with God's plan.

# GENUINENESS IN FAMILY WORSHIP REQUIRED

*"But the time approaches, indeed it is already here, when those who are real worshippers will worship the Father in spirit and in truth."* John 4:23, N.E.B.

Your children will surely be blessed by family worship, provided they see that you are really in earnest. Add the essential thing to your family worship, a life in accordance with the worship that you offer unto God. Be not one kind of person before the family altar and another in the world. Be truly the same Christian at all times. Let your every day be a living commentary upon what you have read and prayed together in the hour of devotion.

If you wish to erect an altar unto the Lord in your house, you must, first of all, erect one in your own heart. You are to be the temple of God. God's Spirit is to dwell within you. So long as there is no altar erected to God in your heart there can be none in your home.

There is one great key that unlocks the secret of family communion with God: a love and loyalty to God and to one another that stands squarely at the heart of all our activities inside and outside the home. Then our family meeting with God each morning makes possible Christ's meeting with us at every turn of the road for the rest of the day.

The voice of God must come into our lives, not just the echo of our own voices. Multitudes arise each day to eat, to go to the office and to work, return to watch the television or go to the sports arena. The next day and the next day they do about the same thing. Does anybody know what it is all about? The issue is that the living God must be written into our life-style.

We are to take all the individual and family problems and talk together with God present. A home is Christian when its members refuse to take things into their own hands only. Family worship means laying things in God's hands. It brings us where God can guide us because we want to know God's will. "I say unto you, That if two of you shall agree on earth as touching any thing that they shall ask, it shall be done for them of my Father which is in heaven. For where two or three are gathered together in my name, there am I in the midst of them" (Matt. 18:19, 20).

# "THE LORD OUR RIGHTEOUSNESS"

*This is his name whereby he shall be called, The Lord our Righteousness.*
**Jer. 23:6.**

The most revealing name in Scripture given to Jesus, the Messiah, is the prophetic title "The Lord our Righteousness." It is given to no one else but Jesus Christ. He is the one and only revelation of perfect righteousness before God the Father, before the universe, and before all men. In His life on earth, He is the one perfect man. Righteousness became a concrete fact, not just a theory. God is not giving us a lecture on righteousness. He Himself is "made unto us wisdom, and *righteousness, and sanctification, and redemption*" (1 Cor. 1:30).

Because He alone is our righteousness, there can be no other source of righteousness whatsoever. The confession of all men must be: "There is none righteous, no, not one" (Rom. 3:10). "For I know that in me . . . dwelleth no good thing" (chap. 7:18).

Righteousness is the one thing that sinners must have to be saved. We do not possess this righteousness on our own. Otherwise we would need to be sinless. This would be another source other than Christ our Righteousness and is diametrically opposed to the teaching of Scripture. In this life we must forever look away from and out of ourselves to Christ. This is the only way we are regarded as righteous before God.

As we become increasingly conscious of the sinful nature within us, our only hope is in Christ. His righteousness is the only emancipation we have from the past. Christ alone takes the sting out of sin and robs the law of its condemning power.

We can never know in this life that we have achieved sinlessness. Therefore we have no safety within ourselves before God or in the presence of God's law. Christ is our righteousness, for the past, the present, and the future. That is our security before the universe. This is our confidence in the hour of death and on the day of judgment. "For I am convinced that there is nothing in death or life, in the realm of spirits of superhuman powers, in the world as it is or the world as it shall be, in the forces of the universe, in heights or depths—nothing in all creation that can separate us from the love of God in Christ Jesus our Lord" (Rom. 8:38, 39, N.E.B.).

13

# FIRST RIGHTEOUSNESS, THEN PEACE

*For this Melchisedec, king of Salem, priest of the most high God, who met Abraham . . . and blessed him; . . . first being by interpretation King of righteousness, and after that also King of Salem, which is, King of peace.* Heb. 7:1, 2.

The Bible has very little to say about Melchisedec. He is an exalted earthly king and priest of the Most High God. His role is one of great dignity. He appears briefly in Abraham's life. The Spirit of God uses him as a type of Christ as king and priest. Christ is king and priest in the realm of righteousness and peace, designed to bring both to men.

The significance is in the order: first, King of Righteousness, and afterwards King of Peace. No peace with God is possible except on the basis of righteousness. God has no pleasure in iniquity. There is no peace for the wicked. The first thing Christ does when He comes into the heart is to create in us the realization of our great need for righteousness in order to find peace with God.

Christ bestows His own righteousness upon us. He acquits the guilty. He forgives and cleanses us. Our only way to peace is union with the King of Righteousness. We cannot be considered righteous unless we have Christ's righteousness. God must deal with the sin problem in our lives before He can manifest Himself as King of Peace. We do not need anything more but Jesus Christ. There can be no deeper desire than that the King of Righteousness should be king in our hearts. Christ cannot be satisfied with less. His nature cannot rest until we have committed ourselves to Him for righteousness. He calls us to accept His righteousness and in so doing He calls us to peace. We cannot merely will to be righteous. We can turn ourselves and our will over to Him, and make Him our King. Christ is not just any king. He is King of Righteousness and Peace.

God had in mind for Israel only one King, the Messiah to come. They were to prepare the world for the coming of the King of kings. Centuries of departure from God prepared the way for the final rejection of King Jesus when He came. The choice is no different today. The King of Righteousness and Peace is on His way back to earth.

# COUNTED AS RIGHTEOUS

*If without any work to his credit he simply puts his faith in him who ac-*
*quits the guilty, then his faith is indeed "counted as righteousness." Rom.*
*4:5, N.E.B.*

Men have sometimes concluded from this verse that
good works are of no importance in the Christian life. Obeying
the law of God has been made light of. This reckoning, or im-
puting to us of Christ's righteousness on faith alone, has been
used to evade rather than to fulfill the law of God. Men have
been told that all that is necessary is to "get on board the gospel train, ride all the way to heaven," while denying the claims
of the law of God.

Is faith, then, to be regarded as actually permitting Christian people to lie, to steal, to commit adultery, in the name of
the gospel? How can we profess to receive the gift of Christ's
righteousness in which we do not ourselves share? How can
any one of us be saved from sin except by not sinning, by not
transgressing the law? How can we desire and claim this perfect
righteousness of Christ unless we want to live that way? How
can we receive it if we lose the distinction between righteousness and unrighteousness? If obedience is not required of the
Christian, then we must admit that Christ does not save from
sin at all, but encourages us in our sins. Such a salvation leaves
us where we are, in our sins. How can we, in the name of
righteousness, believe in such a system of salvation that leaves
us unrighteous?

Nowhere does Christ's gift of righteousness endanger
morality or render men careless of how they live. The moment
we believe, God puts to our account the righteousness of
Christ. We have still a long way to go in the restoration to the
image of God. Faith also means that we see what *is* the righteousness that God desires for us. Under His divine power we
shall increasingly partake of that righteousness of Christ in the
life. Christ has now become the very life and guardian of our
minds, hearts, and conduct.

Do you believe in Christ and accept His righteousness as
your greatest need? To have this righteousness put to our account does not make us careless of how we live. Christ imputes
His righteousness to us in order to work it out in our lives.

# IMITATION OR PARTICIPATION

*Be ye therefore followers of God, as dear children; and walk in love, as Christ also hath loved us. Eph. 5:1, 2.*

Years ago Thomas à Kempis wrote a classic work: *The Imitation of Christ.* It has been translated into more than sixty languages. It is written largely on the supposition that if we look long and hard at the life of Jesus and seek thereby to imitate Him, we can actually do so. But is the Christian life that simple? Is all we need before us an example of righteousness in order to follow it? It will not work in *other* areas of ability and talents.

Suppose someone gives us a piece of canvas, some paint, and a few brushes, and then tells us to imitate a Raphael or a Rembrandt. How many long hours would we need to study their paintings and imitate them? Actually, it is impossible. Or we are asked to imitate the famous violinist Heifetz. How many days, months, and years would we need to practice? We cannot do it. These artists have within them an artistic gift from God. It is part of their very lives, an ability that most of us do not have.

How can we by looking at Christ long enough, examining every move and word He makes, imitate His life? You can try to do it. But such an imitation will not be spontaneous. It will be something put on. You will need continual self-discipline and concentration with little or no time to relax even for a moment. What we really need in order to live like Christ is an actual change in our inner nature, a new life. Only to the extent to which we partake of the nature of Christ can we live like Him. Christ must change us before we can live changed lives.

Christ does not stand in relationship to us as do the great artists of the world. Imitation keeps us at a distance when we endeavor under our own steam to live as He does. The Christian way is to receive from God new life. Outward conformity, a diligent effort to keep the rules, is not the answer. We would not be satisfied with this kind of response from our children. We must have their love and oneness. Nothing else will suffice. So it is in the Christian experience. We participate in the life of Christ. We are one with Him. The work is God's.

# THE ROCK OF OFFENSE—1

*As it is written, Behold, I lay in Sion a stumblingstone and rock of offence:*
*and whosoever believeth on him shall not be ashamed.* **Rom. 9:33.**

Salvation is by way of the cross of Jesus Christ. We do not
find our way back to God by a triumphant march down Independence Avenue. We come to Christ not as a conquering hero
to receive honors from God. We come as penitents, asking
for forgiveness, acknowledging our sinfulness and desperate
need. The way of the cross is the way of surrender of all claims
to our own greatness and personal achievement. We don't
find our way out of sin by a pilgrimage or by the imposition
upon ourselves of some difficult assignment. We come to God
without any claim on God whatsoever.

God's redemption of us by the sacrifice of His Son cannot be
watered down to our meeting a list of requirements. The way
of the cross is rough going on the minds of men. Especially
where men consider themselves self-sufficient and of considerable reputation, this way to salvation is hard to accept. With
the great advancement of science and technology, man tends
to look more to himself. He considers that by his own abilities
and power he holds the key to human salvation and improvement.

A university professor once said to me, "I don't need Jesus
Christ. I am a good man. I don't drink or smoke or break any
of the Ten Commandments. I am faithful to my family. I have
a great mind; am emotionally mature. I write learned books.
What do you have that I don't have?" But such men rarely
comprehend how dangerously self-confident and selfish they
are.

Christ proclaims the bankruptcy of man. The cross of
Christ comes to us with an attack on human independence
and the pride of man. Salvation and the solution to our problems come through Christ alone. This prevents us from ever
remaining independent if we wish to be saved. We put our
"faith in him who acquits the guilty" (Rom. 4:5, N.E.B.). When
God does this He does not justify our ungodly deeds. He acquits us of the guilt that deserves punishment. He restores us
to favor with God. Imputed righteousness means it is His
righteousness, not ours.

# THE ROCK OF OFFENSE—2

*For they being ignorant of God's righteousness, and going about to establish their own righteousness, have not submitted themselves unto the righteousness of God.* **Rom. 10:3.**

The most difficult thing in all the world is the complete surrender of all human pride. Our sophistication is so smart. Our science is so brilliant. Our achievements are so impressive.

Christ is a stumblingblock to men because of the radical nature of the solution to the problem of sin and death that God has proposed: life through death; fulfillment of self through denial of self; exaltation by way of the cross. Christ was put to death by those religious leaders whose vested interests in their own status and superiority prevented them from repentance and commitment. To die to self-will, to self-esteem, to self-sufficiency, is the inevitable problem for all of us.

To be a sinner means we have lost the capacity to find our way back to God, or to make ourselves right. We have lost the will and the power to pull ourselves together and correct our mistakes. Is it too much to accept God's estimate of us—"There is none righteous, no, not one" (Rom. 3:10)? Is it too much to seek to return to our heavenly Father as did the prodigal son?

In his book *Surprised by Joy,* C. S. Lewis tells of his pilgrimage to faith and how God found him. This is how he tells it: "I had always wanted above all things, not to be 'interfered with.' I had wanted 'to call my soul my own.' . . . You must picture me alone in that room in Magdalen [college (Oxford)]. . . . That which I greatly feared had at last come upon me. In the Trinity Term of 1929 I gave in, and admitted that God was God, and knelt and prayed; perhaps, that night, the most dejected and reluctant convert in all England. I did not then see what is now the most shining and obvious thing; the Divine humility which will accept a convert even on such terms. . . . The words . . . 'compel them to come in,' have been so abused by wicked men that we shudder at them; but, properly understood, they plumb the depth of the Divine mercy. The hardness of God is kinder than the softness of men, and His compulsion is our liberation." *

---

* C. S. Lewis, *Surprised by Joy,* Harcourt, Brace and World Inc., New York, 1955, pp. 228, 229.

## GLORYING IN THE CROSS

*But God forbid that I should glory, save in the cross of our Lord Jesus Christ, by whom the world is crucified unto me, and I unto the world. Gal. 6:14.*

The cross constitutes the climax of Christ's work for the salvation of men. Here is God's answer to our sin problem. Thousands of men had been crucified before, but this Man was different. The nature of Christ's death for us is the center of salvation history.

A good many people who wish to shoulder their own sins refuse to come to grips with the problem that our sins are against the God of heaven and that therefore only He can forgive us and save us. I read a story some years ago of a skeptic who entered a cathedral. When he heard the chanting of the Agnus Dei, "Behold the Lamb of God which taketh away the sin of the world," he rushed out exclaiming with an oath, "Suppose it were true." Well, it is true.

We know for sure how the God of heaven feels about us. We know that His love is the source and root of all things good, stronger than hate, mightier than sin, more enduring than hell fire. His love for us is enough for the direst emergency that ever came to man. God's word from the cross is that He refuses to give us up to sin and death. He never despairs of our salvation and recovery. He reveals His one redemptive purpose for our lives, even by the sacrifice of one member of the Godhead; the Son of God staring into the abyss of eternal separation from His Father, refusing to give us up to eternal loss. There is no point in toning down this great truth.

John Newton ran a slave ship between Africa and America. He met Christ and became a minister of the Church of England. Before he died he wrote his own epitaph:

"John Newton, Clerk, once an infidel and libertine,
a servant of slaves in Africa, was, by the rich mercy
of our Lord and Saviour Jesus Christ, preserved, restored,
pardoned, appointed to preach the faith he had long
labored to destroy."

We are all left with nothing but the marvelous grace and mercy of God.

# THE INCOMPARABLE CHRIST—1

*And Jesus stood before the governor: and the governor asked him, saying, Art thou the King of the Jews? And Jesus said unto him, Thou sayest.*
**Matt. 27:11.**

As far as our relationship to Christ is concerned, there is no middle ground. The answer is either an emphatic Yes or an emphatic No. With Pilate the issue arose when he asked of Jesus, "Art thou the King of the Jews?" One thing became clear to Pilate: Jesus was innocent. As he saw the moral and spiritual stature of Jesus, Pilate knew that the only right thing to do was to acquit Him; that is, providing it could be done with no inconvenience and no undesirable consequences to himself. He was convicted as to the claim of Jesus and became profoundly disturbed. He tried to wash his mind by washing his hands. In the end he surrendered his privilege of speaking in defense of what he knew to be right and just.

The choice of Jesus Christ is not a preference, Christ or Barabbas. Do you prefer to become a Christian or not? In a way, that is a foolish question. It is like asking, Do I wish to cheat? Do I wish to lie? Do I wish to betray my family or not? Do I wish to be honest or not? This is not asking the right questions at all.

The claim of Christ is an either/or decision. When the rich young ruler came to Christ he did not contemplate making any radical changes. Nicodemus, who came to Jesus by night, conceded he was willing to accept Jesus as a great teacher. He did not contemplate making a revolutionary change when Christ said, "Nicodemus, you must be born again." That was the one thing he was not prepared for.

There are few things in Christian experience more self-defeating than sitting on the fence. Jesus declared: "A man's foes shall be they of his own household" (Matt. 10:36). He was not talking about Christian homes, but about the unavoidable choice that confronts us sometimes.

It is easy to choose Barabbas when that is what the crowd wants. Often it is costly to choose Christ. Jesus Christ troubled the world back in the first century. He still does. He places before us one great and ultimate alternative: I will or I will not have this Man to rule over me.

# THE INCOMPARABLE CHRIST—2

*Pilate saith unto them, What shall I do then with Jesus which is called Christ? They all say unto him, Let him be crucified. . . . His blood be on us, and on our children. Matt. 27:22-25.*

Christ never allows us to be neutral. In the first century it was Christ or Caesar. To offer or not to offer incense to the Emperor of Rome was fraught with the most terrible consequences. In most Eastern countries the Mohammedan who decides to follow Christ knows he must do so at the price of being cast out by his family, that the funeral rites will be performed for him as for one already dead.

We must decide either to take the kingdom of God seriously or casually. This unqualified rule of God in our hearts Christ took seriously. He wanted no disciple who would not accept this. The neutral attitude that keeps to a few moral platitudes by way of concession can be the most corrupting factor in life. It brings confusion into the cause of God.

"But Peter followed him afar off unto the high priest's palace, and went in, and sat with the servants, to see the end" (Matt. 26:58). At that crucial point Peter did not want to be identified with Jesus. That kind of discipleship is cowardly and weak. There is no place in Christian living for a half-and-half commitment. Feebleness of devotion is utterly inconsistent with the Christian faith. To choose Christ and to follow Him means such thoroughness of spirit, loftiness of life, and beauty of character, that anything like mediocrity is intolerable.

In his denials of Christ, Peter started out by saying he did not know what the girl was saying to him. He ended up by saying of Christ, "I do not know the man." Cowardice, hesitancy when the chips are down, takes us down this road. The master stroke of Satan is to detach us from Christ and get us to accept some form of compromise. The devil cuts off the stragglers. Let us shun neutrality and indecision. This is the fatal attitude that makes the triumph of sin and self possible. Fullness of love and devotion to Christ means the highest and the utmost in Christian character. This is the key to our allegiance. No indecisiveness is there.

Nothing has changed since Christ walked the earth. Jesus spelled out what it meant to be a Christian.

# RELIGIOUS REVIVALS—1

*The king made a covenant before the Lord to obey him and keep his commandments . . . with all his heart and soul.* **2 Kings 23:3, N.E.B.**

This scripture records one of the greatest revivals that took place in the history of ancient Israel. The method by which it occurred is significant: the discovery of the Book of the Law, the reading of it, and the response of obedience to all that was written therein.

The opinion of a well-informed man is more authoritative than that of an ignorant man. The word of a good man has more positive influence than that of a bad man. When it comes to religion, we yield our lives to the highest and most trustworthy authority. Jesus spoke with authority. He is the truth. His word is truth because He gave it. In Him dwelt all the fullness of the Godhead bodily.

Today, authority, for the most part, has shifted to the individual's so-called experience of the supernatural. The claim to have made a personal encounter with the divine is becoming increasingly the basis for belief that one has met God. There is an easy access to the spirit world, which tends to make each person feel sufficient in himself.

This type of experience is frequently emphasized at the expense of God's communication to us in His Word. The Word of God is reduced to a place of secondary importance. Many who sincerely seek to follow Jesus Christ are being deceived by an appeal to other people's sensational experiences. They say: "Why does not God come to me this way? I too desire to be turned on." Consequently, doctrines, objective truths, and ideas on religion are said to be inadequate. So people are not satisfied just to read about God. They want to meet Him.

The God of the Bible is the speaking God. He communicates intelligently with us. This is how we are able to communicate with one another, through the medium of language that can be understood. Human thought and language are our only means of apprehending the revealed truths of God. The Holy Spirit makes vital and spiritual the Word of God. First we learn about Him and His truth from the Bible. Then we go on to know Him and obey Him.

# RELIGIOUS REVIVALS—2

*Wilt thou not revive us again: that thy people may rejoice in thee?*
*Ps. 85:6.*

We are seeing two types of religious revivals today: first, that which looks to and depends upon the claims of men and churches to encounter directly the supernatural in what seems like miraculous and unexplainable manifestations. And second, that which depends entirely upon the revealed word of God in Scripture and is tested by it.

The shifting emphasis in modern revivals from God's Word to the claim to personal contact with the supernatural tends to silence God's claim to our obedience to His commandments. Under the glow and excitement of a supposed contact with and direct sign from God, people tend to become a law unto themselves. For these individuals the call of obedience to the truth of God's Word becomes a rather cold, intellectual affair.

We have no wish to pass judgment on the claim of other people to have experienced a relationship with God. But it must be tested as to its truth or falsity. Only the truth from God can determine that. This does not disparage the deep feelings we experience in our devotion to God. Any swing of the pendulum toward the sensational and the spectacular in relation to the spirit world should be halted at the Word of God and tested by it.

Neither Christian faith nor experience emanates from within ourselves. It rests on and proceeds from God's Word. Genuine Christian experience is never divorced from the teachings of the Bible. It is dependent upon that Word for which God alone is responsible. The truth from God carries more power for the life than a million human experiences of the supernatural. No religious revival is true that ignores or departs from obedience to the law of God. The religious experience of all peoples in the world can never become the center of authority or of spiritual power. In this direction deception lies.

Unrestrained emotionalism, spiritistic sensationalism, are manifest in almost all the pagan religions of the world. We need that inner poise and calmness of the Holy Spirit, the peace of mind so essential to understanding truth and committing ourselves to it.

# YOUR HALL OF FAME

**Wherefore God also hath highly exalted him, and given him a name which is above every name. Phil. 2:9.**

Suppose you were to outline your Hall of Fame on a written document. Whom would you put on it? On the left side of the document write down the names of those whom you believe to be the greatest that the human race has produced. If you were born in America you would probably include Washington and Lincoln. If you have studied philosophy you would likely think of Plato, Aristotle, Socrates. If you have studied history you would think of Hannibal, Julius Caesar, Charlemagne, and others. If you have studied religion you would, no doubt, include St. Francis of Assisi, Martin Luther, Calvin, John Wesley. If you have studied sports you would include some of the sports champions.

On the right side of the document write down Jesus Christ. Where would you place Him in relation to all the others? Should Jesus Christ be placed in a column all by Himself? Would you want to measure all other men by Him? Is Jesus Christ the yardstick for all of us?

The world has changed a great deal; people have changed very little. Study the life of Jesus, then write down what you think He was like, the things He stood for and sought to communicate to others. The words to describe Him will include love, integrity, purity, humility, kindness, mercy, compassion—all values that people need as much today as when He walked the earth.

The world is in a very bad way. What man would you choose to show us the way out? No one should be counted as essential unless he understands our problems and can give us the right answers. Christ is the supreme human being of all who ever lived on earth. The best we can say of any other person is that "he is Christlike." How many of us want to live like Christ? If we are to change our own lives and the world we live in we must live the kind of life found in Christ.

The sustaining power in Christ's life was His faith in the Father. He came to empower us to live by the same kind of faith. Who among us can afford to want anything less than this?

# GOD IS AFFIRMATIVE

*Fear thou not; for I am with thee: be not dismayed; for I am thy God: I will strengthen thee; yea, I will help thee; yea, I will uphold thee with the right hand of my righteousness.* **Isa. 41:10.**

God is faithful. His love, forgiveness, and mercy never change toward us. If we are lost at last, it will not be because God has cut us off from His love or severed us from His mercy, but because we turned from Him with the full light of His love and grace shining in our eyes. God is always affirmative in His attitude toward us. The truth of an ever-present Christ is true and sure, unless we break the link with God ourselves.

God is true. Therefore with Christ in us we also are true. God is eternal love. Therefore we love because "the love of God is shed abroad in our hearts by the Holy Ghost" (Rom. 5:5). God is righteousness. Therefore Christ in us means we are righteous too. We cannot have His life in us and be absent from His love, His mercy, His righteousness.

There may be times when we are in doubt. Yet we can say with assurance, "God is true." His word to us is acceptance. He still loves us. He never stops caring for us. His love to us does not change because we do wrong, any more than we as parents change our love toward our children when they do wrong.

Let us not believe Satan's lies that, because we have fallen short, God has separated Himself from us. I want to bring you face to face again with our heavenly Father, for God is true. He is faithful to His character of love and mercy. God does not love us less because of our failures. He is saddened when we go our own way. Not until we believe that God loves us in spite of all our infirmities and imperfections can we find strength to be different. Let us not say to ourselves: "Now I will mend my ways. I will improve myself. Then God will love and accept me, approve of me."

Let us not try to change ourselves. God's love heals. Selfishness destroys. Love expands the life. Selfishness binds and cramps our style. Selfishness pours out anger, hostility, misunderstanding. The love of God pours out mercy, grace, and kindness. Selfishness uses emotional pressure. The love of God uses forgiveness and sacrifice. Our love is a response to a Person and to a life so wonderful that we become changed.

# IN THE NAME OF THE GODHEAD

**Go ye therefore, and teach all nations, baptizing them in the name of the Father, and of the Son, and of the Holy Ghost. Matt. 28:19.**

When we were born again, we were baptized in the name of all three members of the Godhead. We believe there are three Persons in the Trinity: the Father is God, the Son is God, and the Holy Spirit is God. All three are one in an unbreakable unity. We cannot know how They feel toward us as sinners except what They choose to make known. In the revealed Word of God They have done that in a very special way to those of us who live on this planet. Each of Them has declared what He is to us personally. In this way They have opened to us the very doors of heaven with an everlasting invitation to return home to live with Them forever.

What would it profit us to think and speak of Them as if They were to be feared and dreaded? As exiles from the Garden of Eden and from the presence of God, what if all we knew was the divine sentence of death for our sins?

What would it avail if every day you had this to look forward to, if as a sinner, on waking each day with your sins before you, you did not know yourself to be forgiven? The Bible makes clear that every sin we have committed is registered in the books of heaven. How utterly overwhelming in despair to hear the words, "The hour of God's judgment has come for you. God will not clear the guilty." Yet this would be the situation if the Father, Son, and Holy Spirit had not visited us with the good news of pardon, forgiveness, and acceptance through the shed blood of the Son of God.

While telling of God's judgment on sin, the Bible also presents a divine plan worked out by our heavenly Father, the Son of God, and the Holy Spirit for our redemption and reconciliation. All members of the Godhead refuse to give us up to eternal damnation. Instead of looking on ourselves as outcasts from the Garden of Eden, we are now restored to oneness with God.

To estimate the value of the God you believe in, consider His influence upon yourself. We are His children, not His slaves. We are acquitted, not condemned. We are accepted, not rejected. We are children in our Father's house.

# WHAT ARE YOU WORTH TO GOD?—1

*I will make a man more precious than fine gold; even a man than the golden wedge of Ophir. Isa. 13:12.*

Of far greater value than all the gold of Ophir, with which Solomon overlaid the sanctuary in Jerusalem, is the human soul.

The poet Longfellow could take a worthless sheet of paper and by writing a poem on it make it worth $6,000. That is genius. A Rockefeller can sign his name to a piece of paper and make it worth millions. That is capital. Uncle Sam can take silver, stamp a symbol on it, and make it worth one dollar. That is money. An artist can take a two-dollar piece of canvas, paint on it, and make it worth $100,000. That is art. But God can take young men and young women, wash them in the blood of Christ, capture their hearts and minds, put His Spirit and mind within them, transform them, make them like unto Joseph, Daniel, Paul, or Himself. That is redemption. What is the history of Egypt without a Moses or a Joseph? What is the record of the city of Babylon without a Daniel and the three Hebrews, men of truth, honesty, fidelity, and purity?

At Calvary we witness the highest price paid for anything— the blood of the Son of God, the ransom paid for our redemption. With God we far outweigh in value the sum total of everything that is in or on this earth.

One of the most important questions we can ask is Who am I? Do I have value for God or just for myself and for the state? What is personal fulfillment for me? Evolution tells us that man is a little higher than the animals, a thing of earth and returnable to dust, a child of the beasts. The Bible affirms that we were made sons and daughters of God. God made us in His image. So when we come to worship, each Sabbath, we know who we are. We can say: "I am a child of God. I have a capacity to respond to Him and to love Him in return." Our being born in sin and living in sin is not mere misfortune. It is a departure from God.

The coming of Christ into our world, assuming our nature and living as a man, means that we have a heavenly Father who has taken sides with us. We are not alone. This is seen in the greatness of the salvation provided for us in Jesus Christ.

## WHAT ARE YOU WORTH TO GOD?—2

*He that spared not his own Son, but delivered him up for us all, how shall he not with him also freely give us all things? Rom. 8:32.*

We cannot compass all this verse means to us. Yet this promise is a reality. We can actually experience the truth of it. God loves us as He loves His Son. He loves man just as he is, in whatever state he is, whatever he has done. In Christ man has his greatest possibilities.

This love is more than nature, more than duty, more than wealth and human ability. He loves until the worthless becomes of supreme worth, until the insignificant becomes of great significance.

Claim the promise of this text. Within the realization of it the Christian is not surprised at his best moments and his noblest acts. He is not amazed when he does the brave thing or the unselfish thing. He is not astonished when he does the clean thing and the loving thing. But he is amazed at himself when he is dishonest, when he hates instead of loves, when he hurts people instead of helping them.

If it be asked what we receive from Jesus Christ, we can answer, "All things." We see within ourselves all too often the undesirable and the selfish. Yet we have no doubt about what we have in Christ. Our sins may obscure this fact. But we do have Christ. We do have His righteousness and the fruit of the Spirit. If we really believed this verse and committed ourselves to Christ, our lives would be filled with love, joy, and peace. All too often we look too much at our failures and the failures of others. This tends to turn us away from the "all things" we have in Christ. But the text does not change. The promise is forever valid. The believer who lives by this promise can bear witness to it. He passes from doubt to certainty, from sadness to joy, from hate to love.

There are no virtues that Christ does not provide. There are no lasting joys that Christ does not include, and pleasures forevermore. God never asks more of a man than he can give. He offers him first "all things." Then the Christian exclaims, "I can do all things through Christ which strengtheneth me" (Phil. 4:13).

# THE FATHER'S NAME ON THEIR FOREHEADS

*And they shall see his face; and his name shall be in their foreheads.*
**Rev. 22:4.**

When do you put your name on a thing? You buy a book.
It belongs to you. So you write your name on it. You receive
a gift of a leather-bound Bible. You have your name embossed
in gold on the cover. You own it. The Father's name is written
in the foreheads of those who belong· to Him. He owns us.
He purchased us with His blood. It is as serious an affair to
belong to God as when two people get married, even more
serious. They belong to each other. They are one.

To belong is a word that has great meaning. Love, joy,
fulfillment, flow from the experience of oneness. Frustration,
disorder, illness, flow from the experience of isolation. Belonging is personal. God is our Father with all the love and concern that this involves. The Christian never denies this ownership. He approves the things that are more excellent because
he belongs to such a wonderful God.

Men get much satisfaction and pleasure out of things they
own. But one is not made to love things, only persons. Things
cannot meet our need for oneness. Real life is found in the
quality of the people to whom we belong and who belong to
us. It is persons who make the difference.

It is possible to own many fine things, and yet be the loneliest person in the church or the community. Some of the
richest men in the world are among the loneliest. Nothing can
make up for this lack. There are those who feel not loved or
wanted, who go through life isolated, neglected, estranged
from persons; Jesus Christ came to change all that. The church
is not an institution for perfect people, but a communion of
love where people experience oneness with God and with their
fellow men. Persons weighted down with sin and guilt are not
helped by others who judge and condemn them. Denuncia-
tion and rejection never helped anyone.

In His last prayer just prior to His crucifixion, Jesus Christ
prayed for oneness and belonging among His people and in
the world: "I in them, and thou in me, that they may be made
perfect in one; . . . that the world may know that thou . . . hast
loved them, as thou hast loved me" (John 17:23).

## GOD'S SEARCH FOR US—1

*"What do you think? Suppose a man has a hundred sheep. If one of them strays, does he not leave the other ninety-nine on the hillside and go in search of the one that strayed?"* Matt. 18:12, N.E.B.

The story of God in the Bible is the greatest love story ever written. Almost all of God's acts reveal His endeavor to find men, to win men, to reconcile men to Himself, and to give men eternal life. God is always trying to hand us His calling card in one way or another. What a marvelous approach God makes to us in sending His own Son in search of us!

At the same time the Bible is an account of man's flight from God. When men sin they try to hide from God. Adam started it. In the Garden of Eden God came looking for Adam. God offers men the bread of life, and they stay hungry. He offers them the Light of the world, and they prefer to remain in the shadows. They don't want the exposure that the Light might bring. Men sin. God comes offering forgiveness and acceptance, but all too often men despair of themselves. God offers to carry their burden of sin, but they refuse to give it up.

"O Jerusalem, Jerusalem, thou that killest the prophets, and stonest them which are sent unto thee, how often would I have gathered thy children together, even as a hen gathereth her chickens under her wings, and ye would not" (Matt. 23:37). Why does man take flight from God? For two reasons: his fear and his pride.

Satan persuades men that God is a hard taskmaster. Christ asks men to take up the cross and follow Him, and men are persuaded to believe God will strip them of all they have. None of us like deals unless they are to our advantage. We do not want to lose. Often we are afraid that we will lose, especially in light of all the claims Christ makes upon us—the surrender of self, and death to the world. Following Christ means sacrifice. Many people do not like that.

Sometimes it appears that God has a disconcerting way of keeping out of sight. But the fault is ours. He continues to wait and to knock, still caring. At the end of the road He is our heavenly Father who has wanted us all along. Why not let ourselves be found?

## GOD'S SEARCH FOR US—2

*If I take the wings of the morning, and dwell in the uttermost parts of the sea; even there shall thy hand lead me, and thy right hand shall hold me.* **Ps. 139:9, 10.**

We cannot evade God's love. There is no way to do that. God wants our love. He is perfectly honest about it. He created us. He brought us forth into the world. We are His children. God does not give up on us.

Francis Thompson, in his poem "The Hound of Heaven," describes the man trying to run away from God:

"I fled Him, down the nights and down the days;
I fled Him, down the arches of the years;
I fled Him, down the labyrinthine ways
Of my own mind; and in the midst of tears
I hid from Him . . .
From those strong Feet that followed, followed after."

We may think that God hides His face from us. What we mean is that we have lost contact with Him. Because of our sinning and neglect of Him, we say that God is no longer there. He has gone back into the heavens, which are as brass. But it is false to suppose that God finds us when we are good and bows Himself out of our lives when we are not good. Granted that God hates sin and sin separates us from Him. But the choice is ours, not God's. God still seeks us. He still loves us.

"I have loved thee with an everlasting love" (Jer. 31:3). If we end up in eternal darkness it will be because we have shut God out even when His love shone in our eyes. He is the eternal Shepherd who misses the one lost sheep, the Shepherd who goes through the night of storm and peril to find us. There is still time for all of us. It is not too late. God never rests until He finds us and we find Him. This is what really matters. Christ came all the way from heaven to find us. That is God's way with us. He wants us back home now and for eternity.

> "Mine is an unchanging love
> Higher than the heights above,
> Deeper than the depths beneath,
> Free and faithful, strong as death."
> —WILLIAM COWPER

# LIFE AT ITS BEST

*I am come that they might have life, and that they might have it more abundantly.* John 10:10.

We should remind ourselves each day of Christ's gift of life and the quality of it. Nothing men do and are by themselves is abundant and lasting, however admirable. Without the life that comes from Christ everything crumbles away to dust. This is the significance of Christ's account of the two men who built their house, one upon the rock, and one upon the sand (see Matt. 7:24-27).

We do not live the abundant life unless it has the quality of eternity about it. If our life is hid with Christ failure is impossible; for in Him is the highest and the best. In Him we become new creatures with every aspect of life abundant. In our gardens we have rosebushes, and flowers loaded with buds. Daily we anticipate their opening, the petals' unfolding, the delicate colors' developing, their fragrance exuding. But these must first answer the call of the warm sun and the gentle rain. So to live the abundant life, the mind and heart must respond to the Sun of Righteousness, who comes with healing in His wings.

Edvard Grieg, the Norwegian composer, wrote: "I passed my childhood among some of the grandest scenery of the North; and ever since I can remember, the beauty of my country has impressed me as something wonderful and magnificent beyond expression. It is our mountains, our lakes and forests, which have influenced my work far more than any human being has done; and even now, though I am forty, they have the selfsame power over me."—Quoted in D. S. MARDEN, *The Secret of Achievement*, Thomas Y. Crowell and Company, p. 195.

So it is under the influence of the living Christ. What a man lives in Christ is forever right and true. The millenniums to come bring man only to greater glory and eternal possibilities. Men may spend their lives to multiply possessions, power, and popularity. But the secret of life is not here. Life at its best must have the pervading presence of Jesus Christ.

# "MY CUP RUNNETH OVER"

*Thou preparest a table before me in the presence of mine enemies: thou anointest my head with oil; my cup runneth over.* **Ps. 23:5.**

In our world and on our behalf God has made everything to overflow. A legend tells us that prior to the entrance of sin the head of wheat extended the whole length of the straw. Because of sin the heads grow as we see them now. This legend reflects the truth as to the generosity of God. He has overflowed to us in all things.

The cup of salvation overflows. The plan of redemption is not merely to save us, to rescue us, but to restore in and to us all the fullness in which He made us. God's forgiveness is without reservation. He is not limited, hesitant, reluctant.

God's love and mercy toward us immeasurably transcend our own. They stand in immediate and immense contrast to the limited love of man. The free gift of Christ's righteousness in the gospel is God's everlasting masterpiece. When God clothes us with His righteousness the joy and glory of the new life leaves no room for hesitation and doubt. Here we see how the riches of grace go beyond our deepest needs and desires. We "rejoice with joy unspeakable and full of glory" (1 Peter 1:8).

We are heirs of God's unbounded love and eternity. How foolish to live away or apart from God, to depend on our own meager resources. Let God fill the cup of life, and forthwith it overflows. Let us not live by the temporal and limited offerings of man.

All of God's gifts to us are in cups that run over. All of us are vessels for the reception of His overflowing blessings. "The lines are fallen unto me in pleasant places; yea, I have a goodly heritage" (Ps. 16:6).

God has gone beyond all that we can think of for the fulfillment of our lives. The divine overflow is an invitation to bring a larger cup, the widening and deepening of our hearts and minds. What remains is a response in kind. We are to give Him all the love we have, a spontaneous obedience that runs beyond all the small limits of calculated rules and careful regulations. "I beseech you therefore, brethren, . . . that ye present your bodies a living sacrifice, holy, acceptable unto God, which is your reasonable service" (Rom. 12:1).

# HOW GOD TREATS MEN

*He maketh his sun to rise on the evil and on the good, and sendeth rain on the just and on the unjust. Matt. 5:45.*

Does God regard all men the same? Does He treat all men the same whether they obey Him or not? Does not God render to every man according as his works shall be? Has not God so ordered the universe and the world we live in so as to bless the good and punish the wicked?

To be sure, God loves all men the same, whether they are obedient or disobedient. We parents feel that way toward our children. But the consequences are different with different people. If we live in sin, though God loves us, His love loses its transforming influence and power because we refuse to let that love possess us. If we choose Christ and His righteousness, if we seek first the kingdom of God and His righteousness, then all these things shall be ours, as well. All the blessings of God have access to us. All His love, mercy, and forgiveness minister to us. These things can get through to all men; that is God's intention. But whether they do or not depends on our attitude and response.

If we open our hearts to His love He will save us from anxiety and fear. If we refuse His love our anxiety will increase. If we accept God as our heavenly Father, then we receive the benefits of children. But if we choose to rebel, then God will not force upon us either His presence or His love. If we go the way of the prodigal, then we separate ourselves from the Father-child relationship and from the blessings that come to us in such a relationship.

God is ever seeking us, knocking at the door of our heart. He ever seeks to awaken trust in us, a confidence that makes it easy for Him to pour His blessings upon us.

Adversity should not cause us to change our mind about God. On the contrary, we are increasingly more sure of Him. Every situation and experience draws us nearer to our Lord. We have such trust in Him that we need not trust in riches, in position, in popularity, or even in good health. Such trust in Him is the antidote for all our care, fear, grief, or loss of everything. "All things work together for good to them that love God" (Rom. 8:28).

# THE REACH OF GOD

*This is a faithful saying, and worthy of all acceptation, that Christ Jesus came into the world to save sinners. 1 Tim. 1:15.*

Two fundamental truths are stated in this verse: first, Jesus Christ came into the world; and second, He came to save sinners.

Almost two thousand years ago the second Person of the Godhead invaded this world in disguise. He Himself descended from a sphere quite beyond this earth. In Jesus Christ the invisible God became visible in human form. He is "God with us." He came to effect man's salvation. Only the God who had been sinned against could save. Only the God who lost a world could redeem it. Because God Himself came down, salvation is certain. God stepped down to save sinners by a supreme act of extraordinary grace and love.

The church is a community of the redeemed by virtue of the saving action of Jesus Christ. In 1959 the newspapers in Sydney, Australia, carried the account of a remarkable rescue of a 16-year-old girl. A young lifeguard, seeing her swept out to sea, plunged into the ocean. A strong riptide carried them farther from the shore. According to the account, sharks circled them, often brushing their legs. The girl fainted from the terror of it. The young man held her up for three hours. Finally he brought her to shore. The newspapers called it a record in the history of lifesaving in that country. The lifeguard did not send the girl a book on lifesaving with the counsel to read all about it. He acted. He made a supreme effort and saved the girl. She would never again be the same. One cannot pay off that kind of debt.

The gift of Jesus Christ is God's supreme act to save us. To believe this means that you can never be the same again. Beyond this God cannot go. Christ has done for lost men more than all the great men of earth. He has redeemed us. In place of death He brought eternal life. In place of sin He brought righteousness. In place of disease He brought health. In place of darkness He brought light. What stirrings of heart the good news should create in every life! We have an eternal inheritance in Christ. Let us claim it.

# THE SIN OF MAN, AND THE MERCY OF GOD

*And the Lord sent Nathan unto David. . . . And Nathan said to David, Thou art the man. Thus saith the Lord God of Israel, I anointed thee king. 2 Sam. 12:1-7.*

The Bible never conceals the faults and sins of its noblest characters. The Scripture never flatters its heroes. It tells the truth about each one in order that against this background of human failure we may see and magnify the grace and the mercy of God. We see how God loves men as they are. We learn how graciously God deals with all of us.

Few men have sinned as grievously as David. Few men have so totally returned to God to seek forgiveness, cleansing, and inward restoration. He is the man who wrote most of the Psalms, the devotional book of the Bible.

Certain things become clear in the experience of David: first, sooner or later our weaknesses will be exposed. Second, we have to live with the consequences of our sins and our turning away from God.

The first two decades of David's prominence as leader and king were marked by brilliant conquests. The second two were dark as midnight. For years Satan had probed a vulnerable spot, gradually leading him toward disaster. Finally, he is broken before God and confesses: "I have sinned against the Lord." The amazing grace of our Lord drew him back. By the power of God's Spirit he is made new. God made him a changed man, a converted man.

We are a new creation by the power of God. We may despair over our sins, but God does not. God works and moves upon us to restore us to the image of His Son. Let us not fear the pressure of His hand. For it is employed in tenderness and love.

God always takes the initiative. He continually calls upon us to look to His Son, in whom is all the wisdom, power, and love of God. We cannot atone for our sins. We cannot blot out our transgressions. We cannot cleanse our hearts.

Salvation is a personal matter. We must say: "This love of God concerns me personally. This means life for me. This I must embrace. I cast the ultimate responsibility for my life on God. 'Thou, O Christ, art all I want.' "

# SALVATION, THE GIFT OF GOD—1

*For if by the wrongdoing of that one man death established its reign,*
*through a single sinner, much more shall those who receive in far greater*
*measure God's grace, and his gift of righteousness, live and reign through*
*the one man, Jesus Christ.* **Rom. 5:17, N.E.B.**

Two things are required for us to be saved. First, we must
have a perfect righteousness. But "there is none righteous, no,
not one" (Rom. 3:10). Christ provides this righteousness for
us in His own perfectly righteous life that He lived on earth.
Therefore we receive "the gift of righteousness . . . by one,
Jesus Christ" (chap. 5:17).

Second, because we are sinners, we are under sentence of
death. "The wages of sin is death" (chap. 6:23). On Calvary
Christ bore our sins and paid the penalty for them. "Christ
hath redeemed us from the curse of the law, being made a
curse for us" (Gal. 3:13).

Therefore our salvation is complete and secured for us by
Christ alone. Hence the fundamental proclamation of the
gospel: "God so loved the world that he *gave* his only begotten
Son" (John 3:16). It is left to us to receive salvation as a gift
from God. We must not try to earn it. We receive it by faith.
We live by faith. We walk by faith.

Christ offers new life if only we will receive Him. Now if a
man is born without any artistic ability there is little hope of his
becoming an artist. If a man has no ear for music he cannot be
educated to be a musician. If he lacks creative imagination and
thought he will never become a poet. Nothing but a miracle
from God can change that.

So we come into the world spiritually dead with a carnal
mind at enmity against God (see Rom. 8:7). Unless Christ gives
us new life from above, and unless we receive that new life,
there is no way to be saved. Christ is the opening of the eyes to
men born blind. Christ is the life that raises us from the dead.
His pierced hand strikes the missing chords to bring forth
heavenly music in our lives. We receive the gift of salvation by
faith alone.

# SALVATION, THE GIFT OF GOD—2

*Blessed are they that do his commandments, that they may have right to the tree of life, and may enter in through the gates into the city. Rev. 22:14.*

This text speaks of a specific fitness for the heavenly city, for life in the new earth. A certain quality of life is required in contrast with those who must remain outside. "Nevertheless we, according to his promise, look for new heavens and a new earth, wherein *dwelleth righteousness.* Wherefore, beloved, seeing that ye look for such things, be diligent that ye may be found of him in peace, *without spot, and blameless"* (2 Peter 3:13, 14).

Our receiving the gift of Christ's righteousness means that we truly want to live that way. That is why we accept the gift. By the power of the Holy Spirit we intend to live accordingly. Our receiving the gift of acquittal from sin's condemnation and the death penalty means that we stand with Christ in His hatred and condemnation of sin. We are not alone in working out our salvation. We are one with Him. The gift of Christ's righteousness guarantees the solution to the sin problem in our lives.

To us as Christians who live on the earth now, this is particularly significant. Now is the preparation time for the life to come, on the new earth. By our lives here we become fitted for that life. This is the worth of man's obedience. The life we live now is of vast importance. Our right to the kingdom of heaven is not founded on our obedience. That right was won for us by Christ. But obedience proves that we are in possession of that right.

An adequate preparation is necessary to practice medicine. The purpose of that profession is to practice medicine efficiently and skillfully. An adequate preparation is necessary to fit oneself to be a good teacher. The purpose of teaching is to educate students well and fit them for whatever profession they choose. The purpose or work of salvation is to prepare us to live in harmony with God, for life on the new earth.

These works of obedience earn no merit. God does not bestow eternal life on the basis of our obedience. But obedience is the beginning of a life here and now that is to continue in the hereafter.

# SAVED OR LOST

*Jesus said to him [Zacchaeus], "Salvation has come to this house today!
. . . the Son of Man has come to seek and save what is lost." Luke 19:9, 10,
N.E.B.*

There are many questions we can ask about our faith
without asking the main question. It is possible to join the
church, to take a willing and cheerful part in its work, and yet
fail to understand or to give the primary purpose of the church
proper and due consideration. It is possible for the church to
occupy itself with social reforms, charities, industries, and all
forms of uplift work, and yet overlook the vital principle that
underlies all these, which alone can make them effective. It is
possible to replace the gospel with such activities. It is possible
to achieve improvement in life here, yet have no guarantee
for any hope beyond. The main question of all is this: Are men
being saved or lost?

The theme of man's salvation from sin runs through all the
pages of Scripture. God has organized and directed all the
energies of heaven for this one purpose. Moral and spiritual
redemption is a real, living, tangible reality in Jesus Christ.
There is no limit to the saving power of His righteousness,
His abiding love for sinners, and the transformation of our
individual lives by His presence. We have the assurance that
these things are true and certain, that Jesus Christ can and will
save us from sin unto righteousness from day to day.

Is salvation a mere word or a reality? Is Christ really able to
make us different persons? Is He able to deliver us from all
those defects that are a result of sin and selfishness under
which we have suffered and caused anguish to others?
Throughout the history of the Christian church, multitudes of
believers have testified to the reality of salvation in Christ.

Whatever else we do by way of resolutions toward self-im-
provement, let us drop all illusions that we can do it on our
own. Let us drop all trust in human projects, human support
and excuses. Let us surrender ourselves with complete abandon into the arms of God's love and mercy. Let us really and
truly desire to be saved from our sins. Let us not put this off.

# WHEN CHRIST MARVELS

*The centurion answered and said, Lord, . . . speak the word only, and my servant shall be healed. . . . When Jesus heard it, he marvelled.* **Matt. 8:8-10.**

Only twice in the Gospels is it said of Jesus that He marveled: when the centurion responded to His promise to come and heal his servant (see Matt. 8:5-10), and at the unbelief of His own kinsmen and neighbors in the city of Nazareth (see Mark 6:4, 6).

The case of the Roman centurion is significant. He did not belong to the Jewish race. He had no religious background or education that we know of. Yet he exercised a faith that was not found in Israel. In the case of Jesus' hometown folks, they never seemed to be able to get over the fact that He had grown up among them. They were not impressed by what they knew about Him. They had associated with Him for thirty years. They had seen His spotless life, His character of love and obedience. They lacked the spiritual insight to recognize Him as the Messiah, the Son of God. "He came unto his own, and his own received him not" (John 1:11).

The Bible does not record that Christ marveled at the miracles He wrought. When He healed the man born blind, when He raised Lazarus from the dead, these seemed to Him to be the most natural thing to expect. We ourselves marvel when we see miracles of body healing, a restoration to physical health. We tend to be more impressed by these external manifestations than by the spiritual restoration of a diseased mind and sinful spirit. People are far more impressed by outward wonders. It was not so with Christ. He marveled at people's lack of faith.

What we marvel at is an indication of the kind of person we are. What really impresses us? What captures our attention and interest? We stand overwhelmed by the tragedies of life. "Why does God not do something?" we ask. But our great need is the miracle of spiritual rebirth and transformation. Not the loss of property, health, money, or position is our greatest concern. Far above all these things is a divine course of limitless spiritual power adequate for every test and crisis.

Because faith in Christ means so much for our salvation and daily living, He marvels when we readily exercise it.

# COMMITTED TO RIGHTEOUSNESS

*God be thanked, you, who once were slaves of sin, . . . have become slaves of righteousness.* **Rom. 6:17, 18, N.E.B.**

What we are saved for is equally as important as what we are saved from. The Christian experience is not an escape, but life more abundant. We are saved from death in order to live for Christ. We are saved from sin in order to live in righteousness. Life in and with Christ is more significant than the death we are delivered from.

Many are reluctant to talk of works of righteousness because they have the idea that one thereby moves from salvation by grace and is once again "under law." We do not need to put a restraint on works, provided they are the product of our relationship to our Lord and the fruit of the indwelling Spirit.

Furthermore, good works are not ends in themselves. They will not save us. But they are the best evidence that we have experienced Christ, the best recommendation of our faith. The church can be greatly advanced in the community by genuine Christian examples of what it means to follow Christ. Few things avail to inspire others as does a life where the priority is eternal values. The Christian counts in this world to the extent that he is committed to righteousness, to purity, to honesty, and to love for his fellow men.

That we have committed our lives to righteousness is evidenced by the strength and beauty of the moral life we live. The conduct of many professing Christians is less than desirable. That is what might be expected from a vague or misconceived idea of what salvation is. We are so to trust in our righteous God and in His saving grace that we remain completely loyal to Him and hold fast our integrity. Every moral principle of God's law comes to its fulfillment in the life of a true Christian. The purpose of the gospel is to commit us to Christ's righteousness in every way. Every faculty and affection of our natures is delivered from sinful ends. We are transformed and pressed into the glorious service of purity, unselfishness, love, and peace.

# STRONG IN FAITH

*[Abraham] never doubted God's promise in unbelief, but, strong in faith, give honour to God, in the firm conviction of his power to do what he had promised.* **Rom. 4:19-21, N.E.B.**

It was high noon with Abraham when on Mount Moriah the Lord provided him a lamb for sacrifice and saved his son. Then he lived in the full assurance of faith. But there were times when his faith seemed to fail. We tremble to think how nearly he came to the brink of disaster on several other occasions.

Men who have won great honors in life have cause to wear them with humility when they recall the occasions of their poor judgment and lack of courage. We all have experienced difficult times in our spiritual life. Our faith was in danger. In dark hours we have doubted the goodness and the guidance of the Lord; our interests were absorbed in the secular. The love of the world seemed to master us.

In the mirage of the desert, objects become strangely distorted. A mud bank exhibits the appearance of a magnificent city with domes and towers. A few stunted bushes are transformed into a forest of stately trees. So it is with worldly fame, treasures, and pleasures; the importance we attach to them is false and exaggerated.

Often we find it almost impossible to resist the illusion. Little by little we yield to the tyranny of worldly interests, to the indulgence of questionable pleasures. Prayer becomes infrequent and unreal. The house of God is neglected. The Scriptures lose their relish. The family altar drops stone by stone into the dust. We remember how nearly we were betrayed by appetite, passion, covetousness, and pride. The partition between the true and the false became very thin. We slipped on brinks over which others had fallen. We singed our wings in flames by which others had perished.

But in Christ we have found victory. The Christian life ought not to be a series of narrow escapes from sin. We are to run with sure step and confident hope. By this time in the world's history we should have discovered the faith that overcomes the world. We have a sure basis for our faith. Christ is sufficient for every trial and temptation, and deeper than all the conflicts we have.

# KEPT FROM FALLING

*Now unto him that is able to keep you from falling, and to present you faultless before the presence of his glory with exceeding joy. Jude 24.*

Many Christians know what the scripture "scarcely be saved" means (1 Peter 4:18). There is something wrong with the Christian who lives always in peril of falling into sin. We should not be only just saved. There is a safe margin clear and distinct between the spiritual strength of God and the gulf of sin. Where the Christian is ever backsliding and stumbling into sin, there is real weakness of character, a central lack of spiritual power.

We would falter less if we prayed more. We would find safe living in this world of sin if we were more devout in our worship of God. We would triumph more with complete confidence in God's truth and His promises.

He who is rich in mercy, for His great love wherewith He loves us, is not willing that we should lapse into sin. We are to live in the fullness of the divine resources that God has provided for us. Men give their blood to the blood bank for the sake of saving other lives. Yet, whenever man draws off this precious fluid, nature seems always ready to make up the deficiency, so that the donor shall not suffer injury. The body has this recuperative power. However, it is in such a surplus spiritual resource that many followers of Christ are lacking.

"Be filled with the Spirit" (Eph. 5:18). Such a spiritual endowment from God means we should possess an abundance of spiritual power that keeps us strong to resist every attack of the enemy, triumphant over the severest trials to which we may be subjected.

Faith in God makes a strong Christian. Faith unites us with the greatness of divine power. The victorious power of faith was revealed once and for all in Christ when He lived on the earth. In Christ, God has given us everything. That is what Pentecost proved. Weak fishermen and tax collectors were endowed with a divine, victorious power that enabled them to pull down the strongholds of sin and build the kingdom of God in human hearts. Ever since then, many Christians have been victorious. Joined to Christ, there is no need to fail. All of us are to bear the likeness of our King.

# IN GOD WE TRUST

*O Lord my God, in thee do I put my trust.* **Ps. 7:1.**

A person can have faith in many things. Most of us do. We have faith in our friends, in our doctor, in the businesses that sell shoes, clothing, food. We have faith in the car that takes us to work or to church. We believe that the created wonders of our age will do for us what they have always done. This faith endures in spite of the fact that people, machines, and organizations often fail.

Yet how little faith we seem to have in God at times, in the One who has never failed, who has never let us down. The Bible continually calls upon us to "trust in the Lord with all thine heart; and lean not unto thine own understanding" (Prov. 3:5).

The human heart is the only spot on earth that can properly be called the dwelling place of God. "I dwell in the high and holy place, with him also that is of a contrite and humble spirit" (Isa. 57:15). Our greatest honor is to be the dwelling place of God.

To live by faith means we cannot be holy at a distance from God. We cannot be righteous and live apart from God. Faith means we have accepted Christ as the center of our life and living. We are to be noted in heaven for our firm faith, not for wealth; for righteousness by faith, not for ritual. Faith means we consent to allow Christ to renew us in spirit and in mind, to wash us from the power of sin. Faith unites us to God. We cannot be sons and daughters of God without belonging to God.

We may conceive of God as an easygoing, lax, and kindly Deity—a good-natured Being who bends over His rebellious children and says, "My children, it does not matter. I forgive you." That would probably make it easy, but it would never make us holy and victorious over sin. When by faith the presence of Christ abides in us, there is the fullness of spiritual life like unto that of our Lord. Our living, exalted Lord restores in us the essential greatness of humanity. The whole secret of salvation and redemption is disclosed in Him who sends forth His Spirit for our restoration to the image of God.

# LIVING BY FAITH

*The just shall live by faith.* **Rom. 1:17.**

Ever since Adam and Eve sought life apart from dependence on their Maker, man has been self-determined, not subject to the law of God or to the perfect righteousness provided by another, Jesus Christ. This continues our separation from God. We are dead in trespasses and sins. Regardless of how good or how bad we might consider ourselves, anything that keeps us apart from God, even trust in our own righteousness and good works, continues the original sin of Adam.

Men are not willing to come to terms with their own bankruptcy before God. Any religious system or formula that fails to shift a man's center from self and his own efforts back to Christ and His righteousness is not of God. All such efforts are humanistic and become at last demonic in a final separation from God.

Faith comes to rest on Christ, not on ourselves. Faith involves believing the truth, but it is more than assent to the truth. Faith means that we sense a personal Presence. Two persons are involved with each other, Christ and you. To be truly Christian, faith must bring Christ, His life, and His death, within reach of our own involvement. Unless the living Christ takes over in our life through the power of the Holy Spirit, there is no point of contact between us and God. Christ grips us at the center of our life. We cannot do for ourselves that which only Christ can do.

Abraham and Sarah both realized that they could have no children. Yet God had promised them a son and heir. If they were to have a son, it would have to be by an act of God, by the power of God. Christ alone could do that. They were helpless.

Without faith we have no way of becoming righteous regardless of how hard we try or how well we do. The basic problem of sin is not only the failure to do the best we can. It is a broken fellowship, a ruptured relationship, a separation from God.

Christ is not personally our Saviour and Lord unless we are really dependent upon, and changed by, Him. Faith turns us completely away from ourselves back to trust in, and dependence on, Christ. We are one with Him.

45

# CENTERED IN CHRIST

*So then they which be of faith are blessed with faithful Abraham. For as many as are of the works of the law are under the curse. Gal. 3:9, 10.*

When we say that we are saved by faith alone without works, we mean without our own works. However, faith makes the works of Christ and of the Holy Spirit possible in us. That is why God requires only faith on our part. Not because works will not follow, but because Christ works in us "both to will and to do of his good pleasure" (Phil. 2:13).

In other words, there are works produced by the natural man, which God says are "filthy rags." They are our own righteousness. There are also works produced by Christ in us that belong to His righteousness and not ours. Faith, therefore, stands in contrast to any supposed independent good works of our own. The cause of our salvation is not something that God sees in us. Our faith does not give God anything from within us whereby He now approves of us. Faith makes possible Christ in us, who lives a godly life in us, the "faith which worketh by love" (Gal. 5:6). Faith brings works of righteousness from Christ, not from ourselves. That is why faith alone pleases God. We are now centered in Christ, restored to God. This makes all the difference in the world so far as our relationship to God is concerned. Faith makes God the ruling center of our lives, not self. We no longer own ourselves.

Living by faith in Christ our center is a matter of first importance. It is a personal matter. Dependence upon a power outside of ourselves is an individual experience. We may partake in some general call to stand up for Christ, to join a revival movement. At the same time we may be aware that we have not personally allowed Christ to possess our life.

Will the last revival of true godliness be ushered in by some General Conference session and action? The coming of Christ and the Holy Spirit cannot be organized. Our great need is for individual Christians who have discovered the reality of the transforming power of Christ's righteousness. This is what constitutes the backbone of the church. One Christian who has Christ at the center of his life, who has Christ's righteousness in his life fully, led by the Holy Spirit, can transform the home, the community, and the church.

# SALVATION BY FAITH ALONE

*He that believeth on the Son hath everlasting life; and he that believeth not the Son shall not see life.* John 3:36.

The gospel meets us at every turn with an imperative demand for faith. Our very life and salvation depend on the exercise and response of faith. Why does God make our fate depend on faith? Why can we not have salvation without it? Why is it we cannot please God without faith?

Let us bear in mind that we can expect no miracles from God for our salvation regardless of our attitude. God sincerely and spontaneously seeks to communicate not only salvation but all spiritual gifts. But even God Himself cannot give us what we are unable to receive. The reception of any spiritual gift needs a hand and a mind to take it. The goodness of God meets the freedom of man. God will not force the gates of the mind. He will not force His way upon the man who chooses to walk in darkness.

Faith is the instrument of the mind that receives the gift of God. There is nothing unreasonable when God insists that the reception of His gift of salvation needs a corresponding attitude on our part called faith. Once we admit that faith is the hand by which we receive from God, then God's demand for faith becomes wholly reasonable, because it is grounded in our free will.

We can enter into the world of music, art, medicine, only by an attitude of mind that desires to receive what these areas of life have to offer. The very desire to be loved means that we are prepared to receive that love. In our salvation Christ is everything—our wisdom, our righteousness, our sanctification, and our redemption. Salvation means a lifelong reception of all these things.

This in turn often requires sacrifice. When Christ enters our lives, evil tenants must leave. Christ dwells with the holy, but not with the impure. If we wish to have Christ dwell in us, then we must part with those guests who are enemies of Christ. He knocks at the door of our heart. Let us not say we have faith if we keep the door closed. Christ reveals to us whether we have true faith that accepts Him. At that point we are to give up everything that is contrary to His life and character.

47

# FAITH FULFILLED BY WORKS—1

*But can you not see, you quibbler, that faith divorced from deeds is barren?* James 2:20, N.E.B.

We are saved by faith, not by our own merits. Faith is the gift of the Holy Spirit. Faith is the rope thrown to the drowning man, by which another pulls him safely to shore. Christ is the object of our faith. Faith is that response which brings us to the Saviour. It lays our sins on Jesus. It takes off the rags of our own righteousness and puts on us Christ's righteousness. It covers us with a robe provided only by Christ. So what must we do to be saved? "Believe on the Lord Jesus Christ."

Consequently, many conclude that men are saved without works of any kind. But let no one deceive us. Works are the fruit of faith. "No whoremonger, nor unclean person, nor covetous man, who is an idolater, hath any inheritance in the kingdom of . . . God" (Eph. 5:5). Christian experience without a sound morality is phony. Faith without a godly life, that never touches or changes the conduct of a man, is lifeless. True faith walks in the path of the Ten Commandments. Faith that works is kind, not selfish, obedient, not disobedient. Faith that works keeps husbands loving, wives patient. It banishes sin and evil in the home.

We believe that God will have mercy on the chief of sinners; that all the sins we have committed may be washed away by the blood of Christ. We believe that God's redemption in Christ and the gift of righteousness is sufficient to bear all the sins ever committed; that God despairs of no one; that whoever turns to Christ, may be saved to the uttermost.

Unchristian people often indulge in a loose morality. The gospel without a sound morality is totally unchristian. It is strange indeed to believe that such people who claim to accept Christ could possibly continue to live like that. If such a person can claim to have experienced salvation, then the seed of the Word of God sown in the heart yields no harvest, the Holy Spirit produces no fruit, the power of God gives no solid moral backbone to keep the spiritual frame erect.

God always communicates His saving grace and power with a view to the restoration of men to the image of God.

# FAITH FULFILLED BY WORKS—2

*Seest thou how faith wrought with his works, and by works was faith made perfect?* James 2:22.

It is easy to repeat the words "Jesus is Lord." But the gospel requires more than the formation of words, more than the ability to repeat so many texts from memory. Take the rather mischievous word "surrender." To say "I surrender" or to sing the hymn "All to Jesus I surrender" can sound like a way of relaxing one's way into the kingdom of God.

We speak of "letting go" and "letting God." But Christians are forged on the anvil of commitment rather than by any method of passive relinquishment. Decision is a much-abused word. If it comes easy, it is most likely to be false. Deciding to live for Christ is no easy matter. It involves the most ruthless examination of oneself and an equally total commitment. It is a very personal affair.

True Christians are lovely in their lives, kindhearted, generous, just in their dealings, honest to a penny, and in their allegiance to God and to His will, true as steel. No teaching of religion, no preaching of the gospel, can be more pernicious than that which puts obedience and disobedience on the same plane, truth and falsehood in the same company of saints. To believe there is no connection between faith and good works, between truth and conduct, is to make of no consequence either the discovery of Bible truth or the saving work of Jesus Christ. What we believe and what we do relative to the truth of God's Word are united in any genuine faith. No man who trusts in Christ has the license to break the law of God. Not thieves, not killers, not adulterers do we want in life; but virtuous, honest, pure, and unselfish Christians. And this does matter. It makes all the difference in the world, in the home, in the church, and in the community.

Our eternal destiny is bound up with a faith-love response that we give to the truth and to the law of God. We are Christians by faith only when we become God's man, God's woman, when the sovereign rule of God becomes effective in our lives. This is what salvation by faith alone means—the indwelling life of Christ, who keeps God's commandments.

# GOD'S GOOD WORK IN YOU

*He which hath begun a good work in you will perform it.* **Phil. 1:6.**

Paul calls conversion a good work. It ends a life of sin and darkness. We were without God in the world until Jesus came into our lives. But now we see love, mercy, righteousness, the gift of God to us. Such mercy as we could never imagine has come to us. Now we enjoy fellowship and communion with Him. We are His children, His friends.

Paul emphasizes the fact that it is God who begins this good work in us. "No man can come to me, except the Father which hath sent me draw him" (John 6:44). God makes the first approach. He takes the first step. He is in all our lives "the first and the last," "the beginning and the ending," the "Alpha and Omega" (Rev. 1:8, 11). "God . . . worketh in you both to will and to do of his good pleasure" (Phil. 2:13).

The work of salvation is begun and continued by God, not by us. Let us not venture to do it ourselves. Of ourselves we could never begin it, nor could we continue it. Let us stand by God's Word. Let us be attentive to what God does and to what He says. Let us fear lest God may often have been willing to do His work in us, but we would not.

The work done by God and not by us—what an antidote to pride and self-righteousness this is! Who of us can fail to humble himself and say, "If God had not called me, I would not have come. If God had not worked this change in me, it would never have taken place. If God by His Spirit had not led me to a life of trust and obedience, I would have continued in my enmity against the law of God." Who of us can ever glory in himself?

What good news it is: He who hath begun the work will finish it in our lives. We will meet with many difficulties. There are many obstacles. But we have put our hand to the plow. We have fixed our eyes on the incorruptible riches of heaven. We seek not the glory that the world gives, but eternal glory with Christ. He will not suffer the enemy to regain his power over us so long as we commit our lives to Him. Let us not wander from God. Neglect not the study of God's Word. Let not our prayers become cold, less earnest, and less frequent. God has no intention of leaving us to perish.

# FULLY PERSUADED

*For I know whom I have believed, and am persuaded that he is able to keep that which I have committed unto him against that day.* **2 Tim. 1:12.**

At times the temptation is to get discouraged and give up. We are tempted to feel that we are not going to make it. The apostle Paul is fully persuaded of the keeping power of Christ. This is the privilege of us all. Be assured that He who loves us so greatly as to call us to Himself, will henceforth love us enough to keep us safe. "Why art thou cast down, O my soul? and why art thou disquieted within me? hope thou in God: for I shall yet praise him, who is the health of my countenance, and my God" (Ps. 42:11).

His arm is not shortened that he cannot save us to the uttermost. He is near to us when we pray. If we kept a daily record of all His mercies, we would never doubt His faithfulness. There is not a page of Scripture that does not speak of His love and power to save. "He that spared not his own Son, but delivered him up for us all, how shall he not with him also freely give us all things?" (Rom. 8:32).

That we will accomplish all we undertake here and now is by no means certain. When the time comes for us to go, everything about us is incomplete. But God never leaves the work of His hands imperfect. He never grows weary in well doing. He never gets discouraged with us because of our failures. The more we need Him, the more certain we are of securing His help. "This is the Father's will which hath sent me, that of all which he hath given me I should lose nothing" (John 6:39). "I give unto them [my sheep] eternal life; and they shall never perish, neither shall any man pluck them out of my hand" (chap. 10:28).

In this very day, God is sealing His children here below with a seal that no power on earth will be able to break. Take courage. However small the progress, do not lose heart. Be assured that He who has lighted your lamp, though it may burn dim at times, will never extinguish it, but will pour fresh oil into your lamp that it may give more light. Trust in God. What you cannot do by yourself, God can do. He is your strength. Your responsibility is to commit your life to Him, to walk with Christ.

# GOD WORKS IN YOU

*For it is God which worketh in you both to will and to do of his good pleasure.* **Phil. 2:13.**

For ten years or more Paul had labored in Philippi to win people to Christ. He was now a prisoner in Rome. The believers at Philippi regarded Paul with tender affection and deeply sympathized with him in his trials. Desirous of knowing his condition, they sent one of their brethren, Epaphroditus, to Rome. Paul sent him back with this Epistle to the Philippian believers. It is full of confidence in God's continuing power to keep and to transform them unto the day of Jesus Christ. This continuing work of Christ in the life involves sanctification, obedience, increasing love for one another, and the working out of the fruits of the Spirit.

There are many works performed in the universe and in the world, in heaven and on earth. But this is not the work of which Paul speaks. He says that the work must be performed *in you.* It is within your heart and life that Christ continues to perform His work. He is satisfied with nothing less. He must take possession of your inmost heart and life.

The Scriptures speak of two works: one was performed without us, independent of our response. The other must be performed within us. The first is the work of redemption, which was wrought by Jesus Christ when He reconciled us to God on the cross. It is the work of Christ's perfect righteousness to meet our lack of it.

But we cannot profit by it so long as the work within us has not taken place. Unless the work of Christ has made us acknowledge our need of His righteousness, led us to forsake sin and to be born again to a new life, the essential work of Christ is wanting. It has not been performed in us. It is vain for us to be perfectly knowledgeable as to the gospel, to be able to reason with ease respecting all the religious ideas involved. It is vain for us to say with our lips, "Lord, Lord," unless the redemptive work of Christ is being done in our hearts. Unless we daily present our bodies and lives a living sacrifice, holy, acceptable unto God, all the rest is nothing but show and lip service. "The kingdom of God is not in word, but in power" (1 Cor. 4:20).

# "NOW I SEE"

*Whereas I was blind, now I see.* John 9:25.

These words were uttered by a man who was born blind, and miraculously healed by Christ. In the previous chapter Christ had publicly declared in the Temple, "I am the light of the world: he that followeth me shall not walk in darkness, but shall have the light of life" (John 8:12). He was immediately challenged by the Pharisees. They took issue with Him, denied His claims, taunted Him to the point of ridicule, and said He had a devil. Finally, they became so incensed that they took up stones to cast at Him. Christ then walked out of the Temple with His disciples.

There on the steps lay a blind man. The claim of the blind man upon Christ was irresistible. As "the light of the world" He must give light to the man who from his birth had sat in darkness. Christ not only proclaims the truth but works the truth. He not only teaches truth. He enables us to experience the truth.

Christianity consists of two things: a true knowledge of Christ and an experience of Him. Christ comes not merely with information. He comes so that we exclaim with delight, "Once I was blind, but now I see." The Christ who conquered sin for us is the Christ who conquers sin in us. The Christ who proclaimed Himself the Light of the world has changed our darkness to light. The Christ who in His life on earth wrought out a perfect righteousness is the Christ who works His righteousness in us. The Christ who is the Truth, leads us into all truth.

This experience is ours as much as it was that of the blind man or any other man in the Bible. There is no reason why it should not be. There is no presumption in reaching out your hand and taking Christ as your Saviour and Lord. We have, each of us, a whole salvation and redemption. Christ's only intention in all His deeds and words is to make us living witnesses of His marvelous grace and strength. Christ, the Light, shines into our hearts and minds, and keeps on shining with ever deeper meaning. All this comes to us like the wind across the strings of an Aeolian harp, until we are constrained to proclaim, "Once I was blind, but now I see."

# REPENTANCE

*Him hath God exalted . . . for to give repentance to Israel, and forgiveness of sins.* **Acts 5:31.**

Christ came proclaiming the good news of resurrection to a new life, to free those enslaved and held prisoners by the prince of darkness, to make the weak strong, to open the ears of those who are deaf to the love and mercy of God. Christ came bringing God to us. He wants us to return to God. Therefore, He calls, "Repent ye."

The original word means a change of mind, of heart, a complete shift at the center of our lives, a return to God. Repentance is the highest creative activity of which we are capable. It is not only a passing outburst of emotional regret for past sins that quickly wears away. It is not simply saying, "I am sorry for what I have done." There are momentary feelings of regret, the stings of remorse, the fear of punishment. Thus repentance has been thought of as a sad, painful, humiliating experience.

Repentance does include true sorrow for sins committed, but Christ has much more in mind. He calls for a complete turning to God and acceptance of His mind in place of our self-centered mind—total commitment to His side. Repentance is not a word to be feared and avoided. It is a wonderful word. When we turn to God with all our hearts and minds, that is repentance. When we make Christ our center of reference, that is repentance. When we make the mind of Christ our mind, that is repentance.

The concern of repentance is a change of mind that prepares us to judge and condemn sin before we have actually committed it. We recognize the seed of sin the moment it enters the mind, and we condemn it right then. We face the problem of sin at its source. Therefore we refuse to go into sin. We have the mind of Christ. "As he thinketh in his heart, so is he" (Prov. 23:7). True repentance is aimed at motivation, changing the motivation before we have committed the sin itself. We need more than forgiveness for past sins. We need the mind of Christ that keeps us from getting into sin. That is what Christ offers to us in repentance.

# FORGIVENESS

*If we confess our sins, he is faithful and just to forgive us our sins, and to cleanse us from all unrighteousness.* 1 John 1:9.

Forgiveness and cleansing are two of the most important blessings we have in Christ. They form the heart of Christ's redeeming work.

He who desires to begin a new life in Christ becomes conscious of a past that he cannot change. Sin is a dark and slavish reality. Nothing short of a miracle of God's grace can purge our guilt and set us free from sin. God loves us as a father loves his son. An earthly father should have no difficulty forgiving his son who may run wild. As Christian parents, our love for our children never ceases. It is always there. So much the more is it with our heavenly Father.

"Despisest thou the riches of his goodness and forbearance and longsuffering; not knowing that the goodness of God leadeth thee to repentance?" (Rom. 2:4). If we are "in Christ" all our sins of the past are utterly past and forgiven. In forgiving us, God does not make light either of His law or of our sins. In forgiving us, God does not mean that he no longer remembers our sins. He does. God does not suffer a case of amnesia as to the kind of life we have lived or are living. He does not ignore what we have been.

When our children sin against us and ask our forgiveness, we grant it immediately; but we still remember what they have done. In Christian forgiveness these forgiven sins are no longer an issue between father and son. So it is with God. Forgiven sins are no longer an issue so long as we maintain the right relationship with God. We must know that our Father has really forgiven us. Men speak of forgiving but not forgetting. By this they mean that they still hold men's sins against them. But to say this of God is not the same thing. To say that God does not forget is explained by the fact that He keeps a record of the sins of all men in the books of heaven. This does not mean, however, that they stand as an issue between us and God. God goes all the way in forgiveness. Once we sincerely confess, God makes no reservations. The freedom He gives us from guilt and condemnation is complete.

# CLEANSED FROM SIN

*The blood of Jesus Christ . . . cleanseth us from all sin.* 1 John 1:7.

Forgiveness and cleansing go together. God is not content with just forgiveness. God's purpose is to go further and cleanse us from sin. Christ's treatment of the leper illustrates the point. "Once he was approached by a leper, who knelt before him begging his help. 'If only you will,' said the man, 'you can cleanse me.' . . . Jesus stretched out his hand, touched him, and said, 'Indeed I will; be clean again.' The leprosy left him immediately, and he was clean" (Mark 1:40-42, N.E.B.).

God stamped leprosy as unclean, and using this as an object lesson, we may understand God's abhorrence of all the forms that sin takes. Leprosy was then a living death. It was a gradual and horrible dissolution, the body rotting out of the grave instead of in it. Sin is like that. It destroys a man before it destroys the body. Christians are made alive in Christ, a new creation. The leprosy of sin is truly dealt with.

But a sick man forgiven of his sins could never be content to remain a sick man. Consider the paralytic man let down through the roof to reach Christ. First, his sins were forgiven, then he was healed. If we have faith to believe that Christ has forgiven our sins, we trust also that He will surely heal and cleanse us. Forgiveness is costly business, based on the sacrifice of Christ. God is not dealing carelessly with sin.

When we come to Christ, cleansing is equally as certain as is forgiveness. God does not give us one without the other. For the paralytic, Christ did both. When we cry, "O Christ, make me clean," God always answers, "Be thou clean." We say as did Peter when Christ knelt to wash his feet, "Not only my feet but my head, my hands, and my heart." Let us not settle for less.

We have to quit playing around with our sins. If we really want a way out from our sins we must let Christ cleanse us completely. He is never satisfied to remove one sinful spot at a time. He makes sure of a whole cleansing if we commit our lives to Him. To cleanse our whole lives is God's way. Let us say with David: "Create in me a clean heart, O God, and renew a right spirit within me" (Ps. 51:10). God will reply, not by making us a little cleaner, but by making us every whit clean and whole.

# THE SENSE OF GUILT

*O wretched man that I am! who shall deliver me from the body of this death? I thank God through Jesus Christ our Lord.* **Rom. 7:24, 25.**

The chronic sense of guilt that is characteristic of sinful man is more prevalent than we are ready to admit. What is the nature of guilt? First, there is a guilt we feel before God. Truth and conscience have been tampered with. Maybe we have broken the moral law or violated the principles of righteousness that we find in God's Word. When we have sinned against God in this way, the guilt is clear for most of us. There is a sense of inner disquiet. Guilt also grows out of feelings, attitudes, and thoughts that we know are not Christlike, from all that registers as shame, inferiority, or feelings of worthlessness and rejection.

Guilt must be fully forgiven and removed or it will find ways to create more inner problems. God has so constituted us that guilt must be resolved. Our sins and our sinfulness can become greater than we can bear. Suppose that in walking to school every day, or at work about the house, you are compelled to carry a fifty-pound sack of sand on your shoulders. How long before you would break under the load? Unless you could find some way to get relief the burden would finally crush you.

Guilt can act the same way upon the heart and mind. It presses down so heavily that it creates emotional and physical problems. No Christian should carry a load of guilt around with him day after day.

We must accept God's forgiveness of us and also forgive ourselves for the sins we have committed. In Christ's day the woman taken in adultery was dragged before Him by the Pharisees. The law affirmed that the guilty woman be stoned to death. Her condemners sought to trap Jesus in His judgment of the woman. But He wrote in the sand. When they read what He had written they felt themselves guilty. There was no condemnation of the woman on the part of Jesus. He did not condone her sin; neither did He reject her. People do not need either advice or judgment so much as they need love and acceptance as a person. Because God is like this, we must do likewise.

# GUILT FREE—1

*There is therefore now no condemnation to them which are in Christ Jesus.* **Rom. 8:1.**

Much of the guilt we feel arises from our relation to one another, to society, and to the religious requirements that prevail. Some of the standards are legitimate. Some of them are not. The guilt we attribute to others is quite unwarranted when it is our own rules that we seek to proclaim as God's standards. Also, the stricter the religion to which we belong, the easier it is to regard every infraction of a rule as the violation of a principle, and the easier to make people feel guilty when they fall short. Without the love of God in our hearts and in our religion, the easier it is to become judgmental of people who do not live according to the rules we have set up. The higher the standards, the more we automatically sense the wrongdoings of people. The temptation is to sit in the judgment seat and play God. People sense it without our saying a word.

False guilt feelings are created by poorly based perfectionistic attitudes and unbalanced comprehension of doctrine on the part of parents toward children, religious leaders toward their church members, professed Christians toward the less morally favorable and the spiritually inadequate. The tendency is to communicate rejection, disapproval, of those who may appear to us to be "too liberal" in their thinking and living. Judging, criticizing, and condemning are common practice among many professed Christians. When this happens we destroy personal relationships.

There is a Christian and an unchristian way of treating the failures of other people. The unchristian way is to express the registration of faults and failings, either in attitude or in words of scolding, disapproval, rebuke, and slighting remarks. We tend to make capital out of little things. Nothing gets by us without our taking note of it.

We who daily walk with Jesus Christ are always drawing others to Him, to live in harmony with Him, always leading them back to our heavenly Father. Sin, guilt, and condemnation are discredited, not love, mercy, and forgiveness. Christ wins by redeeming love, not by condemnation.

# GUILT FREE—2

*Who shall lay any thing to the charge of God's elect? It is God that justi-*
*fieth.* **Rom. 8:33.**

Too many people take everything on the side of anxiety
and are guilt-ridden. They do not know how to forgive themselves. They are forever coming short of the ideal. To be guilt
free they need the loving forgiveness and acceptance of our
Lord and of fellow Christians.

There are those respectable Christians who have ceased to
love the unlovable and the wayward. They no longer feel
deeply or care greatly for sinners. The love and compassion of
Christ has pretty well faded away. They become constricted
and contracted in their religion and in their judgments of
people.

People on every hand want someone to love them as they
are. God's rescue of us will seem great only in proportion to the
acknowledgment of our own need for forgiveness and mercy.
If we come to see ourselves as we really are, disfigured by
selfishness, pride, conceit, envy, and lack of love in the face
of all that Christ's love means to us, then we ourselves can
find freedom and can communicate it to others.

Freedom from guilt comes when we open ourselves to
Christ, to acknowledge the kind of persons we really are. The
great enemies of life are not our refusal to conform outwardly
to church standards, although standards are important. The
real issues do not reside here. The great enemies of life are
within us: fear, anxiety, guilt, insecurity. These destroy all
that is beautiful in life. Back of emotional problems for many
people is the unwillingness or inability to accept themselves
for what they are, to acknowledge this before God, and to
allow God's love to take over. There can be no freedom from
guilt and from the sense of rejection unless we are willing to
face the truth about ourselves, accept God's forgiveness, and
then forgive ourselves.

In Jesus we have forgiveness for what we are. To experience God's love, mercy, and acceptance is to meet our emotional problems squarely. To feel the forgiving way in which
God looks at our lives means we have overcome one of the
most serious handicaps to emotional recovery.

# CHRIST MAKES ALL THINGS NEW—1

*A new commandment I give unto you, That ye love one another.* John
13:34.

Is this a new commandment? John also writes, "Brethren,
I write no new commandment unto you, but an old commandment which ye had from the beginning" (1 John 2:7). The
same commandment to love was given to the children of
Israel (see Deut. 6:5). What is meant, then, by its being new?

The New Testament Greek has two words that are translated by the word "new" in the English. One means new in
time. That is, it has not been known or given before. The
other means "anew, renewed, restored to newness." The
second word is used in the scriptures quoted above. The commandment is an ancient one, the same they had from the beginning. But when Christ comes into our lives all things are renewed. We are a new creation (see 2 Cor. 5:17). This is God's way
of stating what Christ does when He comes into our lives. We
become new men and new women. We are in one way the
same person, in another sense we are renewed. So it is with the
commandments. Some people would like to replace the Decalogue with a new one, but there is no such thing. It is the same
law, but renewed, restored to its freshness in Christ.

This great truth is emphasized throughout the Bible.
"Bless the Lord, O my soul, and forget not all his benefits;
who forgiveth all thine iniquities; who healeth all thy diseases;
who redeemeth thy life from destruction; . . . so that thy youth
is *renewed* like the eagle's" (Ps. 103:2-5). God's love and mercy
are "new every morning" (Lam. 3:23). They are extended
afresh to us every day. Isaiah speaks of the coming of the new
earth. It is the same earth that God created, but it is restored
to its original purity and perfection.

The Bible speaks of our being "dead in trespasses and
sins" (Eph. 2:1). Christ redeems us. He restores and renews
spiritual life in us. Nothing significant will happen until Christ
makes us new. Suppose we have a revival? In what would it
consist? The discovery of truth we have never known before?
Not necessarily. We should experience spiritual renewal that
would make our whole lives new, our homes new, our relationships with people new. This is what God offers us.

# CHRIST MAKES ALL THINGS NEW—2

*And he that sat upon the throne said, Behold, I make all things new.*
**Rev. 21:5.**

As we usually think of the term, it is not new husbands, wives, children, that we need; not a different family to live with, but people in the family made new by Christ; not different teachers and preachers, but men and women renewed by the Holy Spirit. It is not a new church we need to attend, but a renewed church. We do not need a new Bible, but the same Word made new to us by the Holy Spirit. Truth becomes vibrant and alive with the reality of Jesus Christ. Doctrines that have become old and decrepit, that have lost their vital freshness, become new by the Spirit of God. In our hands the Bible becomes a new book by the Spirit.

We have a built-in capacity for what is right and wrong. We have a built-in capacity in our conscience that makes us feel guilty and inadequate when we sin. But we have no natural equipment for dealing with our sin and guilt. Zaccheus must have known he was a dishonest man. As a tax gatherer he had hired himself out to the Romans. He squeezed extra money for himself. He knew that he ought not to take money that did not belong to him. It was not until he met Jesus Christ that he found the power to become a new man. He found acceptance, forgiveness, love, and a new heart. He gave half of his goods to feed the poor. He restored fourfold his ill-gotten gains. Jesus made a new man out of him.

Paul knew that his hostility toward Christians was wrong. He must have felt condemned for being an accomplice in the death of Stephen. But it was not until he met Christ in that momentous face-to-face encounter on the Damascus road that he could do anything about it. Then he became a new man and one of the greatest Christians of all time.

The urgent need of the church is not new gadgets, new programs, new machinery; but new life and the renewing love of God flowing through us all. Whatever else our church accomplishes or undertakes, if it fails to make new men and new women in Christ, it fails altogether. Our great need is not a new message, but a renewed message by the Holy Spirit.

# LIFE ONLY IN CHRIST

*For in him dwelleth all the fulness of the Godhead bodily. And ye are complete in him.* **Col. 2:9, 10.**

Whistler, the painter, once remarked that art critics are often artists who have failed. I suppose that this may be true of most of the critics of the Christian religion. But God has not failed. Christians are born of God, not self made. Only God can make a flower. We cannot. Only God can make a real Christian. Only in Christ have we a perfect righteousness, never in ourselves. If we depend on our own ability we must surely fail.

When we turn and commit our lives to Christ an entirely new life begins. To experience new life from God is one thing. To develop a moral personality by our own power is another. To receive the approval of men for our self-styled good living may be considered enough for many people. To share in the life of Christ is the one and only requirement in living the Christian life.

The Christian life is the greatest supernatural adventure known. It requires a clear conviction about Christ as Saviour and Lord, openheartedness to Him, and total commitment. Living the Christian life is always the work of the Holy Spirit. It is something spiritual and supernatural. Living that endures and triumphs is the work of God.

Christ's work in us virtually concerns the whole of our lives, keeping us spiritually prime and vigorous seven days of the week. In the maze of daily activities our energies are frequently dissipated. Keeping spiritually vigorous depends on our daily living with Christ. All the Biblical terms that describe the Christian life are personal. Forgiveness, regeneration, sanctification, justification—all have a personal meaning. They all speak of Christ's work experienced in our lives.

Who will deny that at times the Christian life appears hard to maintain. To meet every situation in life, to fulfill all our duties, to be a loving friend at large to all men, to face and overcome temptation, all this, we are often told, is hard work. I agree that it is. In fact, it is impossible if all this is done apart from the life of Christ in us. Only our Lord is sufficient for these things.

# O DIE WITH CHRIST—1

*then? Shall we continue in sin, that grace may abound?*
*ll we, that are dead to sin, live any longer therein? . . .*
*ur old man is crucified with him, that the body of sin*
*that henceforth we should not serve sin. Rom. 6:1, 6.*

ficance of living entirely by Jesus Christ does
on us unless we see the utter bankruptcy of
human effort, and human righteousness. We
mplete dependence on and union with a life
above and not from within ourselves.

gic cries that go up to heaven, none is more in-
than the cry that began with Lucifer and has
since: "I will ascend into heaven, I will exalt
e the stars of God: . . . I will ascend above the
louds; I will be like the most High" (Isa. 14:13,
ever overrate the serious problem of pride and
ss. The pride of self-will is where sin began. We
go-centered. It is the basic sin of all sins. All
the outgrowth of this one sin. It is like a crease
a piece of paper. Any tear will the more easily
d follow the crease.

ns that by man's own searching he can know the
and save himself. Unfortunately, all of man's so-
bout truth can become a substitute for depend-
It is quite possible to be loyal to our own ideas
loyal to Christ. In that case, as far as our re-
ience is concerned, we are simply good pagans.
ness to the same thing found in Lucifer. We can
es to the stars without trusting in, living by, or
God at all.

cherished by the world is the self-reliant man.
en call self-reliance never gets beyond man's de-
himself. Man's claim to superior knowledge, the
lf-sufficiency, the flaunting of pride, is fatal to the
e. Any claim we make for the glory of man can only
fall and depravity more complete. To be ruled by
means to lose everything.

s only one possibility left for survival: to find our
Jesus Christ.

# RECONCILED TO GOD—1

**For if, when we were God's enemies, we were reconciled to him through the death of his Son, how much more, now that we are reconciled, shall we be saved by his life! Rom. 5:10, N.E.B.**

Christianity is a religion of redemption, a rescue operation by the Father through His Son, Jesus Christ. This is true because only God can forgive sin. All sin is against God. What makes sin so great is that it is against persons. When we sin, we sin not against rules on a wall, but against a loving heavenly Father. Before Christ we must accept the fact that our sins are very real. They are not merely social errors about which we can say, "It does not matter." The experience of forgiveness is reserved for those who come to understand sin within our relation to a personal God and to our fellow men. Otherwise we will not seek forgiveness with a contrite heart before God.

Redemption also means that only Christ has control over the past. We all have a past. We cannot turn back the pages of time and begin all over again. Sin commands a stiff price. It sinks into our blood stream and into our nervous system. Only God has power to lay remedial hands on the past. We have no power to cleanse our past. Yet the past must be cleared if we are to experience redemption.

Furthermore, only Christ has control over the future. Dreadful as are many of the problems and circumstances of this life, they belong only to this life. Christ offers us life eternal, an entirely new kind of life in the future. In Christ there is a way out of all the agony we see in the world. We are all mortal. We all sin and die. There ought to be a future for all those who die young on the battlefields of the world, and in the deprived areas and dark places of the earth. The Christian looks forward with hope and joy to the future. We know that death comes to us all, but we also know we shall live again. Christ will restore our lives, our loved ones, our lost joys, and the perfection in which He created us. Redemption offers no less than this to us.

## RECONCILED TO GOD—2

*And all things are of God, who hath reconciled us to himself by Jesus Christ, and hath given to us the ministry of reconciliation. 2 Cor. 5:18.*

Redemption is through Christ. We could never have known God's love unless He had come to earth. God stooped down in order that we might draw near to Him. Love and salvation invaded our world and our lives. God in human flesh came close to us so that we might put our hands on His face, as it were. "The Word was made flesh and dwelt among us" (John 1:14). Jesus is love on the move from heaven to us. He is the Son of God, sent from the Father, who has broken in upon this lost world, our one hope for our restoration to God. He did not come simply to tell us about God. He brought God, for He is God. We need no longer live in a state of alienation or despair.

The coming of Jesus Christ has eternal consequences for our lives. Therefore He is to us the "bread of life," "the Way, the Truth, and the Life," "the Light of the world," "the Shepherd of the flock," "the King of kings," "the Sun of Righteousness with healing in his wings." He is righteous love, who will never let us go, who yearns to restore us to His own likeness. He has given Himself to us at the cost of His own life, to be the life of our lives. Our religion of redemption is not our search for a better life. It is our complete response to the God of heaven who comes searching for us.

Finally, redemption means not only that Christ must come to the earth to find us but to suffer and die for us. No one else could redeem us. Only a member of the Godhead could reveal and confess to the universe the eternal love of God for man, and reveal at the same time Their willingness to bear sin's penalty rather than to execute it upon us. Here the inmost nature of man's sinfulness is revealed. The cross is the center of all human history, the supreme crisis of God and man. His death was for us. We cannot forgive ourselves. We deserve to die. From the cross God speaks to us: "You can spit in My face. You can place a crown of thorns upon My head. You can nail Me to a cross. But you cannot stop My loving you. There is no way."

# TO DIE WITH CHRIST—2

*For ye are dead, and your life is hid with Christ in God.* **Col. 3:3.**

The question Who am I? cannot be answered by man outside of Christ. From within our sinful state we are tempted to believe that our true self is the self apart from God. Such a life only distorts and warps our identity.

Therefore man puts total stock in himself. Self is his chief interest and center of reference. His basic loyalty is to himself. The higher the position he occupies, the more important his status, the greater the desire for recognition and the more he exaggerates his own importance.

This exaggerated importance attached to the self is wholly contrary to our Lord and His chosen role as servant. Christ's disciples had trouble with pride and the quest for self-recognition. "Who should be the greatest?" All too many times this question motivated their thinking and actions. Everywhere, this spirit destroys and divides, whether in business, in the church, or in the work of God. The surest way to distort the gospel and make its power of none effect is to seek self-exaltation by means of religion.

To be crucified with Christ is the absolute, final, unconditional end of self-glory and every form of self-worship.

Life is always confronting us with the opportunity to reflect Jesus Christ. The whole adventure of living the Christian life is a continual challenge to die to self and live for Christ. This problem is not solved by human wisdom, but by the power of God. One ounce of turning from self to Christ is far better than a pound or a ton of human strategy. Nothing but a miracle can free us from self-centeredness. But God is used to working miracles of this kind.

Let us accept the challenge of every day to let Christ live His life in and through us. Our personal failure, the discouragement resulting from self-will and pride, this sensitiveness that is always getting hurt—face it with Christ. Life with Christ provides us with a margin of power greater than the self-life. Believe that, in spite of all the past selfishness, you are sure to win. Fashion your life with Him at the center. You cannot lose.

# TO RISE WITH CHRIST

*If I must needs glory, I will glory of the things which concern mine infirmities. 2 Cor. 11:30. For when I am weak, then am I strong. Chap. 12:10.*

Only Christians use this kind of language and approve of it. The Christian life is a divine life from God lived entirely by faith. It is impossible to be a Christian and yet be independent. Unless Christ has the sovereign rule over us, we cannot live the Christian life. Nothing but God and His will is to have supreme place in our devotion. We renounce all self-glory in order to prove the excellence of the power of God. We renounce all ego power in order to live by the power of the Holy Spirit. We glory in substituting the power of God for the power of sinful man. We confess the worthlessness of everything that is apart from Christ. It is our self-achieved righteousnesses that God calls filthy rags, not only our obvious transgressions (see Isa. 64: 6). We take the lowest seat as candidates for the highest. We recognize our utter poverty of mind and soul in order to gain the riches of Christ.

Our participation with Christ's death and resurrection is a very real thing. As soon as we discern the ego motive, we ought promptly to take ourselves to the Lord and surrender to Him. Pride and self-centeredness are the basic cause of all our sins: anger, hostility, envy, jealousy, resentment.

We are to see ourselves as new beings in Him, living from an entirely new center. We share the quality of Christ's self-denial. The Holy Spirit provides us with the power and the confidence to enable us to live that way. Christian experience is not an improvement of the self-life that merits congratulations. We affirm our manhood and womanhood always in utter dependence on Christ.

It is not enough to be crucified with Christ. We must also rise with Him to a new life. Seek those things which are above. To rise with Christ is to participate in His resurrection life. We cannot rise to new life without Him. We persevere knowing that nothing can take us out of His hands. "I will say of the Lord, He is my refuge and my fortress: my God; in him will I trust" (Ps. 91:2). "There shall no evil befall thee, neither shall any plague come nigh thy dwelling" (verse 10).

# CHRIST AT THE DOOR

*" 'Here I stand knocking at the door; if anyone hears my voice and opens the door, I will come in and sit down to supper with him.' "* **Rev. 3:20, N.E.B.**

There are two truths in this verse: Christ can be kept out of our lives; and the door can be opened only from within. Christ does not force His way into our hearts. We are told that a man's house is his castle. In countries where personal freedom is cherished, the householder is protected from unwarranted search or interference. Similarly, in regard to our personalities, Christ does not violate our integrity, or our minds. The doors to the chambers of our lives must be opened by us.

A man asked, "Why does God not stop a man from doing the wrong thing, from leaving his family, from being dishonest with his income tax? God is omnipotent. All He needs to do is exercise His power. Why does God let a man destroy himself and others, not only in this life but for the life to come? Why does not God do something?"

The most sacred thing about us is our free will. As parents, we love our children. We do not lock them in the house just in case they plan to do wrong. As children, they have to be told what to do. Abraham was commended because God knew he would "command his children and his household after him." Yet children must develop the ability to make right decisions.

Overprotecting, trying to make all the decisions for our children, can only destroy them emotionally and personally. Ultimately they rebel against us. They resent our denying them their own integrity as persons. God understands this. He will not deny us the freedom so essential to our growth. We may be able to force our children to obey us, but we cannot force them to love us. We may be able to prevent a man from committing a crime, but not from sinning in his heart.

Should Christ come to the door as we watch television, we can tell Him we are too busy, and He will respect our wishes. If we have a quarrel at home and He stops by to help, we can tell Him to mind His own business, and He will. If we go on a picnic and He indicates He would like to go along, we can ignore Him. He will not push His way into our private pleasures. Christ comes, not with a demand, but as a guest. Even the divine Guest must be wanted and welcomed.

# COMMITTED TO CHRIST

*None of these things move me, neither count I my life dear unto myself, so that I might finish my course with joy. Acts 20:24.*

Few men have equaled the depth of Paul's personal involvement with Christ and with His saving program for lost man. Paul was a man completely devoted to Christ. He was a Christian of clear decision, consecration, and wholeheartedness, with a mind single to God's glory.

Commitment means the point of no return. We place ourselves entirely at Christ's disposal. We acknowledge His full claim as the master of our lives.

The concern of Christ is that He should rule in every heart. To be a follower of Christ means to accept the unqualified rule of God.

It is folly to assume that one can be a Christian by some passive attitude toward the claims of God's Word. Christians are to be the most actively dedicated people in the world, manifest in every aspect of life.

Christ works out His will in us only to the extent of our commitment. God will respond to man's genuine response with a reality that cannot be denied. Consecration to Him transfigures the life.

All that is high and noble is possible as we surrender to the living Christ. His power extends to our hands, to our hearts, and to our lives in order that we may practice the principles of truth, uprightness, purity, and righteousness.

Life with Christ is no make-believe. Faith in Him is no dream world. Sin, lust, disobedience, hostility, selfishness, are all dynamic realities.

The answer to all these problems is in surrender to Him in order that the power of God may live in us. There is no such thing as an easygoing Christianity. A conscious choice of Christ and of His claims cannot be imposed from without. Commitment must come from within the believer. That is the one response that God will honor with the fulfillment of all His promises.

# AN UNDIVIDED HEART

*[Jehosphaphat] did what was right in the eyes of the Lord. But the hill-shrines were allowed to remain.* **1 Kings 22:43, N.E.B.**

As to the general piety of King Jehoshaphat, the Bible writers leave no doubt. But he did not make a clean break with idolatry. Wrote James the brother of our Lord, "You who are double-minded, see that your motives are pure" (James 4:8, N.E.B.). The temptation is to be divided in mind. We amend our ways and our doings, yet cling to some aspect of sin. The eye is not single in its spiritual purpose.

It is possible to retain privately those evil practices we have renounced in public. Evils are removed outwardly only to be cherished in the inner life. Religious revivals may appear very impressive without being thorough. Sin is concealed rather than destroyed. Moral compromise tends to the concealment of sin. God cannot be pleased with revivals that simply remove sin into a less conspicuous place, where it is made to lose half of its wickedness before God. Iniquity is iniquity to Him whether done in the public eye or indulged under the cover of situational pressures and a softened terminology.

Often we deal softly with sinful habits, associations, pursuits, pleasures, which ought to be sacrificed forever. God will not be satisfied with less. Moses took the golden calf, burned it with fire, stamped upon it, ground it very small as dust, and then cast it into the river. As Christians we are to renounce sin both in conduct and in thought. Compromise has no place. Whatever pleasantness, fascination, and attraction may be associated with evil places, people, and pursuits, God requires that we make a clean break with them. We must not retain mentally what we have renounced in conduct. It frequently happens that the sins we once actually committed find asylum in our minds and hearts. For various reasons concessions are made to sinful thoughts. Excuses are made according to differing situations. Often men keep an evil imagination quite distinct from their active and outer life. The sensual mind can take the place of sensual practices, in which the mind may revel in sin. We have only concealed the sin that ought to have been totally destroyed.

# OBEDIENCE AND LIFE

*Sin shall no longer be your master, because you are no longer under law, but under the grace of God.* **Rom. 6:14, N.E.B.**

Life is forever confronting us with difficult, unexpected situations. Men argue that we must make moral adjustments because of the type of world we live in. "The moral law does not count in this case. We lie to save someone's life. We act from good intent. The choice is a matter of the lesser of two evils." But does this suffice us? Do the "lesser" sins we settle for give us any rest or satisfaction?

The upshot of the matter is the same as if our choices were intentionally on the wrong side. If we get lost out in the desert or in the jungle the result is the same for an innocent sheep as for a willful man. We all pay for our mistakes. Of course, God considers our motives and our situations. He will judge, acquit, or condemn accordingly.

But Jesus said, "One jot or one tittle shall in no wise pass from the law, till all be fulfilled" (Matt. 5:18). We have to believe that back of that requirement God has provided the power to make it so in our lives. If our human weakness and sinfulness arise to undermine confidence in the law of God, ultimately there will not be much left of it. Men will not stick to the Ten Commandments on such terms. Jesus would have nothing to do with the idea that breaking the law in this or that particular case did not count.

Self-deceiving as we are, stained and fettered with self and sin, we ought to understand what the Bible says about knowing and loving God and keeping His commandments. Such loving obedience is not performed with the listless necessity of slaves, but with the joy of sons of God. If we really believe in Christ's power to save from sin, in faith that works by love; if we have entered into life with Christ, then we will keep His commandments. The love that binds us to keep His commandments is meant to hold life, home, and character together. In Christ we gird ourselves for moral victory, not moral defeat.

Are we pure in our lives? Are we kind, fair, and honest in our words and actions? Are we obedient to our heavenly Father? If not, what else can avail us at last? What is the worth of the everlasting gospel that is to save us from sin?

# THE CHRISTIAN CANNOT BE NEUTRAL

*Not every one that saith unto me, Lord, Lord, shall enter into the kingdom of heaven; but he that doeth the will of my Father which is in heaven. Matt. 7:21.*

Jesus does not look for cleverness in His followers. He requires total obedience to His way and His will. There is no such thing as Christian experience by proxy. We can never be certain until we make the commitment ourselves.

One of the disturbing factors in the church is that of professed Christians with great abilities and possibilities never yet released to the cause of Christ. One of the most serious deterrents to witnessing to a triumphant Christian life is neutrality on great issues and truths that affect our loyalty to Christ and the eternal destiny of others.

Evil is no vague, dormant principle that is hard to find; but something savagely, energetically offensive. When we surrender to a climate of apathy and lukewarmness, then evil seizes the chance to get us to deny our Lord. Martin Luther, in one of his legends, tells of Satan, who called a council of his chiefs to defeat the Christian.

Said one, "I let loose the wild beasts on many Christians. Their bones now bleach the sands in the arena." "What of that?" said Satan. "Their souls are still saved." Said another: "I drove the storm against a shipload of Christians, and they all perished in the sea." "What of that?" said Satan. "Their souls are all saved." Said another: "I have labored for ten years to lull Christians to sleep and get them to be neutral. At last I have succeeded." Then Satan shouted for joy and all the angels of hell rejoiced together.

Nothing can be stronger than our Saviour's words on the need to banish everything that would undermine our allegiance to Him. If our right eye offend us, that is, if it tempts us to sin, we are to pluck it out and cast it from us. If our right hand prove a temptation to us, we are to cut it off.

If we remain neutral and do nothing about sin we shall be destroyed. We must tolerate no indifference, no apathy, and no delay. Unqualified commitment to Christ and to His truth is the guarantee of perfect security and ultimate salvation.

# NOT WITH ME MEANS AGAINST ME

*He that is not with me is against me; and he that gathereth not with me scattereth abroad.* **Matt. 12:30.**

In the great controversy between Christ and Satan, between truth and error, there can be no neutrality. We cannot belong to both sides. We might be tempted to believe we do not have to take open sides with Jesus against sin and Satan, that one can still be friendly to the other side. But neutrality in such issues amounts to opposition. The gospel is of such a nature in its claims upon us that it cannot tolerate indifference and lukewarmness. If Christ is indeed what He claims to be, then He deserves our entire and unreserved acceptance and commitment. Neutrality cannot generate the conviction that makes genuine Christians. The martyrs of the early church did not go to the stake because they remained neutral. The significant thing was their total allegiance to Christ, even to the dungeon and the fiery flame.

In issues that concern the welfare of our souls, our friends, the church, and the cause of God, there is no room for sitting on the fence. So long as you ask, "What harm can there be if I refuse to commit myself when God has made clear the issue?"; so long as you say, "I am not prepared to take a stand; I am no worse than a lot of other professed Christians," you are taking a stand against Christ. Unless you are heartily on the Lord's side and on the side of truth, it is mere pretense to say that you are a follower of Christ. Sacrifices must be made.

On the three-hundredth anniversary of their university, a group of students carried a banner bearing the inscription "This university has waited 300 years for us." They considered themselves keepers and champions of the lofty purpose of that institution.

Well, God has been waiting two thousand years for us. We are that important. This is no time to strike our colors, but to join the ranks of those "who through faith subdued kingdoms, wrought righteousness, obtained promises, stopped the mouths of lions, . . . out of weakness were made strong, waxed valiant in fight, turned to flight the armies of the aliens" (Heb. 11:33, 34).

# COURAGE

*And I said, Should such a man as I flee? and who is there, that, being as I am, would go into the temple to save his life? I will not go in.* **Neh. 6:11.**

There is a spirit of courage in these words. Nehemiah was rebuilding the walls and setting up the gates of Jerusalem. He was opposed by foes within and without—Sanballat the Moabite, Tobiah the Ammonite, Geshem the Arabian, and others. They charged him with treason before the Persian king. They tried to kill him. They bribed a false prophet to deliver a message supposedly from God in order to stop the building program. He rejected all this and said, "I will not run. I will not come down."

There are few virtues we admire more than courage born of clear convictions of the truth and the will of God. There are few things we despise more than cowardice and selfishness in such situations. Christian courage never trembles before men. Love of the truth never betrays personal integrity. It is only selfishness that grasps at personal gain that denies the faith.

What are we supposed to do in a difficult situation? We admire a man who faces terminal cancer with a brave heart and confident faith. A man is crippled by an accident, but he can do nothing about it. He is a Christian. He sees everything in the light of Christ's suffering for him, accepts what life brings to him, refuses all expressions of self-pity. Such people are much to be admired.

In Nehemiah's case it was not that inevitable. He could have quit in face of the opposition. But he was quite prepared to make sacrifice inevitable because of his convictions.

Christ promises us power, courage for every situation. His power transcends every other kind of power known to man. Christ is not just someone to be admired, but to be followed. The most magnificent act of courage the world has seen was our Lord's commitment to go to the cross to save us all. He could have refused it. He could have stayed in Galilee and not gone to Jerusalem at all. No Roman soldier would have gone looking for Him. He was under no external compulsion. His decision was absolutely free.

Christian courage is marked by a loftiness and a firmness that distinguishes it from any kind of moral compromise.

# GOING ALL THE WAY

*He that endureth to the end shall be saved.* Matt. 10:22.

Starting out on the Christian way is not all that is important. The rest of the journey counts even more. We hear a lot of talk about dropouts. It does not take much for people to enroll in a course. But it takes a great deal more to stay with it. Along the way there are a lot of opportunities and temptations to drop out. It does not take much courage to quit. It takes all we have to endure to the end.

We have far too many dropouts, people who once belonged to the church. Ask the pastor of almost any church. He will tell you he has a large number of names of people who have dropped out along the way. Why do people do that?

For one thing, if anything goes wrong in the church, for some people this gives them a way out. According to the individual, the church did not measure up; so what is the use? However, those who know Christ and have found in Him the satisfaction for all their needs are not easily moved or disturbed. Those who are easily shaken out have, most often, not been firmly established in the faith, have not been that serious about going the whole way.

Life for us is a continued journey into the light of Christ. We have staked our all on Him and on His truth. We have no intention of moving from that foundation. Each event and occasion provides us with the opportunity to move closer to the gates of heaven, to grasp ever more fully God's will for us.

These days there is an impression given that we do not have to do anything to be a Christian. It has an element of truth in that Christ alone has redeemed us and provided a perfect righteousness for us. There are two ways you can try to get people to become Christians. You can tell them that God does it all, that it is easy, that being a Christian is a very comfortable way of life. Or you can challenge them to a life of warfare, that we are a fighting force under the Captain of our salvation, that Christianity is a life for heroes. It demands the best of us, an endurance test; it confronts us with the greatest adventure known to man, that Christianity is a cause to live for, fight for, and die for.

# RELUCTANT DISCIPLES

*Pilate was approached by Joseph of Arimathaea, a disciple of Jesus, but a secret disciple for fear of the Jews, who asked to be allowed to remove the body of Jesus. . . . He was joined by Nicodemus. John 19:38, 39, N.E.B.*

Very little is said about Nicodemus or Joseph of Arimathea, although they are mentioned as disciples. One could wish to know more about them, particularly Nicodemus. He is reputed to have been a very wealthy man. He did not want to be seen with Christ. He came to Jesus by night. He condescended to call Jesus a teacher. He cannot be ranked with the other disciples. For a long time he appears to be an undeclared disciple.

Silence is a position whether we like it or not. Silence cannot be interpreted to mean commitment to Christ. This restricted loyalty, if you wish to give it a name, is not the ideal thing. Our witness to the effect that we have accepted Christ and experienced His saving power is to avow Him, to stand for Him, to confess Him at all times, especially when the issues call for it. We must give expression to our commitment. We must not leave our friends and neighbors in doubt on such an issue as this. It is of vital consequence that we openly and spontaneously honor our Lord in word and deed. We must not shy away from full-square allegiance to Him and to His Word. The cause of Christ never needed courageous witnesses more than now.

For Christians, there are three unpardonable attitudes today: first, to be superficial, indifferent, and flippant about the world peril and the human situation of our time. Second, to live and act as if the status quo would avail to meet our Christian responsibility. Third, to lack the moral courage to rise to the occasion and the opportunity God has set before us.

Everything about our world today is critical. To be slothful in our thinking and our mode of living is surely to play the coward. It takes courage to live openly and unashamedly for Christ in a world that is foolish, immoral, and cruel. We are not asking for fanaticism, but for a daily choice toward righteous living and away from sin, toward love and away from hate, toward self-sacrifice and obedience and away from disobedience, toward compassion for the lost and away from indifference.

# WHO STANDS HIS GROUND?

*Shadrach, Meshach, and Abednego, answered. . . . Be it known unto thee, O king, that we will not serve thy gods, nor worship the golden image which thou hast set up.* Dan. 3:16-18.

One of the proverbs people quote from time to time is "When in Rome do as the Romans do." When you are with the gang, do as the gang does. When you are with the crowd, do as the crowd does. When the majority vote a certain way, vote along with them.

To say No when everyone else says Yes requires the clearest thinking and the highest form of courage. Everywhere in government, in business, in pleasure, and even in education, men easily compromise principle.

As followers of Christ, we need the clearest convictions and strongest determination to stand firm. The three Hebrew slaves in the city of Babylon stood alone. They would neither bow down nor bend before the idol that King Nebuchadnezzar had set up. The God of heaven was their only Master.

The Christian life is a life inspired with courage from God, a life reliable in all situations. There is no more persistent obligation for us than to take our stand for Christ with all the integrity we can muster, regardless of the consequences.

The German count Moltke was arrested and charged with involvement in a plot against Hitler's life. Just before he was taken out to be hanged he wrote his wife a final letter that described his stand before the Nazi judge. "The entire room could have roared like Judge Freisler, and all the walls could have trembled—it would have meant nothing to me. I found it was actually true what is said by the prophet Isaiah: 'When thou passest through the waters, I will be with thee; and through the rivers, they shall not overflow thee: when thou walkest through the fire, thou shalt not be burned; neither shall the flame kindle upon thee. For I am the Lord thy God, the Holy One of Israel, thy Saviour' " (Isa. 43:2, 3).

Let us reject all vacillation when confronted with the truth. Let us exercise the strength and uprightness of a firm faith in God; courage to be loyal to the best and to the highest, to break with those who would betray our Lord. Let us not be ashamed of Jesus Christ. Let us be wholly on His side.

*78*

# ONE MASTER

*No man can serve two masters.* Matt. 6:24.

Jesus did not want anyone to follow Him under false pretenses. Our choices must center in Christ. We begin here. The real problem is not lack of knowledge of the truth so much as the warping of our judgment. When a man has seared his conscience, it is no trick at all to rationalize or fool himself into choosing the wrong master. Men pay a frightful price for their illusions as to what they accept as the way of truth.

Neither serving Christ nor serving the world and the devil is an accident. We will only sink deeper and deeper in the mire if we choose the wrong master. In 6,000 years we have fashioned more than twenty civilizations and destroyed every one of them. And now for this twentieth civilization we are nearer than man has ever been to total destruction.

"Thou shalt have no other gods before me" (Ex. 20:3). Stake everything on this. This must be the rock-bottom of all choices: Christ as our master; Christ the one priority before possessions and things, good or bad. Many of the choices we are asked to make are tied to things and activities that in themselves are quite innocent. I knew a young lady with a wonderful head of hair. She spent two hours a day taking care of it. But she had no time for the study of the Word of God.

To young people in particular, the world offers a fascinating and glittering array of temporal pleasures. The offer that Satan made to Christ is still in season: "The devil . . . showed him all the kingdoms of the world in their glory. 'All these,' he said, 'I will give you, if you will only fall down and do me homage' " (Matt. 4:8, 9, N.E.B.). Satan says, "Just include me in your many things. Give me a small portion of your devotion, and I will give you all that the world has to offer. Why take the hard road? What is wrong with a little concentration now and then upon giving priority to what the world has to offer? Why not call a moratorium on your religion, on your Christian witness, once in a while? Just do not plan on reaching the standards all the time. Why stand up against the crowd? Would you not rather be a living neutral than a dead hero?"

But we cannot serve two masters. This is where the final choice is made.

# "THE VALLEY OF DECISION"

*Put ye in the sickle, for the harvest is ripe. . . . Multitudes, multitudes in the valley of decision: for the day of the Lord is near.* Joel 3:13, 14.

The keynote of the book of Joel is "the day of the Lord." The world is moving fast toward a divine climax. It is a time of crisis, of sifting, of separation. Therefore we must make the right decisions.

In order to live right one must choose right. In the realm of the great controversy between good and evil, the side a man chooses is crucial. It all seems quite simple and straightforward. It would be if the choice were either black or white. But in many areas the line between right and wrong is quite blurred these days. Also the mind can become so warped that it no longer is able to distinguish the fine shades of color as to what is right and what is wrong. There is much that is on the borderline.

The prelude to Lowell's "Vision of Sir Launfal" reads:
"At the devil's booth are all things sold,
Each ounce of dross costs its ounce of gold;
For a cap and bells our lives we pay,
Bubbles we buy with a whole soul's tasking:
'Tis heaven alone that is given away,
'Tis only God may be had for the asking."

If you want to buy a washing machine or an electric mixer you go into a store and compare various makes. You might study the *Consumers' Guide* and get the rating on all the various models. How much do they cost? Which is most nearly worth the price? You finally make a choice, hoping that you have bought the best. Maybe you bought a "lemon," losing money on the deal. "Each ounce of dross costs its ounce of gold."

Similar choices must be made in regard to character. If you want to be intelligent you must give up being ignorant. If you want to be courageous then give up being weak and cowardly. If you want to be patient, give up being impatient. The reverse of this is that if you choose to be dishonest, you surrender the idea of being an honest man. If you choose to be immoral you give up the idea of being pure. If you desire to be a Christian through and through you will have to give up that which prevents you from becoming one.

# "SEEK YE FIRST THE KINGDOM OF GOD"

*But seek ye first the kingdom of God, and his righteousness; and all these things shall be added unto you.* Matt. 6:33.

The words of Christ are full of significance. He had just counseled against preoccupation with the temporal things of life—"What shall we eat? or What shall we drink, or Wherewithal shall we be clothed?" (Matt. 6:31).

The Christian does not work for money alone, or measure his achievement by it. The appeal of Christ to us is "Don't make things the most important factor in life."

To unite with Christ in concern and compassion for people takes precedence over affluence and status. I knew a man who refused a large salary, many times more than the church could pay him. He took a position that offered the opportunity to serve people and lead them to Christ.

We cannot afford to make a mistake here. To end up the richest man in the cemetery is no accomplishment. If a man has nothing that he can take with him beyond the grave he is poor indeed. Bacon said, "It is reserved only for God and the angels to be lookers-on." But they are not merely spectators. The angels are ministering spirits sent to those who should be heirs of salvation (see Heb. 1:14). We are invited to unite with them in this service.

But this is man's folly: to turn to his wealth, to his sports and his amusements, then to count them the principal thing worthy of his time, his energy, and his thought. We ought to listen to Jesus Christ with the utmost earnestness. We ought to consider the carrying of the gospel to men as having absolute priority. There is no quicker way to spiritual disaster than to treat the spread of His kingdom and the triumph of His righteousness as simply a matter of personal convenience. That we should consider these life-and-death concerns as casual, as objects of passing interest in a world that is hastening to its final destiny with God, is unthinkable. There seems no mood so tragic as a bland tolerance of God, an easy indifference to His cause for which He died, a bored disdain for eternal realities.

On the other hand, nothing is so satisfying as to bring God's transforming grace to lost men and women.

# WANTED: A LIVING VERDICT
# CONCERNING CHRIST

*Choose you this day whom ye will serve; . . . as for me and my house, we will serve the Lord.* Joshua 24:15.

To be a Christian means to be brought face to face with the greatest decisions in life. One cannot be a Christian without the ability to make the right decision now and always. Our thinking must lead to moral and spiritual conclusions. There is a lot of discussion about religion and moral problems that never gets beyond words and is never tied together into a final knot.

The mind may be likened to a court of law. The evidence has been presented, the witnesses heard, the conclusions reached. It is time for a verdict. Men must make up their minds. The Bible speaks of those who are "ever learning, and never able to come to the knowledge of the truth" (2 Tim. 3:7).

Our study of God's Word must not be allowed to go on day after day, month after month, with an undecided mind and heart. In the Holy Scriptures the path of truth and the way of salvation are unmistakably clear. It is the single eye that ensures the body to be full of light. It is the committed soul that makes sure of the truth.

When we come to the Bible as guests to partake of the bread of life, enlightenment will attend our steps. Reason and conscience will be exercised under the Spirit of God. Personal responsibility to the truth will become as clear as the noonday. It is well that our minds should be so awakened as to know the truth. It is good that the eyes of the mind can distinguish between truth and error. But now comes the time to stand. Exercise the most careful judgment on what the Word of God reveals. The Holy Spirit has promised to lead us into all truth. Now is the time to determine the direction of our lives. A higher power is before us to make all things work together for good. It is not enough to know what is truth. We must decide. Now there must be no drifting, no moving timidly. Christian living is not a life of chance or fate. It involves the right exercise of the will committed wholly to Christ, the Way, the Truth, and the Life.

# FAITH IN ACTION

*So with faith; if it does not lead to action, it is in itself a lifeless thing.*
**James 2:17, N.E.B.**

It is possible to claim to have faith and still fail to produce works of obedience and love. The result is deception and hypocrisy. The Pharisees of Christ's day held a false faith. At no time in the history of religion have pride, greed, covetousness, hostility, impurity, and disobedience been more tolerated than today.

To profess faith in God and in His Word either makes us more like Christ or worse off than we were, depending on whether it changes our lives or leaves us unregenerate and unsanctified. Faith in Christ must exalt Christian character and personal holiness. It must reject all that would suppress the truth and righteousness. The Bible insists that we hold the right kind of faith—the faith of Jesus. Let us study the life He lived on earth. We see the most perfect character. We discover full obedience to His Father's commandments. In Him truth is clear. Biblical morality is revealed. All that is virtuous and Godlike is seen in His life.

Christ said that even if we have only a grain of genuine trust in God, works will follow, obstacles will be removed. Out of genuine faith will spring purity and righteousness, victory over sin, unselfish service and a life of good works. How wonderful it is when a person is born with musical talent, artistic ability, or any special quality. But much more significant is the gift of true faith, even though it be the size of a mustard seed. We may be sure that our Lord will not give us faith that fails to extend God's truth to our lives, to our hands, and to our hearts. We need to take care when we claim to hold a faith that does not change our lives. We are no better than the genius with unique talents that lie dormant and are not exercised.

Faith in Christ means trust in Him, fellowship with Him, devotion to Him. Such a dynamic relationship is the guarantee of righteous living, and of loving obedience to God's commandments. "Ye shall know them by their fruits" (Matt. 7:16). All our good works are traced to our faith union with Him. Nothing is real in the Christian life except as it grows out of our faith in Christ.

# "YE ARE NOT YOUR OWN"

*Ye are not your own? For ye are bought with a price.* 1 Cor. 6:19, 20.

Being a true Christian is not a matter of preference. One may prefer one book above another, one kind of food above another, one game above another. We all have preferences. But to acknowledge God's lordship is more than a personal preference. When receiving a call to visit the President of the United States, or when given a presidential assignment for one's country, there is an extra plus involved: inescapable responsibility and personal destiny.

God redeemed and bought us with His blood. Our lives are henceforth not our own. We are part of His plan. The nature of our response affects every part of life's purpose. His call should be listened to with reverence and respect—it is the Lord of the universe who addresses us. The invitation is a gracious act on God's part. God is perfectly sincere; our response should be the same. Many voices call to us day by day. Often we are attracted by them in a way that makes us neglect the call of God.

Arthur was a genius with radio. This hobby absorbed most of his time and most of his money. The skill and facility he had inherited worked out much to his advantage. But he had no time to pray or study the Word of God. Grudgingly he came to church. He had his heart in the wrong place. There is nothing wrong with radio, but this was his central and all-absorbing interest. Finally he drifted away from Christ.

William Carey, who became the first great missionary to India, was a shoe-repair man. But his primary interest was the spread of the gospel. It was said of him that he cobbled shoes only to pay expenses. Paul was a good tentmaker for the same reason.

A man should take heed to his vocation in which he can work diligently and successfully. A man's talents should inspire him to do his best. At the same time a Christian lives to the glory of God and bears witness to the Lord who died to save him. Failure to acknowledge this reveals a serious defect in character. Whatever our talents and skills, we are partners with the God of heaven, who made us all we have and are. "Where your treasure is, there will your heart be also" (Matt. 6:21).

# NO MORE DELAY

*He that is unjust, let him be unjust still: . . . and he that is righteous, let him be righteous still. Rev. 22:11.*

There is such a thing as a last chance for us all. Only God knows when it has passed, but one day all of us will pass that time. Daily the Spirit of God moves upon our hearts. Divine visitation does not leave us where it found us. It always leaves us better or worse. To come into contact with truth, to hear God's voice speaking to our hearts, leaves no room for delay. To brush God aside in this way always leaves us weaker, poorer spiritually.

Many people are found following the church who are not actuated by love for Christ or by devotion to His cause. This is an imperfect attachment to our Lord. At such a time as this we ought not to hesitate. We are to know Him as our Saviour, our hope, our life. We are to come to His sanctuary because we love His word, not because the respectable people are there. We are to give and work for His sake. We are to be captured by His truth and love and beauty, which is the true attachment.

When Christ was on earth He achieved a certain degree of popularity with some because He healed the sick and fed the hungry. They were not captured by His person and His mission to save the lost, or by His redeeming grace. Christ looks deep into our hearts to see whether we truly love Him, love Him for His own sake.

The preparation necessary to meet Christ is to love Him with a true heart. True love thinks nothing of the loaves and the fishes. We belong to Him and to His church, not for the sake of what is profitable, but because we want more than anything to be like Him. We cling to Him, not because it is fashionable to do so, but even when it is unpopular to do so. His righteousness is our salvation, His love for us our inspiration, His approval of us our supreme satisfaction, His life our greatest need.

Everything is possible in the power of His love and grace. We are no longer moved by every wind of doctrine. We are no longer anxious as to the day of His coming. Having this certainty with Christ, we enjoy stability and peace. We are not perplexed by the conflicts in the world.

# THE TIME OF GOD'S VISITATION

*"If only you had known, on this great day, the way that leads to peace! But no; it is hidden from your sight. . . . You did not recognize God's moment when it came." Luke 19:41-44, N.E.B.*

We ought to know more than anyone else about the time of God's visitation. The idea of visitation in the Bible usually implies some special intervention on God's part in the affairs of men. Failure to know the time is followed by grave consequences. Such failure implies a serious decline in spiritual insight and experience.

The occasion for Christ's statement was His visit to Jerusalem following the raising of Lazarus from the dead. The people of Bethany led a triumphal procession and sang praises to Christ, "Hosanna to the Son of David." As they came within sight of Jerusalem, Christ stopped. He gazed intently at the Holy City. Then His eyes filled with tears. He saw beyond His day some forty years hence when the city would be destroyed. There followed His solemn words, "Thou knewest not the time of thy visitation." "Behold, your house is left unto you desolate."

Let us put the question to ourselves, to our families, to our places of business, to our pleasures, to our comings and goings. Is our insight into the times any better than that of the Jews? The extraordinary thing would be if we are now unable to recognize that again we have come to the time of Christ's judgment and visitation to our world. To live in expectancy of the soon return of our Lord should motivate us to prepare to meet Him. This is the time to gain new spiritual power and insight. This is the time to acquire a warmer desire and love for Christ.

If we daily respond to the voice of God, if we daily dedicate ourselves to Christ and to His service and count the world but loss, then when Christ comes our hearts and lives will easily and naturally make the transition from this world to the next. We are to make sure it will be well with us. Seek Christ first and His kingdom. Make life with Him your ruling and supreme purpose.

# WISDOM OF THE UNJUST STEWARD

*And the lord commended the unjust steward, because he had done wisely: for the children of this world are in their generation wiser than the children of light.* **Luke 16:8.**

In this parable the rich landowner entrusted the management of his estate to his steward. Then later he brought charges against him for the abuse of his stewardship. He ordered him to give account. The steward knew that this would mean the loss of his position, so decided upon a scheme. He sent for his master's tenants who still owed goods and money. He reduced their indebtedness and had them settle for much less than what they owed. In this way, when dismissed from his position he would still have friends among the tenants, who would provide for him. Granted that the unjust steward had little to commend him in the way of honesty. But the master commended him for his ingenuity and diligence for his own future benefit.

The issue involves a contrast with the Christian entrusted by God with the management of His estate and eternal business in this world. Christ said that the children of this world, in their own line of work and business, and according to their own standards, act more wisely than the children of light. They are diligent, active, persevering, hard working. They set their whole heart upon getting economic security for themselves. They watch for every opportunity to make headway. One does not say, "I have an opportunity in a business deal to make a lot of money if I act now. My friends agree with me. But I will wait a year to see if the price comes down." He has no intention of letting the deal slip out of his hands, so he immediately engages in the transaction.

Do we as Christians manifest the same interest, thoroughness, and diligence as do the children of the world? Do we strive to obtain eternal riches with the same commitment? Do we serve our Lord with less zeal and His cause with less devotion, than the man of business, the man of pleasure, or the man of sports serves *his* cause?

Let us be determined to please God every bit as much as men are set to please themselves. When we are called to account, Christ will receive us into His everlasting kingdom.

87

# THE RACE SET BEFORE US

*Wherefore seeing we also are compassed about with so great a cloud of witnesses, let us lay aside every weight, and the sin which doth so easily beset us, and let us run with patience the race that is set before us, looking unto Jesus the author and finisher of our faith.* **Heb. 12:1, 2.**

The steadfast pursuit of our high calling in Christ is the central truth of this scripture. Paul's appeal to Christians was by way of illustration: the race run by athletes in an amphitheater of one of the cities of Greece. The spectators sat on seats that sloped upward, tier upon tier, as they do in the great sports stadiums today.

What is meant by our running the Christian race? How do we win the race? By looking steadfastly to Jesus, "the author and finisher of our faith." We are to keep our eyes and minds fixed on Him. We are not to allow ourselves to be diverted from Christ and His righteousness.

To win this race, we must first put aside, strip off as it were, every weight, everything that would hold us back, that hinders us in the Christian life. What is the sin that so easily besets us? In the Greek, it is the sin that surrounds us; the sin that the majority of people are involved in; the sins that, because they are the common sins of our day, we persuade ourselves are not so bad. Everybody does it. We are all involved. With so many doing it, it cannot be that bad. They are the popular sins, the successful sins, the sins that seem to pay off.

Therefore, why alienate ourselves from the respectable people around us? Let us be all things to all men. So we surrender a little to the popular pressure. Keeping in harmony with the right people is more important than keeping in harmony with God. These common sins include everything that can be called in question, from display to entertainment.

They are the most dangerous because they are attractive to the multitude. Unfortunately, they lead us to conceal our Christian witness. They gradually erode away our relationship with Christ. They make us ashamed to look unto Jesus.

The greatest hindrance to running this race is found within our own life, not within the world. Our peril is that we forfeit our dependence on Him, our looking to Him. We know that our right relation to Him each day is our vital need.

## "LET US RUN WITH PATIENCE"

*Let us run with patience the race that is set before us.* **Heb. 12:1.**

The word *patience* in the Greek is a very strong word. It means diligence, steadfastness, endurance, resolute and whole-hearted allegiance that will face every trial, every disapproval, every temptation, rather than deny Christ. It is not enough to make a good start. We must keep in shape day after day, spiritually, morally, and mentally.

There is to be no slothfulness in our Christian life. Life is fleeting, short, and swift. If we see a man building a house we can tell by the way he goes about it whether his heart is in it or not. We can tell whether he has a will to do the work.

A man who is swimming for his life will strike out with determination and strength so long as he has hope of saving his life. When he despairs, he is in danger of sinking. Let us not lose confidence, let us not lose our trust in our God. He loves us more than we can ever know. He desires our salvation more than we do. He guarantees that the prize will be ours.

"Here is the patience of the saints: here are they that keep the commandments of God, and the faith of Jesus" (Rev. 14: 12). If we would truly enter into eternal life, if we desire to escape the loss of our souls, if we prefer the honor of God rather than the praise of men, if we would live the Christlike life, if we would stand at last in the sunrise of the splendor of the heights of heaven, we must run with patience. We must never give up.

In this race we are surrounded by a great cloud of witnesses. Those Christians who have finished the race are pictured as though they were holding us in full survey, urging us on. As we study the great men of God who have gone before us, let us take heart. We too can receive the crown. They were all men of like passions, but they found Christ more than sufficient. These men like unto ourselves won the race. What happened to them will surely happen to us, providing we look unto Christ. He is the author and finisher of our faith. "Consider him, . . . lest ye be wearied and faint in your minds" (Heb. 12:3). He never forsakes us, He never gives up on us. He never ceases to train, to direct, to encourage and empower us. Let us press on with certainty of victory through Christ.

# DISTINGUISHED CHRISTIANS

*These are they which follow the Lamb whithersoever he goeth.* **Rev. 14:4.**

What is the standard by which we measure ourselves as Christians? Let the Bible show forth its true men. Look into the face of Joseph. That married woman came to him and offered him a shrunken womanhood for a sterling manhood. Without hesitation he said, "Woman, my decision is on the side of God." Think of Daniel, in the full bloom of youth, with head up and shining eyes: "Thank you, gentlemen, I do not drink." Consider Moses, with all the education of a great civilization. The queen mother rises to place upon his brow the crown of the Pharaohs. Immediately he declares, "I am not the son of Pharaoh's daughter. I am the son of the living God."

Would that there were great multitudes of Christians who could stand these tests, who could be really trusted for honesty and purity, who rise conspicuously above the vulgar standards of the world, whose faith in God is unmovable. The world in admiration, if not in imitation, will stand bareheaded to admire and respect them, simple people though they may be.

At the religious rituals, the external observances and multiplied church functions, men of the world will only look on as at some passing show. By such things they will not be impressed or moved. They will not be converted. But let the remnant church produce one Joseph, one Moses, one Daniel, or one Paul, and more will be converted to Christ than by all the evangelistic programs.

Like them we are to render a living verdict for Christ and His righteousness at all times. Is it any use to call oneself a Christian and not be a distinguished one? At the solemn bar of divine judgment we will not be asked about our theories, but about our commitment to Christ.

There is a lot of discussion on religion that never amounts to much. The might-have-beens in the Bible reveal the tragedy of failing to stand true when brought into the valley of decision. There was Esau, who sold his heritage for a mess of pottage; and Gehazi, private secretary to Elisha, who sold himself for a new suit and a wedge of gold. There was Judas Iscariot, who had the glorious privilege of walking with Christ on earth. He threw it all away for thirty pieces of silver.

## "WE KEEP HIS COMMANDMENTS"

*For this is the love of God, that we keep his commandments: and his commandments are not grievous.* 1 John 5:3.

How beautiful is the law of God to the Christian. Every commandment is a revelation of the character of God, a light shining in a dark place to guide our lives. "Wherefore the law is holy, and the commandment holy, and just, and good" (Rom. 7:12).

But there is another side to the story. Ours is a pagan civilization marked by the prevalence of sin and indifference to sin. Multitudes have drifted into a neutral attitude in the breaking of God's commandments. For many, sin and transgression are fossil words. They are regarded either as not too important or as curable by the methods of human therapy.

The Bible affirms human depravity in the most strenuous terms. Redemption in Christ is based upon the fact of man's sinful lost state. Therefore our spiritual understanding of sin and law is of first consequence. The law is like a torch carried into the dark corners of human nature to reveal the sin that lurks there. "I had not known sin, but by the law: for I had not known lust, except the law had said, Thou shalt not covet" (verse 7).

The law was never intended to propel us to righteousness. The law convicts of sin. This was intended to prepare us for a righteousness from heaven, a gift from Jesus Christ. The man who has passed from under the condemnation of the law to under Christ and His righteousness does not wish to lie or steal.

The reason now for obeying the law of God is that these moral principles are part of our lives. The question of obedience has been decided on higher grounds. We are constrained by love for Christ. The Christian life is just the opposite of moral anarchy and disobedience.

We no longer want our own way. We want God's way. Mere external conformity to rules is insufficient. United with Christ, we share in His life and His righteousness. Before God we are accepted as righteous, not through our own merits, but through Christ's.

# THE KEY TO VICTORY

*How then can I do this great wickedness, and sin against God?* **Gen. 39:9.**

These words spoken by Joseph in the hour of temptation hold the key to victory over sin. Joseph's religious commitment led to his great moral character. He was perfectly assured when he met with temptation. His responsibility to God effected in him strength for every trial and victory over every sin. In spite of his being sold as a slave at 18 years of age, he was never inclined to give way to the idea that God had forsaken him. He was so absolutely sure of God that his loyalty never wavered.

This is a perfectly sound Christian principle by which to face temptation and trial. If you have not done so, try it. You will stand amazingly firm. You will shake off the influence of public opinion that pressures you to go the wrong way. But standing consciously before the face of the eternal God is no light matter. It is not done with a superficial air or a taken-for-granted assurance. With Joseph, his was no milk-and-water religion. All he did was under the clear conviction: "Thou God seest me," as Hagar had realized.

What people think or say about us is not the supreme consideration. The position we take in terms of our responsibility to God does matter. Men have grown used to setting up their own moral standards. All too often men assure us that moral commitments depend largely on their moods and tastes. The whole catalog of modern sins is dressed up so as to look quite proper. And all the time there is a righteous God who has determined the moral character we are to develop and the moral code we are to obey. This is far more final than any appeal to man.

It is not necessary that we should be rich, but that we should first be a firm and true Christian. It is not essential that we should prosper, be popular, or famous. That may be detrimental to us. But it is essential that we live in the sight of God. He is the witness to our thoughts and actions. The eyes of God, of the angels, of a multitude of heavenly witnesses, are concentrated upon us. When tempted to sin let our most powerful restraint be: "How can I do anything so wicked and sin against God?"

# CHRISTIAN MOTIVATION

*Lord, thou hast examined me and knowest me. Thou knowest all, whether I sit down or rise up; thou hast discerned my thoughts from afar. . . . For there is not a word on my tongue but thou, Lord, knowest them all. . . . Where can I escape from thy spirit? Where can I flee from thy presence?* Ps. 139:1-7, N.E.B.

The great men of God in the Bible all felt this way. They judged their thoughts and actions, not by what the world thought, but by what God pronounced them to be.

There is no end of gifted and educated people who deny or ridicule the claim that the moral code of the Ten Commandments is still valid for people today. But the Word of God is clear. "By this we know that we love the children of God, when we love God, and keep his commandments. For this is the love of God, that we keep his commandments: and his commandments are not grievous" (1 John 5:2, 3).

At the core and center of our faith is this kind of righteous love. There is a communion and a fellowship with God and with His children that keeps these divine moral ideals alive. You will meet people along the way who will tell you that if two people love each other they are a law unto themselves and can to a great extent do what they like. Christian young people who live with a clear sense of responsibility to God, to His moral character and law, will stand against such folly.

There is no way you can stand alone and hold onto your moral integrity if you lose a sense of the living God and your accountability to Him. There have been too many wretched consequences along the road for anyone to suppose that you can take liberties with God's commandments. It isn't enough to set up your own moral standard. God is the one who is involved. Nothing so restrains sin and transgression as seeing it all in the light of how God looks at it. Our life is a divine calling. We are responsible to Him alone. We are conscious of a new and conquering force in our lives. Where other men are cowards and yield to temptation, we are confident, assured, and invincible in Christ. God has left us only one possibility: in every situation and before every temptation we will be true to Him and to our fellow men.

# THE FULLNESS OF CHRIST

*To know the love of Christ, which passeth knowledge, that ye might be filled with all the fulness of God.* **Eph. 3:19.**

The Christian faith destroys no natural relationships, denies no human obligations, makes void no moral or spiritual laws. It elevates all of these into a new sphere—"in Christ." "Of his fulness have all we received, and grace for grace" (John 1:16).

Christ, in taking us up into Himself, takes all that belongs to us except sin. He sanctifies all. Christ never touches any part of our lives without transforming it. He recreates us "in righteousness and true holiness" (Eph. 4:24). Christ and His righteousness never part company. It is impossible for us to be in Christ without our being made like unto Him.

Sometimes we buy a house but do not live in it. We rent it out. Usually, however, we buy a house to live in. Now Christ has bought this temple of ours with the cost of His sacrifice. His plan is to dwell in it, not to have others occupy it. Christ promised He would dwell in us through the Holy Spirit. The more we are filled with Christ, the more we belong to Him and the more we acknowledge His ownership.

One of the great problems we face is that while we acknowledge that He has redeemed us, we live much of the time as if we owned ourselves. We go off on our own to do "our own thing." But there can be no separation from our Lord without Satan's moving in to take over. Failure to let Christ own us completely is responsible for most spiritual problems and lapses into sin. If Christ is not master at any point He is not master at all. If He is not the master of our pleasures He is not the master of us. If He is not the master of our money He is not the master of our life. God does not want all our time, money, or pleasures; but we must acknowledge Him to be the master over all.

Daily we are to open our hearts and minds fully to the Holy Spirit. Christ must truly possess us. We are possessed either by Christ or by Satan. We never get to the place where we can go it alone.

# REMEMBER JESUS CHRIST

*Remember that Jesus Christ . . . was raised from the dead.* **2 Tim. 2:8.**

Is there any likelihood that we should forget Jesus Christ? The possibility seems altogether out of the question. That sounds like a hungry man forgetting to eat, a tired man forgetting to sleep, the ship's captain forgetting his compass. Is it true that we do forget our Lord?

Many times I think that we do. Other earthly responsibilities and problems compel our attention. They come to have a power over us, many times quite out of proportion to that of our need for divine help.

"When Jesus then lifted up his eyes, and saw a great company come unto him, he saith unto Philip, Whence shall we buy bread, that these may eat? And this he said to prove him: for he himself knew what he would do" (John 6:5, 6). All that was available was a boy's lunch of five loaves and two fishes. Philip replied that they did not have the money to feed so many people. Dismiss the crowd to get bread any way they could.

Jesus told the people to sit down. Philip had not given much thought to what Jesus would or could do. The disciples had seen Jesus perform miracles before, but they had evidently forgotten about that.

Sometimes the situation recurs within our own lives. In our anxiety we cry, "I do not know what to do. I hardly know which way to turn." For us it should not matter what the problem is or how big. The question is How do we meet it? We ought to know by this time that there is no use searching for answers from within ourselves. One bit of genuine faith in God, the size of a grain of mustard seed, is worth a ton of human wisdom and effort.

But no, we become so engrossed and overcome with our difficulties that we forget Jesus Christ. When, to no avail, we have exhausted our energy and our thinking, we appeal to God. We go on until we are at the end of our rope. Then it is time to pray and call God in. Anyone who has used this human strategy will tell you how foolish it is. Human effort alone comes to nothing, exactly nothing. The issue seems clear enough. Why not count on God from the start?

# THE REALITY OF JESUS

*Wherefore henceforth know we no man after the flesh: yea, though we have known Christ after the flesh, yet now henceforth know we him no more. 2 Cor. 5:16.*

Paul had never seen Jesus in the flesh when He was on the earth. In those days it seems many Christians made a big issue about that. That is how they claimed to know Christ. That was the extent of their knowledge: His birth, race, position, life, and death; His natural, human appearance. Paul's knowledge of Christ was essentially spiritual; a living Christ, not outside of him, but inside of him.

"If only Jesus were here visibly!" we tell ourselves. "If only we could see Him heal the sick, and raise the dead! If we had but felt His hands in our hands! If we had actually heard His voice say to us, 'Thy sins be forgiven thee. Go in peace.' If we had heard Him say to the tempestuous sea, 'Peace be still,' and then had seen the sea get suddenly calm. All this could never be forgotten."

We are to know Jesus with equal certainty. If we have experienced at His hands the forgiveness of our sins, the new life in Him, the transforming power of His love, there can be no doubt. He is very real to us. Ignoring or forgetting Jesus is not because our memory is not working. We remember a thousand and one things of comparatively trifling and minor importance, such as a slight or a favor given us. But we forget God at times. We ought not to have to prod our memories and agonize when it comes to Jesus Christ and His meaning for our lives.

Where problems persist, His grace is sufficient for us. Trials must come to all of us. Temptations never fail to raise their ugly head. Perhaps God is testing us. We are to fill our minds each day with thoughts of Him. He is an antidote for all our sins. Is much of modern life so gripping and captivating that we feel no need of Him?

God has not given us simply a list of texts to memorize, a set of rules to be remembered. What God has promised to us is Himself. "I will not leave you comfortless: I will come to you" (John 14:18).

# IN THE NAME OF JESUS

*"Not everyone who calls me 'Lord, Lord' will enter the kingdom of Heaven, but only those who do the will of my heavenly Father."* Matt. 7:21, N.E.B.

The name *Jesus* has become in our time a popular name to use. There is a tremendous vocal enthusiasm for Jesus, with a repetition that might be either real or assumed. The name *Lord* conveys the idea of rightful ruler, master, sovereign. The point of the text is that if we call Jesus Lord and do not what He says, then we do not accept His claims upon our lives. We are just pretending. We are phonies.

There is a new type of "Christian" attracted to the name *Jesus* without being attracted to His character and His teachings. We must not silence the truth while using His name. Much of the difficulty in getting to know Jesus is that His professed followers know little or nothing of the Word of God and feel no loyalty to it.

What it amounts to is this: "Let us call on the name, Jesus, but not get specific as to what it means to follow Him. Do not bother doing what He says, or keeping His commandments. Let us do good and love everybody, but do not trouble us with moral standards." This permits much of life to remain remote from His control and direction.

An easy use of His name without accepting His claim as Lord of our lives carries with it great peril. "I never knew you," said Jesus. "Out of My sight." Much of modern religion has lost its grip on Jesus Christ. The commanding note that compels obedience to Him has faded. We can be sure that the devil approves of a religion that *uses* the name *Jesus* but leaves people with only a good feeling.

If we are to be the elect of God it will not be because we use His name frequently or plaster Jesus slogans on our cars or on the rocks along the highway. Jesus is both Saviour and Lord because He so profoundly and completely deals with man's experience as a sinner. Jesus is more than a name, more than some magic word. What does Jesus require us to do? How does He require us to live? Many do not put into this word the truth that it stands for. Following Jesus Christ is a completely new life-style in terms of moral and spiritual transformation.

# "WHO CALLS ME, LORD, LORD?"

*When once the master of the house . . . hath shut to the door, and ye begin to stand without, and to knock at the door, saying, Lord, Lord, open unto us; and he shall answer and say unto you, I know you not whence ye are. . . . Depart from me, all ye workers of iniquity.* **Luke 13:25-27.**

These verses raise the question as to who has the right to enter the heavenly mansions. The Master has shut the door knowing that His household is complete. Others outside, professing to be members of His family, continue knocking. Not having been workers of righteousness, however, they are of necessity workers of iniquity, in spite of the fact that they used His name. They did not belong in His house.

To be a follower of Christ is a wonderful thing, a new creation. It is a serious thing. It involves the development of a Christlike character. Life as Jesus lived it and as we are to live it are the same. To follow Jesus means to know where we stand on integrity, morality, righteous love, and obedience.

We cannot afford to belong to a church or a religion that uses the name *Jesus* and neglects His power to save from sin. Young people, with all the enthusiasm that comes to people of that age, call "Jesus, Jesus" with the uplifting of hands and emotionally filled voices and radiant faces. There is nothing wrong with that, of course not. But the day has come when Christ our Lord stands out against the sky asking for total allegiance to His way of life and truth.

The truths and teachings of Jesus Christ bear the same relation to our lives as does the rosebush to the rose, the tree to the fruit. Without the bush or the tree, reaching down deep and bringing nourishment from rich soil, there would be no rose and no fruit. This is no time to take such a light dose of truth that it does not count for much.

Let us have no limited use of His name, no use that does not involve us in His truth. We have accepted the name *Seventh-day Adventist* because we cannot be Christian in any other way, because this church offers that religion which is the closest to the life and teaching of Christ our Lord.

Jesus has the first claim upon the whole of our lives. Keeping the seventh-day Sabbath is a sign of it.

# ABLE TO STAND

*Put on the whole armour of God, that ye may be able to stand against the wiles of the devil. Eph. 6:11.*

The worth and the reality of the remnant church is directly in proportion to the number of genuine Christians who make up our fellowship. There was a time when this question could be discussed on the theoretical level, but not any more. We have now come to the place where, first, the true church of God is the only body of Christians who know the whole truth by which everything else in the world must be judged. And second, the Christians who make up this body have repudiated religion as a neutral state, who bear witness to the sovereign rule of Christ over the whole of their lives.

We have to make up our minds whether we are going to fall victim to the Laodicean mood or consider this hour the finest opportunity for the highest and freest devotion to Christ. This much we know: the remnant church is here to prove to the world and to the universe that God's supreme purpose is being fully realized in His people. In the midst of a world now fully secularized, show us the Christian who can lead others to an unparalleled allegiance to God; who can offer to men the faith of Jesus; a life cleansed from low, degrading passions; a pure mind and steadfastness of life.

The life of the people of God is not a soft life, though men sometimes seem to think so. God's last movement is a challenge to exercise our best powers, to inspire others to stand for the truth. Let no one think lightly as to what it means to be a Seventh-day Adventist.

Back in the days of the second world war, the Government drafted many of our young men, taking them from college and sending them to the battle front. One of these men had attended one of my Bible classes. He had given his heart fully to Christ and dedicated his life to the service of God. In the arenas and battles of the war, young men faced temptations that defied description. But he never wavered. Later, when he came back to finish college, he told me, "In my group of soldiers there were only three of us who stood loyal to Christ and to any kind of high moral standard. I was one of them. Thank you for making Christ real to me."

# HAVE YOU RECEIVED THE HOLY SPIRIT?

*And it came to pass, that, while Apollos was at Corinth, Paul having passed through the upper coasts came to Ephesus: and finding certain disciples, he said unto them, Have ye received the Holy Ghost since ye believed? Acts 19:1, 2.*

So crucial was the Holy Spirit a test of church membership that one must inevitably ask Paul's question of new believers. The question is still valid today.

Just prior to His leaving the earth to return to His Father, Christ promised that the third member of the Godhead would take His place. In this way Jesus would continue to be a reality and a power to His church. For unless God has some way to make possible our connection with the living Christ now in heaven, Jesus remains a person of history rather than a divine power in the present. What Christ offers us is not a man out there in space, but a personal Christ within us. "I will pray the Father, and he shall give you another Comforter, that he may abide with you for ever. . . . I will not leave you comfortless: I will come to you" (John 14:16-18).

The Holy Spirit came to bear witness to Christ. His work is to glorify Christ. "He shall glorify me; for he shall receive of mine, and shall shew it unto you" (chap. 16:14). The Holy Spirit is not to focus the spotlight on Himself by sensational manifestations. "For he shall not speak of himself; but whatsoever he shall hear, that shall he speak" (verse 13). The Holy Spirit does not work in isolation. He does not say or do something different from what Christ said and did. He unites with Christ to make the life and teachings of Christ real to us. He does not work independently.

While on earth, Christ wrought out for us a perfect righteousness and a complete redemption. The Holy Spirit makes this real to us. This is why "no man can say that Jesus is the Lord, but by the Holy Ghost" (1 Cor. 12:3). This close cooperation and identification of the Holy Spirit with the living Christ prevents the Christian faith from degenerating into a vague mysticism and perilous spiritism. The Spirit does not seek to catch the headlines or startle the mind. He is never a blind, unintelligent force. He comes to us in terms of our personal relationship to Christ.

# FINDING POWER FROM GOD

*Ye shall receive power, after that the Holy Ghost is come upon you.*
**Acts 1:8.**

What does it mean to have power from God? How shall this power from the Holy Spirit be interpreted? What manifestations should we expect?

Multitudes are being deceived by offers of spiritistic encounters with the supernatural. Because one is beside himself with religious ecstasy almost to the point of loss of self-control does not mean that he has met the Lord Jesus Christ.

It is never God's intention to coerce or excite the mind as an end in itself, while ignoring the claims of the Scriptures upon the whole of life. No crescendo of emotion must be allowed to bypass sound thinking on the Word of God. The Holy Spirit does no violence to the mind. He leads into all truth. We should refrain from all expressions of religion that imperil the sanity and the serenity of the soul. This is not intended to disparage the emotions. Fellowship with Christ does not chill the emotions. The Holy Spirit is present in love, joy, and peace. But these are not surface emotions that pass with the mood. Temporary emotionalism does not resolve the problems of life, or bring victory over selfishness, impurity, hostility, and disobedience to God's will.

The power of the Holy Spirit means adequacy for service, for Christian warfare, power to meet all the demands of life. There is a release of spiritual and moral resources to the life. There is a new mastery over sin and self.

There is nothing so ominous as man's misuse of power, especially in religion. The human mind is easily conscious of its sufficiency, but not its insufficiency. We tend to have revivals by placing ourselves at the center, rather than our Lord, Jesus Christ. How do people see us as Christians? Spirit-filled Christians have the spirit of Christ, not to be ministered unto but to minister to others. This implies a willingness to forsake the privilege and the exaltation of self, to renounce prestige. We center our lives in Christ.

# POWER BY THE HOLY SPIRIT—1

*And, behold, I send the promise of my Father upon you: but tarry ye in the city of Jerusalem, until ye be endued with power from on high. Luke 24:49.*

Christ promised us power, but power for what? How shall this power of the Holy Spirit be interpreted? What manifestations should we expect? The New Testament gives two areas in particular where the power of the Spirit is to be exercised: first, it is His work to fill the lives of Christians with the fullness of God, the fruit of the Spirit; and second, to fulfill the gospel commission to the world.

The fundamental fallacy is to interpret the power of the Holy Spirit in terms of experiences, manifestations, sensations, that the Spirit never promised to perform. Many people are not content unless they possess power to perform magical feats. Actually, the closer we get to the power of the Holy Spirit, the less we will talk about the power revealed in us. The Spirit does not turn us back upon ourselves to determine what is truth or what it means to be baptized with the Spirit. "For God hath not given us the spirit of fear; but of power, and of love, and of a sound mind" (2 Tim. 1:7). Is there anything more than this we could wish for from the Spirit? Think what it would mean to find in our experience adequate love for every situation and a sound, balanced mind, an integrated mind that functions at full capacity. This is the power God promised, complete adequacy available twenty-four hours a day to meet every experience and every situation.

The power of the Spirit provides us with the fullness of Christ to meet all the demands in life, power to live victoriously and radiantly.

The issue is this: How can we live like Christ in the modern world? How can we live to the glory of God and not for ourselves? It is quite possible to lack the power of the Holy Spirit but have great confidence in our own strength, capacities, and abilities. We read that to live by the Holy Spirit is to have all the fruit of the Spirit: "love, joy, peace, longsuffering, gentleness, goodness, faith, meekness, temperance" (Gal. 5:22, 23). There is so much that should belong to our daily lives that we do not yet possess.

# POWER BY THE HOLY SPIRIT—2

*Ye shall receive power, after that the Holy Ghost is come upon you.*
*Acts 1:8.*

When we study the early Christians we discover that the power of the Spirit was not given as an end in itself, to shock, to surprise, to overwhelm the individual, but to fulfill the great commission. One hundred twenty disciples filled with the Spirit shook the world. What a triumph was there.

The indwelling of the Holy Spirit is pre-eminently calculated to fashion men and women of great dedication to God. Everything about the presence and power of the Holy Spirit is calculated to unlock the mind, to evoke all our powers, to bring out all the possibilities for doing the work of God in the world. The Spirit is strong to enlist people in the service of God. "The people that do know their God shall be strong, and do exploits" (Dan. 11:32).

The presence of the Holy Spirit makes a strong church. It makes strong Christians. What was the great blessing of Pentecost? Cowardly, weak, timid, ignorant men; fishermen; taxgatherers—by the power of the Holy Spirit they became the majestic apostles whose mighty work and witness changed the face of the world for all time. They endured to the end, to martyrdom, to face every possible sacrifice to build the City of God. The Spirit led them to the most magnificent triumphs for the Kingdom of God, greater than anything ever seen before. Under the latter rain the remnant church of God is to exceed this.

Without the Holy Spirit the world is too strong for us. All through the Bible God gets things done in a remarkable way by an odd group of men and women filled with the Spirit, who never could have gone very far by their own efforts and under their own steam.

Jesus Christ is not asking for our strength, our wisdom, our power. When Gideon went to war with the Midianites, their armies "lay along in the valley like grasshoppers for multitude" (Judges 7:12). Yet God utterly defeated them by three hundred men empowered by the Spirit. What you and I can do on our own for God will never amount to much. Only the power of the Holy Spirit can make the difference.

# INVOLVED WITH GOD—1

*"I will not leave you bereft; I am coming back to you. In a little while the world will see me no longer, but you will see me; because I live, you too will live; then you will know that I am in my Father, and you in me and I in you."* John 14:18-20, N.E.B.

Today people want to get involved. They no longer wish to sit as spectators, particularly in religion and in relation to God. This is a day of encounter with the supernatural. Millions claim to experience the supernatural. Flushed with emotion and excitement, people seek involvement with the spirit world.

Naturally, people would prefer to meet God personally and directly rather than receive letters such as Paul's Epistles to the churches. But the visible Christ no longer lives among us. How do we experience oneness with Him? Christ affirmed that the Holy Spirit, the third member of the Godhead, was to be this living connection between Himself now in heaven and the Christian on earth. He becomes a living reality and power for the present. The Holy Spirit makes Christ as real to us as when He lived on earth. No Christian experience is possible without Him.

Regeneration and sanctification are the work of the Holy Spirit. He alone lives Christ's life within us, produces the fruit of the Spirit. The Word of God without the Holy Spirit is just information in the area of religion. God promises us far more than that.

"It was through one man that sin entered the world, and through sin death, and thus death pervaded the whole human race" (Rom. 5:12, N.E.B.). This is a statement about the mortality of all men. We all die because of sin. Man is not immortal. That is part of our creed. You can discuss the subject, write an essay on the subject, without getting involved. But one day the doctor tells you that you have a terminal cancer. This is different. You are no longer discussing man's mortality. You are involved in death itself. You cannot dismiss this with a shrug.

But this is true about the whole of the Word of God. Salvation, regeneration, obedience, sanctification, the writing of God's law on our hearts, must equally involve our whole lives. This is what the Holy Spirit came to do—to make all truth a dynamic power, and Christ personally real.

# INVOLVED WITH GOD—2

*For we wrestle not against flesh and blood, but against principalities, against powers, against the rulers of the darkness of this world, against spiritual wickedness in high places. Eph. 6:12.*

Involvement with the supernatural brings us face to face with two supernatural forces—the powers of light and the powers of darkness. On this crucial point more than on any other, Satan seeks to deceive us. He too seeks to get us involved with the supernatural. How shall we know which encounter with the supernatural is true and which is false?

"The last great delusion is soon to open before us. Antichrist is to perform his marvelous works in our sight. So closely will the counterfeit resemble the true that it will be impossible to distinguish between them except by the Holy Scriptures. By their testimony every statement and every miracle must be tested."—ELLEN G. WHITE, *The Great Controversy,* p. 593.

Christ has given us two witnesses to Himself which belong together: the Holy Spirit and the Word of God. They are with us until Christ returns. We must live and test our Christian life, our encounter with God, in relation to both of them. So long as you seek for the fullness of the Spirit to lead you into all truth from God's Word, you will not be found on the wrong side in the controversy between Christ and Satan. There is no possibility of losing your way.

The devil's counterfeit of the Holy Spirit is dangerous in proportion to the skill and subtlety with which it is put forth. It is more likely to pass unnoticed and unchallenged when it is more nearly identical with the true. These counterfeits are becoming more successful in deceiving people. Any type of involvement with the supernatural that bypasses the truth of Scripture is false.

At this point we are not asserting that all the adherents of others' faiths and creeds are not Christian. We pronounce no judgment. But we do insist on testing all claims to truth by the Word of God. A man may be better than his creed, just as he may be worse. But what we believe about the word of God in the Bible will determine the genuineness or falsity of our Christian experience. Every claim to an encounter with some form of the supernatural must be tested by the Word of God.

# INVOLVED WITH GOD—3

*And when they shall say unto you, Seek unto them that have familiar spirits, . . . should not a people seek unto their God? . . . To the law and to the testimony: if they speak not according to this word, it is because there is no light in them. Isa. 8:19, 20.*

Certain forms of encounter with the supernatural enjoy a high degree of popularity today. They promise the exciting and the sensational, unnatural phenomena that excite the mind. At the same time this kind of experience may require no deep repentance for sin and no obedience to the truth of God. It may affect a high degree of religion, but the Bible exempts no one from the claims of God's moral law by a promise of some glowing crescendo of emotion. The peril is that this inner subjective experience of the supernatural so involves the individual as to lead him to be indifferent to Bible truth.

In this sinning world we need salvation and deliverance from sin and error twenty-four hours a day, not just a few moments of professed encounter with the supernatural. Any religious system that fails to require obedience to the Word of God cannot meet either the moral law of God or the moral needs of sinners. All types of religious ecstasy, excitement, and euphoria are but a mockery if they do not bring men into harmony with God and with His truth.

Christ cast out demons, but He was no sensational, loud exorcist. He used no spells nor incantations. He spoke in clear words that called upon the demons and false spirits to release sinners from their bondage. He was filled with the Holy Spirit, yet gave way to no sensationalism or irrational bypassing of the mind. He aroused no excitement and emotion that silenced the restraints of reason, purity, integrity. He refrained from all expressions and types of ritual that would imperil the normal operations of the mind and the clear serenity of the soul.

Christ's appeal was always to the Scripture—"It is written"— and never to subjective experience. He gave priority to the Word of God. Experience involved hearing and obeying that Word. He claimed to be the Truth. The Scripture spoke of Him and witnessed to Him. He opened the minds of His hearers that they might understand the Scriptures and the truth from God.

# TRUTH BY THE HOLY SPIRIT

*"However, when he comes who is the Spirit of truth, he will guide you into all the truth. . . . He will glorify me, for everything that he makes known to you he will draw from what is mine." John 16:13, 14, N.E.B.*

Time and again in His last words to His disciples Christ associated the Holy Spirit with truth. The term "Spirit of truth" means the Spirit who communicates truth. He leads us into the truth on all the eternal issues found in Christ and in the Word of God. Christ and the Holy Spirit stand as our supreme teachers. They disclose clearly to our minds our relationship to the spiritual world. " 'Your Advocate, the Holy Spirit whom the Father will send in my name, will teach you everything, and will call to mind all that I have told you' " (John 14:26, N.E.B.).

At the very core of the Christian faith is God's respect for man as a rational and responsible person. God can use no methods or bring to bear no pressure that violates our personal integrity. The Christian faith is supernatural, but it is never irrational. False doctrine must be met by the authority of the truth of God's Word. The Holy Spirit does not allow feelings or emotional excitement to form the basis for a sound choice as to what is truth. Only by balanced emphasis on the Word and the Holy Spirit can God be glorified and men be sanctified by the truth.

The Bible is God's book. It is heaven's light for a dark world. God's Word is a path of light laid at our feet to lead us to God and to our eternal home. The Word of God is the sword of the Spirit (see Eph. 6:17). Whenever the Holy Spirit seeks to communicate with us, the truth of the Bible has priority, not some other professed "truth." The Spirit seeks to bring about our total allegiance to the truth of God.

The source of authority for our lives and for the church is the Bible, and the Holy Spirit who leads us into Bible truth. Truth does not change. Time does not destroy its relation to life itself. It is not for more religious information that men perish. We need always to hear the voice of God speaking to us through the Word by the Holy Spirit. We must be prepared to pay the price for firm allegiance to the truth. God will take it from there.

# THE FORM AND THE POWER—1

*Having a form of godliness, but denying the power thereof: from such turn away.* 2 Tim. 3:5.

The Christian religion can be either a form or a power. The "form of godliness," of which Paul writes, refers to external appearance, the outward form of religion without the reality. The Pharisees had the outward form. They were very zealous for the traditional ritual, the established order and routine. That is what mattered to them. They had none of the power of their religion in character, conduct, and life.

One of the great defects in religious experience may be the lack of power to change and transform our lives. We may become satisfied with adhering to the letter of the law. Then our religious life is artificial. We can go through the form of baptism without the regenerating power of the Spirit to which it points. We can observe the form of the Sabbath without any vital energy from God. When this happens, the power of the Spirit-life is ignored. Outward conformity is stressed rather than the insistence upon a vital experience with Christ. This has often been the tendency among religionists. Then people get bored and weary with the form of religion. The form alone has nothing to offer. If that is all there is, religion becomes an empty thing.

The power of the Christian faith comes from the Holy Spirit. The essential thing is our surrender to, and possession by, the Holy Spirit. He alone makes a real Christian experience possible. Most of us are aware of spiritual inadequacies, of failures that never seem to be resolved. We must acknowledge before God that we are at the end of our resources. Living victoriously comes only through the power from God. This means death to human effort to bring our lives into line. We must forfeit all self-dependence.

"He that loveth his life shall lose it; and he that hateth his life in this world shall keep it unto life eternal" (John 12:25). Christ here states a truth of momentous importance, fundamental for Christian living. It points to a life contrary to all self-culture, self-esteem, and self-exaltation. Christ asks us to reverse the whole bent of our thinking, to die to every expression of the self-life that prevents the control of the Holy Spirit.

# THE FORM AND THE POWER—2

*Now unto him that is able to do exceeding abundantly above all that we ask or think, according to the power that worketh in us.* **Eph. 3:20.**

In the Christian life nothing exists for or by itself. No part of our being can fulfill its true function until the Spirit of God is given His rightful place. Everything we know and find out about ourselves proves how much we need a power from beyond ourselves. We are most likely to go astray in this respect.

The power to live for Christ is not natural, but supernatural; not inborn, but God-born and nourished by our continual dependence upon Him. A victorious Christian is a person in whom God rules. No professed Christian can triumph in life except as he is Spirit moved, Spirit controlled, and Spirit led.

Spirituality cannot be reduced to a system or to church machinery under the control of men. The form of religion in terms of ritual, institutionalism, and organization is a means to an end. Most religious systems tend toward the excess of machinery and the parasites of form. Truth hardens into a hopeless routine. There lurks in the form of religion an inherent falsity as a result of the misrepresentation of spiritual life. There is no greater waste of mind and power than to reduce religion to externals.

The Jew had the law, but did not recognize the spirit deeper than the law. He discerned the God of the law, but not God as his heavenly Father. So the Jew never discovered the real answer and meaning to his religion. Our religious life cannot take root in form. Behind all the forms of religion, God presents Himself as a living personality, very real indeed.

Only the reality has any lifting power. Reality does not lie in repeating the ritual and going through the forms. There is no benefit to our Christian experience by carrying a cross around our neck. Our Lord left a cross on a hill a long time ago upon which and beyond which the living God actually committed Himself to us for our redemption and salvation. God knew that His love was the only hope we would ever have, the only revelation that would make a difference. In its very essence the Christian faith is committed, not to a form, but to reality that really makes a difference in our lives.

# FILLED WITH THE SPIRIT—1

*Be not drunk with wine, wherein is excess; but be filled with the Spirit.*
**Eph. 5:18.**

The Christian life is nothing except as it is the fruit of the Spirit. A great lack is frequently felt and expressed by God's people. Somehow, the Christian life is not what we expected it to be. Instead of the abundant life, it is often a meager life. Instead of inner satisfaction, it is one of increasing hunger. Instead of a life of peace, it is often disquiet and discontent. Instead of love and compassion, life is marked by irritation and hostility. Some Christians live and die spiritually poor.

Christ is glorified when we experience His presence and fullness. Fathers in their work and business, with the pressure of a thousand responsibilities, need the fullness of the Spirit if they are to give glory to God. Mothers in the home, with the demands of children upon them, need this fullness to give glory to God. Young people in all their associations at school and in their pleasures need the Spirit for the same reason.

To be filled with the Spirit is to experience what Christ promised us: "Out of his belly shall flow rivers of living water" (John 7:38). The promise is for us. "Rivers of living water" —not a trickle or an almost-dry stream. Life abundant, not a cramped life.

Christ gave the promise Himself, so it has to be genuine and it has to be vital. A promise from God never used is like a check never cashed. "I will pour out of my Spirit upon all flesh" (Acts 2:17). "Have ye received the Holy Ghost since ye believed?" (chap. 19:2). This is one of the most important questions we can ask of ourselves. The emphasis is upon receiving, not achieving. The word *receiving* is used in accepting a gift.

In this respect the gift of the Spirit is not different from the gift of salvation. As salvation is a gift based on the completed work of Christ's redemption, so is the Holy Spirit. There was a time when we had not heard of God's gift of salvation offered to us. When Christ came to us we gladly accepted the salvation and forgiveness of sins. Accepting the gift of salvation, being born again, is our starting point. The acceptance of the gift of salvation and of the Holy Spirit is the same in both cases.

## FILLED WITH THE SPIRIT—2

*Be not drunk with wine, wherein is excess; but be filled with the Spirit.*
**Eph. 5:18.**

Having the fullness of the Spirit is never an end in itself. God never endues us with the power of the Spirit simply to satisfy us with some temporary euphoria. The Holy Spirit always witnesses to Christ, not to make His own impression on people's emotions. Many people seek for the exciting and the sensational by which they claim to be possessed by the Spirit. But it is no part of the Spirit's work to glorify us. His work is to glorify Christ. God will not let us use the Holy Spirit for emotional purposes. If we seek to appropriate Him magically, we shall not receive Him. He will not come to us.

We can be trusted with the Holy Spirit only to the degree that we let Him use us for the glory of God. We need to pray, "Father, glorify Thy name in every experience that comes to me." If we can honestly say, "Father, glorify Thy name; let Thy life and love shine through me," we are in a position to receive the fullness of the Spirit.

What greater thing can we do than to let Christ take all that happens to us and all that we are, and fill us with Himself? The fundamental issue is: Can we accept so great a loss as dying to self-sufficiency and self-will in order that the Spirit will wholly possess us? This is the Spirit-filled life. It is not necessary to expect the spectacular, the obvious, the exaltation of ourselves. Life by the Spirit may be just the opposite.

Do not think of this life as an unnatural, strange thing, or a unique thing. The strange thing is that we should live in the world without being filled with Christ.

Men talk about having the power of the Holy Spirit and seem to lift themselves up and say, "I am baptized with the Spirit. I have His fullness." I am not at all sure that it happens this way. There is one real and true strength in this universe, and that is God's strength. No Christian ever did any powerful thing yet that God did not do in and through him. We have the power of God only as we let ourselves be held in the hand of God. As the chisel is powerless if it tries to carve a statue by itself, so is the Christian who seeks power for himself.

# THE SEAL OF THE SPIRIT

*Ye were sealed with that holy Spirit of promise.* **Eph. 1:13.**

It is quite probable that in his use of the word "sealed" Paul alludes to the custom of his day. Impressions made in wax or clay were placed on documents as a mark of authority. They were also placed on goods to show ownership. Paul uses this term to speak of Christians as belonging to God, bearing a sign of His ownership. Christ impresses upon our hearts and lives His eternal purity and righteousness, just like the impression that is left upon the wax of an official seal. This seal is evidence by which we are known. We have the image of Christ stamped upon us by the Holy Spirit. We are truly His.

In the Apocalypse, John speaks of the saints' being sealed with "the seal of the living God" (Rev. 7:2) of "having his Father's name written in their foreheads" (chap. 14:1). We write our names in books and on things that belong to us. So it is with God. "Those who love God, have the seal of God in their foreheads."—ELLEN G. WHITE, in *The Youth's Instructor,* July 26, 1894. People who love us belong to us and we to them. Only in love relationships do people belong to each other or to God. Only love makes possible our total response and commitment. Nothing else really does.

God wants us to love Him, not simply to conform to the rules. The Holy Spirit makes us loving and lovable persons. In this way He restores us to a right relationship in God's family. We belong to a holy fellowship. Within this family we are fulfilled as persons and our lives fully realized. We can be lost in a crowd. But love is such a personal thing. As individuals we do count with God and with all members of His family. Nothing that is personally worthwhile is denied us.

God has written His name upon us. The Spirit has placed the seal of God upon us. We revel in the beauty of Christ's character. We appreciate with love the wonder of His wisdom, power, and presence. We identify ourselves with His cause on the earth. Our lives are redeemed from the superficial, the trivial, and the temporal. We are lifted into an eternal sphere of life. Through the Spirit, Christ inspires all the possibilities and potentialities in us to greatness that otherwise might never be realized.

# THE EARNEST OF THE SPIRIT

**Ye were sealed with that holy Spirit of promise, which is the earnest of our inheritance until the redemption of the purchased possession, unto the praise of his glory. Eph. 1:13, 14.**

The word translated as *earnest* means literally "money given in advance as a pledge or security that the full amount promised will be paid." It is part of the price to be paid as agreed on by buyer and seller.

The Spirit is given to us now as the pledge and guarantee of our future heavenly inheritance. The ultimate blessing, of which the Holy Spirit has given us a foretaste in our lives, will not fail. The very work of the Spirit in our lives is God's pledge to us, "being confident of this very thing, that he which hath begun a good work in you will perform it until the day of Jesus Christ" (Phil. 1:6). The Holy Spirit in our lives now is the guarantee of complete redemption. We have this security from God, the completing of that which has already begun in us.

This blessed down payment takes the weight of doubt and uncertainty off the heart. We know for sure. There are no "if's" and "but's," only genuine, solid conviction and assurance. No better proof could we have than this work of the Holy Spirit in us. We are fully persuaded, completely convinced. God has actually come to us in the presence of the Spirit. God meant by this to give us certainty.

We are never sure when we make a down payment on a house or a car that we can go through with it. Problems and difficulties may arise that will make full payment impossible. But not so with God's down payment. Only God can make and keep such a pledge to us. He intends to go all the way with us. He will stop at nothing less than complete restoration and redemption. He will never go back on His promise to us. Nothing can separate us from the love of Christ, absolutely nothing.

Therefore we become the bearers and witnesses to an eternal hope. We are messengers of certainty. We have the most glorious news in the world for all people: the sure pledge of the earth made new; an eternity of harmony with the most loving persons in the universe, beginning with God our Father, Jesus Christ our Elder Brother, and the Holy Spirit our unbreakable pledge.

# WALK IN THE SPIRIT—1

*There is therefore now no condemnation to them which are in Christ Jesus, who walk not after the flesh, but after the Spirit.* **Rom. 8:1.**

The figure of walking is frequently used in the New Testament to describe our daily Christian experience. We walk by faith (2 Cor. 5:7). We walk in love (Eph. 5:2). We walk in Christ (Col. 2:6). We walk in newness of life (Rom. 6:4).

We are commanded not only to have the Spirit but also to walk in the Spirit. That is, we form no character, we follow no course, we perform no acts, but such as the living Holy Spirit produces and inspires in us. Walking by the Spirit means dependence on Him as our way of life. Daily we allow the Spirit to possess our minds, to guide us at all times. We stay on the narrow path with Christ.

But it is not always easy. Paul counsels us to "walk not after the flesh, but after the Spirit."

Here are two tendencies in the life, or two powers as it were. On the one hand we are tempted to walk or operate from our own center, independent of God. This is always a possibility even for us as Christians. Our most frequent lapses are in this area. "Flesh" does not mean our being sensual or physically degenerate. It has primary reference to the whole person dependent on himself, his own wisdom and ability; to seek glory for himself, the praise and the approval of men.

The devil continually tempts us, as he tempted Christ, to look to ourselves, even in religion. We find satisfaction in those things that we can do without any help from God. Our obedience to the law gives us something to be proud of. We can point to our religious achievements with a sense of self-satisfaction. It is amazing how many good things we can do by sheer will power on our own. We thank God for giving us the Ten Commandments. We tell Him that we intend to do our best; we will go as far as we can on our own; then when we get in difficulty, we will call on Him for help.

But walking with the Spirit and by faith means we are in cooperation with God in living the Christian life. We don't live in anxiety wondering whether we are going to make it or not. That is not our responsibility. The Holy Spirit is the only one who knows just what God can make of us here on earth.

# WALK IN THE SPIRIT—2

*Whatsoever is not of faith is sin.* **Rom. 14:23.** *We walk by faith, not by sight.* **2 Cor. 5:7.**

We do not know how strong our dependence on self is until the Holy Spirit seeks to replace it. The substance of Christianity is the complete supremacy of Christ and the Holy Spirit. Our primary problem is how to walk this way every day.

Sometimes we hear men speak of salvation by character, but there is no such salvation. The character we develop as we walk in the Spirit is not our own. It is not the result of our education and discipline. Christian character is Christ's and the result of Christ's living in us by the power of the Spirit. It is Christ's hatred of sin that expresses itself through us. It is Christ's love of righteousness that is lived in us by Him. The Holy Spirit builds us up into the fullness of Christ. We are "rooted and built up in him" (Col. 2:7).

Walking by the flesh determines our destiny on the side of sin, self, and death. Walking by the Spirit determines our destiny on the side of eternal life. "If any man be in Christ, he is a new creature" (2 Cor. 5:17). We are transformed into Christ's likeness only as far and as fast as we walk in the Spirit.

The Spirit sets our affections on things above. The flesh sets them on things on the earth. As we walk by the Spirit, we become clearly aware of the change in our lives. The still small voice of God daily reminds us that we are never to depend on ourselves; but always to depend on Him, give place to Him, trust Him, commit ourselves to His guidance and control. There is no part of our lives at any time, day or night, that is to be kept apart from Him.

Therefore we waste no time depending on ourselves, no time on worthless or corrupting things in the life. We learn the way of life in the Spirit. He is always before us and with us.

The Holy Spirit pervades our whole life. He ignores no part of us. The whole life is brought into harmony with God. Any attempt to keep the law on our own is out, not because the law no longer applies, but because the Holy Spirit within us answers to all the demands of the law. Saving righteousness is always in Christ, not in us, even when we are made partakers of it by the indwelling of the Holy Spirit.

# "PRAY WITH THE SPIRIT"

*I will pray with the spirit.* **1 Cor. 14:15.**

To pray with the Spirit means to pray from a nature inspired and moved by the Holy Spirit. The Holy Spirit imparts new life in us. He quickens our dormant powers. Therefore we pray in newness of Spirit, not in the oldness of the letter.

Prayer often becomes cold and formal. It degenerates into mere words. Then it is an unprofitable religious exercise. Saying prayers is no more praying than a corpse is a living man. Would a creature that had only seen a corpse be able to make out from it what a living man is? No more can a person, who is accustomed only to say prayers with his lips, understand the life and power of prayer that bursts forth from a spiritual heart and mind. Real prayer involves spiritual ardor. Deep emotions are expressed out of a capacity and spiritual appetite for God.

The psalmist declared: "Bless the Lord, O my soul: and all that is within me, bless his holy name" (Ps. 103:1). David praised God with all that was within him. We are to do the same with prayer. Is our understanding within us? Then we are to pray and praise with an active, alert mind that has been fully awakened to the privilege and responsibility of prayer. Is our memory within us? Then we ought to remember all God's goodness to us, and all His promises. Is the capacity to love and adore within us? Then we ought to love God as we pray to Him. All our capacities are put on the stretch to know God.

Prayer with the Spirit employs our minds and hearts in proper balance. We must worship and pray to God in spirit and in truth. To pray without understanding can lead to fanaticism and deception. To pray with the Spirit is to have Christ come alive to us, to know that all the channels to God are open. Such prayer banishes coldness and indifference. Our lives are united with God, where His love, mercy, and grace can flow into us. We are no longer uncommitted Christians. We have reached the point of no return with God. We are totally involved. We really need Him. We enjoy Him. We come believing Him to be absolutely reliable, that we cannot live without Him. He is the One who will never let us down.

# "PRAY WITH THE UNDERSTANDING ALSO"

*I will pray with the understanding also.* **1 Cor. 14:15.**

If there is any place where we need to be understood and to understand God's will for us, it is in prayer. Understanding makes prayer intelligible. It is essential to communication. We are to pray intelligently. We must give thought to what we need to say to God. God's mind and our mind must operate on the same wave length. We are not to babble incoherent sounds to God. We are not to let the mind wander. We are to lift our minds in clear understanding and complete trust to our heavenly Father.

If there is some place where life has become difficult, where things have gone wrong, where some uncleanness has possessed us, where some hostility or hate has entered our hearts, or some sin that needs forgiveness, we are to face it with God. God moves into the picture with forgiveness, with new hope in place of despair, with love instead of fear, with divine strength instead of weakness. A clear knowledge of what we say and what is taking place is needed. Prayer is a very real and practical thing.

Before all the disorders of mind and heart that assail us, the temptations that make life difficult, prayer must be real and genuine, intelligent and understandable. We need the clearest minds possible when facing our personal problems. If there is a rift between us and God, we need to understand why. If we need forgiveness for a specific sin—and all sins are specific—we can have that from God. If we lack wisdom in some particular situation, then we ask God and we have that. We need a poised spirit and a mind at peace with God. We have that through prayer. It is a great blessing to bring our minds into harmony with God's mind.

Contact with God means we are prepared to see and understand God's will in specific situations and to do God's will instead of our own. There is so much in our lives that stands in the way of God's will and the fulfilling of His purpose for our lives. We need to face that. Prayer means we are prepared to let those things go. We withhold nothing from God. We accept His responsibility for our lives. In turn God makes Himself responsible for us.

# WHO ARE THE SONS OF GOD?—1

*For as many as are led by the Spirit of God, they are the sons of God.*
**Rom. 8:14.**

The importance of being led by the Holy Spirit cannot be overestimated. For the Spirit creates within us the clear conviction that we are indeed the sons and daughters of God. This implies living now as a conscious member of God's family. We are the special concern of our Father's love. The right of inheritance for the children of God is the very law and plan of heaven. It is sure and it is unerring.

Said Christ: "And think not to say within yourselves, We have Abraham to our father: for I say unto you, that God is able of these stones to raise up children unto Abraham" (Matt. 3:9). No one can be a child of God by calling himself one. God looks not at what we call ourselves but what we actually are.

The Scripture states that the Holy Spirit must settle the matter. If we are led by the Spirit, then we are the sons and daughters of God. If we are not so led, then we are not His children. How do we know when we are led by the Holy Spirit?

Which way are we taking, the narrow way or the broad way? If we knowingly continue in sin, then we cannot be led by the Spirit. We can no more be walking toward and with Christ when following any sin than we can be walking east when we are going west.

To be led by God is the divine principle that operates throughout all of God's creation. In the natural world God gives life to every flower, regulates every cell of plants and animals. He orders the grandeur and the beauty of the natural world. Then who should doubt for a moment the leading of the Spirit in our personal lives? Will not the Lord who guides the birds in their migrations, do much more for us? Will He who pilots all the stars in their courses hesitate to pilot our lives?

Place the right book in your hand, with Christian people as your companions. If a book is tainted with evil, let it alone. If a worldly place of amusement caters to the ugly, the cheap, and the impure, keep away. Listen to the still small voice of the Spirit. Wait upon Him sincerely, obediently. Everything depends upon your cooperation with Him.

# WHO ARE THE SONS OF GOD?—2

*Now we have received, not the spirit of the world, but the spirit which is of God. . . . We have the mind of Christ. 1 Cor. 2:12-16.*

If we are led by the Spirit we will become spiritual. Our life-style is not that of the world. The spiritual man has his thoughts and purposes in harmony with God and eternal values. Life with meaning is life with Christ.

To be led by the Spirit means to know Christ, to enjoy His love, to hold fellowship with Him, to find Christ real. Eternal reality is ours. But the natural life apart from God is ever changing, temporary. The fashion of it passes away.

God made us to live in fellowship with Himself. The heart and the flesh cry out for the living God. We are forever incomplete and unfulfilled without Him. Life has meaning only as we are led by the Spirit. Before Columbus came to America this great country was little more than a dream, a fabled world of gold and treasure. The truth of this suddenly became a reality when Columbus returned to tell his story.

Jesus Christ is the great discoverer to us of the eternal world of God. He came down from heaven and brought life and immortality to light through the gospel. Christ made known to us the things unseen and eternal.

How perilous is the hold and attraction of the temporary world around us. Secularism pleads that our lives be given entirely to earthly interests. "But thou, O man of God, flee these things; and follow after righteousness, godliness, faith, love, patience, meekness. Fight the good fight of faith, lay hold on eternal life, whereunto thou art also called, and hast professed a good profession before many witnesses" (1 Tim. 6:11, 12).

The Holy Spirit lifts our minds to eternal realities. He leads us deeper and deeper into a life with Christ, into a life of compassion for men everywhere. As sons and daughters of God we are to advance in righteousness and holiness. Our progress toward heaven may be slow sometimes, but it must be real and true. We must increasingly hate sin, become more diligent in the discharge of our Christian responsibilities to those around us. We will pray more meaningfully, love the Word of God more, walk firmly and boldly for the right, always keeping a sense of utter dependence on the Spirit's leading.

# TOGETHER WITH CHRIST

*For if we have been planted together in the likeness of his death, we shall be also in the likeness of his resurrection.* **Rom. 6:5.**

The first man was the first Adam. Christ is the second Adam. Both are heads and representatives of the human race. Adam stands, on the one hand, responsible for a race of sinners. After sinning, Adam could not transmit to his posterity what he did not have. Separated from God, his descendants suffered the same alienation. Christ, on the other hand, as the second Adam, brought new life to the race, for those who believed in Him. We are said to be planted together with Him in the likeness of His resurrection. That is, we share in the very experience and power that raised Him from the dead. We are also said to be crucified with Him; that is, we die to self-will in order to live in harmony with God.

We are what we are because of Adam's alienation from God. Equally so, as Christians we are what we are because of Christ and His righteousness. Jesus, the second Adam, has the right to be our Redeemer and our Lord.

Whether Christ can release in us His resurrection power depends upon our staying together with Him. We choose Him. We commit our lives to Him. We place ourselves at His disposal. We respond with glad obedience to His will. We burn our bridges behind us, in that our past life is rejected and done with. We never withdraw ourselves from His control, from His loving hand. We cultivate the habit of doing His will in every situation. The weakest Christian may have this power from God. We henceforth and forever accept Christ as the center of our purposes, decisions, and activities.

There are two possibilities for our lives. One is that we consider the life we have as our own, to do with it as we please. The other is that it belongs to another just as definitely as when we commit our lives to another in marriage. Drifting away from Christ is always a possibility. To be casual about this relationship with Christ means to drift. No one in the world ever drifted into a great achievement. None of us drifts into Christlikeness. This comes by a daily choice, commitment, surrender, personal initiative to walk with Christ. As we do this, we experience His transforming presence.

# "GIVE GLORY TO HIM"—1

*Fear God and give glory to him.* **Rev. 14:7.**

The Holy Spirit is God's best gift to us. What happens when the Holy Spirit possesses our lives? How can we tell whether this fullness of the Spirit is of God or of Satan?

We must not seek the fullness of the Spirit from wrong motives. Power from God is not anybody's possession. God cannot give us spiritual power unless we know how to use it and unless we are fit for it. We must desire to be filled with the Spirit for one supreme purpose: to give glory to God. If self motivates us, God will surely withhold the gift. We cannot be filled with the Spirit while we are filled with ourselves.

We need first a true cleansing of our hearts and lives. "When he [the Comforter] is come, he will reprove the world of sin" (John 16:8). Our hearts may partially belong to God and yet not be clean. The Holy Spirit first convicts us of sin, then cleanses us. To be empty of self and sin is the first requirement for being filled with the Spirit. If we are filled with one thing, we cannot at the same time be filled with something else. To be partially controlled by selfish motives means we cannot be fully controlled by the Spirit. The fullness of the Spirit is not some temporary excitation of the mind, some passing emotion. This calls attention to people, not to God.

The Holy Spirit's presence brings glory to God. His name is love, whose doctrine is truth, whose essence is purity, whose character is like Christ. The cleansing of the Spirit is from ugliness to beauty, from gross pleasures to eternal values, from stale worship to genuine devotion, from anxiety to peace, from hate to love, from disobedience to obedience. The whole life is purged, harmonized with God. In all of these there is no seeking for power and self-exaltation. There is no passion for public display.

To glory in His truth, His righteousness, His love, His kingdom, and His coming, this was the atmosphere that the apostles breathed as they were filled with the Spirit. They knew themselves to be nothing. The closer they came to the power of the Spirit, the less they talked about it. To God was the glory. God will not share His glory with another.

# "GIVE GLORY TO HIM"—2

*Ye are bought with a price: therefore glorify God in your body, and in your spirit, which are God's.* 1 Cor. 6:20.

The fullness of the Holy Spirit, possession by the Spirit, means to belong wholly to Christ. Nothing is withheld. We must consecrate, dedicate, our whole lives to God. Dedication is another word for sanctification. "The very God of peace sanctify you wholly" (1 Thess. 5:23). To cleanse is to separate from sin. To sanctify is to dedicate one's life to God. This belonging involves transference of ownership. To live as if we belong in part to ourselves or to the world means we are not fully possessed by the Spirit. We are to consider ourselves purchased by the blood of Christ. We are His property. Our whole life is lived in the light of this fact.

"He that believeth on me, . . . out of his belly shall flow rivers of living water. (But this spake he of the Spirit, which they that believe on him should receive: for the Holy Ghost was not yet given; because that Jesus was not yet glorified)" (John 7:38, 39).

This outpouring of the Spirit depended upon Christ's being glorified. This is true in us. We must see that Christ is enthroned in our hearts. When we make this possible, then the water of life will flow like a river. The dedicated life, the life set apart, belonging to God, is the Christ-centered life. Every other kind of living is self-centered. Have we stopped halfway in giving ourselves to God? We must be honest with ourselves and with God. Then the Holy Spirit will take it from there. It is our responsibility to make the commitment. It is Christ's responsibility to give us the Spirit. Then Christ will keep us filled and overflowing.

The fullness of the Spirit is no temporary excitement. It is like the water coming into the reservoir. What reservoir is there that does not need daily replenishing. We need to be filled all the time as we give out to others the fruit of the Spirit. Let us not limit God and the Spirit. Let our Christian lives be like an abounding river that cannot be contained, refreshing our homes, our children, our friends, and our churches. Then our witness to the indwelling Christ gives glory to God.

# "GIVE GLORY TO HIM"—3

*I seek not mine own glory.* John 8:50.

Our Lord's life is full of what it means to give glory to God. "The Son can do nothing of himself" (John 5:19). "I receive not honour from men" (verse 41). "Neither came I of myself" (chap. 8:42).

The quest for the glory of self in the long run will destroy us, as it did Lucifer's position in heaven. Christ lived wholly to the glory of His Father, never for the glory of Himself. The problem for Jesus exceeds our own. Jesus had every reason to exalt Himself. He was God. He was the only perfect man who ever lived on earth. How different with Lucifer: "I will exalt my throne above the stars of God" (Isa. 14:13). This was the sin on which Adam and Eve stumbled to the ruin of the race. "Ye shall be as gods," Satan told them. Ever since, man has centered life in himself. Man has assumed an impossible independence. Through the centuries man's pride has defied solution.

When we see the way Christ lived, we can see our predicament in self-seeking, self-glory, self-exaltation. The life and death of Christ is the most penetrating revelation to us and condemnation of the way of pride, the quest for self-glory. Those who seek to stand proudly before God in their own goodness, their own ability and self-esteem, have no way of finding that righteousness by faith that gives all the glory to God and lays the glory of man in the dust. God's last message, "Fear God and give glory to him," aims to expose the pride that divides families, workers, teachers, students, and professed Christians.

The love of learning, of scholarship, of position, of status, can indeed be full of pride and deeply selfish. True Christian education is based on a radically different foundation than a program of self-esteem, personal superiority, or a religion that tends, by adding virtue to virtue and knowledge to knowledge, to make us feel superior. Christian education is never a substitute for personal dependence on Jesus Christ. It is the dynamic condition for giving glory to God and not to ourselves.

# THE EXALTING POWER OF RIGHTEOUSNESS

*Righteousness exalteth a nation: but sin is a reproach to any people.*
**Prov. 14:34.**

Whenever the Bible records and unfolds the greatness of men, or singles them out as doing a service for the world or for the nation in which they live, it invariably points to the quality of their lives.

In the world men are usually selected on a different basis and according to a different standard. Were we to be introduced to a sports champion or to a multimillionaire we would probably give him a little more adulation than we would to a more ordinary man. If it were announced that one of the great entertainers was to give a program in a public meeting, the auditorium would probably be more crowded than it would be to hear the most learned scholar or the most dedicated evangelist. If some of the movie stars were to be the town's guests of honor, no doubt large crowds would pour forth into the streets to welcome them, and that without any question as to their moral character. People are easily dazzled by outward show and accomplishments.

Everything about the truth of the Bible and the faith of Jesus is calculated to unlock our faculties, enlarge our capacities, bring out the best possibilities within us. The Christian is a strong man. The Christian faith quickens the powers of the mind. Our moral life becomes a conquering force. The Bible speaks of humble shepherds, farmers, unknown men. Under the action of God and the power of the Holy Spirit, they became commanding characters in the controversy between truth and falsehood, between Christ and Satan. They became men with firm resolutions and convictions, intellectual and military geniuses.

Righteousness exalteth a nation. Sin is a reproach. At no time is sin a positive factor for the improvement and the exaltation of man. Wealth without integrity, without compassion, without spirituality, destroys and degrades. Outward splendor and luxury without character can only falsify life. Pleasures that compromise one's character are a ghastly fiction. The end is ruin and spiritual bankruptcy. There are no lasting pleasures outside of a life of righteousness.

# CAPACITY FOR GOD

*A man who is unspiritual refuses what belongs to the Spirit of God; it is folly to him; he cannot grasp it, because it needs to be judged in the light of the Spirit. A man gifted with the Spirit can judge the worth of everything. 1 Cor. 2:14, 15, N.E.B.*

The reception and enjoyment of anything depends on our capacity to receive and enjoy. This is true in music, art, literature, religion, Jesus Christ. Our capacity of heart and mind precedes the bestowment of whatever blessings and inspirations are contained within these riches. The appreciation of these things depends upon the state of our minds.

The fruit of the Spirit is love, joy, peace. Do we have a spiritual mind to receive it? He who is capable of the highest emotions can feel the beauty of God's world that He created. He who becomes a son of God and develops a spiritual mind, can freely enter into all that which is of God. God gives to us the riches of His kingdom only as our minds are fitted for them. God will not let us inherit the new earth unless we have a taste and an appetite for it. To the carnal-minded, heaven would be totally at odds with their desires and hopes. Who can possess beauty but those who love beauty? Who can possess love if he is possessed by hate? Who can possess the love of a good woman except a good man?

"Blessed are the pure in heart: for they shall see God" (Matt. 5:8). Only the pure in heart can stand to see God. Only those who develop a spiritual mind can enjoy God. Since God is love, how can God dwell in any heart but that which has the capacity for such a love? How could a man enjoy the harmony of heaven who is not in tune with God?

Religion can easily be a superficial thing, a mere veneer that we wear to church. It is possible to pick up a few religious facts and texts so that we are not strangers to religion. For fellowship with God and fellow Christians there must be a new capacity for God and for His truth.

We may talk about religion. We may study the doctrines. We may go to church and listen to sermons on the fundamentals of the faith. But do we have a capacity for Christ in our minds and lives? Ceremonies are nothing. Christ means very little to the man who has little or nothing in common with Him.

# THE OVERFLOWING LIFE

*In the last day, that great day of the feast, Jesus stood and cried, saying, If any man thirst, let him come unto me, and drink. He that believeth on me, . . . out of his belly shall flow rivers of living water.* John 7:37, 38.

The Christian life is a full life, an abundant life, an overflowing life from God. We cannot help getting the message. Our life in Christ is to be like an overflowing, irresistible river. We have a lot more of life than we can keep to ourselves. The abundant measure in which His life and love have been shed abroad in our hearts we are bound to share with others.

Christ does not give His life to be contained within ourselves. We no longer live unto ourselves. We are constrained to witness. We are ambassadors of Christ.

The Christian who has no life to give away to bless and save others is open to question. Taking the name of Christian in itself does not make us living witnesses. Any self-engineered effort to witness usually feels awkward. It tends to repel or irritate those to whom we seek to witness. Well, is it worth trying? Let us go back to Christ's promise that once we have Christ's life within, "out of . . . [our] belly shall flow rivers of living water." This is spontaneous. It is not put on at all.

"But this spake he of the Spirit, which they that believe on him should receive" (John 7:39). "Not by might, nor by power, but by my Spirit, saith the Lord of hosts" (Zech. 4:6). Christ did not begin His ministry until He was baptized with the Holy Spirit. He was fitted for the overflowing life by the Spirit. The Scripture says that "God giveth not the Spirit by measure unto him" (John 3:34). At His baptism the Holy Spirit descended upon Him like a dove and from then on abode in Him. This is similar to what happened to the apostles and disciples of Christ at Pentecost. Until they received the Holy Spirit they could not begin their work for others. When the Holy Spirit filled their lives, three thousand were converted in a day. Soul winning is the work of the Spirit. It is a very moving and rewarding experience.

To some extent, we all face a problem here: our timidity, fears, self-consciousness, the inhibitions we feel. The Holy Spirit changes everything in terms of Christian service and witness. He gives us new boldness for witnessing.

# THE LIVING CHRIST

*I am he that liveth, and was dead; and, behold, I am alive for evermore, Amen; and have the keys of hell and of death. Rev. 1:18.*

Beyond all the differences in man's understanding of the Bible, there is alive today, and in the world, the same Jesus Christ who lived on earth almost two thousand years ago. The Christian receives this life and divine presence and sets his feet upon the new path that leads to life. Christ in our lives is a power, not a problem. The world needs new life. But it must be Christ's life. He is the one Person who can be trusted with the whole of our lives.

The reason Christ does not win out with us and live His life through us is that often we want our own way. When we desire the living Christ, then Jesus is no longer only a man of history who lived so long ago. He becomes contemporary with us once we acknowledge His Lordship. This is no time to play games. We must be prepared to go all the way. Jesus has significance for us personally as we identify ourselves with Him as He lives today. Identification takes place as we receive Christ's life.

Here there is no generation gap. Life in Christ is not a matter of age. It has to do with our commitment. We hear people say that they will accept Christ and His love, but not His law. But when we truly want Christ and His life, we must want His purity, His righteousness, His honesty, and everything that He is in Himself. His love is the most righteous and mature love ever seen on earth. The claim of Christ is all inclusive.

Five minutes of total acceptance of Christ's claims on our lives would solve almost all of our problems. What kind of relationship with Christ do we want? It is no use trying to shop around for some limited commitment. It simply will not work. We would not do this when getting married, and still expect to have a truly love relationship. A partial recognition of the claims of husband and wife upon each other spells failure. The real problem for many is that they do not wish Christ to rule over them. Only the Lordship of Christ carries within itself the motive and the power for a changed life.

# LIVING ON GOD

*As the living Father hath sent me, and I live by the Father: so he that eateth me, even he shall live by me. This is that bread which came down from heaven. John 6:57, 58.*

Eating the flesh and drinking the blood of Christ means to live by Jesus Christ. The Christian faith is life, the life of Christ in us.

In this age we are always in danger of substituting something else for this vital power from God, of living by other sources of power than God. It is possible to live on the husks of piety, to bustle in religion without any spirituality. We need that which will resist the superficial tendencies of this age. Living on God means we have a deep sense of dependence on Him, and no dependence on any other source. Why should we trust to the floating reed, when we can stand on an immovable Rock? We must learn to go daily and directly to God, to derive from Him the entire support of our spiritual life.

With many the love of things is in the driver's seat. We little realize what this does to us. We tend to love things and use people, to exploit people for our own advantage. Truly to live by someone is to love that person. We can depend on those who love us because love does not exploit. We can live by them because they are safe to trust.

So it is with Christ. How difficult it is to commit ourselves to others unless we are sure that they love us. For we have faults and wants. We want to be loved and accepted. But we feel that our faults and inadequacies can only merit disdain and rejection. But Christ is not like that. His love for us has nothing to do with what we deserve. He sees our imperfections and our immaturities, but there is no lessening of His love. He ought to reject us for our sins, but He doesn't. He ought to dislike us for our selfishness, but He doesn't.

What kind of faith will teach us to curse pride and sin? What kind of God will provide us the remedy for our lack of love, purity, and integrity? If we are humbled, it is by coming to know the righteous love of God. If we repent, it will be because we trust His goodness. If we face our true condition with hope, it will be because God's love never gives up on us.

# "BE STRONG"

*Watch ye, stand fast in the faith, quit you like men, be strong.*
**1 Cor. 16:13.**

We would expect the apostle Paul to talk like that. He was that kind of man. That is how he lived the Christian life. He was no passive Christian. Morally and spiritually he was a remarkable disciple of Christ. Accepting Paul's advice, we naturally conclude that being strong is one of the essential qualities of the Christian life.

But sooner or later we come to realize how weak we are. So much of the time we seem unable to cope successfully, in any strong way, with the difficulties, trials, and temptations that come to us. The world, the flesh, and the devil are too strong for us. We might as well admit it.

When we study the Bible, we learn how men of God accomplished things. One thing is clear—they never could have gone very far by themselves. Abraham, Moses, Elijah, Peter, James, John—they all had their weak moments. The theme of the Bible is the weakness of men and the strength of God. So we have this scripture exhorting us to be strong.

The twelve chosen men from the tribes of Israel went forth to spy out the land of their enemies that they were to face. Ten of them came back with stories of giants in the land; they saw themselves as grasshoppers by comparison. They were convinced of defeat even before the invasion began. They forgot all about the power of God. In plain words, God promised them complete victory over their enemies. What they could do alone would not be enough.

The Christian church would have perished in the first century without the power of the Holy Spirit. In the hour of Christ's greatest need, all the weak disciples forsook Him and fled. But after Pentecost, Peter and John stood before the Jewish council and boldly proclaimed the name of Jesus. Stephen firmly but quietly awaited his death without fear. It is not human weakness that has spread the gospel around the world. Christians found the perfect satisfaction and fulfillment of their needs in Christ's power and strength. The strength of Christ in us is the strong side of Christianity.

# SECURITY IN GOD'S LOVE

*For thy Maker is thine husband; the Lord of hosts is his name; and thy Redeemer the Holy One of Israel. . . . For a small moment have I forsaken thee; but with great mercies will I gather thee. . . . For the mountains shall depart, and the hills be removed; but my kindness shall not depart from thee, neither shall the covenant of my peace be removed. Isa. 54:5-10.*

God binds Himself to us by the contract of love. When we marry we take our vows to keep our promises, to love forever, until death do us part. Similarly, God binds Himself to us. It is not possible for God to go back on His pledge to love us with an everlasting love.

God so loves us as to give us not only a second chance but many chances. God never misses an opportunity to bestow His love and grace upon us.

At times it may seem that our sins have separated us from Him. We are not worthy of such a love as this. Our hearts condemn us. Our minds are darkened by transgression. We are sure that God has left us. We have forsaken Him from time to time. Why should He not forsake us?

But God is our Father. He seeks in every way to correct our errors, to recover us to obedience and to righteousness. No one can ever pluck us from the heart of God except we ourselves. God continually yearns over us. He seeks us. Why hesitate to return to Him at any time? Are we worse than Peter who denied his Lord? Are we worse than the thief on the cross? Are we more of a rebel than Paul the apostle, who had persecuted the church? Are our lives darker and more burdened with sin than the children of Israel, slaves in Egypt, for whom He wrought miracles of deliverance?

The love of God is never exhausted. It is an inexhaustible fountain that flows on forever. Thousands, millions upon millions, probably billions throughout the universe, drink of it, live by it. It is a living stream from the heart of God.

Remember that the love of Christ for you is the love that caresses a little child, the love that lays hands on a leper, the love that leads a blind man back to sight, the love that accepts a harlot who weeps at His feet, that sits at meat with publicans and sinners, that forgives the thief on the cross. Such love is ours through Jesus Christ our Lord.

# THE SPONTANEITY OF LOVE—1

*And Enoch walked with God: and he was not; for God took him.*
**Gen. 5:24.**

Enoch was perfect in his relationship with God. He was translated by God to heaven without seeing death because he was fitted for the company of perfect beings. He walked with God in love.

The gift of salvation in Christ means that we actually share in the essential life and quality of God's love. We are committed to Him with unreserved devotion. We know that Christ will continue to work out His own righteousness in us. We are sure of the sufficiency of His love. The everlasting love of God for us, the eternal vigilance of the angels toward us, both unite us to the living God. We will not allow anything to come between us and Christ. We know exactly what this means within the family relationship. The love relationship that exists between husband and wife, parents and children, prevents any divisive, separating thing to come between them.

We do not think of this love relationship with Christ in terms of a point system, conformity to rules and norms. Loving Christ with all our hearts, minds, and strength does not issue in isolated religious accomplishments. To have Christ in our hearts means that it is with Him that we are concerned and occupied. We witness to Him, not to ourselves or to our achievements, even in religion. Our love for Christ does not focus the spotlight on ourselves. We are not attempting to square our lives with any rule of law. We have become one with Christ in life and purpose. We glorify Christ, not ourselves.

To believe that we have finally arrived at perfection in all of God's requirements so that we are now superior and among the top people religiously is not the answer. Christ alone is our sole and sufficient perfection and righteousness. Our lives are hid with Christ in God. Walking with God in love is the principal thing. "Looking unto Jesus" becomes the measure of the ideal we wish for ourselves. All we can do is to permit Christ to love and to save us to the uttermost. In our possession of Him and His possession of us, faith and hope work continually toward the Christlike ideal.

# THE SPONTANEITY OF LOVE—2

*Jesus answered and said . . . , If a man love me, he will keep my words: and my Father will love him, and we will come unto him, and make our abode with him.* John 14:23.

To seek always for the supremacy of Christ and Christlikeness is the finest and most inspiring spiritual exercise we can know. This is the certainty, not in and from ourselves, but in the sovereign love that has come to rule our hearts and lives. In our weakness we are allied to His strength. Even though we see through a glass darkly, we have a clear knowledge of Christ and His righteousness.

One of the dangers to the Christian life is the keeping of a watch on self without walking with God. In this approach, it is easier to sacrifice ourselves on the altar of religious extremism than to love God and to love our fellow men. We need to face frankly the peril of making perfection a self-centered process, something to be attained by much effort and rigid concentration.

By this method we may win attention and admiration for our efforts. But where is our love for God and man? Loving others does not draw attention to ourselves. Always to calculate, to analyze, to judge the mistakes of ourselves and others, never carries us beyond ourselves.

Conformity to a perfect norm does not satisfy the heart of God or even ourselves. God wants the loyalty, the love, and devotion spontaneously given to Him. The true Christian is not concerned only with his efforts to achieve sinlessness. We make Christ our end, not only perfection.

We cannot bring to God a nature with sin completely eradicated. But we can bring a love and devotion to Christ and His righteousness that can never be satisfied with less. God then accepts and regards what we really mean, desire, and intend as though it were really accomplished. At His coming He will make it so. We are complete in faith that works by love to the best of our ability. We are one with God.

This means that we want Christ, that we love Christ, that we enjoy Christ. We walk with God as Enoch did. We are never alone. This is the supreme thing, the crucial thing, in our lives.

# THE TEST OF LOVE

*By this shall all men know that ye are my disciples, if ye have love one to another.* John 13:35.

The disciples had just celebrated the Lord's Supper. At its conclusion Christ gave His disciples the true test of being His followers, His disciples. If you were looking for the right church to join, what test would you apply so as to make sure it was the right one? To become a Christian is so vitally important that the non-Christian should have a simple test by which he can tell who are real Christians. If a man had just a short time to live and came to you to find God, you might find it no simple matter to give him the whole of what you believe. In this case, make it simple.

Christ Himself gave us no complicated examination, but a very simple test. Ellen White said about the same thing but in different words: "The last rays of merciful light, the last message of mercy to be given to the world, is a revelation of His character of love."—*Christ's Object Lessons,* p. 415.

This does not mean that we are to neglect all other aspects of the truth. But the first thing that people need to know is that God loves them. God must represent Himself as love before people can comprehend Him. He has done so supremely in His beloved Son, Jesus Christ. Jesus was the most loving Person in all the world. No one ever had any hesitation in seeking His help. Love opens the door of people's hearts. We must begin here, also. This is the first thing people should experience at their first contact with us.

Our church as an institution must not stand as an end in itself. It must lead to God. Organization, machinery, ritual, order, can represent that which is external and material, but not the personal God. If the love of Christ is not present in us as church members, then all we have for people is an organization to join. We can almost sense the anxiety that Christ's test brings to us. But the unbeliever will apply the test even though he has not heard about it. He will measure the character of God by those who claim to be His disciples. Said one interested man, "There is something about this remnant church. Her members have in their lives something akin to Jesus Christ. I want it."

# LOVE THY NEIGHBOR—1

*But he, willing to justify himself, said unto Jesus, And who is my neigh-bour?* **Luke 10:29.**

This discussion began when a "certain lawyer stood up, and tempted him, saying, Master, what shall I do to inherit eternal life?" The answer to the question is not as simple as we sometimes would believe. A true moral and spiritual response to the demands of Christianity is more than an intellectual nod of the head. It calls for personal involvement.

First Christ said, "Make Me master of all your money." This is not easy. Second, "So love Me as to put Me first above everything else." That is not easy, either. Third, "Love your neighbor as you love yourself." Now that is getting rough.

For instance, we are required to love God and our neighbor for billions of years. How do you love—and live with—the same people for a billion years? Some don't seem to be able to do it for a year. We all have the invitation from God. He has gone to prepare a place for us. That means our heavenly mansion is going to be open to everybody on the planet. Every day will be open house. We are going to love everybody without exception.

However, Christ is talking about life down here. "Love thy neighbour as thyself." Who is our neighbor? Or does it make any difference? What race? White, black, yellow, red? The text does not say. What is his creed? A Baptist, a Mormon, a Roman Catholic, a member of Jehovah's Witnesses, an unbeliever? Member of Campus Crusade; Jew or gentile? The text does not say.

In answering the question Who is my neighbor? Christ gave the story of the good Samaritan and his treatment of the man who had been beaten by robbers. Today there are a lot of people in a similar position to the man on the Jericho road— people who go to bed hungry, people stripped of security and happiness, people ground down by the pressures of life.

When we are involved with God we are involved with people. Jesus had compassion. It was something that He was, not just something that He taught. Love is something we are and do.

# LOVE THY NEIGHBOR—2

*Which now of these three, thinkest thou, was neighbour unto him that fell among thieves? And he said, He that shewed mercy on him. Then said Jesus unto him, Go, and do thou likewise.* **Luke 10:36, 37.**

The church is not for perfect people. It is a healing center, a saving center. All of the people in the world are God's lost sheep. To help find the lost is our primary duty. As Christians we are face to face with Christ's command in the above scripture. To be a Christian minister, nurse, dentist, doctor, laborer, engineer—is that not part of it? Or have we taken up a position within a religious system that does not deal with the issue at all?

It is dangerous to speak of loving our neighbor as ourselves as if that is a logical consequence of belonging to the Seventh-day Adventist Church. All too often we become eager to defend our doctrinal position from the security of our own religious establishment. Often the point at which people begin to talk about how their religion differs from others signals some sort of surrender of human sensitivity and Christian concern.

Christian concern stays close to human life, human suffering, human hopes, and human salvation. When we view the great truths God has given us, they are tremendous. But God judges nothing by itself, but only in the totality of our own moral and spiritual attitudes and the way we communicate these truths to others.

Life's greatest blunder is to live just one life when you can live a thousand. We who have experienced the saving love of God are to enter the lives of those around us, to take upon ourselves the needs and the burdens of those who know not Christ.

To give a dollar in the offering or to return one hundred dollars in tithe may be either a true Christian service or it may be an escape. To give money to the church as a substitute for caring about people is a denial of what is really meant by being a Christian. To dismiss a person's needs by giving him a tract of literature is unchristian. The money we have, the ability we have, the Christian experience we have, should never be an escape from any human situation but should represent real love and compassion for other people.

# LOVE ONE ANOTHER

*A new commandment I give unto you, That ye love one another; as I have loved you, that ye also love one another.* John 13:34.

Without love we may increase the externals of religion but not spirituality. Without love we may impress others with the financial growth in tithes and offerings, but not win men to Christ.

God's standard is that we love one another *"as I have loved you."* But to love as Christ loved is quite beyond our power and ability to perform. Love comes from being loved. Christ's love for us is the source of our love. "We love him because he first loved us" (1 John 4:19). To the degree that we believe the love God has for us and let Him truly love us, to that degree we have the capacity to love others. "The love of Christ constraineth us" (2 Cor. 5:14).

For the natural, unconverted man, the best he can do is to love the lovable. He cannot love the depraved, the emotionally sick, the unlikable personality. This is quite beyond his powers. But Christ's command is to love our enemies. Of ourselves and by our own efforts we can conform outwardly to the rules and standards of the church. We really do not necessarily need help from God to wear the right kind of clothes, to eat the right kind of food. By actual personal discipline, it is amazing what we can do in keeping the rules. There are many professed Christians who would not think of violating the rules and regulations of the church, particularly in dress and diet. Yet for some of these people, it is of little importance that they are easily jealous, hostile, envious, critical, impatient, selfish, and overbearing. What kind of religion is that? These inner problems require a complete change of heart and motivation. This change we cannot bring about ourselves.

How do we become loving and lovable Christians? "The fruit of the Spirit is love." Love is a gift of God. It is a spiritual fruit. It belongs to us only when the Holy Spirit dwells within. It is not a matter of how good we are. We cannot even tell that. The Spirit loves in us and through us. It simply is not possible to let Christ down anymore, or anyone else, for that matter.

# LOVE AND KNOWLEDGE

*Of course we all "have knowledge," as you say. This "knowledge" breeds conceit; it is love that builds. If anyone fancies that he knows, he knows nothing yet, in the true sense of knowing. But if a man loves, he is acknowledged by God.* **1 Cor. 8:1-3, N.E.B.**

As far as knowledge is concerned, Paul is perfectly clear in his own mind. For him an idol means absolutely nothing. There is only one true God, the God and Father of our Lord Jesus Christ. When Paul sits down to eat, since he knows there is only one true God he can eat food offered to idols for one reason: he is hungry and needs strength and sustenance to carry on his gospel ministry. Paul never gives any consideration to the idol. Food is just food for him and nothing more. Therefore when he eats such food it makes him neither better nor worse spiritually.

But Paul does not stop there. He says, "All things are lawful for me, but all things are not expedient." Knowledge by itself is quite insufficient to guide us to the right judgment in such things, because from this point of view alone we are simply concerned with ourselves and no one else. But such knowledge must be balanced with love for people.

Two questions arise when one is faced with such a choice. Does it hurt me? Does it hurt my neighbor? You may be able to say No to the first without reservation. But the answer to the second is not that simple. Paul understood that. When he thought of his responsibility to others who might misunderstand his action, love for them became the deciding factor. Suppose that certain people who were easily thrown off stride saw him eating some of the food that had been offered to idols. Some doubtless would misunderstand and lose their faith or lower their standards in other lines. Because Paul loved them, he took a stand: "If meat make my brother to offend, I will eat no flesh while the world standeth, lest I make my brother to offend" (1 Cor. 8:13).

Love is the one thing that establishes a man in Christ, and leads him into the truth. God offers us more than information, more than knowledge that satisfies our logic. He insists that we communicate also love, which perfects our judgment and leads to the right stand.

# THE ELEVATION OF LOVE

*Set your affection on things above, not on things on the earth.* **Col. 3:2.**

If I could wish one thing for all the young people who have sat in my classes through the years, it would be a capacity to love and to receive love at its best. Only righteous love is adequate for life and religion. Only by love does one make the right response to God and to man. "God so loved the world that he gave . . ." In the Bible God is not only lecturing us; He is giving Himself.

Paul speaks of our being able to comprehend the height of the love of God (see Eph. 3:18). One of the great scandals of our day is the perversion of what people call love because men will not relate it to the purity of God's love and grace. All men need to surrender their basic needs to the elevated love of God.

Love is the gift of God. But no gift has been so warped and perverted by man. When men say they love, they mean they want to possess, they want to gratify themselves, to exploit the functions people perform. Everyone has functions—religious functions, money functions, sex functions, social functions. Today the functions that people perform have become more important than the people themselves. But people don't like to be used. Using people destroys their sense of self-worth.

The love of Christ gives people a true feeling of self-worth, a sense of well-being. God never limits or cripples a man's basic needs. Always there is a new capacity, an enlarged emphasis on love. It is the work of Christ to make people loving. It is the work of the devil to debase men's urge to love.

The perverted love of our day is best vanquished by the pure love of God. The immorality of this generation is most effectively eradicated by the Spirit who sheds the love of God abroad in our hearts. To the heart fully opened to the uplifting power of Christ, no sordidness can mar it; no evil can pollute it; no fear can make it afraid; no temptation betray it. "Know and believe the love that God has to us, and you are secure; that love is a fortress impregnable to all the delusions and assaults of Satan."—*Thoughts From the Mount of Blessing*, p. 119.

## "AS I HAVE LOVED YOU"—1

*A new commandment I give unto you, That ye love one another; as I have loved you, that ye also love one another.* **John 13:34.**

We are to love as Christ loved. The first transformation effected by the power of the gospel is to make us loving Christians. Our capacity to love becomes noble and unselfish, gentle and gracious. Such love becomes an irresistible drawing power upon others.

Christ enlarges our capacity to love. The devil restricts, debases, and dishonors it. All perversions of love are from the devil. Christ never impoverishes our ability to love. He enriches it. As it is in nature, so it is with our hearts and lives.

No one has ever passed such a judgment on our quality of loving as did Jesus in His acceptance of a harlot, condemning the sin, but offering rescue to the sinner; His making a friend of the thief who was crucified alongside of Him; His glad forgiveness of Peter who had betrayed Him, who prayed for those who crucified Him. Jesus' standard of love prefers a sinner who loves to a "saint" who does not.

We repeat that to love as Christ loved is quite beyond our power and ability. But we can approach it by giving ourselves over to His love and letting it work a response in us. To the degree that we let Christ love us, to that degree we have the capacity to love others. "We love him, because he first loved us" (1 John 4:19). "The fruit of the Spirit is love" (Gal. 5:22).

Christian compassion and love for others goes to the very root of our relationship with Christ. Christ put this test to Peter at His first meeting with the disciples after His resurrection. "Simon, son of Jonas, lovest thou me more than these? . . . Feed my sheep" (John 21:15, 16). We must first love our Lord and then we can love people.

It pleased Christ to redeem us in order to make us loving persons. His love forgives all our sins. His love triumphs over the selfishness of our hearts, our impatience, hostility, resentment, jealousy, and envy. His love breaks through into our lives, so much so that we can respond to God and to our fellow men in love. What do we think about most? Is it our business, our money, our pleasures, or people—people who need to meet the love of God in us and be redeemed by it?

# "AS I HAVE LOVED YOU"—2

*If a man say, I love God, and hateth his brother, he is a liar: for he that loveth not his brother whom he hath seen, how can he love God whom he hath not seen? 1 John 4:20.*

If you were looking for the right church to join, how would you test it to know whether it is true or false? Where would you begin? If someone had but a short time to live and asked to know the way to God, what would you tell him? It would be no simple matter to give him the whole of what we believe.

For people looking for divine help, the first thing they need to know is that their heavenly Father loves them. That is why Jesus came to earth. God must personally represent Himself as love before people can comprehend Him. That is why we as Christians are to be filled with love for people.

The church as an institution must not stand in the place of God, as an end in itself. It must lead to God. To furnish other people with a test of truth and of the right church to join, we must furnish them with a living Person from whom they can receive love and to whom they can express love in return.

Organization, machinery, ritual, can represent that which is material, the externals, but not the personal God. If Christ is not represented and reproduced in church members who know how to love, then all we have for people is an organization to join.

We face one of our more serious problems here. We have an inclination to do good works by way of organizations. We work by groups. I suppose it cannot be otherwise. Christ's work for the most part was with individuals. We preach to the congregation. We instruct by classes. We give out tracts and literature by congregations. We raise money by groups. I am not saying that something is wrong with that, provided all this is not a substitute for personal work for individuals. We must not allow our personal witness and love for people to get lost in the group or in the organization.

Loving concern for people is a personal thing. Passion for the lost does not belong to groups as such, but to individuals.

# THE GOSPEL OF LOVE AND OBEDIENCE—1

*By this we know that we love the children of God, when we love God, and keep his commandments.* **1 John 5:2.**

Love and obedience are the key words in this verse. Love leads to obedience. Obedience is the test of one's love. Neither love nor obedience is to be isolated from the other. The gospel aims to increase the righteous love in our lives.

In considering this question of obedience, there are three possibilities. First, we can preach obedience to the law of God apart from Christ. We can transform the good news of Christ into the demands of a cold law. We can take our motivation from the law and become legalists. Second, we can preach the gospel without obedience. We can tone down the will and the law of God and settle for a sentimental softness that has neither discipline nor moral backbone. We mistake license for freedom. Third, we can show that the gospel and obedience to the law of God go hand in hand, that without obedience we make a farce of the gospel itself.

Many have a marked tendency toward legalism. Sin has separated us from God. God now confronts us with the revelation of His law. We can respond to the law in order to gain merit, to seek justification before God by doing the best we can to conform. But strict adherence to the law does not mean that we are legalists. A person who never misses a Sabbath school or a prayer meeting is not necessarily a legalist. Only when obedience is done to gain advantage or merit with God are we legalists.

Legalism has a deadly effect upon the human spirit. It involves us in a preoccupation with our own moral balance sheet. It amounts to a competition for virtue. The mask of virtue can provide the perfect disguise for the most unlovely motives. It often leads to seeking satisfaction through a personal advantage over someone else by means of religion. It lacks compassion. The Christian life is considered to be unswerving obedience to duty.

"While the claims of the law of God are to be presented to the world, we should never forget that love, the love of Christ, is the only power that can soften the heart and lead to obedience."—*Evangelism*, p. 57.

# THE GOSPEL OF LOVE AND OBEDIENCE—2

*And hereby we do know that we know him, if we keep his commandments. He that saith, I know him, and keepeth not his commandments, is a liar, and the truth is not in him. But whoso keepeth his word, in him verily is the love of God perfected: hereby know we that we are in him.* 1 John 2:3-5.

John warns against preaching the gospel without obedience. All over the world the law of God is being silenced. People are being fed a type of gospel with little or no appeal to obedience. One of the most frightening perils of our day is the spread of the climate of compromise between sin and moral standards. There is an abundance of cheap Christianity and religion with just enough prayer and church attendance to get by. Salvation is free, but it is not cheap. Much religion is in name only. Ours is a time when it is counted a virtue to be so broad-minded as to say a good word for everything. The eternal antagonism of God against sin is easily dismissed.

Finally, we can believe and live with the conviction that the gospel and obedience to the Ten Commandments go together. Throughout the Bible great emphasis is placed upon obedience. Salvation by grace means that God gives Himself to us before He requires anything from us. Our response to Him is always within the framework of a personal relationship to God. God commits Himself to us with compassion, patience, love. Therefore God seeks true obedience from us. God is always true to us. We are to be true to Him. Our response for His gift of salvation is expressed in terms of loving obedience born of a grateful heart. The law of God is no longer a power outside of us. We now have the inner resources for doing God's will and keeping His commandments. Christ does not give us a new law, but a new power.

The spirit of Christ is the spirit of love. The very genius of Christianity is that of compassion, patience, conciliation. In Christ we apprehend the infinite love of God. We are made to understand somewhat our mighty debt to that love. Christ envelopes us in an atmosphere of love. It is impossible to be a true disciple of Christ so long as we are disobedient to Him.

# LOVE FULFILLS THE LAW

*Owe no man any thing, but to love one another: for he that loveth another hath fulfilled the law.* **Rom. 13:8.**

None of us should have any difficulty understanding this passage of Scripture. If you love a person you will not try to kill him; you will not steal from him; you will not seek to draw the attention and affections of his wife from him; you will not tell lies about him. For "love worketh no ill to his neighbour."

What does the text mean when it says that love fulfills? It means to fill it full, so that no part of it is left void or empty. No act of ours, no business dealing, no social relationship, will be empty of love. All will be made sacred by the loving spirit of Christ.

The psalmist said, "Thy commandment is exceeding broad" (Ps. 119:96). What did he mean by that? A mere external conformity to the requirements of the law is a very narrow understanding of it. We may point to the fact that we have not killed a man, nor have we actually committed an act of adultery, nor stolen anything. Now add love to our life and see what happens.

Love makes the keeping of the commandments easy and delightful. The inner power of the Holy Spirit within us is equal to all that the commandments require. The weight of the atmosphere around the earth is equal to fifteen pounds to the square inch. The adult person sustains a total weight of about fifteen tons pressure. But we don't realize it. The pressure of internal fluids and other forces within press outward, balancing the external pressure. This leaves us to walk at liberty. The atmosphere is not a burden to us. What is lighter to us than air? If we suddenly lost these inner forces and power, the atmosphere would crush us.

So it is with the pressure of the moral law. In our unregenerate state the pressure of guilt and condemnation, owing to our transgression of the law, weighs upon us. When we are born again and have the Holy Spirit within, our minds are so filled with the power of God's love that the requirements of the law become as light as air. Every one of God's commandments is intended as a blessing to us. For love is the fulfilling of the law.

# THE HARMONY OF LOVE AND OBEDIENCE—1

*For this is the love of God, that we keep his commandments: and his commandments are not grievous.* 1 John 5:3.

Love is the great commandment from God. The main work and purpose of the church is to shed the love of God abroad in the earth. In and through the church of Christ is to be manifested the full and final display of the love of God. But the response of love is not exactly under our direct control. We do not love people simply because we will to do so. It is not that simple. Love is something we grow into by being loved. Every true relationship both with God and with people is dependent upon our capacity to love and to accept love. Love is not effective simply by talking about it. We must let God love us and respond to it.

Love costs. There is no such thing as cheap love. Our sinful condition, our situations of envy, jealousy, hostility, anger, can be transformed only by love. Who by taking thought can love his neighbor as himself? Who by taking thought can love all men in all situations? The human situation is too badly out of hand to be overcome by our tugging at our own boot straps. God's first work in and for us is, by loving He gives us the power and the capacity to love. For "the love of God is shed abroad in our hearts by the Holy Ghost which is given unto us" (Rom. 5:5). God's love changes us into loving persons.

Love is both response and responsibility. Obedience isolated from love tends toward legalism. Then we take our motivation from the law and not from love. We can never relax our grip on the claims of the Ten Commandments and our need to obey them. Obedience without love means obedience to the letter of the law, the imposition of rules and regulations from without. In such obedience formal conformity to the law is the main thing. Almost always this makes a mockery of the deeper content of the law and the need for a new heart. Such external obedience exerts a deadly effect upon the human spirit.

We are to be willing to pay the price that love demands: the sacrifice and giving of ourselves. A loving Christian does not use attitudes and emotional devices for the repression of himself or other people. He affirms himself and others as sons and daughters of God, redeemed by love.

# THE HARMONY OF LOVE AND OBEDIENCE—2

*If ye love me, keep my commandments.* John 14:15.

The emphasis on love and obedience is not milk for babes, but meat for mature Christians. The combination of rules and regulations is for children. When we are children we have to be told what to do. When we grow up in an atmosphere of love we should not have to be told. The fundamental issue is whether our obedience constitutes an expression of love for God and man.

When people get married there is a change in relationship. This involves a new set of mutual responsibilities. Each has entered a new type of living, one of total self-commitment to live for the other's best welfare, security, and integrity as a person.

And when we accept the Christian relationship with our heavenly Father our life changes. Obedience on a legal basis and obedience on a love basis are based on different principles. The first operates outside a personal relation to Christ. The second derives its power from a personal love relationship to Christ, which is the primary thing.

Our relationship with Christ cannot be secure in an atmosphere of dishonesty, impurity, disobedience, hate, and hostility. It will not work in our homes, either. If our homes are ever going to be safe, if our Christian experience is to continue, we must discover the power of God's love to make us obedient to His will and His law.

In our time it is not the lack of the use of the word *love* that worries us. It is the perversion and adulteration of it that robs lives and homes of its vitality, that practice of a certain laxity and license that we as Christians are in no position at all to defend.

Over and over again in our lives and in our homes, it is not the use of the word *love* that is important. It is the urgent necessity of sticking by the kind of righteous, trustworthy, high love that Christ talks about. The tragedy of our day is that people continue to use this supreme word *love* that describes God, after they have dropped God's meaning out of it. God's final word of love to us has to do with an eternal quality of love that honors the everlasting moral principles of the moral law.

# LOVE WITH KNOWLEDGE

*And we know that the Son of God is come, and hath given us an under-standing, that we may know him that is true, and we are in him that is true, even in his Son Jesus Christ. 1 John 5:20.*

Sometimes one of the greatest hindrances to a Christian experience is contentment with a superficial knowledge of religious truth. Some of the severest casualties are among those who never get beyond the wisdom of man. It is possible to know many things about God without changing our basic attitudes and lives.

Paul speaks of the conceit that can arise by way of the claim to a superior mind and knowledge. The achievement of the human mind is not to be disparaged at all. God needs the finest minds possible. But Jesus did not look simply for cleverness in His disciples. He asked for total commitment, obedience, the response of love. Christianity is something we are, in the whole of our person.

It is comparatively easy to take the Bible without its vital power. The issue has to do with the exposure of the whole of our lives to God. God is not the end result of our speculations about Him. We cannot reduce God to an idea and still know Him. When religious knowledge becomes an end in itself, religious experience becomes coldly intellectual. Then we become proud by virtue of our great intellectual insight. We acquire a knowledge of Christ and of religion, but lose the spirit of Christ.

Paul said, "I know whom I have believed." He is not simply giving out information. He is totally involved with Christ. He has taken Christ into his innermost being. God laid siege to his whole life.

The foundation of all Christian experience is the conviction that the meaning of life lies in an intelligent love relationship to a personal God. Out of this relationship, God does transform us. In our witness we do not offer people just a neat bundle of foolproof doctrines. To be saved and to become Christians, people need more than information.

We make people hungry for God and for His love, for the truth as a way of life. Christianity is a life that has been deeply stirred by God's mercy, love, truth, and goodness.

# LIFE IN DEPTH

*The spirit of the Lord God is upon me because the Lord has anointed me;
he has sent me to bring good news to the humble, to bind up the broken-
hearted, to proclaim liberty to captives.* **Isa. 61:1, N.E.B.**

One of our needs is the deepening of our moral and spiritual lives. Sensuous, pleasure-loving attitudes have weakened
the character. We need young people with great moral and
spiritual compulsions driving them to witness for Christ. A
great spiritual hunger exists among millions of young people
today. To a large degree, some youth are more honest about
life than some adults. Christian young people are to stand for
things that are big enough, clean enough, noble enough, and
true enough. The kingdom of God is soon to be established.
We must give ourselves wholly to it. We must refuse to play
games to amuse ourselves. We are to unite ourselves to divine
resources by means of a deepening prayer and study life.

All too often the temptation is to take our life-style from
the prevailing life around us. Christ calls us to abandon petty
aims and shallow living, to lose ourselves in the glorious Christian adventure in preparation for our coming King. The
strength of Christ is ours. Divine resources are available.

The call is not to compete with the world's great minds and
men. Much as we admire them, this achievement is not
enough. How lofty the intellects that have searched out the
great discoveries in science, in medicine, and in every field of
endeavor. Even without their admitting their dependence on
God for what truth they do find, how impressive are some
parts of the philosophies of a Plato, an Aristotle, a Seneca! How
sublime are the literary geniuses of a Homer, a Dante, a
Shakespeare, a Keats, and a Shelley! How superb are the artistic talents of a Michelangelo, a Raphael, a Christopher Wren!
How frequently the brightest minds have the saddest lives.
How might such talent have blessed the world if it had been
fully dedicated to Christ!

Have you found Christ worth living for? Think what you
will about Jesus Christ, no man on earth has ever so inspired
men to such great sacrifice and dedication, to such transformed
lives. Is He doing that for you?

147

# VITAL CHRISTIANITY

*I am crucified with Christ: nevertheless I live; yet not I, but Christ liveth in me: and the life which I now live in the flesh I live by the faith of the Son of God, who loved me, and gave himself for me.* **Gal. 2:20.**

Are we able to say with conviction, "I live by the faith of the Son of God, who loved me, and gave himself for me"? This scripture must always stand as something fundamental in our Christian experience. Our distinct witness is that Christ actually lives His life in us. We experience nothing less than the supremacy of Christ over every part of our lives.

It will not do for us to say, "My religion is a private matter between Jesus Christ and me," that is, if you mean by private that no one else seems to know what you are standing for. Granted that the Christian faith is between you and Christ. But it is not a private affair, by any means.

If we are employed by a business firm or in an important profession, we do not say that the quality of service we render, the fraudulent work we cover up, the sabotage we cause, is our private affair. Neither can we say that our experience with God is our own private affair. There is no part of our lives that is not affected by our being a Christian. We cannot say that what we watch on television, what we read, what we do for recreation, how we spend our time, is our private affair.

We are to be genuine through and through. Everything we do, every transaction we make, every business deal we engage in, every sport or pleasure we enjoy, becomes significant because Christ rules in all of these.

Christ is not communicated by argument. If our friends see no Christ in us, they are not likely to listen to our arguments on religion. On the other hand, if our religion is an example of Christ's very life, no one can reduce our faith to a set of opinions or ideas. They see that this same life can be theirs as well. Such a life will gain a ready hearing from men.

This last generation of people on earth must have the opportunity to see the saving truth of God in their own situation. Profession without reality detracts and denies the genuineness of the Christian religion. We must reject everything that contradicts living by faith in the Son of God.

# THE CONDITION OF YOUR HEART

*And ye shall seek me, and find me, when ye shall search for me with all your heart. Jer. 29:13.*

A few years ago *Life* magazine ran a series of articles with some remarkable photographs of the human heart. It also pictured the main arteries that carry blood to and fro throughout the body. Then the article went on to show why heart disease is the number one killer. The arteries become blocked with cholesterol. The flow of blood slows down until it stops. Then the heart stops and dies.

The Bible has a lot to say about the heart of man in relation to God. However, God is not speaking of the physical organ. The Bible reads, "Keep thy heart with all diligence" (Prov. 4:23). "From within, out of the heart of man, proceed evil thoughts" (Mark 7:21). Our relationship to God is spoken of in particular in relation to our heart, not because the Christian experience is located in the emotions or in some part of the body but because genuine Christian experience must come from the very center of our lives and is not something put on externally. When the heart obeys, the whole person obeys. When the heart is in a wrong relationship to God, the whole person is wrong. When God writes the law in the heart, He writes it in the whole person from the inside out. Unless the inner part is captured for Christ, there is no way that we can be Christians at all.

So the Bible urges us to serve and love the Lord with a perfect heart. Certain men of the Bible are stated to have "served the Lord with a perfect heart." Of others it is said, "Their heart was not perfect with God." The Bible is speaking of man's whole life and character: the thoughts, the desires, the imaginations, the will. The reference is to the whole inner life as contrasted with the outward expressions. A person can put on a front in religion as in anything else.

How to restore a heart life, that is the question. The question is charged with moral and spiritual urgency. It is a matter of life or death. Age will not wait for improvement. Time will not wait for spiritual health in the heart. Spiritually, the only way is to make sure that our heart, our inner being, belongs to God.

# "WITH ALL THY HEART"

*Thou shalt love the Lord thy God with all thy heart, and with all thy soul, and with all thy mind. Matt. 22:37.*

The problem for many in the church is a heart problem. There is an increasingly slight attachment to Christ, to truth, to purity, to honesty, and to righteousness. "Then shall the kingdom of heaven be likened unto ten virgins, which took their lamps, and went forth to meet the bridegroom. And five of them were wise, and five were foolish" (Matt. 25:1, 2). Christ draws a clear distinction between the two groups in the church. Both groups look quite similar. They profess the same religion. But the five foolish virgins did not get in to the wedding.

We are appalled to learn that by the slam of that door, five girls are shut out of the kingdom of heaven. It was not because God wanted it that way; it was the result of a great spiritual indifference in their lives. The five foolish virgins failed to have that inner heart experience that is made possible only by the indwelling of the Holy Spirit.

Church membership will profit nothing in the final analysis. We may bear the honored name of Christian. We may hope that the church may have Christ's righteousness and the Holy Spirit available somewhere about for everybody who joins the organization. The church has no more of the indwelling Spirit than each of us brings to it. We may enjoy a good choir and good social fellowship, but fail to make a full heart response, to love God with all our heart.

We surely know what such an act of the heart means. It needs no explanation. This is no mere knowledge, but a commitment, a companionship with Christ. In my Christian experience I must be beyond any arguments about the furniture and the veils in the heavenly sanctuary. I do not go to my own home and say: "How are the draperies? How are the bed and the couch?" I meet a *person* and have companionship with a *person* —my wife. Is not this the way it must be between us and the Lord? The heart motive is love to God and to man.

Such a heart response and commitment is crucial. We are no longer doubleminded, unstable like the waves of the sea. Our heart is fixed. "My heart is fixed, O God, my heart is fixed" (Ps. 57:7).

# HEART RELIGION—1

*But this shall be the covenant that I will make with the house of Israel; After those days, saith the Lord, I will put my law in their inward parts, and write it in their hearts; and will be their God, and they shall be my people.* **Jer. 31:33.**

One of the most striking truths of the Christian faith is that we human beings can have and keep a genuine personal relationship with members of the Godhead. It is called a heart relationship, where divine realities are experienced in the inner man as contrasted with mere surface, external religion; what we are in our entire being as opposed to what we outwardly profess.

The heart Christian is a very impressive person. What we are tells far more than what we say or do. Heart in the Bible refers to our depth dimension, the real person we are inside. The law written on tables of stone is not as impressive as the law written in the whole of our inner being, so that we are basically spiritual, not simply religious; basically honest, pure, unselfish, loving. The Ten Commandments written on the wall of the church may be very attractive. But the Ten Commandments as part of our very being, the kind of obedient Christian we are inside, that is the greatest work of God that can be seen.

"That Christ may dwell in your hearts by faith" (Eph. 3:17), that is, in the inner life where thoughts, desires, motivations, arise, where affections have their beginning. We can never cleanse the water in a well by painting the pump. We cannot change the bareness of the trees in winter by hanging leaves on the branches. We must have a revival of life at the roots. We can never redeem man by external adjustments.

Not the turning of water into wine, not the raising of Lazarus from the dead, are Christ's greatest works. But Mary Magdalene given a new heart and made pure throughout forever, the thieving Zacchaeus made basically honest, the cowardly Peter made to have a heart of courage, the apostle Paul given a new heart of love for Christ as opposed to enmity and opposition. Completely new persons inside and out.

We should seek and pray to reflect the living Christ in the whole of our being. Christ will settle for no less. Why should we?

# HEART RELIGION—2

*For with the heart man believeth unto righteousness; and with the mouth confession is made unto salvation.* **Rom. 10:10.**

A verbal confession of Christ without a heart experience lacks genuineness. We are to have both the inner experience and the outward confession.

Unfortunately, the heart has been interpreted to mean the emotions. Consequently, much of religion is aimed at arousing the emotions. The craving for excitement is universal. We find it in sports, certain types of music and music festivals, and religious revivals geared to arouse the emotions. Here people experience highly fantastic moods, beyond what they are able to live each day. To "get in the spirit" is to feel intoxicated, to experience thrills that go beyond the boundary of the rational and intelligible. For a short time people are distracted from their troubles of life, but the problems are never resolved in this way. Nothing is really changed. Emotional excitations in religion do not solve the inner problems of the mind, the un-christian attitudes, the inner discords that cause so much agony.

A genuine heart religion means a permanent change in the life throughout. No epidemic of emotionalism will ever justify the slightest departure from obedience to the law of God. The permanence of heart religion is the result of Christ within, of the Spirit's indwelling, which empowers the whole of our inner selves. A heart religion makes us faithful in our responsibilities to God and to man. Where Christ rules within, there is a quiet peace and gladness, an abiding beauty of spirit. There is no excitement, but a permanent charm, a dignity of soul that lifts us above the sinful excitements of the world.

A heart religion is "known and read of all men" (2 Cor. 3:2). It is fit for all places. It does not belong to occasional re-vivals where excitement is aroused and people tend to lose self-control. Heart religion is for all people on all occasions. It can grow in a dungeon. It can bloom in a palace. It bears its fruits in the workshop, in business, in the office, and in the home. A prison can become a paradise.

Christ in us is something far beyond any passing excitation. He fills the whole of our lives with likeness to Himself.

# LIVING EPISTLES

*You are all the letter we need, a letter written on our heart; any man can see it for what it is and read it for himself. And as for you, it is plain that you are a letter that has come from Christ, given to us to deliver.* **2 Cor. 3:2, 3, N.E.B.**

When Paul came to Corinth and established the church, he had no letters of recommendation from the church leaders at Jerusalem. When challenged on this point, he replied that his converts were his epistle of commendation. He had living epistles to show for his work. These converts could be read and known of all men. This should be sufficient.

One of the most effective arguments for the Christian faith is the Spirit of the living God in the lives of believers. They are living epistles to the world, to all men.

What does Christ seek to write on our hearts and minds and in our lives? That we are reconciled to God, that we love one another, that we value the best things in life, that we have the mind of Christ. So when people read our lives, they see that God loves them and will forgive them. Christ communicates these truths to the world through us. He writes our love of righteousness, our trust in God, our love for people. We are Christ's epistles, written by Him, read and known of all men. Each of us is a separate living epistle, a center of light, shedding brightness and warmth, cheerfully, loyally, persistently, unceasingly, round an ever-widening circle.

During the second world war an air pilot was shot down while flying over one of the islands in the South Pacific. He bailed out and as he drifted down he wondered what kind of reception he might receive. He had heard of cannibals living on these islands. He landed in rough terrain and broke both his legs. The natives found him and carried him in a sheet back to the village. On the sheet he saw printed the name of a missionary society. He learned that years before, a missionary had come there, a loving, living epistle. Under his Christlike ministry the people of the island became Christians. The missionary had died and was buried there. When the pilot recovered, he walked out to the cemetery. On the tombstone the natives had written these words: "When he came there was no light. When he died there was no darkness."

# FILLED WITH THE FULLNESS OF GOD

*To know the love of Christ, which passeth knowledge, that ye might be filled with all the fulness of God. Now unto him that is able to do exceeding abundantly above all that we ask or think, according to the power that worketh in us. Eph. 3:19, 20.*

The gift of Christ in His fullness contains the secret that distinguishes it from all other religions. No other religious leaders in the history of the world have ever had a perfect righteousness to offer to sinful men, let alone the unsearchable riches of heaven. They have no inexhaustible wealth to give away. They are sinful men like ourselves. They can make no offer to make us rich.

The apostle Paul puts it this way: "Unto me, who am less than the least of all saints, is this grace given, that I should preach among the Gentiles the unsearchable riches of Christ" (Eph. 3:8). These are riches that cannot be counted. No amount of extravagance can exhaust them. No length of time can count their value. The riches of Christ are boundless, immeasurable, inexhaustible.

Christ in us is the fullness of wisdom, the perfect righteousness, the fullness of all truth. Everything man needs, comes to us in Him. Christ is a great treasure mine containing all the wealth of heaven. When we accept Christ, we have all this too. "And of his fulness have all we received, and grace for grace" (John 1:16).

Faith is the means by which all His wealth becomes ours. Faith, that word so easily used and casually referred to. That word which is always on our lips and always in our ears. Some of us have lost the very reality of it by reason of having heard it so often—that simple act of trust and commitment to Christ, in whom are hid all the treasures of heaven as in a boundless mine of wealth. He unites us with Himself. His wealth passes over into our lives. We are joined to the wealthiest Person in the universe.

When I dilate my lungs, the air comes in; when I open my eyes, the light comes in. When I open my heart, Christ comes in. When I trust Him, He pours His life and riches into my life. When I stretch out my hand to Him He fills it with the blessings of heaven.

# GOD MAKES THE DIFFERENCE

*For the same God who said, "Out of darkness let light shine," has caused his light to shine within us, to give the light of revelation—the revelation of the glory of God in the face of Jesus Christ. 2 Cor. 4:6, N.E.B.*

The great contribution that Christ makes is not only that He died for us but that He also gives us power to be and to do that which, until we gave our lives to Him, we had never been able to be and do on our own. God so loves us as to change and transform us. Men and women spiritually dead, lost in a round of secular and worldly activities, ambitions, and pleasures, become new men and women with all the power of God available. Prophets, apostles, missionaries, martyrs, gave their lives and spilled their blood.

When Christ comes into our lives, this does not necessarily mean we must change our work or the place where we live in order to escape difficulties and temptations. We may have the same job, the same home, the same community, the same people to live with. But there is the power of God added, a new dimension to life. There is something thrilling about life with Christ. We can throw ourselves into our job, singing our way through the days and weeks and years.

In Christ's time, to the Greek, the only man who counted was the one who could think. To the Roman, the only man who counted was the one who had power to conquer. To the Jew, the only man who counted was the man who knew the law and kept it. Then came Jesus. He cares for the lilies of the field and clothes them with beauty. Not even a sparrow falls to the ground but what He knows. Even the hairs of our head are numbered. Christ left the ninety-and-nine sheep in the fold and came to our world searching for His lost children. It is this that makes the difference in our world and in our lives.

I have read that in the field of botany, radium is sometimes used with plants that are warped and stunted. Then the flower or the plant comes to bloom and to fullness in a way never seen before. Similarly, when God walks into our lives, nothing is the same again. Nothing makes life so abundant as the coming of Christ into our hearts.

# CONFORMED OR TRANSFORMED—1

*And be not conformed to this world: but be ye transformed by the renewing of your mind, that ye may prove what is that good, and acceptable, and perfect, will of God. Rom. 12:2.*

Conformity to the world has a great attraction for a vast number of people. Conformity will reach its maximum when the two-horned beast of Revelation 13 comes to power. "He causeth all, both small and great, rich and poor, free and bond, to receive a mark in their right hand, or in their foreheads: and that no man might buy or sell, save he that had the mark, or the name of the beast, or the number of his name" (Rev. 13:16, 17).

Men's minds are being conditioned. This trend is already greatly advanced in the world. One of the prices we pay for the complexity of modern life is the production of mediocre personalities and mediocre minds. The trend is to conformity in everything, from our clothing to our thinking. The development of an independent personality is difficult to achieve.

Conformity is dangerous when it is of the worldly kind and is applied to the church and the Christian. The world is ever seeking to bring people to its ways of living. It has little or no concern for the individual. The world offers a great deal of success provided we allow ourselves to be enslaved by its ways.

Let us not underestimate the seriousness of the Christian adventure and the cost thereof. It is quite possible to become passive subordinates in a religious environment we take for granted. All but one of the twelve apostles were killed because of their stand for Christ against the crowd. John, the last of them, was exiled to a concentration camp on the Isle of Patmos. Almost all of the martyrs of the early centuries were slain for just one reason: they would not conform to the imperial pattern.

We must not be afraid to stand alone. Let us not call compromise diplomacy when it is cowardice. We are to be transformed by the renewing of the mind. We are not different just to be different. We are different where the choice is between truth and error, between Christ and the world, between the Lordship of Christ and the rule of the world, the flesh, and the devil.

# CONFORMED OR TRANSFORMED—2

*The messenger sent to fetch Micaiah told him that the prophets had with one voice given the king a favourable answer. "And mind you agree with them," he added. "As the Lord lives," said Micaiah, "I will say only what the Lord tells me to say." 1 Kings 22:13, 14, N.E.B.*

The setting is a meeting of Jehoshaphat, king of Judah, with Ahab, king of Israel. Ahab seeks to get Jehoshaphat to join him in a war against Syria. Jehoshaphat first asks that an inquiry be made of the Lord through the prophets. Four hundred come. With one voice they tell Ahab what he wants to know: victory over Syria should they go to war.

But Jehoshaphat is not satisfied. He asks, "Is there not here in Samaria a true prophet of Jehovah besides these four hundred self-styled prophets?" One true prophet remained— Micaiah. Ahab had imprisoned him for his opposition. So Micaiah is brought from prison, his hands tied. He rejects the counsel given by the four hundred. He will not be of those prophets with a smooth tongue who say and do what Ahab demands. Alone, he unfolds the vision God had given him. He bears testimony to the truth without fear and without hesitation. If Ahab and Jehoshaphat go to war against Syria, they will lose. Ahab is furious. Micaiah the prophet is taken back to prison. The two kings reject God's word. They unite and go to war with Syria. They are defeated. Ahab is slain.

Faith in God does not consist of a mere conformity to a doctrine. We must desire above all else to be delivered from our errors and our deficiencies. We must be prepared to pay any price to be guided by God's truth alone. Transformation of our lives is never something achieved en masse.

The good news of God's redemptive love in Christ may be had for the taking, like a gift freely offered. All we have to do is to reach out and take it. It is as simple as that. Yet perversely enough, it is not simple at all. To respond personally to Christ, to be transformed by His love and power, can be the most difficult thing in all the world.

When the final test comes, the majority will go along with the crowd. The true Christian will have to stand alone, undaunted, immovable, because his mind and heart have been captured by God.

# SECULAR OR SPIRITUAL

*Lest there be any . . . profane person, as Esau, who for one morsel of meat sold his birthright.* **Heb. 12:16.**

The Bible story of the two brothers, Esau and Jacob, often elicits our sympathy for Esau who was cheated out of his birthright by his brother. But there was a fatal weakness in Esau's character. He dismissed the importance of the birthright with insensibility and scorn. The birthright brought with it certain moral and spiritual responsibilities on which the home was founded.

The family heritage went back to God's call to Abraham. When he and Lot were confronted with a choice, Abraham had decided for eternal values, looking "for a city whose builder and maker is God" (Heb. 11:10). Lot had chosen temporal, material wealth. Esau followed in Lot's footsteps, and is referred to in the Bible as a profane person.

The *New English Bible* translates the word "profane" to mean "a worldly-minded person." It has no reference to one's use of language. Esau was wholly secular in his philosophy of life and outlook. The manner in which the secular man treats God's gift of life and salvation reveals a serious defect in character. The secular life is not necessarily wicked. The secular man relates his meaning of life to things. In actuality he says to God, "I have heard of You, learned of You, but You have no meaning and value for the kind of life I want to live."

There is nothing more disturbing than this despising of one's spiritual birthright. It creates blindness of mind and has fatal consequences. So long as we are secular we cannot respond to what is divine and spiritual.

All of us are familiar with the expression "the handwriting on the wall." It refers to a young man, Belshazzar, who already at his age had sacrificed eternal values and passed the point of no return.

Only those who have been born again by the Spirit see clearly and steadily eternal values. We experience them as the true life. This is our birthright because of what we are in Christ.

## "THE BEAUTY OF HOLINESS"

*Worship the Lord in the beauty of holiness.* **1 Chron. 16:29.**

Much that makes up life today has nearly annihilated respect for the beautiful. We need daily companionship with Christ, His quiet sensitivity toward the beautiful, His reverent poise. If we are to overcome the flippant rowdiness and the impetuosity of man's hectic existence, we must learn to worship God in the beauty of holiness. It has been observed that men who serve and work in great cathedrals develop a poise, a grace, and a majesty consistent with the beauty of the place where they work.

Our faith is not advanced by some cheap form of religious entertainment. To live our lives in company with the beauty of His character, and in the poise that stays upon God through all the pressures of life, that is to be our witness. Not all Christians are scholars or artists, but beauty of character and life are within reach of all of us.

A professed religionist may be esteemed for his brilliance even if he is rude and ungracious. But it is very doubtful if anyone desires his type of religion. Beauty of mind and manner are the most visible aspects of the Christian. We like to dress well, to look attractive. To be well-tailored is at least a sign of a person's good taste. It indicates a measure of social refinement. The beauty of one's religion is more than any kind of external appearance, however. It is more than good manners. It includes a sensitive taste for the virtuous and the beautiful. It involves kindness, thoughtfulness, unselfishness, and sincerity.

There is at times a false piety that repels. The words men speak may sound right but the spirit may be wrong. It is possible to communicate one's religion in the spirit of the enemy. Something is wrong with a professed Christian who is fond of discord and whose manner of life promotes it. The beauty of holiness passes into our being a certain quality of person. This requires that we be just and true, gentle and courteous, unselfish and loving. The beauty of holiness is not a voice, but it affects the voice. It is not manner, but it dignifies the manner. It is not conduct, but it beautifies the conduct.

# TRIUMPH IN CHRIST

*But thanks be to God, who continually leads us about, captives in Christ's triumphal procession, and everywhere uses us to reveal and spread abroad the fragrance of the knowledge of himself! We are indeed the incense offered by Christ to God, both for those who are on the way to salvation, and for those who are on the way to perdition. 2 Cor. 2:14, 15, N.E.B.*

In this scripture, Paul regards his conversion and complete surrender gained over him by our Lord, and his subsequent life, as celebrating the Lord's triumph in his life. Christ is the Conqueror. We are the conquered. Paul likens our status as trophies of Christ's victory, to the processions in which those who had been conquered by the Romans were led in triumph down the broad avenues of the imperial city of Rome.

The fact of our being led in triumph as trophies of the grace of God is a truth of exceptional moment for all of us. It involves the complete surrender of ourselves to Christ, our Lord and King. No one but Christ has the right to lead us in triumph. The basic issue is the type of commitment that brings this about. All too often we are subject to the rule of self and pride. But we are summoned to renounce all other lords and masters for the rule of the Lord Jesus. We do not truly live the Christian life save as we are led in triumph by Jesus Christ. There can be no place for any other master.

We must give up all desire to have other powers capture and lead us. We must be ardent in our desire to be led in triumph by Christ. We are defeated if we live for ourselves. We are victorious when we have surrendered ourselves to the control of the Holy Spirit. Self-will is so hard to surrender to another master. We are reluctant to be brought into subjection to Christ. How hard it is to forfeit the rule of self and pride.

Let us seek now to accept and cherish the triumph of Christ in our lives, to become His captives. Let our burning desire be to have Him as Conqueror. Christ came into our midst and defeated Satan to whom we were in bondage. He has delivered the captives out of Satan's power and seeks to lead them in triumph under His sovereign rule. Christ Himself has done it that He might lead us in triumph through the streets of the New Jerusalem. This is to be the witness of the remnant church, a spiritual body led in triumph by Christ.

# CHRIST CAME TO MINISTER

*For even the Son of man came not to be ministered unto, but to minister,*
*and to give his life a ransom for many.* **Mark 10:45.**

The two disciples James and John had requested to sit on
the right and on the left in Christ's coming kingdom. This
created resentment and confusion among the other disciples.
They were much displeased. Even in the presence of Christ,
the struggle for self-esteem and personal position prevailed.
Thus division developed among them. Once we set our eyes on
ourselves and allow room for selfishness and pride, others are
displeased and angered.

To be in the presence of Christ does not mean that all our
problems of selfishness are automatically resolved. Many
Christians presume that no effort is required to avail His grace
and power. It is possible to go on an ego trip at any time. When
we violate the unselfishness that Christian love requires, antagonism and controversy are the result.

Christ came to make us different. He performed fewer
spectacular miracles at the end of His ministry than at the beginning. He made no defense of Himself. He trod the last road
alone. No service was too mean or too long. He became the servant of all. He made no claim to greatness. He was meek and
lowly in heart. For more than three years the disciples had
lived with Him. They claimed to have forsaken all to follow
Him. Then the devil of pride aroused. They could not see beyond themselves, even at the time when Christ humbled Himself to the death of the cross.

To follow Christ means that we do not seek praise and
honor from men, to receive attention and flattery. Christ had
one destiny, to minister to others.

Christ speaks to those who are captives of self. If we think
more highly of ourselves than we ought, we have need to study
this text. Christ does not free us from pride and selfishness
automatically. Only as we take the same road with Christ and
die to self-will, when we seek no help from man but yield our
claim to superiority and self-importance, do we become like
Him. Let us not witness to ourselves, but to Jesus Christ our
Lord. When all of us in the church are doing that we shall
shake the world.

# UNTO THE LEAST OF THESE

*Inasmuch as ye have done it unto one of the least of these my brethren, ye have done it unto me. Matt. 25:40.*

There is need for real Christians who love and live to reconcile others to God. Our religion comes, not as a luxury, but as a power that transforms lives for eternity. Only when our faith has this power will we walk in the streets and in our household as we should.

Are we not the servants of men for Christ's sake? This much is certain. In the kingdom of God we will be able to look around the universe; nothing will be found of our sins, but our loving service for others will endure forever. We will meet those who will say to us, "I am here because you cared about me and loved me. You were hardly aware of what you did." One day it will be revealed, when you move out into eternity holding by the hand those for whom Christ lived and died.

I have developed grave suspicions of late about some of the ideas and things we have been trying to hold onto. With the fast deterioration of the value of money, our personal savings are hardly worth trying to keep for happy days ahead. One thing is sure to me: to invest everything we have in the kingdom of God, retaining just enough to live on, is worth trying. Giving our money, time, effort, and ourselves to get people to join us on the last trip to the New Jerusalem has a great deal in its favor. This is the way we feel about our loved ones. We cannot think of a future without them. There is little else that is more important in life.

In the communities where we live, people really need us. This is not a matter of pressuring ourselves to do what is difficult and distasteful. We offer men and women new life, eternal life through Jesus Christ. All the sacrifice Christ made in order to come face to face with individuals He never considered wasted—the woman of Samaria at the well, the woman taken in adultery, the little children who ran to Him. Jesus never left a solitary soul with the impression that he or she did not amount to much, or that He had more important things to do. It is no use hoping that one of these days something will happen to make Christian living worthwhile. Now is the supreme moment to serve and save others.

# THE ROAD TO EMMAUS

*And they said one to another, Did not our heart burn within us, while he talked with us by the way, and while he opened to us the scriptures?* **Luke 24:32.**

The hearts burning within the two disciples while on the way to Emmaus denotes that fervor of religious interest awakened by the clear apprehension of truth as Christ opened the Scriptures to them.

In the hearts and minds of millions today there is a fresh yearning to study and to know the Bible. They have a genuine craving to hear the voice of God, to understand His will for them. They desire not only to know something but to *be* something, to know how spiritual truth can be related to their everyday living.

We owe these people an answer to their hunger. The third angel's message is a concern about righteousness and a commitment to righteousness. To communicate it to others, it must be real to us. We are not in this world merely to mount guard around the Adventist doctrines; to sit inside our little compounds and look anxiously to see if our religious position will still hold. Our God-given assignment is to set a fire in people's hearts, to set their faces toward Christ and His Word.

To walk the road to Emmaus today is to have our own eyes opened—so to be taught the truth by the Holy Spirit that our hearts burn within us. Our lives are lit up with the glow of spiritual health and living truth; they give strength to our character, a boldness of witness that no worldly power can ever create.

Consider Paul before Festus and Agrippa. What matters is Paul and his witness. This man in chains really matters. The light from God's Word, as it shone through this man, kindled fire and conviction in those who heard him.

There is something thrilling about the truth when it takes hold of people. We must see ourselves as part of God's purpose and plan. We know that God is going to do something with us and for the people we meet. Like the prophets and apostles who had messages from God to man, we too are sure of the message. Voices by the thousand cry for light and press for an answer from those who have the truth of God.

# THE GOD OF ELIJAH—1

*Where is the Lord God of Elijah?* 2 Kings 2:14.

This was a question asked by Elisha, the young prophet who had been selected to continue the work of Elijah, the most famous prophet in Israel. Elijah was expecting to be translated to heaven. Three times he sought to get Elisha to leave him rather than have him on hand when the great moment came. "Tarry, I pray thee, here." But Elisha would have none of it. "As the Lord liveth and as thy soul liveth, I will not leave thee."

So they journeyed on together until they came to the river Jordan. Elijah smote the waters with his mantle. They divided, and the two men went over on dry ground. Finally, Elijah, about to be taken, said to Elisha: "Ask what I shall do for thee, before I be taken away from thee. And Elisha said, I pray thee, let a double portion of thy spirit be upon me. . . . And Elijah went up by a whirlwind into heaven. And Elisha saw it" (2 Kings 2:9-12).

Elisha then took up Elijah's mantle that had fallen, and went back and stood by the banks of the river Jordan. He too smote the waters as Elijah had done and cried out, "Where is the Lord God of Elijah?" The waters parted as before, and Elisha went on his way.

We do not know how long Elisha had been servant with Elijah. During this time he learned a great deal about the God of Elijah. Elijah had exercised a great influence on him. There was no escaping that. But now he was to find out for himself about the Lord God of Elijah. Because Elijah had so faithfully represented his God, Elisha asked the important question, "Where is the Lord God of Elijah?"

That is a fundamental question to ask. Christian men and women who are nearest and dearest to us convey an impression of the God we claim to believe in. As representatives of Jesus Christ, we believe in love, righteousness, purity, honor, integrity. We ourselves claim to walk with God. Our lives witness in one way or another to this quality of life. The people with whom we live and work are thus led to ask the question, "Where is the God of this Christian?" We will not be confronted with a more fundamental question than that.

# THE GOD OF ELIJAH—2

*But as for you—you may bear the name of Jew. . . . While you take pride in the law, you dishonour God by breaking it. . . . "Because of you the name of God is dishonoured among the Gentiles." Rom. 2:17-24, N.E.B.*

Much of the influence of the Jewish leaders, the chosen people of God, became wholly ineffective because by word and deed they profaned and misinterpreted the character of the God they claimed to believe in.

Adventists represent to the world the character of our religion. It follows that we also represent the God who is the founder of that religion. The picture of God in the minds of people has rarely if ever exceeded the quality that has been manifested in His followers. People are more influenced to seek the God we serve if our witness is true to His character of love and mercy as well as to His standards of refinement.

Elijah little realized the unconscious influence he had exercised on the other prophets and also on the seven thousand who had not bowed their knee to Baal. The scepter of righteousness that had ruled his life did not depart from Israel. It was taken up by Elisha and other prophets.

We are all Elijahs in our own little way. Others will follow in the way we go. Are people grateful that we uphold the truth of God? What if our children and our friends felt as Elisha did of Elijah, so that from our witness they would be led to cry: "Where is the God of this Christian mother, father, brother, sister, friend?" Because of our influence and witness, thousands may refuse to bow the knee to Baal.

We see at once the importance of our entire dedication to Christ, to that which is highest and noblest in life. No halfway religion will do. Not merely attending church on Sabbath. Nothing less will do but that we witness to Christ seven days a week.

Can we really expect our friends and loved ones to reach a higher standard in life than we set for ourselves? In every deed, word, and movement, our family and friends have their eyes upon us. If they are saved in the kingdom of God, it may be because they have caught from us some devotion and personal loyalty to Christ, some loving concern. They will smite the waters that stand in their way of becoming Christians and say, "Where is the Lord Jesus Christ of that man or woman of God?"

# STRENGTHEN YOUR BRETHREN

*And the Lord said, Simon, Simon, behold, Satan hath desired to have you . . . : but I have prayed for thee, that thy faith fail not: and when thou art converted, strengthen thy brethren. Luke 22:31, 32.*

These words were spoken by our Lord to Peter by way of caution and also encouragement. The counsel opens with Satan's plan for Peter's life and Christ's purpose to have him stand firm. With characteristic promptness, Peter assures Jesus he is ready to go with Him both to prison and to death. Then come the key words: "When thou art converted, strengthen thy brethren."

We cannot communicate to others what we do not have ourselves. In proportion to our firmness in Christ, to the degree of our self-control and Christian character, does the responsibility lie upon us to strengthen those around us. Joseph was taken as a slave into Egypt. His stand before the court of Pharaoh was a preparation for the coming of his father and brethren and their own destiny.

Moral greatness never appears so magnificent as when it keeps others from falling, when it inspires them to take the same stand. Young people who follow in the footsteps of Joseph, Daniel, Moses, and Paul, amid the downward moral trend of our times, are more majestic in the sight of heaven than all the cathedrals of the world. We have every reason to be converted to Christ.

Every sound has an echo. Every light has a shadow. Every act we do, every word we speak, every thought we think, effects consequences upon others, as well as upon ourselves. Refuse to take one step that will weaken another's character. Nothing pays off so miserably as that which weakens and destroys another person morally and spiritually.

Are we Christians salt? Then it's ours to give the savor of life. Are we light? It is that others may be lightened. Are we converted to Christ? It is that we might communicate spiritual and moral strength to others. Have we been lifted up from the miry clay of sin and our feet established upon the Rock, Christ Jesus? It is to enable others to do the same. A man converted to Christ is different. The most illustrious names of history are not of the rich or the learned, but of those morally and spiritually like Christ.

# A REALISTIC FAITH IN A REAL WORLD

*And they . . . did eat their meat with gladness and singleness of heart, prais-*
*ing God, and having favour with all the people. And the Lord added to the*
*church daily such as should be saved. Acts 2:46, 47.*

Not long ago I happend to be in the office of a travel agent discussing an overseas trip (that never materialized). The agent
presented me one brochure after another with the most inviting
descriptions of the countries I planned to visit. Her own ani-
mated comments whetted my appetite.

"I suppose you have been to all these places," I said.

"No," she replied honestly, "I have not." In a moment created
by her candor I thought of the possibility of our operating as
Christians on the same basis. It could be that one of the obstacles
standing in the way of selling others on the faith we believe is
what some people consider "not for real" religion. The world is a
difficult place in which to live.

The distance from the Christian to troubled souls is reminis-
cent of the New Testament story of the prodigal son. Among the
lonely and tragic lives of lost men, the Christian is asked to make
his way in the world. Real Christian living teaches us not to build
our silly castles in the air. There are too many needy people of
all ages crying for help. Attending church each Sabbath and
paying our tithes and offerings is only part of our religion. We
cannot exactly call that the whole of our Christian experience.
Enter into the lives of people and you will see for yourself.

The great things, the true things, the loving things, about our
religion are the reaching into the lives of lonely and needy people.
Whatever you do, don't call loving concern for people unreal or
visionary.

I have always been impressed with the practical, down-to-
earth Christianity of the early disciples after Pentecost. Nothing
about their ministry or their witness drags or bores me. Against
the most impossible odds, they increased and rejoiced. Ours is
no other-worldly religion, the kind that is half miserable and
gloomy today for the sake of "eating pie in the sky" sometime in
the future. It is not a religion that withdraws itself to some isolated area of special privileges. Ours is an engaging world of people. We will not turn our backs on them.

# "WITNESSES UNTO ME"

*But ye shall receive power, after that the Holy Ghost is come upon you; and ye shall be witnesses unto me both in Jerusalem, and in all Judaea, and in Samaria, and unto the uttermost part of the earth. Acts 1:8.*

If Christ were walking down here with us today, we would be taking the long march with Him to see the Syrophenician woman, to Jericho to see Zaccheus, and to a host of other bright prospects for the kingdom of God. The time has not yet come to escape from our responsibilities to the world.

Granted that we have little relish for what the world offers; but the people in it are something else again. We could witness with an infilling of apostolic fervor that feared no one and loved all men. We are not ready to flee to the mountains. There are too many people yet to be won to Christ. As Christians, time should not hang heavily on our hands anymore. We cannot sit down and stay where we are. There is too much at stake in the world. The devil has come down with great wrath and destructive power.

It is not hard to believe that the church is not going to save the world. But we cannot leave people behind to perish. We might be tempted to believe at times that the church has proved its impotence by not being able to make a great impression on the world. However, against all the evil forces in the world there is the power and the presence of God, of Christ, and of the Holy Spirit. The triumph of the everlasting gospel and the third angel's message in the lives of multitudes is still to be realized.

There is a very realistic way for our lives to go. Wherein and wherever sin has deceived and led us, none of it is complimentary. We tremble to think of how our sins outgrow themselves and run far away into other lives where we can never follow them. Thank God, Christ will wipe out that record for eternity. Throughout the universe, when sin is ended we shall not be confronted with gossips who never let rest our mistakes and our sins. In Christ we are assured that God will not later dredge the depths of the sea for our sins and bring them up against us. We know for sure that in the ages to come they will not arise and condemn us. We will be able to look around the universe and see no trace of the evil we have done. Thank God we will stand clear, amazingly clear, for all eternity.

## SALT OF THE EARTH

*"You are salt to the world. And if salt becomes tasteless, how is its salt-ness to be restored? It is now good for nothing."* **Matt. 5:13, N.E.B.**

No doubt we have all met people who have asked with a shrug of the shoulders, "Why should I be a Christian?" The indication is that they have never found any good and sufficient reason to be one. Christ stated that Christians have two distinct roles—salt and light. What do these types of Christians prove about Jesus Christ that is worth having? Does Jesus Christ make that much difference in people?

For one thing the function of salt is to preserve that which is good. Salt acts against corrupting germs. Salt also brings out the taste. It flavors. So Christ said that Christians are to fulfill this role. We act against evil, against those forces that corrupt life. We live actively and dynamically against spiritual disease.

Salt can also lose its usefulness. Instead of bringing out the full flavor of the Christian life, the professed Christian can dull the taste of life. We can live in a way that fails to meet people's needs. Poor lawyers make poor mediators for their clients. Poor physicians make poor instruments for healing people. Poor Christians are poor influences, poor keepers of the truth, poor in acting against those forces that corrupt life.

Christ meant our lives to count. So much of life is stale and flat for many people, unprofitable and useless. So much of life is futile. We are to be different. To become salt in the earth is certainly worth trying. Let us forget about the grabbing and the self-ishness. Let us sweeten and purify life for all the people we meet. Let us change the corrupting forces in other lives. There is a way to get rid of the staleness and the dullness of life. We can do it by functioning as Christ gave us the power to do.

"The fruit of the Spirit is love, joy, peace." Well, that is a pre-servative, healing force, all right. Everyone will admit to that. We are to purify life, not corrupt it. We are to preserve our love re-lationships with one another so that life is sweet and not sour.

Seldom if ever has the world been so rich in possibilities, yet so torn with strife and so dark with despair. Nobody seems to know what to do except the Christian. Our experience with the living Christ offers to men the fullness of life both for time and for eternity.

# YE ARE THE LIGHT OF THE WORLD

*"You are light for all the world. . . . When a lamp is lit, it is not put under the meal-tub, but on the lamp-stand, where it gives light to everyone in the house. And you, like the lamp, must shed light among your fellows, so that, when they see the good you do, they may give praise to your Father in heaven." Matt. 5:14-16, N.E.B.*

What does it mean to be a light to the world? Obviously it means that we dispel the darkness in whatever situation we find ourselves. As lights we live in such a way that we show others the way to God. We are concerned to communicate Christ, to create fellowship, to raise the level of truth in the minds of people.

We are not to be an island unto ourselves. We are to be noticed and known as Christians, not for our sakes, but for the glory of God. We are to be so spiritually alive as Christians that there is no possibility that people will take us for unbelievers. We are to capture the attention of people for Christ.

If as Christians we are married, there will be light in the home—the light of love, joy, and peace rather than hostility, darkness, and discord. What are we to do with situations that bring gloom into the home, the church, and the community? Precisely here we are to be the light of life, the hope of people's tomorrow.

Every time Christ came face to face with people He brought light to darkened minds and hearts. He sat one day with the woman of Samaria and opened one chapter after another from her life. He met the woman taken in adultery and knew everything about her. With one word Jesus could have called up the long record of departures from integrity, but He said, "I do not condemn you. Go and sin no more." The life of everyone who met Christ was enlightened in some way. In place of bitterness and hostility there was love and friendship. The sorrows and sins that weighed men down disappeared.

How practical it is to be that kind of Christian—to shine for Christ. No complicated theology is required here. Jesus wanted the life of His followers to be radiant. The Christian is really made for life and living. We cannot keep company with Christ without this happening to us. Christ in us will make us a light to the world.

# "HE PASSED BY ON THE OTHER SIDE"

*And by chance there came down a certain priest that way; and when he saw him, he passed by on the other side.* **Luke 10:31.**

We cannot be Christians alone. None of us who profess to follow Christ can dodge the responsibility for the people who come our way. We are thousands of miles away from the people in Africa and India. But when men, women, and children starve to death, when children born of American soldiers in Vietnam are dying because there is no one to care, that too is our business.

Once we fall into the habit of not caring about people whose destitution and misery are a burden on the world, we deserve no peace. We achieve nothing but lovelessness when nothing that happens around us is our concern. Every situation that prevails in our world ties in somewhere with people. If there is tragedy in a family we are to be there with compassion. If there are young people who carry loads greater than they can bear we are to be there with our presence, our prayers, and our love and acceptance.

The priest and the Levite in the story probably felt themselves right with God. Certainly they were considered decent persons, respectable, moral, except for one thing—they did not intend to be found where human need was the greatest.

The idea of leaving everything to God can be pretty disastrous so far as Christian love for others is concerned. It is not true that if we pass by chances to bring people to Christ, God will step in and do the rest. Let us not assume that because God loves all people, that love will reach them independently of anything we care to feel or do. After a while we come to believe there is little or nothing we can do. The tendency is to relax behind the façade of the church.

Many who make no profession of being Christians live more compassionately than those who bear the name. No large talents are required. No great public assignments are necessary to challenge us; just compassion on the road of life.

Under the transforming power of Christ's love, people come to believe that the Christian faith is genuine. These broken fragments of humanity become of great value. Are we investing our lives in needy people for Christ's sake?

# WINNING MEN TO CHRIST

*Jonah was greatly displeased and angry, and he prayed to the Lord: "This, O Lord, is what I feared when I was in my own country . . . ; I knew that thou art 'a god gracious . . . and always willing to repent. . . . ' And now, Lord, take my life: I should be better dead than alive." Jonah 4:1-3, N.E.B.*

It was payday for Nineveh. God commissioned the prophet Jonah to go and call on the city to repent. On hearing God's judgment message, all the people turned to God. As their heavenly Father, God showed mercy and saved them.

But Jonah was angry with God because His love and mercy was wider than his own. Men would fain cut God down to their own size. Jonah was honest enough to explain his refusal at first to go to Nineveh. But his explanation is almost beyond belief: "I fled before unto Tarshish: for I knew that thou art a gracious God, and merciful, slow to anger, and of great kindness, and repenteth thee of the evil" (Jonah 4:2).

Because Jonah was a prophet of God, his lack of compassion for the wicked people of Nineveh condemned him. Do you believe that God loves all men without distinction of race or creed? Do you believe that the love and mercy of God is as wide as the world? Do you cherish the hope that God will be gracious and full of mercy to your opposers and enemies? Better be an unbeliever than a professed Christian who has not learned "there's a wideness in God's mercy like the wideness of the sea."

The vitality of our faith depends on the success with which it succeeds in providing real answers to the disturbing conditions in human lives.

Christian experience can neither be imposed nor imputed from without. It is possible to advocate truth in a spirit that is not really Christian, to hurt the cause of Christ by the way we advocate Him. The presence of judgment and condemnation when seeking to communicate the truth to others discloses our own lack of trust and peace with God. To be able to express love while seeking to win others to Christ is a mark of a mature Christian. No technique for taking the gospel and the message to others is of any use in the hands of a critical and judgmental operator. The atmosphere of Christian love is Christ's only method of conveying the truth to people.

# A RELIGION THAT WALKS THE EARTH

*Those who have come to believe in God should see that they engage in honourable occupations, which are not only honourable in themselves, but also useful to their fellow-men.* **Titus 3:8, N.E.B.**

The truth we believe should unfold before men in a life of holiness, honesty, righteousness, usefulness to men, exercising a Christian influence, and in all other ways beneficial. Christians should follow honest occupations and should be honest in those occupations.

God's last message cannot carry out the will of God if it cannot be true to itself. The kind of life that results in loss of moral and spiritual strength can help no one's faith. We are not to modernize our content of truth so that God's will is no longer understood. Tolerance of other people's views must not mean laxity with our own. Much of so-called religious tolerance is indifference to the truth.

Christians of the first century clearly understood this. They branded many of the common and popular practices as dishonest. They could accept no public office that involved the burning of incense to Caesar. They could obey no command of any official that would make them untrue to God or to His commandments. They refused any work that might connect them with the degrading shows and features and crafts of that day.

If a slave became a Christian, he had to risk the whip, the dungeon, heavy labor in the quarries, and death itself rather than comply with many of the demands made upon him. Obedience to Christ forbade the Christian to take part in the evil and suggestive pleasures of Rome. They were bound, by their very faith in Christ, to be honest in their occupations, to please God in all the details of daily life. The Christian would not indulge in questionable amusements.

Their concern was for the success and triumph of the cause of Christ. They feared lest evil should overcome the truth. They abstained from every species of wickedness that put the gospel in a bad light.

Christians in every age are to bind themselves to that which is pleasing and acceptable to God. The influence of our faith must enlighten, sanctify, and purify life.

## "I AM A DEBTOR"

*I am debtor both to the Greeks, and to the Barbarians; both to the wise, and to the unwise. So, as much as in me is, I am ready to preach the gospel to you that are at Rome also. Rom. 1:14, 15.*

Our task as Christians is not to lecture people or to get into an argument or even a discussion about our religion with an approach that is detached from people. Like Paul, we are witnesses. We confess our indebtedness to love the unlovable, to strengthen the weak, to be a faithful friend. We are to care so much about people that we cannot go to heaven without them.

To feel ourselves debtors to God and man is to possess the highest qualifications for success in the Christian life. Several years ago a student named Chang came to America and attended Princeton Theological Seminary. He had been a flaming political revolutionary in an Asian country. Captured and put in prison, he was abandoned by his former friends. As he lay in prison a man began to visit him. Later Chang said: "Every now and then he would drop in, and seemed to be interested in me. It was the first time in my life that someone cared for me as a human being. For the first time, I became an individual, loved for my own sake. I asked the man: 'Why do you come to see me?' He replied: 'I am a Christian. Jesus Christ, who is my Lord, told His disciples to visit those who are in prison. I like to do it.'" Said Chang: "Tell me more about this Jesus." This gave the Christian man the opportunity to open up the gospel and tell the revolutionary that nobody ever loved people as Jesus did, even to the point of giving His life for man. This captured Chang's heart. He entered the ministry. The last that I heard of him, he was teaching in a seminary in China as a professor of religion and a witness for Christ. He found Christ because someone cared enough.

Paul does not call upon us to be fanatics. He asks for no unattractive intensity of mind that pressures people unduly or unkindly. Have you considered how responsible we are for one another? That if we fail in our witness, if we allow any personal deflection from principle, love, and kindness, everyone about us suffers? Christ needs us to be undismayed and unashamed.

# EVANGELICAL CHRISTIANITY

*And as he thus spake for himself, Festus said with a loud voice, Paul,*
*thou art beside thyself; much learning doth make thee mad. But he said, I am*
*not mad . . . ; but speak forth the words of truth.* Acts 26:24, 25.

What made the early church not only powerful but invincible was its sense of the profound obligation to proclaim the gospel everywhere. The evangelical Christian of the past was a person of passionate devotion to the truth, to the cause of God, and to the salvation of men.

Years ago in New England, when a certain minister preached they called him a "mad man." He protested with the words: "When I passed yonder gravel pit and saw it cave in and bury three men alive, I shouted for help till they heard me in the town nearly a mile away. Nobody called me a mad man then. But when I see destruction about to fall on sinners and entomb them in an eternal mass of woe, I cry aloud. Then they say I am beside myself. Perhaps I am, but I would that all God's children might be on fire to save their fellows."

John Knox would pray in agony, "Give me Scotland or I die." Scotland, in spite of its mind set, yielded to the "fervent, effectual prayer" of this righteous man. I hate to hear the inane compliment to a sermon, "I enjoyed your lecture." We need to be graciously but firmly possessed with Christ, who is so wise, and who loves us with such an eternal compassion, that He ought to be loved and obeyed by everybody in return.

No Christian organization has ever succeeded in preserving its spiritual vitality where it has lived unto itself. Jesus gave us the secret of spiritual success and triumph when He said, "Except a corn of wheat fall into the ground and die, it abideth alone: but if it die, it beareth forth much fruit" (John 12:24).

Formality, aimlessness, indifference, are the enemies of a dynamic faith. Nothing brings us up more sharply as to the depth and genuineness of our Christian experience than when we seek to bring Christ to others. The world needs not only religious information but the power of Christ to change lives.

# OUR GOD-GIVEN TASK

*"For myself, I set no store by life; I only want to finish the race, and complete the task which the Lord Jesus assigned to me, of bearing my testimony to the gospel of God's grace."* Acts 20:24, N.E.B.

The evangelism of Christ's disciples was regarded as supreme folly to most people of that day. That Jesus the crucified should engage His followers in an enterprise that required the total surrender of their lives, seemed madness; to renounce every worldly prospect and advantage in devotion to such a Person seemed folly of the worst kind. Paul said that for Christ he had suffered the loss of all things, including a leading position in the Jewish Sanhedrin. This kind of commitment obviates all neutrality and indifference.

The professed Christian who thinks of the third angel's message as a plan to play safety first, or a postmortem passport to Paradise, has not walked the way of the cross with Christ. We are face to face with the most compelling hour since Christ died for us. Can we deliberately elect to stay poor, if necessary, to be content with less of this world's goods?

The materialistic secular man does not understand that all our money should be dedicated to evangelism, that so many lives should be sacrificed in faraway unprofitable mission enterprises, that people would be ready to perish in disease-racked places of the earth or become victims of pagan hatred or finally return with nothing of this world's goods. The natural man is convinced of the madness of such a sacrifice. "Others, again, had to face jeers and flogging, even fetters and prison bars. They were stoned, they were sawn in two, they were put to the sword, they went about dressed in skins of sheep or goats, in poverty, distress, and misery. They were too good for a world like this" (Heb. 11:36-38, N.E.B.).

To become possessed by Christ and by the Holy Spirit is to overflow with love for people and to make any sacrifice in order to bring them to Christ. There is no fanaticism, no extremism; but dedication unsurpassed. The divine call to exalt Christ and draw all men unto Him does not repress ambition and desire. On the contrary, it develops excellence in the service of God. It requires more mental strength, more force of character, more courage and audacity, than any other enterprise in the world.

# VIRTUE WENT OUT OF HIM—1

*And the whole multitude sought to touch him: for there went virtue out of him, and healed them all.* **Luke 6:19.**

When a man establishes a business he first considers the operating costs. If he makes only 2 per cent profit he will probably soon fail. If he makes 8 per cent he can remain solvent. If he makes 20 per cent or more he will soon be rich.

Man's investment in the kingdom of God involves a similar principle. If a man uses seven days a week, 365 days a year, to make money, to build his house and garden, to build a portfolio in the stock market, he makes no investment in the kingdom of God. He simply lives on the physical plane, which has no future.

If we give one tenth or more of our money and one seventh or more of our time, investing them in God's program to save men, if we inspire the discouraged and lift up the fallen, we are investing for the future. We are putting money in the bank of heaven where it will not rust or decay. There in eternity we will get the full investment, some 50 and some 100 per cent. If we invest life in ourselves alone we will be bankrupt for eternity.

There are many people, diligent and successful in this world's business, who have ceased to care about other people, whose influence for God and for the good of others has ceased to function. We are to be different. Give out your Christian influence as freely as the sun gives its heat and light over the earth. Develop loving atmosphere and spread it everywhere as the flowers pour forth their perfume.

In the garden, a week is enough for the rye grass seed to sprout and the lawn to begin to green. Three weeks will answer for most flower seeds to burst forth; and it will take the summer for the corn to mature, four or five summers for the peach tree to reach maturity, and perhaps fifty years for the oak tree to reach majestic proportions. In the realm of personal relations, the sweetening of the lives of our children and our friends, the uplifting of others, requires a lifetime. The investment of ourselves in the transforming of people is never impaired by a stock market crash. Here the annual dividend is never suspended. This is where we make an eternal profit.

# VIRTUE WENT OUT OF HIM—2

*I perceive that virtue is gone out of me.* **Luke 8:46.**

Jesus never failed to enter into the lives of people. He saw with their eyes and felt what they were feeling. He realized their problems, sensed their needs, reached out to them with warmth and love.

All of us have an influence that goes out of us, falling either like a light or a shadow. Unconsciously we exercise a healing spirit or one that may create anxiety and fear. Whatever the spirit is within us, whether of selfishness or unselfishness, of love or hostility, of humility or pride, of concern or indifference, it makes itself felt upon those around us.

From this spirit within us an atmosphere is created, which either lifts people up or drags them down. We can either warm people or chill them, relax them or tense them. We are responsible for whatever spirit and influence we exercise upon others.

For us Christians, there is to be a virtue that goes out from us, an influence born of the reality that is in our own hearts and experience. We are to exercise a loving and gracious atmosphere, so that we will draw others to Christ even without knowing it. There are people around us who need to be softened, whose lives have been hardened by circumstances. We are to inspire them with hope and courage, love them into new life and sweetness. This is the best communication of the gospel there is. When Jesus walked the earth little children ran to Him. He was always the One with shining eyes and loving words. None came into His presence without feeling better.

I am told that the Tate Gallery of Art in London has on display the paint box used by the great painter Turner. The box is nothing to look at, but smudged and marked with old paint and pigments. It really does not belong among the works of art. Yet from it, Turner gave expression to his unexcelled paintings of nature and pastoral scenes. At his hands, the beauties of art came forth.

Paul put it this way: "We have this treasure in earthen vessels, that the excellency of the power may be of God, and not of us. . . . That the life also of Jesus might be made manifest in our mortal flesh" (2 Cor. 4:7-10). In the hands of the Master Artist, glorious possibilities are realized in our lives.

## LET ME BE AWARE

*I am a free man and own no master; but I have made myself every man's servant, to win over as many as possible.* **1 Cor. 9:19, N.E.B.**

It is time to take the Christian offensive in love. There is no profit in bracing ourselves, warding off the blows and the words we do not like. By the grace of God and the love of Christ we must turn the battle around, loving our enemies and those who do things against us. We cannot turn our lives into some sort of fortress as a means of self-defense. We cannot continue protecting ourselves against hurts and insults and injustices by reacting in the same spirit.

The love of God in our hearts is God's kind of security. That is how Christ faced the opposition and the hostility of men. We do not need anything more than that. Selfishness is always defensive. Love is outgoing and puts first the welfare of the other person.

We are not here to save face, position, or prestige. Our lives are renewed in Christ for one reason: to pour them out for the healing and transformation of others. Pride will not accomplish that. Rejection will not do it.

The spontaneous love of Christ in our hearts makes us aware of the deep needs of others. We go forth to meet people each day without thinking about ourselves, pouring out the loving-kindness born in our hearts by the Holy Spirit. People seeing us will then say, "This man had reason to be resentful, but he was not. This woman had reason to become angry, but she did not. This young person had reason to get bitter, but he did not."

Christ's way is the way of patience, long-suffering, compassion. We are to travel this way with those both inside and outside the church. In face of all the abuse He received, one of the supreme moments in the life of Christ came at the cross: "Father, forgive them for they know not what they do." Christ took people captive by His love. It was not only His teaching. It was more than that. Those who are captured by the love of Jesus Christ do not want to be free from it.

There is a price to pay to be this kind of person. Maximum value in the cause of Christ is never achieved at minimum cost. It requires that we be genuine Christians, loving and radiant, because people really matter most with us.

# WITNESSES UNTO CHRIST

*Ye shall be witnesses unto me.* Acts 1:8.

Christ's life was one of incomparable beauty, righteousness, and love for sinners. He is the greatest man the world has ever known. The lives of other men have left impressions and memories for a short time. In the end they are forgotten. But not so with Jesus Christ. His command to His disciples to be His witnesses is just as meaningful and urgent as when He gave it. The world cries out for divine realities. The divine command to witness presses upon every situation in which we find ourselves. If we want to make our years count, we must witness.

"According to my earnest expectation and my hope, that in nothing I shall be ashamed, but that with all boldness, as always, so now also Christ shall be magnified in my body, whether it be by life, or by death. For to me to live is Christ, and to die is gain" (Phil. 1:20, 21). Paul wrote these words while in prison. His witness to Christ was crowned with abundant success before the eyes of all throughout the universe. The commission to witness never faded from his mind.

We too are to maintain our testimony to Jesus by word and action. We are to witness to Christ as truth, to the Word of God as truth. Opinion is one thing, truth is another. Our views, opinions, reasonings, may capture people's interest for a while. But the Christian faith is on a far different footing.

The Christian faith, whatever else it is, is not a selfish religion. He who is ready to falter at any moment in the cause of the third angel's message does not know what following Christ means. Witnessing to Christ often seems unacknowledged and unrequited, but it spells loyalty to the divine mission of our Lord and Saviour, and that pays all we need by way of reward.

You might aspire to be the best sportsman, the best salesman. You might rise to eminence in your profession. As a man's vision so shall his life be. Now recall the day when Christ came to your heart. You saw His sacrifice for you, His character, His purity, His righteousness. Do not let time or temptation deface your devotion. Do not allow the radiance of your witness to fade away.

# RESPONSIBILITY FOR OUR NEIGHBORS

*If you have warned the righteous man not to sin and he has not sinned, then he will have saved his life because he has been warned, and you will have saved yourself. Eze. 3:21, N.E.B.*

This passage of Scripture reveals a basic moral principle: Man is responsible. He will be judged accordingly. The text speaks of the influence we have on people. God holds us responsible for it. We are to turn men from self-indulgence, unfaithfulness, and sin, to the high and holy way of following Christ. In every life we meet we exercise an influence for good or ill, for obedience or disobedience, for purity or impurity, for humility or pride. Every plant and tree that grows is affected by its soil and environment. There is no way we can escape our responsibility.

Often we dismiss our influence as of little account. If our minds are set shallow, if our lives are superficial, if we lack integrity, all this soils the lives of our children. The moment we belong to Christ we become responsible for the influence we have upon members of our family, upon our neighbors and our friends. In the judgment men will stand up and praise us for our influence of love that turned their feet toward God.

Here is one law for every class—for the rich and the poor, the ignorant and the educated. This matter of influence presses upon us the responsibility for saving men as far as it is possible. Christ requires of us purity, integrity, love, and all the other qualities found in Him. Unchastity, injustice, greed, hostility, dishonesty, in professed Christians have never won anyone to Christ or to the truth. They have driven men away. Let another man enrich himself at our expense, deal unjustly with us, attempt to degrade our children, reject us in anger or isolate us; this kind of professing Christian invariably leads away from Christ and the gospel of salvation.

If we keep close to Christ, walk with God day by day, we find it easy and natural to be patient, loving, honest, and unselfish. Has not Christ come into our lives to make us Christlike? As we consider those Christlike Christians we know, are we not grateful and happy for the influence they have upon us? Their image akin to Christ came to be transferred to our minds and can never be erased.

# COMMUNICATING THE TRUTH—1

*And the servant of the Lord must not strive; but be gentle unto all men, apt to teach, patient, in meekness instructing those that oppose themselves; if God peradventure will give them repentance to the acknowledging of the truth. 2 Tim. 2:24, 25.*

A person said to me some time ago, "I have accepted Christ as my Saviour. I feel no necessity for doctrine." But without Bible teachings or doctrines, religion becomes an affair of the feelings. Doctrine has been abused. Men play with doctrine as something that belongs to the intellect rather than with life. Then people are likely to adopt only what is convenient.

Our text begins with the advice "The servant of the Lord must not strive." Men do strive about doctrine and creedal statements. They get into controversy when others hold religious opinions different from their own. The tendency then is to alienate people. So people come to believe that the best thing to do is to stress Jesus and de-emphasize doctrine. Intellectual knowledge becomes separated from knowing Jesus. Disagreement prevails in the first case; unity in the second.

We are to proclaim the faith in the spirit of Christ, without harshness, contention, or strife. Any separation between Jesus and doctrine leaves much to be desired. It is easy to lose sight of the uniqueness of the faith we hold. We must not shift our message and responsibility from doctrine to Christ. What gives our message its great importance is the whole truth as part of our response to Christ.

This does not mean that Christians will find everything sweetness and light. A man's foes can be those of his own household. But this should be none of our making. We are to have the spirit of love, not strife. This is how Joseph in Egypt and Daniel in Babylon witnessed to their faith. They stood firm for their unique beliefs in such a way and with such a quality of life, that kings and princes were won over to their side.

A Christian without Biblical doctrine is a rudderless man, tossed to and fro. He is not securely anchored. Love does not destroy doctrine or make it unnecessary. It puts life and meaning into it. Let this be so witnessed that men can agree that our specific doctrines have made us more like Christ in every way.

# COMMUNICATING THE TRUTH—2

*Be gentle unto all men, apt to teach, . . . in meekness instructing those that oppose themselves.* **2 Tim. 2:24, 25.**

Wild animals may rave and roar, but it is the little lambs that draw children to the farmyard. We as Adventists must not strive. The whole truth of God given to us is intended to make people whole, not simply to satisfy their sense of logic. How can we lead men to accept the truth while conveying the impression that we are at odds with them, that we cannot love them until they change their minds?

"Be gentle unto all men." There is no real success in communicating the truth by the manifestation of any other spirit. All the angry disputes on religion are like so many winds and waves upon a stormy sea that interrupt and endanger the progress of the ship. Not the religious subject matter makes the difference in communicating the truth, but the spirit of the teacher, the representative of Jesus Christ.

"In meekness"—humility must mark our bearing. We communicate not only ideas on truth but all those qualities of Christ as well: love, patience, humility, gentleness, long-suffering. The work of the "loud cry," calling upon Christians in other religious bodies to come out from among them, is not to be through strife, but through us as living representatives of Jesus Christ. The great error of which churches and teachers have been guilty through the centuries has been the thrusting of religious ideas and opinions into greater prominence than Jesus Christ and His righteous and moral character.

To advance the cause of the third angel's message, two things are necessary: an appeal to the intellect by soundness in teaching the truth, and an appeal to men's hearts in love. How is any spiritual message really proved? Not by intellect and logic alone, but by the spirit of Jesus. We must not only persuade men's minds to receive the truth but actually communicate the very spirit of our Lord. These two together make up the distinctiveness of our message. The touch of Christ on our hearts and His love shining forth from us, together with a clear knowledge of the Word of God, is the only way to be a messenger of God's grace.

# THE GLORY OF THE CHRISTIAN LIFE

*I call heaven and earth to record this day against you, that I have set be-fore you life and death, blessing and cursing: therefore choose life.* **Deut. 30:19.**

Some time ago I was talking with a young man about choosing fully and entirely the Christian way of life. He replied that he did not think it was worth it. In the first place he wanted to make money. Christians are not particularly concerned with that. Furthermore, up until then he had not made the grade as a Christian. He did not think he could make it. He did not wish to lose both the pleasures of this life and those of the next. For him religion was all right for old ladies, sick people, and solemn functions.

There is a false impression that we have to go to the world to find happiness, success, and fame; that we can hardly be expected to be concerned with such things in the Christian faith. Where do people get the idea that riches, worldly success, and fame bring happiness? One New Year's Eve I was in Times Square, New York City. When the clock struck midnight, people were working hard at drinking, dancing, shouting, wearing themselves out trying to get some happiness in the last few minutes of the old year. Personally, for my recreation I prefer working in the garden or chopping wood, or playing a healthy game in the countryside.

In serving Christ there is nothing that leaves a nasty taste in our mouth, a hangover, or a headache. The prodigal son thought he had to go to the world to find happiness and have a good time. He thought he was having the time of his life with his so-called friends—until his money gave out.

"You are young only once." Have you ever heard that statement? Quite probably. Certainly there is only one time when you have the full bloom of youth, when you are possessed with the strength of youth, when your mind, heart, and body are at their best. But why waste all this?

We cannot get happiness by artificial ways of living. Wherever men and women have lived for Christ, they have proved themselves the salt of the earth. They have been the most satisfied people the world has ever known. In the first century they won the world for Christ.

# THE PATH TO GREATNESS

*Happy art thou, O Israel: who is like unto thee, O people saved by the Lord. Deut. 33:29.*

Christian living is greater than wealth, grander than worldly fame, more rewarding than any career in the world. Christ does not demand that you be a doctor, a lawyer, farmer, engineer, scientist, or a business tycoon. No doubt the world will applaud you should you succeed in any of these occupations. But without Christ they cut but a small figure before the universe. High position or a large salary is no indication of success with God.

You have not chosen the path to greatness until all your faculties are awakened by the Spirit of God, and your whole being is committed to the life and the work to which Christ has appointed you. A man cheapens himself by leaving out Christ. Sports, music, social climbing, the ability to make money, can only end in failure unless Christ is given first place. If you are committed to Him, then all of life's abilities, activities, and purposes will find expression in loving obedience to God and loving service for others. A living beauty in your life and a creativity in your heart and mind will be seen because you have added the presence and the glory of the Lord. As the sun unfolds the beauty and the fragrance of the flowers, so Christ unfolds our lives in love, joy, peace, kindness, integrity, and righteousness.

A young woman graduating from college was asked, "What do you want most in life?" She replied with one word: "Fame." The greatest exploits in the history of our world are found in the service of God. If you are asking for lasting fame and greatness, then the Christian faith can give you the sure formula. The fundamental principle for greatness, fame, honor, and happiness is this: These things are best found in bringing Christ's life to someone else.

You may not like to give up many things that the world has to offer. I am not suggesting that you should. But you ought to think and live in terms of God's handiwork in the lives of the great men and women of the Bible and of the Christian church. By all means, find out to what extent God can do the same for you.

# SATISFACTION GUARANTEED

*He shall see of the travail of his soul, and shall be satisfied.* Isa. 53:11.

"Satisfaction guaranteed." In advertising the sale of all manner of goods and articles, this is often promised to us. But in the Bible satisfaction is not from possessions, but from sacrificial service. The prophet Isaiah speaks of the coming Messiah and of the eternal satisfaction that will come with the harvest of souls as a result of His life of service and sacrifice.

Christ "made himself of no reputation, and took upon him the form of a servant . . . : he humbled himself, . . . even [to] the death of the cross" (Phil. 2:7, 8). How could Jesus Christ, a member of the Godhead, do this? How could He accept this humiliation and still preserve a sense of personal significance as God? Because His children mattered more to Him than anything else.

Every time we identify ourselves with others in order to help them and lead them to Christ, there is lasting satisfaction. The happy people are those not occupied with themselves, but those who live lives of unselfish service. We are made to love others. God has no plan to get us to heaven that ignores our relationship to other people. We can have too much money to be good for us. We can multiply riches and possessions on earth. After a while we get surfeited with them. But we can never give too much love to others. We can never have too much of the fruit of the Spirit—love, joy, peace—to shed abroad.

In the Bible God's children are called "servants." This involves a willingness to forsake privilege and status, to renounce position, never to rest satisfied until men and women are won back to God. Because Christ came down, we must come down. Every time we claim special privilege and recognition in order to gain self-importance we are in bondage to ourselves. If we fail to embrace others within Christ's love for us and our love for Him, then He has lived and died for us in vain.

When we view the truths we have in and of themselves, they are very impressive. But God judges nothing by itself, only in the use we make of it. In the last analysis, the central purpose of the church is to share the redeeming love of Christ with those around us. How vast is the worth of a soul before God.

# BORN BLIND

*Jesus saw a man blind from his birth. His disciples put the question, "Rabbi, who sinned, this man or his parents?" John 9:2, N.E.B.*

The disciples felt that someone was to blame for this poor man's condition. Who was it? Someone must have sinned along the way. Who could it be, the man himself or his parents? Jesus answered, Neither did this man sin nor his parents.

Christ is saying this: "Do not be so severe with your judgment of this man or his parents. Love thinketh no evil. God is not punishing these people for their sins." At times every one of us is inclined to call our own trials and tribulations accidents and those of our neighbors judgments of God. We hear something adverse about a neighbor—he was careless in his habits of eating, drinking, driving the car, or keeping the Sabbath. Maybe he had an accident. The temptation is to think that he got what was coming to him. He asked for it and he deserved it.

Christ's explanation for this man's blindness is very revealing: "That the works of God should be made manifest in him." In such cases our Christian attitude is not to criticize, but to go at once to help them. We are to consider that our meeting with such unfortunate people is God's way of providing us with the opportunity to serve.

I heard of a poor boy who became a Christian. He was without decent clothes to wear. One day a critic said to him, "If God is your Father and loves you, how can He possibly let you continue in such ragged clothing? Why does not your God see that you get some new clothes?" The boy finally spoke up and said, "I think that God asked someone to do that, but he has forgotten."

Even if we know that some people's misfortunes are the result of their sins and disobedience, let us not be hard on them. Such people do not need scolding or criticizing. They need loving. Those encompassed with infirmities are not sinners above ourselves.

God does not exploit His children. If through weakness and tribulation we learn of God's power to heal and to save, if through darkness we are prepared to receive the Light of the World, if through sickness we discover the Great Physician, then is it not better for us that we pass through these difficulties?

# BE NOT RIGHTEOUS OVER MUCH

*Be not righteous over much.* Eccl. 7:16.

The Christian life should be taken seriously, but not harshly. It is possible for our beliefs to be sound, our religious responsibility to the church never neglected, our moral conduct beyond reproach, and yet have the tendency to induce irritability, despair, and uneasiness in those about us. We may oppose the way this or that is being done in the church in such a way that is not really Christian.

It is so easy to have disparaging feelings toward another with whom we disagree. People get angry in debate and unchristian in their rejection of people, not because they are defending the truth, but because they defend the importance they have attached to themselves.

Suppose there is a newcomer among us who does not understand the teachings and doctrinal positions of our church, but who loves the Lord Jesus. Do we accept him as a fellow Christian? Well, doctrine is very important. But without love we have merely beliefs in doctrine and do not practice them on the inside. God is not doctrine. God is eternal purity, sweetness, righteousness, and love.

What saves and heals people? What awakens the hearts of people to desire Christ and His righteousness? What makes the flowers to grow? What makes the seeds to sprout after being planted? The frost does not help them. The icy ground does not awaken them. Not until the springtime comes, not until the soft rains find them, not until the sun, returning from the equator, sheds its warmth over them, do they grow. Then, in the warmth of the sun and the beauty of the skies and the gentle atmosphere, the seeds and flowers shoot up their stems and burst into bloom.

So it is with people. Not all the harshness, coldness, severity, and disdain can produce any life at all. It is not until we understand people and care, it is not until they see in us that Jesus loves, not until we share Christ's compassion, that they begin to feel life from God.

# THE GLORY OF ONENESS

*"It is not for these alone that I pray, but for those also who . . . put their faith in me; may they all be one: as thou, Father, art in me, and I in thee, so also may they be in us, that the world may believe that thou didst send me."* John 17:20, 21, N.E.B.

The basic need of us all is to be one with someone, to belong. We are persons. We stand over against one another often in a state of alienation because of sin and selfishness. Even in a crowd an individual can feel himself to be the loneliest person in the world. The world is filled with frightened and lonely people. We so easily create conditions of loneliness by our anxiety, self-reference, and distrust. We cannot hope to find within ourselves the oneness we need.

The good news of the gospel is God's gift of oneness in His Son, Jesus Christ. This is the essential meaning of the atonement—at-one-ment. God gives Himself to us. We become involved in the giving of ourselves to Him and to our fellow men.

God created persons to be loved and things to be used. He made us for personal relations and the world of things to serve a subordinate purpose. The temptation growing out of our insecurity is to love things and to use persons. When that happens we create unhappiness, especially in our homes. We lose our sense of self-worth. We resent being used.

Today man fearfully degrades other men. Men are desired, not for what they are in themselves, but for their functions. Every time we treat another person as a thing we degrade him. Every time we use him for a convenience we deny him dignity as a child of God.

God's supreme gift to us is this love relationship. Oneness is always the result of being loved. We want to be wanted, to be needed, to be valued. We can never reach maturity or fulfillment without the capacity to love and to be loved. We are to witness to this oneness of love with God and man. The test of our Christian experience is not what we do for the church as an institution, but what we do in relation to persons.

The message of the gospel is not what God requires of us, but what He gives to us: Himself, His love, His forgiveness.

# CALLED TO CONFESS CHRIST

*Whosoever therefore shall confess me before men, him will I confess also before my Father which is in heaven. Matt. 10:32.*

These words were spoken by our Lord in anticipation of times of trial. We are living in days that are akin to those of the disciples. Before the return of Christ there will be final conflicts and the great hour of temptation that will come upon the world. It is not enough to believe that we are Christians in our hearts. All men are to read in our lives an epistle written by the hand of Christ. The manner in which non-Christians see us every day is an indication of whether Christ dwells in our hearts. This is more than a simple statement about what we believe.

We confess with our mouths and with our lives. Neither by word nor by conduct are we to hesitate, to keep silent, or turn our backs on our Lord. No man belongs fully to Christ unless he is ready to lay down his life for the purpose of confessing Him. We all confess Jesus Christ in one way or another. We are to live as children of God called out of darkness into His marvelous light. We are to proclaim in all that we do and say the virtues of Him who has redeemed us. Our confession is to be the expression of Christ in us. The confession of Christ can be free and genuine outwardly only insofar as Christ is within us. A confession with the mouth without renouncing sin, without the corresponding heart experience, is hypocrisy.

We are to confess Christ with the spontaneity of love—gladly, willingly, boldly. So let the mechanic confess Christ in his workshop, the businessman in all his transactions, the mother in relation to her family, the doctor in his practice, the laborer in whatever he is called upon to do. Wherever we may be placed we are to consider our situation as an opportunity to confess the Lord.

The times are ripe for the confessing of Christ and His truth to the world. Let us leave behind our petty differences, our self-seeking, and our envies. Let those with whom we associate be constrained to look and to listen. Let there be in the church a great concert of harmony and praise to Him who has redeemed us.

# THE AUTHORITY OF GOD

*For he taught them as one having authority.* **Matt. 7:29.**

God comes first, not law. The Creator is free, but not creation. Creation is held in the grasp of Christ. All nature is under the sovereign sway of Him who made it. God created the law of gravitation. This is the way God runs our world and the planets. He never departs from it. We call this consistent operation "law." The sovereignty of Christ is first; then law, then freedom.

In the moral world the same order and supremacy prevail. The moral law is under Christ, our divine Lawgiver. These moral and spiritual principles are seen in God, in His character. The authority of His own character comes first. This constitutes what is known as truth. Absolute truth can be known. God has revealed it.

The moral law describes what God is, how He lives, how His creatures are made to live. Only as we live in harmony with God's law are we free. Outside of God's truth and authority we are enslaved.

The law of God does not say, "You may or you may not. What you do makes no difference. Just make up your mind." It invariably says, Thou shalt not kill, steal, bear false witness, and so on. We are commanded to believe the truth and then obey it. If we refuse, sin and transgression follow. We do not have the choice of disbelieving and disobeying the truth and still being free from sin.

We fulfill our lives as God intended, not by desiring to go our own way but by desiring to go God's way. The Christ-controlled man is the truly free man. What would happen to an airplane pilot who refused to follow the laws that involve the compass, or the laws of aerodynamics? Or one who insisted upon his freedom to take off in any way he wanted, or to land contrary to the established patterns and laws?

God is our moral and spiritual Pilot. The Bible is our chart and compass. We must not follow an independent course. We must shape our lives by the unerring needle of truth. The security of all life rests not upon human freedom, but upon divine authority; not upon individual caprice, but upon God's sovereign Person and Law.

# THE MORAL CODE: BANE OR BLESSING

*And he opened his mouth, and taught them, saying, Blessed are the poor in spirit: for their's is the kingdom of heaven. Matt. 5:2.*

It might be expected that Christ would call blessed those who have everything; those who are superior in talents and virtues, those with great abilities, those who are attractive and have fine personalities. We do that. We say that this person is blessed with this gift or that capacity. That is how we use the word. But Jesus does not use it that way. The blessed are those who need everything and receive everything from Him.

Christ found us poor and made us rich. He makes us the light of the world because He is our Light. The blessed do not make themselves light, truth, loving, patient, righteous. He also makes us the salt of the earth. We do not make ourselves that. In being made all this by Christ, we give praise to our Father in heaven.

Immediately following the praise of those who have nothing in themselves, Christ proceeds to show that such people must also take the law of God seriously. This seems so incongruous. Why emphasize obedience to the law, the jots and the tittles? How could this be a blessing? By the acknowledgment that in ourselves we are nothing and can do nothing. Totally dependent on Him, we have discovered the only way to obey the law of God.

Christ explains this further by a series of contrasts between the way the Pharisees read and kept the law and the way the Christian keeps it. "Ye have heard that it was said by them of old time, . . . but I say unto you." The Pharisees were motivated by the law. The Christian is motivated by love for Christ.

Jesus never credits His followers with the ability to obey the commandments. He knows we cannot do that. Jesus proclaims the bankruptcy of man to produce this kind of obedience that God requires. Jesus is not imposing a new set of rules on His followers.

But we are blessed because He has entered into our lives with resurrection life and power. In Christ, God has given us everything, including the power to keep His commandments. This is our blessedness.

# THE GOSPEL HONORS THE LAW

**All are justified by God's free grace alone. . . . Does this mean that we are using faith to undermine law? By no means: we are placing law itself on a firmer footing. Rom. 3:24-31, N.E.B.**

Men often speak of the law and the gospel in terms that imply an antagonism between them, whereas there is no antagonism. They belong together in God's plan for our lives. However, there is a difference between them.

There must be some way available in which obedience to the law and the will of God is possible for us as Christians, for the moral principles set forth in the Ten Commandments commend themselves to all sound-thinking men. The law of God condemns us, both Christian and non-Christian, for every violation of the law. Hence the need for the gospel as well as for the law. The law provides us with no power to obey. We must have sufficient resources to keep God's commandments. God has provided this in the gospel. Since Christ came to save from sin and the transgression of the law, we expect Him to do nothing less than that. By the power of the gospel, God promised to put His laws into our minds, and write them in our hearts (see Heb. 8:10).

With every demand that God makes, every requirement of the law that He has specified, He has provided us with the power to fulfill it. God fulfills His promise to do just that. The woman of Samaria asked for water and He gave her living water. David asked for a clean heart and he became a new man. Paul asked for light. Christ met him and enlightened his life.

Do not be afraid that God will make a demand on you that you will not have the strength to meet. God says to us: "Call on Me. Make demands on Me for strength. I will put a new heart in you. I will put a right spirit within you. I will be your patience, your purity, your obedience, your ability to live as I live." God's purpose is to restore men to virtue, righteousness, and obedience. But God alone can do it.

New life from God is brought into us. We are a new creation. We find Christ utterly reliable and trustworthy. "The righteousness of the law might be fulfilled in us, who walk not after the flesh, but after the Spirit" (Rom. 8:4).

7

# TRANSGRESSION OF THE LAW

*Whosoever committeth sin transgresseth also the law: for sin is the transgression of the law. 1 John 3:4.*

The law of God is called the moral law because it sets forth certain fundamental principles that distinguish between right and wrong. For any thought, desire, or conduct to be called sinful requires that moral issues be involved.

I have a tract entitled "One Hundred Sins of Which God's People Are Now Guilty." Why the writer arrived at one hundred and no more or less, is hard to tell. I am not at all sure that all the items mentioned can be classed as sins. The tract includes a multiplication of requirements and an appeal to all kinds of rules and regulations.

We should distinguish between rules and principles. Rules change, and vary in different parts of the world, in different countries and situations. Principles never change. They are eternally binding.

It is possible so to stress obedience to rules as to divert attention from the grosser sins: anger, jealousy, hatred, hostility, lust, idleness, malice, backbiting, and every shade of illicit pride. By accentuating the external "sins" we do not have, we may take an easy attitude towards the inner sins we do have. When every infraction of a rule is treated as a serious violation of a principle, religion increasingly creates guilt, anxiety, and condemnation. People cannot live with that, not for long. The cold morality of rules tends to become undiscriminating and heartless. We tend to become suspicious of people and neglect our responsibility as loving Christians.

A religion that condemns its members to a perpetual spring cleaning and continued guilt feelings is futile. When love to God rules, there is little need for continual purgation as a separate process.

No peril is greater than the substitution of external acts for the sincere commitment of the heart. It is much easier to give lip service to the rules than it is to commit ourselves to the living Christ. The sins of the spirit in Christ's judgment are the skeletons in the closet, the "dead men's bones." By the Spirit we delight in the law of God.

# OVERCOMING

*He that overcometh shall inherit all things.* **Rev. 21:7.**

The Bible closes with a great acclamation of victory. When we consider the triumph of God's last message to the world, it surges up in us with a great outburst of hope and glory. The hour of Christ's return will be the hour of supreme honor and distinction for us. Let us believe that, in the end, every true though obscure disciple will receive direct and personal recognition throughout all the universe. "He that overcometh, the same shall be clothed in white raiment; and . . . I will confess his name before my Father, and before his angels" (Rev. 3:5). Let us banish forever from our mind all doubt as to the Lord's willingness and power to keep us from falling. Let us commit ourselves to be kept by Him. There is one type of Christian no one in the universe will have any doubt about—he whose allegiance is unquestioned regardless of the circumstances.

In our whole life we are to come forth as victor, not as vanquished. It is to him that overcomes that the great promises of the book of Revelation are given. We either overcome the world or are overcome by it. Either we are the master of sin or the slave of sin. The man of the world is either the slave or the master of his business. The man of money either keeps it under his feet or is trampled under its feet. We are to gain the mastery of all these things, to render force to our characters, to make us even better and stronger men and women of God, to mellow our lives into a fuller and deeper relationship to God.

In the cause of Christ, let there be no doubt as to where we stand. We are standard-bearers for God in the midst of a world that is descending into darkness. Every one of us who is in Christ has the divine power to conquer the world, the flesh, and the devil. In Him we are stronger than circumstances, stronger than sin and the devil.

We could not live such a life without God's promises of victory being fulfilled to us. In spite of every discouragement, in spite of temptation, in spite of suffering and death itself, Christ has given us a moral and spiritual vitality and power that overcomes.

# MORAL CERTAINTY

*The Lord is well pleased for his righteousness' sake; he will magnify the law, and make it honourable. Isa. 42:21.*

Christian morality is founded upon the revelation of God at Sinai and the word of Christ in the Sermon on the Mount. Our moral obligation to God is central. Hence the norm for us is Christ, His giving of the law, His exaltation of it. The morality that the Christian faith inspires and demands is never the product of human situations and human experience. Christian morality is always ahead of human progress. It takes into consideration every possible human situation to the end of time.

We need always to be receptive to moral guidance from God and not from man. The free mercy and influence of a loving God exercised toward us in our varying circumstances does not change the moral principles eternal in God. The truth of Christ is to possess and guide our minds and lives. We must maintain the moral law of God pure from all the infiltrations of sinful man, who is at enmity with the law.

The law of heaven should be the law of this world and all the people who live in it. Moral deficiency in all men due to sin is bad enough. But willful departure from the law and rejection is outright opposition to God. Sinful men have an urge to argue against the nature of the moral law rather than to practice it. But no man is wise enough to provide his own moral direction, or powerful enough to obey God's commandments.

We are answerable to God and not to man. We test our lives by God's standard, not by human situations. We cannot have it both ways. When the moral law as God gave it is proclaimed to the world, then men hear the word and the truth from God and not from man.

We seek no continuance or increase of men's guilt and condemnation, but only to show sinners the need for the saving gospel of Jesus Christ. In this way God's law is magnified and made honorable. We cannot know what is good or evil from within ourselves. We can know it only from the Bible. The Ten Commandments are more timely than ever. The law of God is not obsolete and never will be. We have no other God. We worship no other God than the God who gave us the Decalogue.

# CONSCIENCE AND THE MORAL LAW

*And herein do I exercise myself, to have always a conscience void of offence toward God, and toward men. Acts 24:16.*

Today there is great need of a moral sense that fits the mind and the law of God. We are to abound more and more in the moral and spiritual stature of Christ.

The record of man's sinful history is one of setting his own moral code over against that of God. Nothing but a firm belief in the divine revelation of God's moral law at Sinai and in Christ's Sermon on the Mount can cleanse the conscience and develop high moral character. A loss of confidence in, or disdain of, the law of God has always led to a moral decline.

Unfortunately, almost all of us from time to time become affected by the universal letting down of moral standards. We are assailed by the warped moral judgments of men and their moral situation excuses. We need not only the knowledge of moral standards, but the power to obey them. By itself the moral code cannot make us obedient. Without the gospel we are left to do everything ourselves. We must start with Jesus Christ, with the gospel and its saving power.

"Hereby we do know that we know him, if we keep his commandments" (1 John 2:3). None of us can escape this clear statement. If we really claim to know God, we must take His answer. Nothing can exceed the absolute plainness, the simplicity of Christ's teaching. "The end of the commandment is charity out of a pure heart, and of a good conscience, and of faith unfeigned" (1 Tim. 1:5). Let us not argue about the meaning of the word "commandment." When the young ruler asked our Lord, "Which commandments?" He directed him to the Ten. Would that all Christians would ask Christ the same question and accept the same answer.

God could have made it impossible for us to break His commandments. But then God would never find out just what kind of people we are. We are nothing if we are not capable of making the right moral choices and developing a moral character akin to that of Christ. But with people who are like Christ, God will have no problem in creating a new heaven and a new earth.

# THE WITNESS OF OUR CONSCIENCE

*For our rejoicing is this, the testimony of our conscience.* **2 Cor. 1:12.**

"Let your conscience be your guide" is an oft-repeated phrase. Thousands of people believe that if they live according to this principle, they fulfill their moral responsibility to God and man. Yet many of these people lack discriminating judgment on moral issues.

Conscience is not a separate moral faculty, but the function of the mind discriminating between right and wrong. While God speaks to us through this moral sense, conscience does not tell us what is right. We do not possess within ourselves the ability to discover or learn what our moral responsibilities are. Conscience cannot discover what is right and wrong. This we get from God and from His moral law.

Men often assume that the dictate of conscience is the moral standard by which to live. This is a dangerous error, for men may not develop a good conscience but a depraved, weak, seared one. Then the conscience renders false moral judgments or no judgment at all.

God requires that we take our moral standard from Him and not from ourselves. We are to judge the moral situations and acts of men from the immaculate purity and righteousness of God's character, the holiness of His law, and in the light of Jesus Christ.

Every moral act and response becomes significant when illuminated by the revealed truth of God. To neglect developing our moral sensitivity according to the moral perfection of God can only make us a law unto ourselves.

Some years ago I held a series of public evangelistic meetings. A man who held an important position in another religious body attended the services. When I confronted him with God's requirement in the fourth commandment, he said to me, "I know what the law of God says. But I am not going to change. I am not going to let it bother me. I intend to go on letting my conscience be my guide."

It is a small matter that we be judged by man's standards. It is of supreme importance that we be judged by God's moral code. Here we can take our stand. Here we wait for God's final vindication of us.

# OBEDIENCE BY THE HOLY SPIRIT—1

*The commandment of the law may find fulfilment in us, whose conduct, no longer under the control of our lower nature, is directed by the Spirit.* **Rom. 8:4, N.E.B.**

In our day the moral condition of the world is ominous. Morality has become a matter of expediency. Sharp-witted fraud has taken the place of sterling integrity. Self-interest has supplanted allegiance to moral principles. We now face the dread possibility of living in a pagan society.

The morality or immorality of our nation determines its destiny. It reveals whether we have chosen to live under the Lordship of Christ or under the dominion of sin and Satan. So long as we do the first, there remains in the world a people that constitute the church of God. The need in every area of life is obedience to the law of God by the power of the gospel.

Jesus Christ did not come to this earth to release anyone from the obligation to keep His commandments. He came to bring salvation from sin. He sends His Holy Spirit to renew us, so that the law is truly fulfilled in our lives. If this transforming work by the power of the Holy Spirit is denied or rejected, there can be no such fulfillment as is promised by our Lord.

There are two roads we can take. We can let this virus of disobedience and lawlessness infect us. We can let the immorality of the world deceptively invade our lives and our homes, until we are no longer alarmed at the license taken with the moral principles of God. We can then regard sin in a softer light than God does.

Or we can, by our personal commitment, let the Holy Spirit impart moral excellence in us. Jesus is perfect love, perfect honesty, perfect unselfishness, perfect obedience to the law of God. God gave His Son that through Him He could communicate His own character of righteousness to us. Through the Holy Spirit, Christ provides us with the power and the motivation to keep His commandments in the same way that He kept them. This is the proof that we have the Holy Spirit who fulfills the law of God in us. This is one of the great blessings of the gospel.

# OBEDIENCE BY THE HOLY SPIRIT—2

*Do we then make void the law through faith? God forbid: yea, we establish the law. Rom. 3:31.*

There is widespread deception and misunderstanding as to the relation of the law and the gospel. There is a way of interpreting the love of God that fosters deception and leads to continuance in sin. The claims of Christ are ignored.

The religion of some people exhausts itself in amens and hallelujahs. Isolate them from the electricity of certain crowded assemblies and passionate appeals, and their spiritual fervor and devotion evaporate.

Let God's remnant people be aware that no amount of religious enthusiasm can make right any departure from the will of God. We have chosen the moral and spiritual life of our Lord. We have determined to tread the path of obedience under God, regardless of whether we have to do it alone. In reality we can say, "Whom have I in heaven but thee? And having thee, I desire nothing else on earth" (Ps. 73:25, N.E.B.).

Let us cleave to Him when the pulse beats low, when the feelings are depressed and things do not go so well. He will never forsake us. His presence is our joy. Let His approval, "Blessed are they that do his commandments, that they may have right to the tree of life, and may enter in through the gates into the city" (Rev. 22:14), be our exceeding great reward.

There is no guarantee that in the end we shall not have to stand alone. In spite of isolation and solitude on the earth, if we have to take that kind of stand, we can know that morally and spiritually we are one with Christ, that we are never alone.

The Holy Spirit is the key both to our obedience and to our oneness with God. There is no way to interpret this as legalism. By the power of the Spirit our lives are patterned after our Lord. The desire to keep the commandments as an expression of our oneness with God is neither impossible nor hopeless. The experience of living in harmony with Christ distinguishes us from those who refuse to obey God's commandments. "By this we know that we love the children of God, when we love God, and keep his commandments. . . . And his commandments are not grievous" (1 John 5:2, 3).

# ABIDING IN THE TRUE VINE

*I am the true vine. . . . Abide in me, and I in you. As the branch cannot bear fruit of itself . . . ; no more can ye, except ye abide in me. John 15:1-4.*

In our world there is an almost irresistible urge to water down the truth, the genuine thing. Truth has become wrapped up in clichés, phrases, words, cautious statements. It is that error that leads us to believe that we are in the truth by virtue of our sound thinking and arguing for it, rather than upon the spiritual renovation of our lives by the indwelling of the genuine person of Jesus Christ.

The inner transformation of our lives will not be realized by some final consistency in our logic, however important that might be. Being a genuine Christian is beyond the power of merely smart discussion on the subject. The use of a brilliant mind in the search for truth does not guarantee that a man is a Christian or ever will be one.

Valuable as all our discussions about the truth are, we only become genuine Christians when we take our stand within God's saving action in Christ. The consciousness of personal commitment to and personal union with Christ is the unique and distinctive feature of the Christian religion. The reality of salvation is in our relation to a living Person rather than in the adoption of opinions and conclusions of men. We are involved in truth only insofar as we are united with Christ as the branch is to the vine, as the arm is united to the body.

Both an intellectual understanding of truth and our involvement in it are necessary. If we know truth only as information, we have only a partial and restricted view. We are not actually living the truth. The problem for some people is not that they do not believe in God intellectually, but they do not find Him real. Maybe all we have is logic.

Do you believe that nature with her mountains, seas, lakes, forests, and flowers is beautiful? Of course—it is all there to see. But do you get a personal thrill when your heart is captivated by all this beauty? Do you believe in a Christian home? Do you find that Christian marriage is most satisfying and fulfilling? Whatever you are involved with becomes morally and spiritually decisive and controlling. Real friendship does not come at the end of an argument; neither does God.

# "THE WHOLE DUTY OF MAN"

*Let us hear the conclusion of the whole matter: Fear God, and keep his commandments: for this is the whole duty of man. Eccl. 12:13.*

What is the whole matter of which this verse is the conclusion? The matter is Solomon's own experience. He has had every opportunity to enjoy all that the human soul could possibly desire. He has his fill of everything. Finally, he is totally disillusioned with it all. His conclusion: "Vanity of vanities . . . ; all is vanity" (Eccl. 12:8).

In our day of advancement in every field of knowledge and endeavor, we have undoubtedly excelled Solomon. He was convinced, however, that there is no solid happiness or security to be found in this world outside of harmony with God's righteous character as seen in the commandments. To fear God and obey Him constitutes man's whole being. In any case, God will bring us to judgment to reveal what choices we have made.

To speak of keeping the commandments as an essential aspect of our whole duty to God might sound like legalism to some. But this is to miss the point. The issue is: how do we stand in relation to God, which is a moral relationship? Whose righteousness will sit in judgment on our morality?

Every act of obedience and faithfulness to God and His commandments brings us into harmony with Him. Christ came into the world to restore us to harmony with God. Obedience is the best evidence that this harmony is being realized. In proportion as we love God enough to obey Him, He will in the judgment pronounce the verdict in our favor.

The law of God should constitute no problem for Christians. It is a revelation of the very moral heart of God to us. The closer we come to Christ, the more our lives are marked with the same moral principles.

When Solomon wanted to make sure that he was right with God, in harmony with Him as against the world, this statement in Ecclesiastes was his conclusion. What evidence do we have that we have reversed the course of our lives from earthly things to the divine, from sin to God? Indeed, it is a serious thing to live in harmony with God. There is no sanction for transgression either in thought or in deed.

## "SLAVES OF RIGHTEOUSNESS"

*God be thanked, you, who once were slaves of sin, . . . have become slaves of righteousness.* **Rom. 6:17, 18, N.E.B.**

At the heart of being a Christian there lies a seriousness about life. We are summoned to a different kind of life. Commitment to Christ, being born again of the Holy Spirit, always creates in us the desire to obey God and keep His commandments. This is the evidence that Christ lives in us. Disobedience to God denies the existence of this new life.

Unfortunately, too many professed Christians find the word *obedience* not only disturbing but unacceptable. If salvation is by grace and by faith alone, they ask, why emphasize and insist upon obedience? Men tend to reject what they consider as divine pressure. Obedience smacks of the lack of freedom, they believe. People want an easy, relaxed type of living. A disciplined life of obedience to a whole set of commandments and laws seems quite undesirable where love, joy, and peace reign.

This is an age that lacks discipline and hardness, so necessary for good soldiers of Jesus Christ. People have become morally and spiritually soft in so many ways. Almost everything about the present life tends to undermine the moral fiber. It is so easy to allow a touch of this moral sickness to pervade our lives.

Do you think it is of any use to call yourself a Christian and yet not be a Christian in heart and conduct? Have you an enemy? Then this very day forgive him. Have you wronged another? Then this very day make restitution. Have you said things that are not true? Then this very day repent and tell the truth. Are you living two lives, of which one is self-deceiving hypocrisy? Then tear off the mask. Before Christ entreat Him to make you true. Are you stained through and through with impurity? Then come to Him as did the leper and cry, "Lord, if thou wilt, thou canst make me clean." Christ will reply, "I will, be thou clean." So shall you experience salvation from sin, the strength of His presence unto righteousness. So shall you find approval of God and the certainty of His acceptance, "Hereby we do know that we know him, if we keep his commandments."

# "SINGLENESS OF HEART"

*In singleness of heart, fearing God: and whatsoever ye do, do it heartily, as to the Lord, and not unto men. Col. 3:22, 23.*

Where sin is cherished in any form, we are double minded in serving God. We are not altogether committed to Christ. Our sins may be cast down without being cast off. They may be dislodged in part, without being destroyed. Great is the deceitfulness of sin. If all our partially buried idols could be resurrected, if all our secret sympathy with sin could be discerned and acknowledged, we might be shocked to find how adulterated is our profession of the Christian faith.

Wherever we find strength and beauty of Christian character, we may be sure that they spring from the roots of the heart that have struck deep in everlasting truth and love of Jesus Christ. Our life is independent of outward circumstances and what men think. We are no longer moved by every wind of doctrine, nor captivated by lurid literature or corrupting movies. We make no surrender whatsoever to immoral practices approved by law and organizations. The life and beauty of the mountain flowers are safe against the wind and the storm because they are set in the clefts of the rocks. The Christian with singleness of mind is united with Christ, our Rock and our Fortress.

We need to see the importance of complete consecration to Christ. A secret clinging to sin means weakness, peril, and ultimate failure. "A double minded man is unstable in all his ways" (James 1:8). It discolors our judgments, saps our will power, impedes our spiritual progress. The day will come when our secret sins and motives will be set in the light of God's presence. We may disguise our sins before men. We may seek to hide and excuse our compromises. But there comes a time when we can no longer conceal our divided heart.

The consecrated Christian regards the good, the pure, the honest, the beautiful with enjoyment and enthusiasm, the evil and the ugly with abhorrence. We find disloyalty impossible, not only when it involves poverty and sacrifice, but when it is profitable. Paul speaks of our "being dead to sin." How completely this truth cuts us off from sin. How utterly it separates us from all ungodliness.

# THE OBEDIENCE OF FAITH

*And hereby we do know that we know him, if we keep his command-*
*ments.* 1 John 2:3.

Some years ago a minister went to visit one of the poorest
of his parishioners, taking with him a gift of money to pay the
woman's rent. But there was no response to his knocking. So
he finally left. Yet the woman was inside her house all the time.
When she learned later of the minister's call and his generous
intention, she said: "I heard the knocking on the door. I never
thought my minister had come with a gift. I thought it was
the landlord demanding my rent."

Many professed Christians interpret the divine claim for
obedience to the commandments as a demand rather than a
gift of God. They assume that God has laid down a set of laws,
and that it is up to the believer to make the proper payment
by living up to them.

Christianity is not first a demand. It is first the gift of God's
saving righteousness to us in His Son Jesus Christ. At the same
time God insists that if we really know Him, we will also obey
Him. He who truly knows God is to make no truce with evil,
no halting between two opinions.

The Bible says that when the Israelites tramped through
the wilderness for forty years, their clothes and shoes waxed
not old upon them. A later writer wrote a legend embellishing
this account. According to the legend, as the children grew
so did their clothes and shoes—the little Hebrew boy who
crossed the Red Sea in boy's clothes wore the same clothes
when he crossed Jordan into the Promised Land forty years
later. Interpreters of the legend came to regard it as a parable
of a man's life with God. As men grow old in years and experience, the garment of Christ's righteousness given to the believer when he accepted Christ, fulfills all the spiritual needs of
the passing years.

As we hear His call to obedience, shall we reply that it is an
impossible thing? Or shall we say, "O Christ, You are my life. I
truly know You whom to know is life eternal. Your righteousness never fails. You are the same yesterday, today, and forever. Keep me clothed with Your righteousness until the day
when I shall stand in Your presence."

# DO NOT TAMPER WITH SIN

*And Hazael said, Why weepeth my lord? And he answered, Because I know the evil that thou wilt do unto the children of Israel. . . . And Hazael said, But what, is thy servant a dog, that he should do this great thing?* **2 Kings 8:12, 13.**

Elisha the prophet had left Israel and gone to Damascus, the capital of Syria. Benhadad the king was sick. When he heard of Elisha's coming, he sent Hazael, his trusted servant, with splendid gifts, to inquire whether he would recover. The prophet stated that there was no reason why the king should not recover his health. Then he gave Hazael a long and meaningful look, till the latter's eyes fell and his cheeks flushed with guilt. Elisha wept as he foretold what Hazael was about to do, beginning with the murder of the king. Hazael responded with horror. He denied he would ever do such things. But he did.

How can men come to do such things? No man comes to be a thief, a killer, a liar, in a day. He comes to it little by little. Undoubtedly Hazael had entertained an increasing ambition to be king. Lucifer started out this way when he declared his intention to be like the Most High. Eventually he was cast out of heaven to lead a rebellion against God.

If someone came to you and predicted that the time would come when you would leave the church, go the way of the world, become involved in all kinds of sin, you might respond with horror at such a thought. Or suppose you were told that one day you would betray your wife and children, that your home would then be broken up. You might reply: "Am I a dog; am I such a mean and contemptible person as to do such a thing? That is impossible."

No man is safe who does not keep his heart and mind true to God. We must abhor all evil and love uprightness. There are a thousand and one temptations to compromise, that wear away the edges of loyalty to God; thoughts and doubtful liberties that weaken the power of resistance, that lower the tone of morality. They are full of deadly peril.

# THE DECEPTION OF SIN

*Put on the whole armour of God, that ye may be able to stand against the wiles of the devil.* **Eph. 6:11.**

This generation tells us that sin, if it is sin, is safe. It swears to us that sin is innocent. Dishonesty, immorality, all manner of vice, stride boldly in every city. There are thousands of so-called moral adjustments and ten thousand disguised ambiguities to integrity that encourage disloyalty to truth and uprightness. There are millions of liberties that men take that tend to wear away confidence in the moral standards of the Bible, that sear the conscience and destroy sensitiveness to truth.

Alexander Pope wrote:

> Vice is a monster of so frightful mien,
> As to be hated needs but to be seen;
> Yet seen too oft, familiar with her face,
> We first endure, then pity, then embrace.

Satan's technique is to excite the imagination, then arouse the desires and the urges, and finally persuade the will. Achan said, when confronted with his descent into sin, "I saw, I coveted, I took." The ten plagues have visited our literature, our music, our pleasures and entertainments. They have been let loose upon our homes and families. Have any of the commercialized places of entertainment ever made any concessions to virtue and to righteousness? A saint of old reproached the devil for stealing a young man found at a degrading house of entertainment. The devil promptly replied, "I found him on my premises, and I took him."

What kind of husband or wife do we want? What kind of children do we desire to grow up in our homes? What kind of security do we provide for our families? Today there are endless lusts of the flesh, moral deceptions that delude the brain with appeals to license. Pleasure is offered in its gayest, boldest, and most fascinating forms.

Above all this Jesus Christ offers us an abundance of all that is true and beautiful. The power of God "casts down all imaginations and every high thought." The abundance of Christ's purity and love summons us. The eternal love of the Father constrains us. We are to let the elevating power of the Holy Spirit conquer our minds.

# "THE LAW OF THE SPIRIT OF LIFE"

*The law of the Spirit of life in Christ Jesus hath made me free from the law of sin and death. . . . That the righteousness of the law might be fulfilled in us, who walk not after the flesh, but after the Spirit.* **Rom. 8:2-4.**

The Holy Spirit takes the law of God seriously. So must we. The Christian can obey God's will only as he is led by the Spirit. The demand of a cold law as such can only drive men to despair. Men do not have it within themselves to obey God's commandments. Jesus never credited man with the power to keep His law. Spiritually man in himself is bankrupt. He cannot change himself.

This is why the Christian lives by faith. Faith means entire dependence on God. By faith the believer lets the Holy Spirit have His way. The Spirit keeps the believer in a right relationship to God. The gift of the Spirit is not another law. He is a personal Presence, the power by which the Christian fulfills the righteousness of the law.

Can Jesus be that real to us through the Holy Spirit? That is what Christ promised. The Holy Spirit is to be our teacher, our guide, our intercessor, our life, and our spiritual power. He makes real a permanent fellowship and a constant walk with God. There can be no substitute for Christ's presence by the Spirit. That alone makes a man a Christian. That alone deals effectively with the temptations of the devil.

The Christian should refrain from all expressions of religion or interpretations of the Bible that imperil the eternal sacredness of the moral code of the Ten Commandments and the will of God. We do not mean by this to disparage the gift of God or deny salvation by grace alone. What is insisted upon is that a life with God by the Spirit does not deny, dilute, or reject the requirements of God's Word. The Bible knows nothing of faith in Christ that falls short of the moral integrity and good works of a life that is right with God. Obedience is the evidence that one is right with God. It is not the means of making oneself right. The works of faith carry no merit with God. The Holy Spirit ignores no part of man. He directs the whole of man: his mind, his conduct, his basic desires. He fills the life with the noblest ideals. His presence brings the life into full harmony with God.

# THE OBEDIENCE OF LOVE

*For this is the love of God, that we keep his commandments: and his commandments are not grievous.* 1 John 5:3.

Some professed Christians believe that all we need is love, that the Decalogue can be dispensed with. This text asserts that love inspires obedience, which is man's proper response to the law of God. The redeeming love of God that forgives our sins also fulfills in us the righteousness of the law (Rom. 8:3, 4). Without love, the commandments are beyond our power to obey. Class assignments to children are grievous when they are beyond their mental capacity. Government taxes are destructive when they are beyond the power of people to pay.

What the law could not do, the love of God empowers man to do. The love of God is not a theory for the mind to ponder. It is a vital motivating force. Filled with love for God and man, the keeping of the commandments becomes easy. Man delights in the law of God. The inner force of love is now equal to the external demands of the law.

In recent years important undersea expeditions have been undertaken at hitherto unknown depths. There man is conditioned to swim freely at depths that before would have crushed him. Men have now learned to balance and equalize the inner power of the body with the external pressure of the sea. The pressure of the water is no burden to the swimmer.

So it is with the power of God's love and the requirements of God's law. Without the inner power of the Spirit, the demands of the law are an impossibility. It could only condemn and oppress the sinner. Because of God's power in the life, man now keeps God's commandments. The Christian finds the whole of his mind and life so filled with Christ's presence that obedience follows naturally and spontaneously. If we feel that the requirements of God's Word are a grievous burden, then the indication is that our inner life with God needs attention, restoration, and empowering by the Holy Spirit.

Loving obedience is the realization of our true relationship to God. As the earth moves on its divinely appointed axis, so man needs a Center, Jesus Christ. Love to God keeps man on center. He moves from hate to love, from disobedience to obedience, from death to life.

# "AN ANSWER TO EVERY MAN"

*Be ready always to give an answer to every man that asketh you a reason of the hope that is in you with meekness and fear.* **1 Peter 3:15.**

People often conceive of defense in terms of controversy. At times Christians will fight for the truth. But we ought not to conceive of defense of the truth in terms of a controversial spirit. Much controversy loses its sense of proportion. Minor issues become major. Major truths are lost to view. People ride hobbies. Phrases are elevated to the place of facts. Group labels crowd out distinctions of character. Discussion often falls into the hands of incompetent practitioners.

When we think of the throbbing world needs to which our church appeals, and of the restless search of great multitudes for a divine message that has the ring of truth and reality about it, any reduction of the gospel and the truth to the level of bickering is tragic. People get weary of doubt and negation.

Those who habitually raise questions or make denials respecting the Word of God are barren of positive realities. There are times when we need to make a critical investigation as to what we believe. But witnessing positively and constructively from our own experience with Christ gets results. That persuades. That edifies. Nothing so persuades the mind and wins people to the truth as does an enthusiastic witness to the great affirmatives of our message.

Personally, I have always believed that my church is challenging the youth with the greatest moral and spiritual assignment in two millenniums. The third angel's message is for all of us an eternal matter, not of sham or figment, but of life or death. It is supremely needful for men everywhere. It is needful for every professing Christian who would fain hide and pride himself under an easy conformity to the faith. It is needful for every one of us, who, desiring sincerity and genuineness above all things, would fain see the return of Christ in our generation. Are we keeping, not as a dead letter, but as the living word of God to us, those plain, unvarnished Ten Commandments, the laws of honesty, kindness, purity, and truth, without which the gospel message is an idle name? He that abideth in Christ "ought himself also so to walk, even as he walked" (1 John 2:6).

# CHRISTIAN COURAGE

*"My God sent his angel to shut the lions' mouths." . . . So Daniel was lifted out and no trace of injury was found on him, because he had put his faith in his God.* **Dan. 6:22-24, N.E.B.**

No one respects a coward. Whatever else a man may not have, if he has courage he is able to salvage something of his life. These days it takes moral courage to live right. The time will surely come when you will have to stand alone for what you believe.

Daniel and the three Hebrews in Babylon were no followers of the crowd. They did not ascertain first how the others were going to vote before they made up their mind on the stand they intended to take. These men were right. The rest were dead wrong.

Why did not the lions devour Daniel? Why did not the fire consume Shadrach, Meshach, and Abednego? Ask God about that. They lived close to God, so close as to make them independent of men. The Bible tells the fate of two cities where evil and immorality had become their trademark—Sodom and Gomorrah. Remember! Ask God about that, too. Under the rule of Adolph Hitler, millions of Jews were destroyed. Multitudes of decent religious people closed their eyes, their noses, and their ears. They were unwilling to take a stand while there was time. Then it was too late. A Christian has no right to back down on moral issues at any time. We can always be in the right when we do what God wants us to do.

"If we say that we have fellowship with him, and walk in darkness, we lie, and do not the truth" (1 John 1:6). What is the true test of fellowship with God? It is quite simple. "He that doeth righteousness is righteous" (chap. 3:7). He that has the fruit of the Spirit is born of the Spirit.

Daniel and his fellows did something for all of us who have come after. When many others acceded to pagan worship, they stood firm. Because they were true and faithful and strong by God's strength, the cause of God became more triumphant in the earth. God's presence in life is more real to us because they lived. Their courage and integrity can be ours, too, as we walk with God. Faithfulness to our Lord, certainty of divine strength, victory over all our enemies—all this belongs to us.

# GOD'S SABBATH REST

*Therefore, a sabbath rest still awaits the people of God; for anyone who enters God's rest, rests from his own work as God did from his. Heb. 4:9, 10, N.E.B.*

God gave the Sabbath as a sign of that rest that follows His work both in the creation of our world, in a completed redemption, and in our own hearts. Ultimately we will enter into the eternal Sabbath rest of God.

The children of Israel did not rest by faith in God's promises to give them the land of Canaan. They sought it by their own works. Had they looked to Him as their righteousness, God would have fulfilled His promise of rest. "Israel made great efforts after a law of righteousness, but never attained to it. Why was this? Because their efforts were not based on faith, but (as they supposed) on deeds" (Rom. 9:31, 32, N.E.B.).

Truly our own works to gain favor with God and to attain to our own righteousness are a great grief and burden. We double the load on our backs. The effort we put into living the Christian life, effort that never gets us any nearer to the ideal, is discouraging and painful. To work for our salvation is beyond our strength. There is no rest. There follow only fear, anxiety, and condemnation.

We are to live in the atmosphere of God's love. We are to trust and depend entirely on Christ and His righteousness. We find rest and spiritual refreshment in fellowship with Him. Only through the merits of Christ can we find this rest. This is how we prepare for the rest in heaven.

The Christian life lived within the rest of God is delightful. The rest from sin, the rest from our own efforts to achieve righteousness, is one of the great gifts God can bestow on us here below. Paul calls all this a Sabbath rest. For it reveals what it must have been like when God finished His work of creation and rested on the seventh day. Everything in the world was perfect. The only thing left to be done was to enjoy it. Rest in the new earth will be like this.

The Sabbath is a day of well-being and well doing, a day when everyone is made better and happier. We have turned over the responsibility of living the Christian life to Him. The Sabbath rest is always to be the best day in the week.

# GOD'S REST FOR THE WORLD'S UNREST

*Let us therefore fear, lest, a promise being left us of entering into his rest, any of you should seem to come short of it.* **Heb. 4:1.**

You and I are more than beasts that perish. We are the redeemed sons and daughters of God. There is something in us and about us that can only be satisfied with God.

Often the work of the week lays burdens upon us and brings anxiety and care. Each Sabbath we come to cast our load of care on Him. Our hearts are touched with His love. We find rest unto our souls. His peace and presence are given to us. We come to church with no haunting fear that we must effect our salvation, that we must contrive some plan for our release from sin and failure. In Christ our salvation and redemption are complete.

We hear of unfinished symphonies, but there is nothing unfinished in the symphony of Christ's righteousness that He offers to us. When Christ cried out on Calvary, "It is finished," He entered into that Sabbath rest of a completed redemption. The price of sin was paid. A perfect righteousness was offered to us in Christ. Not one thing more needed to be done. Then He rested in the tomb throughout the holy hours of the Sabbath. Was there any more beautiful rest than that? Christ met all the requirements for our salvation.

The Sabbath has always been a sign of God's completed work: of a completed work when He made the earth, of a completed redemption when He died for us. In the earth made new "it shall come to pass, that from one new moon to another, and from one sabbath to another, shall all flesh come to worship before me, saith the Lord" (Isa. 66:23). When the earth is recreated and restored to its original perfection, the Sabbath will still be the sign of God's finished work.

It is urgent that we enter into God's rest here and now. His gift to us is a perfect righteousness in His Son, to which nothing needs to be added. In Him we have complete forgiveness and acceptance. We lack nothing. "With all this in mind, what are we to say? If God is on our side, who is against us? He did not spare his own Son, but gave him up for us all; and with this gift how can he fail to lavish upon us all he has to give?" (Rom. 8:31, 32, N.E.B.).

213

# FREEDOM

*And ye shall know the truth, and the truth shall make you free. . . . If the Son therefore shall make you free, ye shall be free indeed.* John 8:32-36.

Some years ago a student at a university challenged me concerning my faith. He said, "I would not shackle my mind as you do. I am free. You are bound. You cannot do what you want to do. I can do anything that my heart desires."

What is freedom? First, there is freedom as opposed to necessity to think a certain way. We are all free to think either one way or another. We are not bound to think alike. The Christian faith does not deny us this freedom of thought. It asserts it. Man is indeed free to choose what he will believe.

Second, men speak of freedom as opposed to authority. Christianity comes with an offer of freedom, yet with a claim of authority. In life both freedom and authority come together. Everywhere in life we submit to authority. No man begins from scratch to start over again in the sphere of medicine, science, mechanics, or any other profession. The more free we are in our judgments and decisions, the more readily we submit to authority. God comes with authority: "Thus saith the Lord." He submits to our judgment and free thought His reasons why we should believe and build our lives on the truth He gives to us.

Third, men also speak of freedom as opposed to responsibility. This is where the shoe pinches, where the opposition and enmity of men arise. God offers us freedom. He is sovereign. But man is responsible. Freedom is possible only through harmony between God and ourselves.

In the natural world, does freedom from natural law allow freedom from responsibility? Let any man think that water does not drown, that fire does not burn, that sin does not bring disease and death. These laws that govern life will not change by a hair's breadth. We disobey them at our peril.

A man is not free who cannot stop sinning. Transgression of God's law in the name of freedom will not work because it is not true. We cannot say, "I will be free but not through Christ." We cannot free ourselves, else the Son would never have come to free us. We can be free only by the truth as it is in Jesus.

# LIFE AND DOCTRINE

*But speak thou the things which become sound doctrine.* **Titus 2:1.**

A religion without distinctive beliefs is a religion without backbone. A religion without the truths of the Bible is a religion without salvation. People want to be stirred, to be moved. But the stirring of emotions is not enough. We must have a definite form of truth that is clear to the mind.

The realm of faith is not apart from the realm of the best and the clearest thinking on the great truths of the Bible. Faith involves our whole personality. Any appeal for faith remains futile unless it involves the free activity of the mind. Were our faith less than this, there would be no way of knowing whether our religious experience is based on truth or error. Biblical faith comes from the Word of God. The personal understanding of God's truth, the response of our hearts and minds, are embodied in our faith.

Those who do not wish to think through the teachings of the Bible settle for some feeling in the emotions. It is so convenient. Anyone can use it regardless of what he believes.

This is a day when men perish for lack of knowledge of God's Word and truth. Until this is restored, there can be no genuine revival of true godliness. Not that the diligent study of God's Word reduces religion to a letter of the law. Rather it is the refusal to commit one's life to obey the truth. We are to love God with all our minds as well as with our hearts.

There are Christians who fear to bring their minds to bear upon the whole truth of the Word of God lest they should lose their heart experience of God. That reveals a serious misgiving and distrust about their faith. Our deepest love for God and man proceeds from a heart and mind that are instructed in the truth. The greater the experience of love becomes, the deeper and clearer is the knowledge of God and His Word. They love God truly today who gaze upon Him with wide open hearts and minds, who come to understand all that God has revealed of Himself and His will. A religion of feelings and fancies is only for the weaker kinds of people. Men who love the Lord with all their minds and hearts realize supreme satisfaction deep within their lives.

# ROCK OR SAND

*What then of the man who hears these words of mine and acts upon them? He is like a man who had the sense to build his house on rock. . . . But what of the man who hears these words of mine and does not act upon them? He is like a man who was foolish enough to build his house on sand.* Matt. 7:24-27, N.E.B.

Some men build on a divine foundation, some do not. The one group stands firm in the storm of life; the other collapses. Jesus Christ and His Word have decisive importance for all men.

The church of God needs a great many Christians, each at his post, who can be relied upon under all circumstances, who at all times will do the Christian thing, the honest, upright thing, the pure and responsible thing. Life is not ours. It belongs to God. We have no right to do with it what we like, regardless.

One weekend in a certain European country the radio changed its programming from light entertainment to a matter of more serious nature. A catastrophe had hit the country. A ship had been lost with all hands on board. The change in the programming caused a storm of telephone protests to the radio company headquarters. "What is this shipwreck to us?" angry listeners demanded.

Most of life in the world is hanging at the end of a rope of sand. The world of men and nations needs a revival of godliness, of Christian character, of virtue and fidelity. We live this way because Christ is at the heart of our lives. We witness to both the saving power of Christ and our obedience to His will. Recently a man told me that his house was beginning to lean. The walls were cracked and the frame twisted. He called for the city inspector, who crawled under the house and found that termites had eaten out the structure.

Jesus defined the man who built his house upon the rock as one who keeps His sayings. He is always on the right side of life. When Christ tells us that hate will not work and love will, then this is the way we ought to live. When He says that dishonesty will not work and integrity will, we ought to commit our lives to obey. Hate and dishonesty are like termites, doing quiet but terrible damage.

## "SHOW US THE FATHER"

*Philip said to him, "Lord, show us the Father and we ask no more."*
**John 14:8, N.E.B.**

Thanks be to God. The Father Himself initiated the plan of redemption to save us. The Son of God descended to reconcile and redeem us back to God. The Holy Spirit takes us out of the hands of Satan, supports and strengthens us. He takes up His abode within us, purifies us, changes our whole nature, fills us with love, joy, peace. He gives us courage and spiritual power.

Think of it: Jesus our Lord, Friend, Saviour, an ever-present attorney for our defense in heaven. Who can harm us if we belong to Him? Satan cannot, for he has been defeated. Fears as to the future—there can be none.

We now glorify the Father whose name is love. We glorify the Son whose love has redeemed us in order to make us loving persons. We glorify the Holy Spirit who empowers us for love, because He has shed abroad the love of God in our hearts (see Rom. 5:5). Their love for us stands in contrast with our sin and our selfishness. Hope for salvation and restoration is not in our efforts, but in the opening of our hearts to Their love. We love because They first loved us.

That the Father as revealed by His Son Jesus Christ was different, is the ground of the only hope we have. We call His Son not Jesus the Great, Jesus the Philosopher, Jesus the great Teacher. Rather we lift Him above all merely human titles. His is the Name that is above every name. One of His titles is "The everlasting Father, The Prince of Peace" (Isa. 9:6). He brought God to us.

A student said to me some years ago that in a Christian college like the one we were in, the name *God* was used more frequently than anywhere else he had been. In view of that he wondered why it was so hard for him to find God. He finally came to see that Jesus was the answer. He accepted the Son of God as the Father's reaching out His love to him. His doubts were turned into a doxology. He resolved to live and love and plan by faith in such a divine Father revealed to him in Jesus. When he left college, it was God the Father of our Lord Jesus Christ of whom he was certain and in whom he trusted.

# WHAT IS TRUTH?

*Sanctify them through thy truth: thy word is truth.* John 17:17.

Christ bids us to love God with all our minds. God desires from us the enthusiastic use of our minds, intent to know the truth that God has given to us in His Word. When you come to worship and to serve Him, do not leave behind the noblest part of your being, your mind. Insist on understanding all that you can of the Word of God. The mind must learn to love truth and to hate iniquity. No Christian completely and worthily loves Jesus Christ unless he loves Him with his mind as well as with his heart and soul.

A second factor involves the personal attitude of the individual. Pilate asked the question, "What is truth?" But did he really want to know? He wanted his own way, not God's. He feared the multitude. He had his reputation and standing to think about.

The love of sin draws a veil over our minds. Indifference and continued ignorance also darken the mind. Men cannot see the truth except they look for it. The battle between Christ and Satan is a battle for the mind, either to enlighten it with truth or to darken it with error and ignorance. Satan hates the light. He seeks to move our minds into the shadows where truth becomes vague and indistinct.

We are to hold fast to the truth of God. This is certainty. God leaves no room for doubt. The only fixed and dependable truth is that which comes from God and not from men. We talk of men falling into sin. Actually men slide into it. Rarely do people take some precipitous action that plunges them into the darkness all at once. Truth is not abandoned. It is compromised. It is diluted. People are drawn aside by ways that fall short of the will of God.

"I thought on my ways, and turned my feet unto thy testimonies" (Ps. 119:59). When the psalmist saw that he was wrong, he turned his feet unto God's testimonies. Men are not too ready to think about their ways. It is not so easily done as we may imagine. The Word of God casts divine eyes on our own lives. How far short have we fallen of God's truth? What is His Word of truth to us now? We have a right to ask these questions only when we intend to obey the truth.

# THE LIGHTENED MIND

*I am the light of the world: he that followeth me shall not walk in darkness, but shall have the light of life.* **John 8:12.**

F. W. Boreham in his book, *Arrows of Desire,** interprets a French proverb: "At night, all cats are grey. . . . In a poor light, chalk looks pretty much the same as cheese; wine as water; brass as gold; a weed as a flower, a mongrel as a champion. . . . In the grey dawn or the gathering dusk or the falling twilight, foes and friends closely resemble each other. Many a battle has been won, as Gideon won his struggle with the Midianites, by throwing the enemy into confusion in the darkness and turning every man's hand against his brother. . . . A toddler sees no difference between mushrooms and toadstools, between the pretty but noxious berries of the deadly nightshade and the appetizing fruits in his own garden. . . . A baby, unenlightened on such matters, would as soon play with a snake as with a skipping-rope."

Dedication to the truth presupposes a high degree of mind enlightenment and alertness. In the realm of the Christian faith, the issues are final. To remain in mental and spiritual darkness concerning what is truth is folly.

The Word of God has a lot to say about light and darkness. Jesus is the Light of the World. Satan is called the prince of darkness. His followers are said to walk in darkness. Isaiah pictured the whole world lying in gross darkness (see Isa. 60:1, 2). With the coming of Christ the people who sat in darkness saw a great light.

Jesus must be our ultimate point of reference, our fixed Center. Every traveler on land, sea, or in the air knows how important it is to have some landmark or star to indicate where he is. We cannot afford to be blind on what is truth, the way we ought to go. We are always to be open to the light.

We are to develop a mind that can perceive and sense the difference between right and wrong, between the true and the false; a mind that makes it impossible to tolerate the ugly, the cheap, the seductive, and the sinful. By the Holy Spirit we possess a spiritual mind with spiritual insight.

---

* F. W. Boreham, *Arrows of Desire* [London: The Epworth Press, 1951], pp. 9, 10.

# THE RENEWED MIND

*Be ye transformed by the renewing of your mind, that ye may prove what is that good, and acceptable, and perfect, will of God. Rom. 12:2.*

It is not possible to overemphasize what we do with our minds. These words of Paul stand unrivaled as defining the Christian life. An essential aspect of it is the renewed mind, the remade mind. What is more serious than having a mind that is impaired and darkened by sin? What is more significant than to have the mind restored by the Holy Spirit?

Every truth from God is an expression of the divine mind. He has given us these truths that we may know Him, know His character, so that our own minds may be brought into harmony with His. If we reject any truth that He reveals, we fall short of our knowledge of Him. We are to exercise to the utmost the use of our minds toward God. It is not enough to be content with little, to be satisfied with the crumbs that fall from the table.

Our mind is like a garden; it will grow up in weeds or in beautiful flowers. It is like a savings bank. We cannot take out what we have not put in. A renewed mind never occurs in a vacuum. The mind of truth rejects error. The mind darkened by sin rejects truth. Our response to God is not blind obedience. Our minds are open when we can say, "This is the truth from God. This is God's Word to me. God has truly spoken to my heart."

We become renewed persons, not by flights of feeling but by diligent application of the mind to truth and commitment to obey it. This becomes utterly crucial to our own Christian stability and maturity.

Let us not hesitate to accept and obey all the truth of God. There can be no standard of beauty, no standard of desire, but that which comes forth from the mind of God.

The mole grubbing in the dirt cannot discern the world of glory that is disclosed to the eye of the eagle. For us the highest revelation from God is found in Jesus Christ and in His Word. The secret of righteousness, of transformation, of restoration, is found here. Nothing so determines the quality of our lives as what we do with our minds. We are to have the mind of Christ, the key to everything.

# THE NARROW AND THE BROAD WAY

*Enter ye in at the strait gate. . . . Because strait is the gate, and narrow is the way, which leadeth unto life, and few there be that find it.* **Matt. 7:13, 14.**

There are no traffic jams on the narrow way to eternal life. The heavy traffic is all on the broad road that leads to destruction. Only a few take the first; the rest take the second. It is impossible to avoid both. You have to take one or the other. There is no third alternative.

The narrow way is that which is restricted to the will and purpose of God. We must take the field as champions of virtue and righteousness. Whatever is found to be unfit for the Christian life, whatever dissipates our minds or cools our devotion to God, whatever indisposes us to study the Bible or engage in prayer, whatever dulls our need to worship God, whatever pleasures we cannot thank God for and on which we cannot ask His blessing—all these things are not for us.

Never go where you cannot ask God to go with you. Never indulge in any pleasure or entertainment that will not bear the morning's reflection with God. Never be found where you would not like death to find you. Remember that the path is narrow and it is easy to stray.

The time comes to us all when the way of life divides before us. One way only is marked as the strait and narrow way. That moment of supreme decision has arrived. Christ shows us the narrow way. Satan beckons to the broad way.

> Heaven above our head
> Watches us in silent dread;
> While the angels stand around,
> Breathless in suspense profound.
>
> *Author Unknown*

Take the road with Christ. Let us keep company with the great men of God. Men and women who walk with Christ on the narrow way are the greatest need of the church. The narrow way offers us the grandest and most daring enterprises anywhere in the universe. What a prospect for our lives and for enlisting our friends and relatives to take this way into the New Jerusalem.

# NO FAITH WITHOUT RESPONSIBILITY

*Who hath ears to hear, let him hear. . . . For this people's heart is waxed gross, and their ears are dull of hearing, and their eyes they have closed; lest at any time they should see with their eyes, and hear with their ears, and should understand with their heart, and should be converted, and I should heal them. Matt. 13:9-15.*

If a man has ears, can he not hear? That depends. A person with good hearing can readily distinguish hundreds of pitches of sound. A trained musician can multiply that number by many times.

Marius the Roman, as he watched the gladiatorial combats in the arena at Rome, was reputed to have said, "What is needed is the development of a mind that makes this kind of thing impossible for people to watch."

The only avenue that God has for getting through to us is the mind. "God . . . will work by His Spirit through the mind he has put in man."—*Testimonies,* vol. 5, p. 725. The words, "Who hath ears to hear, let him hear," declare that we are personally responsible for the direction and the training of our minds. God will not violate the freedom and rights of the mind. In education, unless the student opens and directs his mind the teaching process will not penetrate.

Faith is no passive submission but a mind active in a responsible relationship to the living God. Prayer, study of the Word, Christian service, require active participation. Apathy, neglect, indifference to eternal realities and issues, neutralize the mind toward God.

Today men are hounded by a thousand and one voices crying for attention. Never was there a time when the minds of men were so captured by the trivial and the worthless. We are bombarded by the most amazing fanfare of shallow interests and vain endeavors that ever confronted any generation. Never was the devil more persistent and overwhelming in his efforts to lure Christian men and women into an irresponsible attitude toward eternal things. The spiritual destiny of the individual is imperiled by a way of life that neglects the capacities of the mind toward God and toward His Word. "For the things which are seen are temporal; but the things which are not seen are eternal" (2 Cor. 4:18).

# WE ARE ALL CHANGED

*But we all, with open face beholding as in a glass the glory of the Lord, are changed into the same image from glory to glory.* **2 Cor. 3:18.**

The calendar is a useful device. It numbers our days. It tells you who are 18 years of age that you have about 19,500 days left to live; you who are 25 have 16,500; you who are 30 have 15,400; you who are 40 have 12,000. This is your capital in time. You cannot add to it. This is all there is. When people meet us after twenty years and say, "You do not look a day older," they are guilty of perjury.

But the calendar is only a pale reflection of a vaster calendar written in our lives. The most significant change takes place in our minds and in our spirits. To some the years have brought greater wisdom, a mature spirituality, the gift of insight, and Christian character. To others they have brought a hard mind and a hard face.

How are we changed? The text says, "We all reflect as in a mirror the splendour of the Lord; thus we are transfigured into his likeness" (2 Cor. 3:18, N.E.B.). This is the basic principle. All of us are prone to reflect our last serious conversation, the last good book we read, the last Week of Prayer we attended. The phrase, "A man is known by the company he keeps," expresses a basic principle. We are nobly or ignobly changed by what we contemplate.

The love of God cannot compete with cheap jazz, cheap reading, cheap and vulgar jokes, vulgarly suggestive and low entertainment. "Blessed are the pure in heart, for they shall see God." That is just it. It takes that kind of mind to see God, to desire and enjoy God.

Impurity always replaces itself with impurity. Fear never replaces itself with love. Error never replaces itself with truth. Vulgarity never replaces itself with Christian refinement.

Jesus dispels our darkness of mind. In His presence it is really difficult to be mean, cruel, hostile, selfish, unclean, or vicious. To keep company with Christ is to expose ourselves to that which restores in us His image. In company with Christ we partake of His love, His righteousness, His character. The direction of our gaze, our devotion, our commitment—that is what needs to be changed, really.

# THE DRAWING POWER OF CHRIST

*And I, if I be lifted up from the earth, will draw all men unto me.* John 12:32.

All that is attractive in grace and personality, or beautiful in character, belong to Christ. He is the "chiefest among ten thousand." He is the Shepherd of the flock, the King of kings, the Husband of the bride, the Morning Star. He is the stream of living water flowing from the smitten rock. He is the Rose of Sharon sending forth its fragrance. He is the Sun of Righteousness rising with healing in His wings. He is the Living Bread we eat. He is the coming of the dawn. He is the essence of everlasting love.

To behold Christ, to exalt Him in our lives, means that we give Him His rightful place. We have accepted an inclusive devotion to Him that lifts us out of our selfishness and our sins. When Christ enters, with Him come in pure thoughts, high desires, true love, an irresistible charm of character.

It is up to us to direct our gaze. To this end we have become followers of Christ. Here is where the life line should be drawn. Christ our Righteousness and His character are essential to our very life. We belong to Him. We cannot do without Him. By the power of the Holy Spirit we are to prevent the appeals and fascinations of the world from displacing our ideals of Christ. We are to hold fast our faith and life direction.

The bravest battles that ever are fought are fought not with hands or with guns, but with a mind and a spirit that are continually being renewed by Christ. Who is to keep the image of Christ from flickering and waning under the stress of temptation and worldly pressures? Who is to keep our Christian characters shining in the darkness, singing in the night, unflinching in the face of error and falsehood? The answer is found in having our minds and hearts continually open to our Lord, Jesus Christ. He is the Rock under our feet, the Light to our path, the Love of our lives, the clean wind that blows through our souls.

Rejoice that He has drawn you to Himself with love. Rejoice that He has unveiled the truth before your eyes. Rejoice that He has purged your life from evil and forgiven your sins. Rejoice that through Christ you are bearing His image.

# THE HIGHWAY OF LIFE

*I am the way, the truth, and the life.* John 14:6.

> To every man there openeth
> A Way, and Ways, and a Way
> And the High Soul climbs the High Way,
> And the Low Soul gropes the Low,
> And in between, on the misty flats,
> The rest drift to and fro.
> But to every man there openeth
> A High Way, and a Low.
> And every man decideth
> The way his soul shall go.
>                         —JOHN OXENHAM

Three classes of persons are referred to here: those who follow the high way, those who seek the low, and the drifters. Those who take the low road tell themselves, "This life is all there is. I am going to live for myself, have the best time possible, cater to my own desires and satisfy myself. I don't care about what happens to anyone else."

The drifters have no particular purpose or goal in life. They get all they can out of life as it comes to them. Someone asked a hobo how he knew which way to go. He replied, "I always go with the wind at my back." The drifter makes no contribution to life. He drifts with the tide from pillar to post without a real purpose. Tomorrow is just another day. The end of life for him closes a book containing an unintelligible scrawl.

Finally, there is the man who takes the high way. Paul stated it thus: "But this one thing I do, forgetting those things which are behind, and reaching forth unto those things which are before, I press toward the mark for the prize of the high calling of God in Christ Jesus" (Phil. 3:13, 14). The really happy people in this world believe themselves to be children of God, created for the highest life possible, kings, vicegerents of God on earth. Whatever they do is for the glory of God and the uplifting of men.

The difference between this group and the other two is the difference between living in a cage and singing in the sky. Life has dignity. Life is meaningful. Christ is the Way.

# THE PRIORITIES OF LIFE

*And they that be wise shall shine as the brightness of the firmament; and they that turn many to righteousness as the stars for ever and ever.* **Dan. 12:3.**

Successful living has to do with what is really essential. Offers of success abound in the world. Suppose you ask a bank president, "I am a young man just out of college. I am eager to make a success of life. Will you please give me your advice?" He might say, "Become economically and financially independent. Get to the top in the houses of high finance. Become a millionaire as soon as possible."

Now ask the same question of a movie magnate. He would probably answer, "Fame is what you need to achieve. Win the plaudits and the adoration of the multitudes." Again, ask a university president for the key to success and his reply would be, "Get the best education you can. Add the highest degrees to your name. Become a scholar in your own right. Win a Nobel prize if you can." In a way, many of these things might be desirable priorities.

Should you not ask Jesus Christ the same question? The prophet Daniel said that the "wise shall shine . . . as the stars for ever and ever." Now go outside and look at the stars. They are the same stars that shone down on Abraham, Joseph, Moses, and the apostles. You are to consider what will really endure.

Suppose you had only one year to live. Would you not seek first the real essentials from God? I read of a ship that sank in the South Pacific. A wealthy woman passenger, waiting for a lifeboat, took time to return to her stateroom nearby. In that room were her diamonds and other valuables. But she returned to get three oranges. In a lifeboat in the hot South Pacific, oranges had priority over diamonds.

When a man hastily chooses a way of life that he must later regret, history properly considers him unwise.

Roses are scentless, hopeless are the morns,
Rest is but weakness, laughter crackling thorns,
If Thou, the Truth, do not make them true.
Thou art my life, O Christ, and nothing else will do.
—*Author Unknown*

# "A SOUND MIND"

*For God hath not given us the spirit of fear; but of . . . a sound mind.*
2 Tim. 1:7.

The Greek word for "sound mind" means a balanced, integrated mind with all its powers operating together. The central idea is that of adequacy for every situation. We are able to use all our mental powers with efficiency and purpose.

We hear and read a great deal these days about unbalanced minds, crippled minds, minds that get short-circuited with disastrous consequences in every aspect of life. Ellen White writes that "nine tenths of the diseases from which men suffer have their foundation here [in the mind]."—*Testimonies,* vol. 5, p. 444. Broken minds are one of the prevailing problems today.

The gift of a sound mind comes from God. The hope of the church and the world lies in our having the mind of Christ. Every difficulty and choice that life thrust upon Christ, He met with freshness, courage, faith, hope, and love. Pain, loss, separation, loneliness, opposition, fear—none of these disturbed His inner peace and tranquillity of mind. He shaped them all to His advantage. He was pressured and hounded on every side. But He sought no escape from life. He ran away from no responsibility because of a sense of insufficiency. He resorted to no withdrawal because of inferiority.

The power of the gospel is intended as much for the healing of the mind as for the healing of the body. Life's problems are not solved unless the solution begins here. Christ's work of redemption includes the restoration of our life resources. Paul put it this way: "Now unto him that is able to do exceeding abundantly above all that we ask or think, according to the power that worketh in us" (Eph. 3:20). Christ never leaves us to become victims of the trials and difficulties and pressures of life. His love possesses our minds. We are in His hands.

If our faith in Christ is to mean anything at all in life, then it must free us from those destructive abnormalities that infect the mind, and make the abundant life impossible. He promised to make us whole.

# "PETER FOLLOWED AFAR OFF"

*This is your hour, and the power of darkness. Then took they him, and led him, and brought him into the high priest's house. And Peter followed afar off.* **Luke 22:53, 54.**

Peter did not wish to be identified with Jesus at this point. He had lost the sense of loyalty and courage. We are glad that Peter changed. Judas, on the other hand, had made a complete break with Christ. He had betrayed Him deliberately and knowingly. Peter never intended to do that. He simply turned coward. Cowardice and disloyalty are intolerable to Christ. None of us can stand friends who are ashamed of us because we stand for Christ.

A good many people are Christians only halfway. Their faith and courage disappear when sacrifice is demanded. Christianity is no halfway house to anything. It requires unswerving allegiance to Christ regardless of the cost. Salvation is free, but it is not cheap. It is either all or nothing. There is a stability and dependability about the man who keeps close to Christ.

In painting, in poetry, in music, in any form of art, unless there is a beauty and a mastery in the artist's work, it can only provoke disdain and rejection. There is no place for a poor performance in sculpture or in any of the arts if one is to command respect. A mediocre piece of work is intolerable. The greater and more demanding the work, the diviner the art, the more perfection and devotion are required. Nothing less than excellence will do. It is unthinkable that God should take pleasure in us if we are mediocre in our faith, lukewarm in our devotion.

Every Reformer—Luther, Calvin, Wesley, Knox—felt the power of an abundant life through Christ. They discovered that they had not come to the Kingdom simply to be happy and have a good time. They came into the arena of life to fight the good fight of faith.

Can a professed Christian who has committed no more than 10 per cent of his interest and life to Christ ever escape denying his Lord? We meet such people. There is something sad about letting an occasional sentiment pass for Christian faith, putting a stone where the heart belongs. That kind of religion is a dead weight. It is of no benefit to anyone.

# THE APPEARANCE OF EVIL

*Abstain from all appearance of evil.* **1 Thess. 5:22.**

The Christian must avoid everything that looks evil. He must abstain from every form that evil may assume. It is not enough to abstain from what we know to be evil. The emphasis in the text is on what *appears* evil.

We can argue that some particular thing is wrong only in appearance, and that is all; therefore to engage in it cannot be wrong. But the text affirms that if there is a doubt about it, we would be wise to avoid it. Some feel that this denies Christian liberty.

Paul wrote to the believers in Corinth, "If meat make my brother to offend, I will eat no flesh while the world standeth" (1 Cor. 8:13). To eat it did not appear to him to be evil. However, if his eating of that which had been offered to pagan idols might cause someone to stumble, then Paul would not eat it. It was perfectly lawful for him but it was not expedient.

People can very well misunderstand what we eat and drink at certain times. They might get the wrong impression should we attend to our secular responsibilities during the week but neglect worship in the house of God on Sabbath. Such a course has, in the estimation of many, the appearance of evil. The principle applies to the amusements in which we engage. To seek relaxation is good. But we have no right to do what may seem evil to others. We must have a conscience void of offense toward God and man. Christ said that it were better to die than to give needless offense to one of our children (see Matt. 18:6).

Many times in the home, parents are not as careful as they should be in their practice and their stand taken before the children. We may argue that looking at certain television programs does not hurt us. But what about the children? As to the books and magazines we read, we may be able to discern between that which is good and that which is evil. But can the children do that? Both the church and the home are troubled at times with what appears like carelessness in relation to Biblical standards. We are commanded to keep the faith. People should have no doubt as to where we stand on moral issues.

# LAYING UP TREASURE

*Lay not up for yourselves treasures upon earth . . . but lay up for your-*
*selves treasures in heaven.* Matt. 6:19, 20.

Christ here gives us a choice: treasure on earth or treasure
in heaven. The rich fool in the parable illustrates the point
(see Luke 12:15-21). "The ground of a certain rich man
brought forth plentifully." He had a problem. He did not
know what to do with all he now had. What should he have
done?

He should have thanked God for His goodness to him.
He should have acknowledged that it was God's sun, God's
rain, God's soil, that brought forth the good harvest. He forgot
all about that. You know how it is. We make a lot of money.
We give ourselves the credit. It is owing to our own shrewd-
ness. We made a successful business deal. We congratulate ourselves and leave God out of it.

Or we have made friends with the right people. Success,
we believe, was the result of our own attractiveness, smartness,
and sophistication. We also left God out of these relationships.

Had the rich man given thanks to God, proceeded to feed
the cold, the hungry, and the destitute, sharing with them the
good things that God had given him, he would have been laying up treasure in heaven.

He resolved to hold on to all his goods, build new store-
houses to keep them all to himself. Not the things that belong
to us are important, but the quality of the people to whom we
belong and who belong to us.

The rich fool has numerous followers. What is the difference between the rich fool who pulled down his barns and
built larger ones and the man who, when he prospers, must
build more costly houses, adopt a more expensive mode of
living, and make this an excuse for not investing in the cause
of God? What is the difference between the rich fool who allowed his mind to be so occupied with temporal riches that he
had to leave to others, and those who amass that which they
will never require in this life, yet have no intention of using
in the service of God? The sin lies in the selfishness.

The only way to enjoy our worldly goods is to share them,
to become rich toward God and bring happiness to others.

# "TREASURE IN HEAVEN"

*Go thy way, sell whatsoever thou hast, and give to the poor, and thou shalt have treasure in heaven.* **Mark 10:21.**

The rich young ruler desired eternal life. Jesus did not object to his having money, but He put the test to him on this basis. The young man did not want his money included in the conditions for eternal life. He preferred not to mix business with his religion. When it came to his relationship to God, he wanted his wealth left out. That is the sum total of the problem.

Of course, such a position can be taken with almost anything—sports, fashions, sex; all of them quite legitimate in their proper sphere. However, when we consider our lives untouchable at any of these points we are putting that thing before God. Nothing we do can conceal this fact. Christ insists that when He is Lord of our lives His rule must include everything we possess. This is where the rub comes.

Christ invites us to become candidates for His eternal kingdom, the most magnificent offer ever made to sinful men. The temptation is to want it on our own terms. To be a dedicated disciple of Christ, including all we possess, must have priority.

This is not to say that all wealthy people, all sports-minded people, have turned their backs on Christ. There are many genuine Christians engaged in secular pursuits who love Christ and bear witness to Him. To them it is not the sport or the money that really matters. It is the Jew from Nazareth, born in a stable, reared in a carpenter's home, who died on a cross to save us. He is the One who gives meaning to life.

We cannot afford to sacrifice Him to any of the things offered by the world. Wealth, pleasures, sports, are not worth risking our chances for eternal life.

Many of the fascinations of the world, quite legitimate in themselves, tend to crowd us to the sidelines of the great controversy. Then our lives have little or no reference to God's final movements in the world. We cannot make up for that kind of loss by shouting ourselves hoarse at a ball game or by collecting a few more gold and silver coins.

Let us keep it straight. Christ's presence and program for our lives and for the church is central.

# HINDERING GOD

*That will do for the present; when I find it convenient I will send for you again.* **Acts 24:25, N.E.B.**

It seems irreverent to speak of man's limiting or preventing God from carrying out His plans. Yet, since God has chosen to work with sinful man to whom He has given freedom of choice, man must do his part and cooperate with God, or His purpose has to be changed or abandoned.

The revelation of God to men does not always call forth a full response from them. Hence the importance of cooperating with God. It is God's will that we be freed from the bondage of sin. But the loss of faith makes this impossible. Man often prevents God from doing all He would like to do.

Many, like Felix, believe they should come to Christ but that this is not the time. Later, they tell themselves, they will face up to their responsibility to God. This is one of Satan's great deceptions. This unwillingness to place ourselves before God, this desire for a delay in having God deal with our problem, is an evil and dangerous frame of mind. Once we practice putting off Christ, believing that we still have time, it results in the hardening of the mind against the persuasion of God's Holy Spirit. It is easier for God to deal with men who are openly and definitely on the side of sin, than with one who trifles with the Spirit. "You have received the grace of God; do not let it go for nothing. . . . The hour of favor has now come; now, I say, has the day of deliverance dawned" (2 Cor. 6:1, 2, N.E.B.).

The only time we have is now. What we do in the future depends on what we do now. Take care lest we silence the voice of God, and miss the supreme opportunity of God's time for us. Let not Satan silence the call of God to your heart.

It is not difficult to appear shocked at the widespread ungodliness that prevails in the world. What is hard to perceive is how the toleration of sin in the life gradually closes the mind to God. We are to be filled with the Spirit so that there is no room for sin. Sin is crowded out by God's presence. This allows of no exception, no hanging on to sin in any part of our lives.

## "THOU GOD SEEST ME"

*The heart is deceitful above all things . . . who can know it? I the Lord
search the heart, . . . even to give every man according to his ways, and according to the fruit of his doings. Jer. 17:9, 10.*

The human heart or mind is the most subtle, the most
crafty and deceptive thing we know. From time to time we
persuade ourselves that we are doing right even when we are
doing wrong. We rationalize our problems and justify our departure from the truth.

Who can tear off the mask? Who can get us to see and acknowledge ourselves as God sees us? Who can heal our hearts?
We cannot, but God can. God searches our hearts to their very
depth. Ultimately God will expose and reveal exactly what our
hearts are like.

We may lay stress on outward conformity to what the Bible
and the church require. We may be faithful in Sabbath ob-
servance. The main question is: what are we like inside? The
fact that God really knows can be very disturbing, or it can be
encouraging.

Many sincere Christians are unhappily placed in life—people with a defect of appearance, a feeling of inferiority, a lack
of charm, an awkwardness or timidity, that prevents them
from showing themselves as they would like to be. They seem
always to take a back seat. They never push themselves forward, never win the esteem of others. Around them are others
with more talent and poise, an easier communication. Those
who feel inferior seem unable to say half the kind things they
think or feel, or to do the service that others do. Other faces
and manners draw a better commendation. Their charm in-
stantly attracts others. We all crave to be that kind of person.
But we shall have to be content with the fact that God knows
our hearts, our motives, our intentions. We need not fear that
God will judge us by our acts that are so limited and inhibited
by uncontrollable conditions.

The Lord looks on the heart. What constancy, what devotion, what honesty, what purity, what allegiance, will He find
there? That is the question. God does not judge our lives on a
point system, but records our compatibility and oneness of
heart with Him.

# TOO NEAR SODOM

*Abram dwelled in the land of Canaan, and Lot dwelled in the cities of the plain, and pitched his tent toward Sodom.* **Gen. 13:12.**

This Biblical phrase has an ominous ring about it in light of what happened later.

The loss of one's wife and sons, as Lot suffered, does not necessarily follow because we live in the city. We cannot isolate ourselves and live apart from the world. As Christ's ambassadors we cannot deny ourselves some intercourse with the worldly and the ungodly. But the peril arises when we absorb the spirit of Sodom, when we come to prefer economic advantages to moral and spiritual values, when we become engrossed with the pleasures of the world and catch the spirit of it, when we find more meaning to life in association with Sodom than with Jesus Christ. Then we have pitched our tent toward Sodom. When the desire comes to rise in the world, to allow ourselves to be compromised by evil influences, then we dwell too near the tents of wickedness.

The word *secularism* embraces all of these factors. Secularism is the domination of temporal things. It does not necessarily deny the Christian faith. It requires that we live indifferently to it, that we spend our lives under some dominating interest other than faith in, and allegiance to, God.

Ours is a secular and materialistic age. Many fail to realize what this secular philosophy is doing to us. In an affluent society, people need a lot of things and want a lot more. The well-being of our families and particularly of our children is at stake. This lopsided preoccupation with things, the submissive deference we give to those who have money, the lengths to which people will go and the sacrifice of integrity they will make in order to get money, all this is destroying family life and character.

Certainly we may acquire wealth and riches and enjoy them as Christians. But we must not make materialistic gains at the expense of our commitment to God and to our family. One has only to remember Lot's choice and the sad tragedy of his family. If you lose your children, what do you have left? Fit them for the Christian life now and for eternity. Then you will have everything.

# GOD COMES TO SODOM

*As things were in Lot's days, also: they ate and drank; they bought and sold; they planted and built; but the day that Lot went out from Sodom, it rained fire and sulphur from the sky and made an end of them all—it will be like that on the day when the Son of Man is revealed. Luke 17:28-30, N.E.B.*

The great calamity that came to Lot in Sodom was not his loss of property and possessions, but the eternal loss of his wife and sons. Nothing could make up for that. The story of Lot, the effort of God to save him and all his sons and daughters, shows how very near to us lies another, invisible, world and another kind of life. For that world angels continually minister to save us and our children. We need to have our eyes and minds opened to see God's agencies at work in our behalf.

There is much around us that makes us forget that other world. Yet God leaves Himself not without a witness as to the importance of the eternal world and spiritual values. Who of us has not felt the desire for the more abiding things that this present world cannot give us? How often do we awaken with a start from our engrossment in worldliness, and become conscious for a moment or two of the hollowness and the unreality of giving ourselves wholly to this world?

The tragic record of Lot's family and the city of Sodom ought to show us that we may be walking blindfolded, conscious only of what this world has to offer. Yet all the time, every day and in every way, the angels of God seek to make us aware of our peril, of the need to choose eternal values a thousand times more important than all else.

Christ, by His Holy Spirit and His angels, is close to us on all sides. If we believe that, then we should find our lives to be in God's hand.

But the angel who seeks to awaken us to the importance of eternal matters must also record against us every wrong choice and every act of disobedience. Possessions do not have to mean that we are not Christian. We can use them as an opportunity to heal the sick, feed the hungry, save lives. We are not to care too much about our hold on things, but about our hold on God. The meaning of life cannot be realized or understood without reference to the invisible world so near to us.

# CHRISTIAN DISCIPLINE

*Keep yourself in training for the practice of religion. The training of the body does bring limited benefit, but the benefits of religion are without limit.* 1 Tim. 4:7, 8, N.E.B.

In this passage Paul compares the athletic exercises and sports of the Greeks with the highest training in godliness. The first can avail for good, but ends in this life. Godliness is profitable especially for the life to come. Two crucial factors are set before us—the right priorities or perspective in life, and personal discipline and self-control.

The present generation devotes far more attention to the discipline of the body than to discipline of the soul. Physical fitness is essential for all of us. The health of the mind depends to a large extent on that of the body. What Paul objects to is a wrong perspective. Where do we expend our time, effort, and money? Are we far less concerned with spiritual fitness than with physical? Has the latter become more attractive than spiritual fitness? What really has priority with us?

Both areas require discipline and self-control, but spiritual training provides us with a far more enduring purpose than any system of physical exercise. No clear-thinking person would deny that it is better to be morally and spiritually good and upright than to be physically strong. Spiritual development is the work of a lifetime. Therefore it involves as much constant and strenuous exercise of the mind and heart as does physical fitness.

To achieve physical fitness we must avoid smoking, drinking, and all those foods and practices that tend to weaken the body. Similarly, in the spiritual life we are to control those appetites and desires that make godliness impossible.

We are spiritual and moral athletes for Christ. Self-control and personal discipline are as much required of us as of the artist, the musician, the scientist, and the athlete. The Lord Jesus is our trainer. The discipline of the Christian life is a grand experience under Christ. It is the invigorated life, the equipped life, the victorious life.

# ACCOUNTABLE TO GOD

*So then every one of us shall give account of himself to God.* **Rom. 14:12.**

When Christ was on earth, a large part of His ministry was spent with individuals. He made extensive trips on foot just to minister to one person, such as to Zacchaeus in Jericho and the Syrophoenician woman in the area of Tyre and Sidon. Each man—every person in the singular—is Christ's concern. Each person is unique before God.

Much of modern life in one way or another operates on a mass basis. We are known and numbered according to the computers. The individual seems less important than the system to which we belong. But the Bible emphasizes one truth with great clarity, that of our individual responsibility to God. When capital and labor try to tie us in a bundle with everyone else, we are in danger of being ruined for time and for eternity. Even when the church does our thinking for us, to tell us what and what not to believe, then the pressure of organization destroys our sense of personal responsibility.

Paul states that we must "work out your own salvation with fear and trembling" (Phil. 2:12). We must solve the problems we have as individuals before God; no passive acceptance of truth because everybody believes it, no sitting in church with hundreds of other worshipers, can take away our sins and give us salvation. We must work out our salvation in personal penitence, personal faith, personal sacrifice, personal obedience. No one else can pray for us. No one can read the Bible for us. No one can do Christian service for us.

The Christian religion is creative. All imitative behavior is inadequate. We must have that inward understanding of the value of God's truth to which we are accountable and must bear witness. All talk of religion is fruitless unless our personal responsibility to God is given first place.

The woman of Samaria at the well might have turned her back on the stranger sitting there who asked her for a drink. But if she had, her life would have been spent in darkness. Mirrored in the eyes and the words of Jesus she caught a glimpse of God's amazing purpose for her life. From then on, that became her personal responsibility.

# PERSONAL RESPONSIBILITY

*Though Noah, Daniel, and Job, were in it, as I live, saith the Lord God, they shall deliver neither son nor daughter; they shall but deliver their own souls by their righteousness. Eze. 14:20.*

There is salvation for individuals only, and there is personal doom for personal transgressions unforgiven. The selection of these three men is significant. One might expect that from three of the greatest men in the Old Testament some credit or merit might have passed over to their families. But these three illustrious men saved only themselves. They could not save others by their own righteousness.

Though Noah is called "a just man and perfect," "a preacher of righteousness"; though Daniel was an outstanding example of living righteously, a man in whom no fault could be found; though Job in the midst of all his suffering and tragedy sinned not; these individuals could save only themselves. This does not deny that they were instruments of salvation to those around them. Noah did save his own sons and daughters. Daniel did undoubtedly influence other Jews, such as the three Hebrews who were cast into the burning fire.

This is why we as individuals are so precious to God; why God spends time and effort with us personally. The only way to act responsibly toward Christ and the truth of God's Word is to read what happened to a man like Paul and make the same decision. This was the most revolutionary event in his life. To hold back on our responsible allegiance to Christ is the greatest sin we can commit. What the crowd thinks does not matter. What Christ wants of us is what matters.

The truth in Christ has actually come to our door. We cannot wait for some greater and more convincing truth to come along. It does not exist. It becomes an alarming symptom when we begin to indulge the idea that we can sit and move with Christians en masse, trim our lamps like the five foolish virgins, participate in the functions of the church—believing that all this is sufficient without committing ourselves responsibly and unreservedly to our Lord. Let us be frank. We are going to come through the time of trouble triumphantly only with a clear personal allegiance to God that we will never walk away from.

# MAKING LIGHT OF RELIGION

*But they made light of it, and went their ways, one to his farm, another to his merchandise.* Matt. 22:5.

In the parable Christ calls us to the marriage feast to fellowship with Himself. He is speaking here particularly of the Jews and their attitude toward God's sending His Son with a divine invitation to oneness with Himself and His Son. They showed their indifference to Jesus and refused to accept Him. The King then ordered the invitation to be given to all those on the highways and byways.

More souls are lost through neglect and indifference than by outright rebellion against God. From our way of life there often comes a complacency that lulls the mind and erodes the will away from a continued effort to grow and achieve spiritually. We can so insulate ourselves by indifference that we are no longer interested in any new incoming of the Holy Spirit.

Making fun of religion is part of the spirit of our age. Sports inspire us, business grips us, pleasures fascinate and charm us. But the salvation of men—why get worked up about that? Indifference casts Christ's invitation into the wastepaper basket. Indifference dismisses Christ politely. There is no greater sin than to reduce Christ's work of redemption to a matter of convenience, or of personal taste.

The whole message of the Bible and the life of Christ is opposed to this light and easy, lilting way of life. Life is more than chasing will-o'-the-wisps. Christian living means a sense of seriousness about life—clear, deep thinking on things that really matter, a deep purposeful living for God. Actions, deeds, are the true indication of how far we wish to get involved.

If our Lord had been satisfied simply with an easy use of His name, most people would have gone home from hearing His teachings in high spirits and on good terms with themselves. Our Lord knew human nature. Religionists could be men of profession without being strictly men of action.

Nothing will help us by way of Christ that has not been made genuinely our own—our own in this sense, that we mean it with all the purpose, intensity, and consistency of heart and life, whether others mean it or not.

# A LITTLE LEAVEN

*The kingdom of heaven is like unto leaven, which a woman took, and hid in three measures of meal, till the whole was leavened.* Matt. 13:33.

Leaven as used in Scripture can be either good or bad. Either the gospel or sin in the life leavens the whole person one way or another. Christ warned His disciples against the leaven of the Pharisees. This would affect adversely their entire lives.

Leaven and yeast are almost the same thing. If you use bad or poor yeast the bread will be heavy and undesirable for eating. When yeast is mixed in the dough it works its way through every part of it to make bread. So the gospel must enter our hearts and work through the whole range of our lives, in church and out of church, at home and abroad, in business and in pleasure.

We must not stop short of this. Christ did not cast only six devils out of Mary and leave one. When He exercised His power to work miracles, He did not partially heal the blind or partly cure the man at the pool of Bethesda. He made them completely whole. There is no such thing as being half leavened, with half our life given to the church and half to the world.

One sin can leaven the whole life, also. We do our best to protect our homes from fire and storm. Yet they are liable to other perils such as dry rot and termites. The tissue of the wood silently deteriorates. Our lives are liable to a similar danger. Spiritual peril does not always arise from enemies without. Not only do thieves break through and steal but moths and rust also destroy.

Some of our most serious problems emerge from within. Some sin eats away the fiber of the will, the conscience, the spiritual sensitivity. We can tolerate certain sins, cater to them, until one day a sudden temptation presents itself. We fall. Our moral and spiritual life has deteriorated. The little rift in the lute slowly widening stills the music. Worship is not abandoned. It just becomes routine. Prayer is not repudiated, only reduced. The Bible is not rejected, only ignored.

The leaven of Christ in us means loftiness of life, beauty of character, thoroughness of devotion, constant obedience to the will of God.

# SPIRITUAL REDUCTION

*"The bed is too short for a man to stretch, and the blanket too narrow to cover him."* Isa. 28:20, N.E.B.

The prophet Isaiah is contemplating the coming judgments, the approaching desolation of Samaria and the crisis for Judah. There was need for moral and spiritual preparedness. But they had not made God their refuge. All the time Israel flattered herself that she had prepared an easy and secure couch to slumber on. How miserably insufficient their own righteousness would prove—like a bed too short and a blanket too narrow to cover herself.

Many professed Christians have been reducing their religion to ever simpler and simpler terms. They are reducing it so much that it is considered enough simply to use the name, "Jesus," or to try to follow the golden rule. The issue seems to be, not how much but how little do we need to believe. How little can a man believe and still be a Christian? The aim is to get by on a minimum; trim down the Christian faith until we have a religious pattern that fits our own way of living.

But this minimum is like setting up a billboard to hold back a tornado. It means little more than blowing on our hands to keep warm. Religion becomes much like Isaiah's bed and blanket.

When a man aims at becoming a sports champion he does not say, "How little skill can I get by with and still be a first-class player or skier?" When a man plans to become a musician, he does not say, "How little music can I know and still be called a musician?" In the area of friendship, we do not say, "How little of a friend can I be and still be called a friend?" When a man has a family, wife and children, he does not say, "How little of a father can I be and still be called a father?" The question is not how little, but how much.

We get from our spiritual life what we put into it. There is every reason to develop the deepest awareness of the presence of God, to feel the stimulation of Christ's life on our own.

Are we really persuaded that our spiritual life should come first? Or do we allow the pressures of life to occupy so much of our time that there is little of it left for God? We need strength from God more than any generation before us.

## "EVERYBODY DOES IT"

*The king should issue a decree . . . that whoever within the next thirty days shall present a petition to any god or man other than the king shall be thrown into the lions' pit. . . . When Daniel learnt that this decree had been issued, he went into his house. . . . And offered prayers and praise to his God as his custom had always been.* **Dan. 6:7-10, N.E.B.**

"Everybody does it." For many this statement seems sufficient reason for changing their code of morals—some in the areas of sex and purity, others in cheating at school, some in questionable business dealings.

We are committed to following Christ, as was Daniel. We will not permit ourselves to think for one moment of undermining the moral foundation of our character and denying our Lord.

What image do you have of yourself? Is it Christ's image for you or that of someone else? The moral and spiritual problems of young people are multiplied when they raise questions about moral behavior: Why can I not do so and so? What is the harm in it? Is it wrong to go to this worldly place, to engage in questionable practices? Where there is no clear line of demarcation between right and wrong, then departure from personal integrity becomes simple.

No more regrettable thing has occurred in this generation than the popularization of sexual freedom and impurity, the disregard for integrity and honesty. What is customary on the part of "everybody" and what is popular in "our set" often sets the standard of life, although contrary to the clear Word of God.

Furthermore, we must guard against the danger of excesses in sports and worldly pleasures that lead us to believe that the supreme purpose in life is simply to have a good time. One of the strongest factors in deciding the direction of life is exercised by the "gang" to which we belong. They are often the deciding factors in some of life's most critical situations.

The followers of Christ in all ages have been men of Daniel's character. The glorious privilege of keeping company with Daniel, Joseph, and the apostle Paul should be coveted by every follower of our Lord. We must be prepared to stand and win for Christ without the help of the crowd.

# GENEROSITY

*He hath dispersed abroad; he hath given to the poor: his righteousness remaineth for ever.* **2 Cor. 9:9.**

All we have is the gift of God. In return He asks only for what He gave us. God is generous and gracious. We can never experience the reality of God's gifts to us until we give everything to Him in return. We live without fear and anxiety in the presence of such a God who has given us everything.

What great things He bestows upon us every day, things that we can never exhaust. We have a great inheritance in Christ. We are the sole heirs of the world. A generous loving spirit tends to make us great. It causes us to forget our sorrows, to banish our weariness, to overcome our indifference to life, to fill our days with Christian romance. The possibilities for living are infinite.

Nowhere does generosity more excel than in the Christian church. We are filled with the desire to give because God has given to us the unspeakable gift of His Son. We come to see that all gifts are of God, and therefore there is no room for greed. Christ who came into the world became poor, that we through His poverty might be rich. Christ gave us everything, including His very life.

The wealth we have in Christ forbids that we should envy anyone. "All are your's; and ye are Christ's; and Christ is God's" (1 Cor. 3:22, 23). The spirit of generosity can only enhance the good and happiness of everyone. Whatever may be our economic state, we can be a blessing to all concerned. The more our generosity is expressed, the more God's gifts to us are magnified. Everything concerning us is touched by the generosity of God. Christ's intention is to make us incomprehensibly wealthy.

Since God has been so magnificent in His generosity to us, how can we fail to abound toward our brother? We must drink in Christ's spirit and follow in His footsteps. Christ creates in us a loving, unselfish heart. Out of this coarse clay of sinful man, He makes the greatest givers in the world. Life is found in friendship, love, compassion for all men, none of which money can buy.

# THE LOVE OF MONEY

*For the love of money is the root of all evil: which while some coveted after, they have erred from the faith.* 1 Tim. 6:10.

The kind of person we are is revealed by the values and the principles that control us. Certain values take possession of us. From then on they determine how we live. The Bible has a lot to say about money. It does not condemn it. The real issue centers in our use of it. It is "the love of money" that is the root of all evil. On this point there is no distinction between those who are wealthy and those who are not.

There are two possibilities: to be Christians with an open hand, or with a closed hand. When dealing with people we all prefer the first. We are not attracted to the man who is tight-fisted; who gathers up every penny he can get; who squeezes out of us, in one way or another, every possible dime; who in our work and dealings with him gives us the bare minimum, even less than we have earned or deserved.

In the story of Ruth, Boaz gave instructions to his reapers not to gather up the wheat in the field too closely; to let some sheaves fall here and there so that the poor people could gather up behind the reapers. We like that kind of man.

However, to get and save with indifference to the value and needs of people, is a corrosive element in the character. When we hoard money and use it only for ourselves, then the virtue of thrift becomes a vice. The peril is in the transition from a normal desire for money to the passion to obtain wealth as an end in itself. To get wealth for no other reason than to increase it, is unhealthy.

Judas became a very covetous man. On condition that he would tell them where Jesus was, the leaders of the Sanhedrin promised to pay him thirty pieces of silver, about fifty dollars in American money. Judas had a talent for handling affairs, the gift of management, a commercial tact; he was a man of business. The love of money mastered his better impulses. It drove him to betray the Son of God, the best of men. In despair Judas hanged himself.

The incident is full of warning. Do you ever sell your conscience for money? Do you ever betray your sense of right for perhaps even less than thirty pieces of silver?

# BY GOD'S WORD ALONE

*" 'Man cannot live on bread alone; he lives on every word that God utters.' "*
**Matt. 4:4, N.E.B.**

We cannot read the Word of God without feeling that the truth that is revealed from God is not to be found anywhere else. The mariner's compass is a very fine instrument for directing the ships at sea. The teachings of the Scriptures constitute God's moral and spiritual compass, giving clear and definite guidance with infallible truthfulness.

Have you ever heard the voice of God? Has He ever spoken to you personally? If God spoke to you, how would you recognize Him? How would you know whether it was His voice or the voice of the devil, whether it was true or false? We surely need to hear the voice of God and the voice of truth.

God has given us a capacity for hearing His voice and for recognizing it. To arrest our attention, God's voice must be recognized. There is great peril in not being able to identify a voice or a sound that purports to be from God. We are to live by "every word that God utters," said Christ. That voice is simple, clear, understandable. This requires that we listen carefully, understandingly. Our minds must be fully alert. In the Bible we notice that when God speaks there is an articulate communication and also a warm intelligent reception from those who accept that word as from God. God came to Abraham and spoke His intention to bring judgment upon Sodom and Gomorrah. Abraham understood clearly what God meant. He became greatly aroused and concerned for the people who lived there.

Christ always spoke the truth clearly and intelligently. He was a convincing and inspiring teacher of truth. He confronted His hearers with the responsibility to listen and to understand, and then to obey His voice. The voice of God and the Word of God are always in complete harmony.

A superior, sublime quality of communication from God to man is contained in the Scriptures that is altogether lacking in all other claims to encounter with God. This quality is none other than the very voice of God. This Word from God gives the Bible a loftiness that distinguishes it from all the words of men.

# THE VOICE OF GOD

*Now the Spirit speaketh expressly, that in the latter times some shall depart from the faith, giving heed to seducing spirits, and doctrines of devils. 1 Tim. 4:1.*

Important as it is to hear the voice of God and follow it, other voices not of God can intrude upon our minds. Men most deeply interested in the spiritual world may, at the same time, be drawn by other powers in high places not of God.

Many people seem to have great difficulty today understanding the voice of God. The plight becomes very serious where people become unbalanced on the side of the sensational, without a rational understanding of the Word of God.

Fellowship with Christ is intelligible. God always seeks to reach us through the faculties with which He endowed us at Creation. Passionate excitement in religion can be very deceptive. The danger is that high, fantastical moods drown out thinking. We need to distinguish between extremes in emotionalism and in mere intellectualism.

Our response to God involves the highest and noblest expression of the whole man of which we are capable. How sorely do men need the scriptural admonition, "Wherewithal shall a young man cleanse his way? by taking heed thereto according to thy word. . . . Thy word have I hid in mine heart, that I might not sin against thee" (Ps. 119:9-11). We are to bring our mind, heart, and soul to bear on the voice of God in His Word. The best thinking and the deepest loving are the indispensable conditions of spiritual soundness and Christian growth.

The moment we permit our emotions to outweigh the spiritual illumination of the mind by the Word of God, we are in danger of all manner of delusions. We come to attach more importance to our feelings than to the truth itself. The truth of God is dearer to us than any excitement we may feel over it. God's Word is God's voice to us whether we feel anything or not.

We are to let God's voice in His Word through the Holy Spirit be our divine teacher. Then we will be kept in the truth. Our peril in religion today is not that we will suddenly apostatize, but that voices not of God will step by step lead us to depart from God's Word.

# LIBERTY OR LICENSE

*How sayest thou, Ye shall be made free?* John 8:33.

Ours is a religion of love but not of laxity. Our freest moment comes when sin has been brought vigorously to account and overcome. License is often confused with liberty. Men around the world have a passion to destroy in the name of freedom. License is rude, reeking with the violation of other people's rights, disdaining others, refusing others their own dignity and value in the sight of God. Liberty is dignified, hallowed, sacred, uplifting, transforming. Christ offers us the only true freedom, freedom from self and sin.

Christ always took people as they were—in prison, in slums, in bondage to sin. To all He gave the invitation, "Come, and I will make you clean. Come and I will give you freedom from all that degrades." Freedom is of God's making, whereby we are recreated for purity and holiness; for love, not hate; for obedience, not disobedience.

To us it seems so obvious that Christ makes us free. The experience of liberty stands in proportion to our acceptance of and obedience to the truth.

Men were freed from slavery, in black ink on white paper, when President Lincoln signed the Emancipation Act. But not until Christ and His truth are brought into the life are men really free. If we extend freedom to mean license at any point, we are in danger of opening the door to a whole swarm of sins. We depart from the truth that makes us free. Freedom is not the unrestricted right of doing as we please regardless of the welfare of other people. Freedom is never the right to exploit others for our own advantage and pleasure. Such so-called freedom, rather than developing a righteous character, degrades it.

God never enslaves us by our obedience to the truth. Out of the midst of transgression and perversity in our world, it is impossible for the natural man to talk of real freedom. One must be a Christian to do that. Freedom in Christ outshines all the wars for freedom ever fought in our world. His purifying and transforming presence brings us to the liberty of sons and daughters of God.

# OUR HIGH CALLING IN JESUS

*I press toward the mark for the prize of the high calling of God in Christ Jesus.* **Phil. 3:14.**

The most glorious moment in the history of our world came when all the beauty and perfection of God was gathered up and illuminated in the person of His Son, Jesus Christ. We are to share in this life. As we see Jesus Christ, who would not rather be a genuine Christian than anything else? John Wanamaker, one of America's great business tycoons and a great Christian, said, "It may be considered by the world a great thing to be a successful merchant, lawyer, or doctor, but I regard the Christian calling as the greatest of them all."

The world today requires men with the mind and compassion of Christ, and with the knowledge of the greatest truths in the world. We are to excel in the elevation of our thinking, in human interest and concern for all men, in making every day vibrant with the life of Christ in us.

The times in which we live are strenuous. People get infatuated with money, drunk with power, with pleasure. No calm reasoning on life will satisfy hosts of people today. They want more excitement, more power, more wealth. At the same time this world is filled with the eternal tragedy of sin, sin that crucified the Son of God, despised His grace, and trod under foot the matchless love of God.

The physician may work wonders on injured bodies, and that is his power. The lawyer may win his case before the bar by virtue of his brilliance in argument and debate and in the presentation of the evidence. The businessman may amass a fortune, and this is his power.

Christ's life in us is everything. We are to possess His life-power in us above business acumen and sports ability. We are to excel in love for people, for what they are in the sight of God and for what they can become in Christ. What it means to be a Christian can only be believed from lips, words, and actions moved by the love of God.

We can be truly great Christians only with Christlike motives, Christlike obedience to the will of God, Christlike love and the divine power to live that way. The good news is that in Christ we can actually live this way.

# TALENTS AND RESPONSIBILITY

*And unto one he gave five talents, to another two, and to another one. . . . He that had received one went and digged in the earth, and hid his lord's money.* **Matt. 25:15-18.**

All too often we tend to identify ourselves with the one-talent man, to deny our adequacy, to wrap our potentials in a napkin and bury them. The problem centers in our need for inner power. The person who feels inadequate, who has feelings of worthlessness, often concludes that it is no use trying anymore. He feels unable to meet life.

To live the Christian life does not mean that we must be capable of doing what the five-talent or the two-talent man can do. The issue has to do with becoming all that we can in Christ. This is all that God expects of us.

As Christians we can afford to acknowledge our limitations, even our failures. We do not need to compare ourselves with others, or to compete with them. Let us not bemoan our limited resources, or go back over past failures. In God's presence and love we find ourselves accepted in spite of our failure and inadequacy. He accepts us this way every day. We find life abundant, not in quantity but in quality. We do not live with uncertainty about ourselves, our goals, or priorities. We have settled that. Christ has taken over. We do not compare ourselves with others as to how good we are.

If we believe that God has taken over the responsibility for our lives, we will have contentment in life, enhance the one talent, and realize the possibility in it. Christ gives meaning and purpose to the one-talent man as much as to the five-talent man. We are happy in Christ as we are. God is pleased to make the one-talent man the means for carrying out His purpose. By consulting our personal pride, by yielding to poverty of mind, we unnecessarily make ourselves miserable and spoil the good work that God could do in us.

We are responsible for one thing: the extent of our commitment to Him. We no longer need to think of failure. We are free from anxiety and fear. In Christ we have a sense of well-being and self-worth. We need not pretend to be something that we are not. God's love can be just as much a living power in us as in anyone else.

# FAITHFUL IN LITTLE THINGS

*He that is faithful in that which is least is faithful also in much.* **Luke 16:10.**

How particular do you think we ought to be in little things? None of us likes a check list. It does not really deal with how to live the Christian life. There is the danger of losing our sense of proportion, of becoming censorious in trifles. How do you suggest we deal with all the frailties and foibles that belong to human nature?

Our text affirms the principle that the individual who senses his responsibility in small matters can be trusted in larger things. What we are habitually in small things determines and affects the whole of our moral and spiritual living. What we really are behind all the words and deeds determines our fidelity all the way through.

Our allegiance to God and to His will leaves nothing out. There are no exceptions. There is no situation and no circumstance in life so small that it is not part of our religion. Our faith takes it all in, all there is of us and about us, small and great. This is very much like sculpturing a statue or painting a picture. Details make the difference between a genius and the average man. Great paintings can stand the test of the microscope in the examination of details.

Especially is this true of what we believe and practice. Those who hold a wrong theory as to what is truth, even in small things, find themselves in error. No chain is stronger than its weakest link. No character is stronger than its weakest point. According to a story, a little Dutch boy in Holland saw a small leak in one of the dikes. He tried to plug it up with his finger. If the hole became larger there was danger of the whole dike giving way. Morally and spiritually this is very much to the point.

We are to call upon God and the help of the Holy Spirit to become strong in the small things as well as in the large. We are to be true to Him in all things. We shall triumph at last if we are willing to make every sacrifice that truth may require at our hands.

In everything, small and great, we cast our life and our fortune with One who is eternal. It is our privilege to walk in the full light of truth.

# THE PRESENT OPPORTUNITY

*Redeeming the time, because the days are evil.* **Eph. 5:16.**

Paul urges us to buy up time; that is, to make it our own. Let no one take time from you, steal your time for unworthy things. When Paul wrote this Epistle to the Ephesians, their great city was given over to idolatry, to the excitement of the Roman world with its theaters, its gladiatorial shows and religious celebrations. Spiritual darkness prevailed along with all kinds of vice. The days were evil. So Paul urges the Ephesian Christians to make time their own and bring forth the fruits of righteousness.

To redeem time requires spiritual insight in order to sense that now is the moment to stand for Christ and for His truth. Evil times tend to dull the mind. All of us can look back on specific times that we thought were of little importance. Had we known it then, we would have done differently. We see now that it was a critical time for us. We had no intention of being spiritually asleep. We had no deliberate plan to neglect prayer and the study of God's Word, but we did. So we were not ready for the challenge. Our Christian experience suffered.

This kind of thing does happen. We had some inkling that this was the moment to trust God, to cast our whole dependence on Him, but we let it go. We should have realized that God planned this time to manifest His saving power, but we drifted into failure.

Evil times are opportunities of pre-eminent value for the alert Christian. We pray that God will make us more like Christ. Then God permits a crisis or a temptation in order to test us and fulfill our prayers, to teach us that His grace is sufficient. God provided us with the opportunity to redeem the time. "Time is short" (1 Cor. 7:29). Youth does not think so. The first twenty years are the longest we ever know. This is when time has no past. It is all future. But these golden years are gone almost before they are well begun. Make them count in a life given to the service of God.

We hear people say that they do not have time. We all have time. We have time to do what we really want to do. What is on trial is our sense of values.

# "NOW IT IS HIGH TIME"

*And that, knowing the time, that now it is high time to awake out of sleep: for now is our salvation nearer than when we believed.* **Rom. 13:11.**

Would you measure life by time? A man who had been held in a concentration camp was asked what he did through the long years of imprisonment. He replied, "I survived." Under those conditions, that was no mean achievement. But it is hardly adequate for us as Christians. We live only as we are redeemed by Christ here and now. We live by expressing His love and purity now. We redeem our possessions by investing in the kingdom of God now. We must be honest with ourselves now. We must be true to God now. We must be committed to Christ now. This present moment is all we have.

The happiness men expect from time and possessions is always a little way in the future, just coming; but it never comes. Both good times and critical times have carried men near to God in gratitude and in a sense of need. Good times have carried hosts of people away from God in pride, in pleasure, and in selfishness.

Now is the time to grow spiritually. A man's life does not consist in the abundance of things which he possesses. You may add another story to your house, but your own stature remains the same. You may give a thousand valuable books to the college library, but your education does not grow with the growing number of volumes.

Our essential development now is to grow into the stature of our Lord. But the devil will see to it that we are not left to a normal development. Our lives are subject to evil influences. We cannot afford to stand still. Growth implies increase in overcoming the enemies of the Christian life, in bringing forth increasingly the fruit of the Spirit. Growth is not always easy, but it is essential now. We either continue to grow or die.

Whatever steals our nights and days from the highest and the best, whatever fills our hours with vain actions, steals from eternity. The time we spend now to reach life's purpose in Christ will be restored to us a hundredfold when He returns and we inherit the earth.

# SPIRITUAL ASSETS

*At midnight Paul and Silas prayed, and sang praises unto God: and the prisoners heard them.* Acts 16:25.

There was nothing stale or flat about the religion of Paul and Silas. The world today needs Christians like that. What a faith to have when we really need it! Bill was a professed Christian. He had been brought up in a Christian home. But he got into serious trouble and went to jail. I visited him. He made one request—could I get him a Bible? He had neglected reading it for years. He now wanted to study, to seek to live by it so that this dreadful experience would never recur. He hoped God would forgive him and that others would still believe in him.

This boy was trying to stock his spiritual bank after it had collapsed. Are we depositing now in our own spiritual bank the spiritual wealth necessary for the evil days ahead? Or do we wait for catastrophe to strike before calling on the Lord? If we did this in the business world, or in any other profession, we would soon go bankrupt. Do we wait until we lose our jobs before taking out unemployment insurance? Do we wait until we have an accident before we take out collision insurance?

Moral and spiritual enrichment in our daily lives is like accumulating interest in the bank. We put it there now. The time to meet and gain victory over temptations that will come a month from this day, is now. Crucial days have dawned for us all. They will not get any better. We need to develop a morally and spiritually sound mind and character now.

Many of our failures may be classed as sins of surprise. We know later that it would never have happened if we had made adequate spiritual preparation. Granted that we do not know what is coming, but we are to cultivate a habit of daily preparation that will prevent us from falling into sin. No treacherous mountains we wish to climb require greater care than do the slippery places of the moral and spiritual life. There is a divine power available to us for every situation. Let us make sure of it now.

# "DRAW NIGH TO GOD"

*Draw nigh to God, and he will draw nigh to you.* **James 4:8.**

What does it mean to draw nigh to God? How can we do it? To know that God desires our communion with Him is cause for joy indeed. God would not issue the invitation if such a communion were not possible. In Christ, God has come all the way to draw men back to Himself.

It is a truth of first importance, that God seeks to draw nigh to us. This is the story of the Bible: God's search for lost man. He has heard our cry in the midst of our sin and death. He has bridged the gap that sin has caused. God draws nigh to us in Christ. In Christ, God comes between us and our sinful past. He draws nigh to us with forgiveness. We draw nigh to Him in repentance. He draws nigh to us in love. We draw nigh to Him in gratitude and humility. We draw nigh to God in prayer and the study of His Word. He draws nigh to us with the still small voice. Each day He awakens the mind and touches the heart. He continually transforms us. Even if a man be overtaken in a fault, He goes before us. He still loves us.

In one of the art galleries there is a picture entitled "The Waters of Lethe." On one side of the river stand the aged, the infirm, the sad, the weary, the crippled, the despairing, and the lost. But lo, as these pass through the waters to the other side, old age is transformed into the bloom of youth, despair and sadness into joy. Failure and deformity are changed into fullness of life.

But the saving, transforming presence of God is more than all the magic waters of any river. Naaman found it so. More than the waters of the Jordan, he bathed his mind and body in the love and mercy of God. He left not only his leprosy but the sins and sufferings of the past. God drew near to him. He found rejuvenation, and once more a life fresh, free, and full of sublime purpose.

Where sin is, there God's grace will be found at work to save from sin. He loves us to the end of our sinfulness and our weakness. We shall yet arrive at our eternal destination. The desire of God in patience, in mercy, and in loving forgiveness is toward us. We draw nigh to Him and know that all is well.

# TRANSFORMING THE COMMONPLACE

*"Martha, you are fretting and fussing about so many things; but one thing is necessary. The part that Mary has chosen is best."* **Luke 10:41, 42, N.E.B.**

During the last war a woman wrote these lines:

> I live on under my great trees,
> Raising my children, tending my garden,
> Watching for my Canterbury bells,
> While half the world bleeds—
> Bleeds and curses.
> Yet all I can do about it
> Is sew a few garments
> And save a little wheat;
> So my soul sits in the ashes—
> Brooding, unconsolable, ashamed.
>
> *—Author Unknown*

This woman craved a much more important role in life; some task worthy of her ambitions. Most of us find ourselves pretty much in the same position.

The crucial decisions are made in the run of everyday activity, decisions that ultimately affect our eternal destiny. The Bible reveals how people made decisions for life or for death. Every situation in which we find ourselves is the opportunity for character development, for or against that which is true or false.

The hope of the church and the cause of God lies in the faithfulness of its members in the commonplace matters of every day. Character, not fame, must have primary consideration. How do we let God transform the commonplace? By setting moral excellence before financial success; by sacrificing cash for the sake of character; by preferring to be "in" with God rather than to be "in" with the "right" people; by declining prominence for its own sake.

We must be thankful for a small place with an opportunity to be loyal to God and to one another. Every situation sets itself to establish the moral worth in our characters. The garlands of heaven are not reserved for the great heroes in fields of human endeavor.

# MADE FOR SERENITY

*Take no thought for your life, what ye shall eat, or what ye shall drink; nor yet for your body, what ye shall put on. Matt. 6:25.*

John Greenleaf Whittier wrote a familiar hymn that suggests clearly the pressure and tension under which most of us live, and our longing for serenity of soul:

> "Drop thy still dews of quietness,
> Till all our strivings cease,
> Take from our souls the strain and stress,
> And let our ordered lives confess
> The beauty of Thy peace."

When Christ came to the earth, men expected national deliverance from Roman bondage. When He performed the miracle of feeding the five thousand from five loaves and two fishes, men hoped they never again would go hungry. But He offered them the Bread of Life, and they felt cheated. He offered them inner rest amidst national conflict and Roman occupation, and they were offended. The Jews felt like men who had asked for money and had been given a tract.

God has placed us in the world, not so much to achieve something, but to be something. Being something always takes more time than doing something. What really matters is to be at peace with God, poised, gracious, kind, and full of compassion.

Jesus Christ wore the garb of our common humanity. But he wore it with a difference. People could touch the hem of His garment and receive healing virtue from Him. So long as we respond with anxiety and tension to life's pressures, taunts, and failures, we are like all those who make no profession of following Christ. We need the serenity of soul that will thrill the hearts of those who come within our influence.

Actually, any admiration and enthusiasm for our church on the part of nonchurch members is almost always for individuals in our church. Such admiration is created by individuals in whom abides a divine Presence. The invisible God becomes luminous in us. Angry reaction never advances anything, including ourselves. In Christ we are made serene and confident.

# OUR DAILY BREAD

*I am the bread of life.* **John 6:35.**

Physically we live by bread. Spiritually, we live by Jesus Christ and by the Word of God.

Many things that we considered luxuries years ago have now become necessities. We live by automobiles, by electrical appliances, by various services of government, all of which we consider indispensable to our daily existence. However, should these things be taken from us, we could still survive. This is not true of spiritual bread. We can never have too much of the bread that comes down from heaven.

Bread is basic. Physical starvation is a very real threat to hundreds of millions of people on the earth. Yet far more people starve spiritually. The greatest threat to spiritual health and life is the seeming apparent limited supply of the Bread of Life. Yet God has provided us with an abundance.

In a way, spiritual starvation depends on our spiritual appetite, on the quality of our appetite. To live by Jesus involves our dependence, our daily surrender. We are to need Him as much as we need physical bread. When we hunger and thirst for righteousness spiritual life is never withheld from us. Christ is indispensable to our everyday life. He really does meet our needs.

Christ came into the world not merely to educate the mind. He is a far more living and virile power than any of the intellectual movements in the world. Christ is not simply a new and more intelligent system of thought. This is involved, but Christ offers us the gift of new life, a new power from above. Christ comes to us not simply to correct our thinking, but to communicate life from God. We live by His life, which He brought into the world. We do not reduce divine reality to a creed. Behind all the truths of God's Word is the living Christ and the Holy Spirit. Our lives are involved with them. In the Bible God does not give us a series of lectures on religion. He gives Himself. There is no substitute for the real thing. The true and living God makes the difference in our lives.

# LET THE BIBLE BE READ

*All scripture is given by inspiration of God, and is profitable for doctrine, for reproof, for correction, for instruction in righteousness.* **2 Tim. 3:16.**

Never were there so many translations and interpretations of the Bible as we have today. A great amount of the seed of God's Word has been sown. Has the increase of godliness kept pace with the increase in Bibles? Has all this seed of the Word produced a proportionate increase in the harvest?

In the natural world, in a world with an exploding population, life depends upon sowing of wheat, corn, and all the other staples. Whole nations depend upon the sowing and the reaping. Failure of the crop must be a result of either bad seed, bad weather, or bad soil. The world today needs abundant harvests.

Spiritually, the seed of the Word of God is as good and vital as it has always been. We have the same Book of God, the same truth, the same gospel, the same Bread of Life. Also the Word of God is good in any climate. Christ and His righteousness still shine from heaven upon the hearts of men. From His throne in the heavenly sanctuary He still sends forth the Holy Spirit and the angels to "minister for them who shall be heirs of salvation" (Heb. 1:14). He pours forth His everlasting love and mercy upon us all. Probation has not closed. It is still open season for receiving the Word of God.

As for the condition of the soil, that is another question. What is the state of your heart and mind? What use do you make of the Bible? Do you study it regularly? Do you read it gratefully? Are you hungry for Christ? Are you prepared to obey the Word of God? Your responsibility is to see that the seed of God's Word does not fall on stony ground, or is sown on poor land, or among weeds. If you seriously consider your responsibility, one of these days just ahead of you, you will be grateful to God.

The farmer who leaves his fields unsown is foolish. Much more so the Christian who fails to sow the seed of God's Word in his mind and heart. All nature cries to be fed. The earth must be fed. Fire must be fed. All life must be fed. So it is with the soul. We never grow spiritually unless we are nourished with the food of God's Word.

# MEDITATION

*But when you pray, go into a room by yourself, shut the door, and pray to your Father. Matt. 6:6, N.E.B.*

Meditation is a lost art. There is tense thinking, a lot of day-dreaming, and a good bit of deep feeling; but meditation is sadly neglected. It is easier to be always doing something than to meditate upon God and His Word. It is possible to spend most of our time in religious activities for the church without any private life with God. We come to be satisfied with that. We need regular times for quiet deliberation upon high themes.

Meditation should be part of our morning devotion. It may mean getting up fifteen minutes earlier. It will make all the difference to our day and our living. Meditation is thinking seriously about God, some truth, some fact of our Lord's life, some promise of God to us—thinking about these things in the presence of God. We are to think God's thoughts after Him.

Let us ask ourselves upon what ground we believe that God is love, that He never stops loving us. The kind of faith that makes us want to live like Him, free from fear and ignorance, is that which comes from assurance received while in the presence of God.

Personal experience with the reality of Christ and the power of God must be revived. We need to re-experience a relationship with God. Here men often speak of feeling. But the experience with Christ never stops with feeling. The whole mind and person are involved.

The church has gone through all manner of pious calisthenics before the altar, wept many tears, called for rallies and meetings that aimed at getting the Spirit, fought for phrases, and erected banners with holy symbols in order to impress people. But it is increasingly important to persuade ourselves that to experience the indwelling Christ, to walk with God, can come only by daily excursion into a private audience with God.

However fervently we sing together and play music together, we are not doing the one thing that transforms and empowers us, increases the radiance of our witness, and sanctifies our friendships. One of the great discoveries is to know that God does truly fulfill His promise to meet with us in secret, and there to dwell within our hearts and minds.

259

# THIRSTING FOR GOD

*My soul thirsteth for God, for the living God. Ps. 42:2.*

Is it true that, in the midst of our worldly comforts, riches, and pleasures, we thirst for God? That we are not satisfied with all the things we have? It seems reasonable to believe that though we may have everything in this life to make us content, without this hunger for God we lack everything.

Has your heart and mind been satisfied lately with God's forgiveness of your sins and the removal of your guilt? Has the love of God enabled you to face the truth about yourself so that you don't need to put on a veneer or a phony front? Has Christ led you to the truth that makes you free? As you come to worship from Sabbath to Sabbath have you heard His voice speaking to your heart? In the midst of toil and care, and the responsibilities in the home have you felt the need for His peace in facing the irritations of life?

You see, deep within us we really cannot be satisfied with anything less than God. We live in a sinful world and have no escape from it. We know that this world has no solution to our inner needs and cravings. Day by day the still small voice breaks in upon our minds, reminding us of our great need of God, that God has a role in our lives and seeks to satisfy us.

This hunger we have for God is not a false feeling aroused by our excited minds and frequent fears, but a great desire that God has placed in our hearts. Ever since Adam and Eve were separated from God, there has been a great lack in the human heart that only the coming of Christ can satisfy. We were never meant to live apart from God any more than we were intended to live separate from our loved ones.

Let us yield to our hunger for God. Let us listen to the cry of our hearts for God and the heart of God for us: two persons meant for each other.

God continually searches for His lost children. Because this is true, we feel a profound need for God. Sooner or later, health, wealth, friends and loved ones, and even life itself, may fail us. The satisfaction God is to you is the destiny of your soul. Right now, would you settle for less than God's satisfaction of your heart and life?

# THE POWER OF PRAYER

**Pray without ceasing. 1 Thess. 5:17.**

What a wonderful privilege it is to pray to the living God and to be heard. The end of the world is near. Judgment for every man has come. Prayer means that we know and enjoy our heavenly Father. We come boldly to the throne of grace to receive help in time of need. We are daily sensible of our dependence on the living God, on that unseen Power who looks from His throne and ministers to us all His love and mercy through His Spirit and the angels.

When the Amalekites battled Israel in the wilderness Moses held high his hands to God till the going down of the sun. God was honored so long as they looked to Him. So it will always be.

We need continually the assurance of God's presence. "The effectual fervent prayer of a righteous man availeth much" (James 5:16). The Lord counsels us to pray to Him, since this is the most reasonable thing for God's children to do. He continually gives us precious promises to induce us to come to Him, find mercy and grace and strength. On almost every page of the Bible there is the assurance that prayer avails with God. Our weaknesses and necessities constitute no barrier to God. We do not need to wait until we feel strong. To come to Him with our needs and desires is entirely agreeable to Him. We affirm that the God we worship is infinitely wise and loving.

God does not fail to answer us, to deliver us from evil, and to guide our lives. Through prayer God's richest blessings flow down to us. Sinful though we may be, we may pray. We should always pray.

We may roll all our burdens upon Him, confident that He will sustain us. We seek divine guidance for our whole life through, rejoicing in the fact that every good and perfect gift comes from our heavenly Father, "with whom is no variableness, neither shadow of turning" (chap. 1:17).

Prayer involves a lifetime with God—a year, a month, a week, a day, a minute of vital contact between ourselves and God. We do not stoop to whine or to beg. We come to see ourselves as we really are before God and still are loved. We come to grow more like Jesus. That is what is bound to happen.

## "BE STILL"

*Be still, and know that I am God. . . . The Lord of hosts is with us; the God of Jacob is our refuge.* **Ps. 46:10, 11.**

We are never more glorified in our Christian experience than when, in a strength not our own, we are quiet and confident before God. Here we resign our opinions, our anxieties, merits, strength, and our resources. We look simply to Him. "Be still" refers to our willingness to let God do for us what we cannot do for ourselves, to let Him fight battles for us that we cannot fight for ourselves.

We have accepted the Lordship of Christ. Our position in the battle of life is never one of anxiety and apprehension. Being still means putting all things into His hands, and with a brave heart biding His time.

There are two sides to the Christian life: the quiet and contemplative, and the vigorous and enterprising. It is of prime importance that both sides receive full attention. The special danger of our time is in our liability to exaggerate the place of self-assertion. We are apt to carry our bustling self-sufficiency into our religious life. In the working out of our salvation we fail to develop quiet thought, silent prayer, and receptive waiting. Might we not progress faster toward Christlikeness by a quiet looking to Him than by all feverish activity? "My soul, wait thou only upon God; for my expectation is from him" (Ps. 62:5).

Working, running, fighting, wrestling, are all words used in the Scripture to describe part of our Christian experience. All of them are easier to do than silently to wait upon God. To lean on Christ's strength is the crowning triumph. It is easier to engage in all kinds of religious work than to fall helplessly at the feet of Christ. It is easier to summon our energies to effect small improvements than to receive Christ's full salvation by faith alone. The supreme moments in our experience are those in which the quiet waiting upon God supersedes all other action.

# OUR FELLOWSHIP WITH GOD

*Truly our fellowship is with the Father, and with his Son Jesus Christ.* **1 John 1:3.**

Fellowship with Christ does not maintain itself. It disappears very soon from the life that does not pray. Prayer is the opening of our whole lives to God each day. Study of His Word is opening our lives to His voice. Life with Christ is a life of love, joy, and peace. It must be maintained by prayer and the study of His Word. Otherwise we are operating under our own steam. The difference is like turning our washing machine by hand instead of plugging it in to the power line. It is like rowing our boat in a storm instead of turning on the motor.

The trouble with most of us is that we operate on our own so much of the time. But our dependence and trust must be in God alone. Nothing is too small or inconsequential to commit to Him. In this way we live by faith. Full commitment and a dynamic faith will not bring freedom from temptation. On the contrary, it may be the occasion for the devil's increased attack.

The Christian life is not without conflict. Christ is our victory. He alone can keep us from sinning. We do not direct all our energies to resist temptation. We direct them to Christ. This is spiritual reliance, dependence on God. Victory over temptation and sin is not an achieving, but a receiving. The more we rely on Christ, look to Christ, the less we depend on ourselves. The living Christ is greater than any power of our own, or any power of the enemy.

Only within this personal fellowship with God are we free from the fear of falling and sinning. If we fear we are going to fall, we are half way there. "Perfect love casts out fear." Life with Christ is an assurance of victory. We are delivered from the futility of trying to live the Christian life without His help. The responsibility belongs to our Lord. Divine guidance becomes a new and vital thing to us.

This awareness of Christ in our lives becomes a reality to us, constant and all-controlling. This is no irksome effort on our part. We live in the love of God. This is the life to which Christ calls us.

# "GLAD IN THE LORD"

*My meditation of him shall be sweet. I will be glad in the Lord.* Ps. 104:34.

The world has need of us, providing we are strong and glad in the Lord. The key to this inner gladness is "in the Lord." Such a spirit is not through self-confidence. Nor is it through the strength and splendor of any actions we have done, nor through the deliberate iron will that marks the so-called man of power. We do not seek the homage of men by brazen courage and self-assertion.

Because our life is in the Lord, we can afford to be sweet and glad and modest. If we boast of our self-confidence, of the strength of our personality, we know only too well in whom we trust. But we have no command over the forces of evil. If we build upon ourselves we have only a tower of Babel for our end.

Are you not glad that you do not have to go it alone? Are you not glad that you have power from God, the fruit of the Spirit, and the very sweetness of our Lord? Are you not glad to cast your fortunes with One who is the very essence of sweetness and love? It is no false gladness that prompts us to exclaim, "I can do all things through Christ which strengtheneth me."

What gladness is ours—His nearness, His glory, His power, His love! All these are known to us and are realized through faith. Christ prayed that "the love wherewith thou hast loved me, may be in them, and I in them" (John 17:26). What a glorious reason for rejoicing and being glad all the days of our lives.

This truth is not a difficult one to understand. We say to our loved ones, "You are in my heart." We know what that means. We have the same relationship with Christ. Because we have Christ in our hearts, gloom and depression have to go out. His presence is inconsistent with all that would make us unhappy and sour.

When Christ comes into our hearts He does not come alone. He brings with Him all those qualities of the abundant life, enabling us to live radiantly. He enters and abides as an irresistible joy. No sooner does Christ enter than gladness begins.

# ALONE WITH GOD

*Give attendance to reading, to exhortation, to doctrine. . . . Meditate upon these things.* **1 Tim. 4:13-15.**

One of the most tragic stories in American literature is recorded in "The Man Without a Country." But a Christian without communion with God is worse off than was that man. No matter how much we may accomplish in our daily lives, without Christ we effect nothing. God asks us to take seriously our life with Him.

With many people fellowship with God alone does not seem to count. Yet all the time Christ keeps on trying to tell us that it does matter. Christ promised that if we daily attach ourselves to Him our lives will be fruitful. If we really believe this why not bring ourselves to act on it? Within the family let us encourage one another to take time with God alone. It certainly is far better than trying to go it alone. "Well," you may say, "it does not come natural to me." But God can change all that. Do we take Him for real? Do we believe what He says? Why should it be so hard to get alone with God?

We wear the Christian label. Often we are merely church Christians. We fall back into comfortable living that seems not to need God. All this rat race, the pushing and grabbing and raging in the world, is utterly futile. This is the story of too many lives.

All the time God is trying to get through to us to save us time, energy, and frustration. The only real solution has been found by the individual Christian who means to let God possess and direct his life in the way of peace, love, and happiness. The interesting thing is that people who do this find the way to make wrongs right so much quicker and their work done so much easier.

Our heavenly Father is no stranger to the way we live with all our pressures and problems. Someone told me that he was too busy to take the time for private devotions. His position comes down to this: "God, You really mean very little to me. I can get along on my own."

But our lives are part of God's plan. We ought to let Him fill our lives the best way He can. We ought to keep the windows of our souls open to Him.

# EFFECTUAL PRAYER

*The effectual fervent prayer of a righteous man availeth much.* James 5:16.

Effectual prayer lies in the fact that we ask that God's will may be done. We learn His will from His Word.

God's will for us is bent on our salvation. We seek God because we have need of help higher than our own. We pray because we believe in Christ as our King who rules and directs our lives. We seek deliverance from those things in our lives that are contrary to Him. We pray because we know that behind all the problems and conflicts of life there stands a loving heavenly Father. We pray to be more like Him.

What do you want most from God?—to live triumphantly? To learn to love God and your fellow men? God's great purpose is to fulfill our lives. Do you find meaning in asking Him to do that, to draw your affections from the things that would destroy your Christian experience? Do you ask Him to possess you by His Spirit?

Our heavenly Father has pledged Himself to hear our prayers and answer them. Ought not this certainty to be our confidence and strength and hope? Have we any other spiritual strength within our reach? Do we have access to any other power like unto this? Can we find anywhere else a love that meets our basic needs for acceptance, for security, and for self-worth? When we are weighed down with our faults, frailties, and failures is there anything more certain and assuring than to come to Him for rest, peace, forgiveness, mercy, and joy?

"I am the vine, ye are the branches" (John 15:5). Are we willing to accept our position as a branch linked with Christ, the true vine? If we live in such a dependent relationship God will give us what we ask for, because we will always ask according to His will.

Some professed Christians live a fairly orderly life by self-discipline. It is remarkable how many things can be done by the sheer force of the will. But this is a cut-flower religion. It has no real roots. It does not last. Christian living is a transformed life. We are linked with the true Vine.

# "A LIGHT ON MY PATH"

*Thy word is a lamp to guide my feet and a light on my path.* **Ps. 119:105, N.E.B.**

The Word of God is the word that comes from God. God speaks, and His word is true. God speaks, and the event prophesied takes place. God's Word is an intelligent communication to us. It contains that which He wishes us to understand concerning Himself and His will. When God speaks we can count on that word. One of God's best gifts to us is His word of truth.

We must not shift our belief in the word of God to the uncertain voices of human councils and critics. To put man's word before God's word is one of the oldest and most effective of Satan's snares. Once people lose confidence in God's Word they soon disobey it. Deny or disbelieve that the Scripture is God's word, and evil will triumph in the end. Was not this the great temptation made to Adam and Eve—"Hath God said?"

Often the temptation to doubt and question the Word of God comes to us through the lips of clever men, able men, attractive men, men to be admired, respectable men. We are tempted to dip our colors. When men do this they may call themselves a church, but it is not the church of God.

People everywhere are in search of the truth. Many grope in darkness. Martin Luther was long tormented by a desperate search for the forgiveness of his sins. When he discovered the Word of God and studied it he saw God's light streaming from the cross of Christ. He believed it. He became a new man.

The psalmist declared, "O send out thy light and thy truth: let them lead me; let them bring me unto thy holy hill" (Ps. 43:3). Is this not also the cry of all our hearts and minds? Here is truth. Here is certainty. Here is the Way, the Truth, and the Life. The Word of God will lead you to Christ, keep you in Christ.

You may hesitate to accept the free and easy words of men. You may be skeptical about the promises of men in high office. But in His Word God speaks to you in hundreds of promises, offering you the truth, the everlasting love of God, the privilege of being led by the Spirit. Christ has sealed and guaranteed every pledge with the power of His own resurrection.

# ASK—SEEK—KNOCK

*Ask, and it shall be given you; seek, and ye shall find; knock, and it shall be opened unto you.* Matt. 7:7.

Jesus knows how often we are reluctant to pray and how we neglect to pray. He does everything possible to get us to pray. This threefold promise embraces all of us: "Every one that asketh receiveth." If God dropped a promise down from heaven with your name on it, would you believe it? Some years ago a young man named Henry came to me. He was going through a period of doubt. He said, "If God's hand would come out in the sky every night and write the words, 'Henry, I love you,' I would believe. That is an easy thing for Him to do. Why does He not do that?"

But there are hosts of people called "Henry." How would this man know the promise was for him and not someone else with the same name, someone more worthy, perhaps? But none of us is worthy. God has no elite group to belong to. The promise is for everyone. You and I are part of that everyone. What God has promised to everyone has to include us. So believe His promise.

How do we know His promises are true? We must ask that question sincerely. Do you really want to know? We cannot get answers simply by having an argument. God does not come to us at the close of an argument on prayer. We are to be concerned with the moral and spiritual aspects. God answers prayer for our well-being. He takes it for granted that we will ask for the right thing.

Do we really desire the best things—love, peace, life, righteousness, and all the fruit of the Spirit? God will give us all this. Without these inner qualities all else goes for nothing. Should you be a mean, selfish, unloving person, yet pray for riches, and He gave them to you, then He would not be the God you really need. He would not meet your basic needs at all. The meaning of life would not be clear to you.

The door to God is always open. The man who seeks for wealth for wealth's sake will probably find it. The man who seeks knowledge with all his mind will find it. And if we wholeheartedly seek Christ's righteousness and all the fruit of the Spirit shall we not also find them?

# THE SPLENDID HUMILITY OF OUR LORD

*He shall not strive, nor cry; neither shall any man hear his voice in the streets. A bruised reed shall he not break, and smoking flax shall he not quench, till he send forth judgment unto victory. Matt. 12:19, 20.*

How sensational Christ could have been when tempted to fling Himself down from the pinnacle of the Temple. He could have displayed His miraculous power before the people! On one occasion His disciples urged Him to call fire down from heaven to bring the unrepentant to their knees before Him. There seem to have been numerous occasions for such demonstrations of power.

Some things are not found in the life of Jesus. He does not strive. He does not wrangle on religious themes. He does not engage in petty dialog. He does not cry. There is nothing loud about Him, nothing overdone, no attempt at self-advertisement. Jesus seeks no self-esteem. In His life and ministry He raised no shrine to the gods of passion, pomp, or popularity. When confronted with Judas accompanied by the mob who came to arrest Him, He said: "Thinkest thou that I cannot now pray to my Father, and he shall presently give me more than twelve legions of angels?" (Matt. 26:53). What an opportunity to dispatch His enemies with a single stroke!

"He shall not . . . lift up . . . his voice . . . in the street." He comes not to startle, to overwhelm people with sensational appeals. Christ plays no part of a fanatic. He comes to win men. His name is the Prince of Peace. His doctrine is truth, His essence is purity, His character is love.

Just prior to His crucifixion, when "the Father had given all things into his hands . . . he riseth from supper, and laid aside his garments; and took a towel, and girded himself. . . . And began to wash the disciples' feet" (John 13:3-5).

When the Father had given Him all power, why not call upon His disciples to acknowledge Him King of kings and Lord of lords? In a few hours they were to forsake Him and flee. Knowing all this, He took a towel and washed their feet. "Having loved his own . . . he loved them unto the end." In Christ the desire for attention does not express itself. The passion of ostentation belongs to the Pharisee, but not to Jesus. Divine humility is in His heart.

# "NOT AS OTHER MEN"

*The Pharisees stood and prayed . . . God I thank thee, that I am not as other men are, extortioners, unjust, adulterers, or even as this publican.* **Luke 18:11.**

The Pharisee was a better man in terms of conduct. If we are to judge men by their works as we do trees by their fruits, the Pharisee was more to be admired for his religion. He was not lying when he said he was an honest man, a good moral person, that he fasted and paid an honest tithe.

The publican was a collector of taxes. This man was hired by the Romans who maintained little or no check on his activities, so long as he delivered the amount of revenue the Romans demanded. The system was open to abuse and extortion. The publicans were a despised and a hated class. They were regarded as supremely selfish and unclean because they had sold themselves to the Romans.

When we come to see the practical difference between the two classes, there is a lot to be said for the Pharisee. The lowly demeanor and self-condemning words of the publican do not lend grace to a dishonest life or any departure from the law of God. Yet the publican "went down to his house justified rather than the other."

Our Lord seeks to impress upon us the fatal danger of spiritual pride. The Pharisee claimed to be a better man before God. Therefore he was farther away from the kingdom than the publican. The text speaks against undue confidence when we are tempted to claim to be superior Christians. This Pharisee made himself, rather than God, the center of his life. He considered himself the measure of virtue and righteousness. Therefore he did not feel a need for God's grace.

The true Christian knows that whatever goodness he has, it is the gift of God. The church needs confident men and women, but confident in the sense that they know themselves to be redeemed by Christ alone. We all need Christian self-respect that is consistent with the life that Christ lives in and through us. Surrender and humility are a permanent and increasing attitude. Of ourselves we can do nothing.

# "MY FATHER IS GREATER THAN I"

*Do you not believe that I am in the Father, and the Father in me? I am not myself the source of the words I speak to you: it is the Father who dwells in me doing his own work.* **John 14:10, N.E.B.**

Christ is making no claims for Himself, even though He had every reason to do so. He said, "I can of mine own self do nothing" (John 5:30). He could rightly have proclaimed Himself God and King, deserving of all the recognition and worship of men. But He "made Himself of no reputation." He says, in effect, "I am only God's servant, God's agent mediating the things of God and the character of God. It is not I, but my Father in Me, that accounts for everything about Me. He is the living fountain out of which I do all My miracles."

Jesus was free from all self-esteem. He had a divine guidance greater than His own. He depended entirely on God. His life gave place to no ego trips or expressions.

We all have to start where the publican started. Self will destroy us unless we do. All we need is Christ and His righteousness, which will give us freedom from our self-centeredness. It is possible to try to hide our self-esteem under such things as fasting, tithing, doing missionary work, with a lot of self-effort in religious living. But before Christ the secret knowledge of ourselves comes out.

The redeeming love and grace of God, by which we are saved, will not permit us to claim a superiority that alienates Christians in other churches and drives them from the truth. We are to obey the law of God in a way that is distinctly Christlike, while at the same time we are not to exclude from our friendship those who may not know the truth as we claim to do. We may condemn the flagrant sins of men but allow ourselves the more subtle sins of the spirit—pride, selfishness, the proud forms of ego, which work the most harm in other lives.

The remarkable thing about the Christian faith is that we are not supposed to cut much of a figure on our own. We are on the center stage in the great controversy, and the universe is watching us, but we are witnesses, not to ourselves, but to God's plan to save us by Christ's righteousness alone.

# HUMILITY OR RECOGNITION

*He . . . went into the borders of Tyre and Sidon, and entered into an house, and would have no man know it: but he could not be hid.* **Mark 7:24.**

There is a modesty and a humility about Christ that asks for no recognition. He never advertised Himself. At the same time He could not be hid. A genuine goodness like that is self-revealing. As Christians we are to be like the Master. Innate Christian goodness is bound to shine through. People will get wind of it. Wherever there is a loyal disciple of Christ, there he will be known.

The world needs, more than anything else, Christians who love and care. The world cries out for such as are like Christ. The true Christian cannot be hid. He does not need to solicit attention or crave recognition. He who knows Christ will be sought from far and wide, as the queen of Sheba came from afar to see the king of Israel.

When the Syrophoenician woman made her needs known to Christ, He helped her. His compassion triumphed over every desire to withdraw into isolation. The Christ who sought to avoid all publicity yielded to the woman's need for love and healing power.

To withdraw into a monastery or a place of retreat can be either an expression of consecration to God or an expression of selfishness. Christianity does not shun the world or seek to escape from its problems by solitude, by moving as far as possible from sinful men. A Christian who seeks a life of retirement from working for others can be a good man. But it must never be forgotten that we are called upon to sacrifice ourselves for the world's need. There is always the temptation to dwell comfortably in our houses, forgetful of the misery and needs of others who stand at our door. We cannot retire in sheltered tranquillity. The world's need made Christ visible and known. It will make His followers visible, too. Granted that great Christians shun observation and publicity. The saving righteousness of Christ lays the glory of man in the dust. Nevertheless, the time comes for our revelation to men. The needs and cravings of lost men and women for what Christ is and has, draw forth the love of Christ's followers.

# MEEK AND LOWLY IN HEART

*Notwithstanding in this rejoice not, that the spirits are subject unto you; but rather rejoice, because your names are written in heaven.* Luke 10:20.

The gift of power from God brings an obligation, not to pride and self-exaltation but to greater humility and holiness. Christ taught His disciples how perilous a spirit of self-glorification can be, particularly in spiritual experiences relating to the power of the Holy Spirit. "Take my yoke upon you, and learn of me; for I am meek and lowly in heart" (Matt. 11:29).

We need to be afraid of any attitude that boasts of spiritual experiences. The joy of being used by the Lord is not wholly without danger. The meek and lowly Christ does not boast of His own spiritual power and experience by the Holy Spirit. Only what Christ is able to do through our weak and feeble selves has any significance. We learn this lesson very slowly.

Any claim to self-exaltation by means of religion, springs from the belief that we are essentially superior because God has favored us with truth and power. God selects His prophets and apostles from among "the weakest of the weak." Christ commanded the man cleansed from leprosy to say nothing to any man, not to publish abroad the miraculous healing. Why, in so many cases, was the miraculously healed person bidden to keep silent? Miracles, sensational manifestations, are just the thing to get a crowd. People are really impressed by this kind of thing. Today there are many occasions when professed Christians have occasion to tell of the sensational work of God, so-called.

It is easier to exalt this kind of startling events than to withdraw into a quiet place away from the excitable crowds. Great spiritual excitement often produces perilous attitudes. When we are drawn the closest to Christ, spiritual excitement and ecstasy are not really important. A sense of awe at God's presence, a quietness of voice and mind, possesses us. There is no occasion to call attention to ourselves, that we have been the recipient of special favors from God. In all our witness we are to give glory to God and never to ourselves. When Christ draws near to us He makes us partakers of His holiness and His humility.

# THE PRAISE OF MEN

*For they valued their reputation with men rather than the honour which comes from God.* John 12:43, N.E.B.

The Pharisees were probably close to being convinced at times that Jesus was the Messiah. But they did not like His type. To espouse His cause would degrade them from their honorable status. They were not prepared to make this kind of sacrifice. Their pride and jealousy refused to receive evidence and listen to arguments that He could be the Messiah. They finally expressed themselves in hostility by planning His crucifixion.

There is nothing wrong with valuing our reputation among men. We should have a good reputation. What is wrong is loving it more than desiring the praise of God. Desire for human favor is not necessarily wrong. We are not required to be indifferent to personal approval. Christ did not seek honor from men, yet the Scripture says of Him, "Reproach hath broken my heart" (Ps. 69:20).

Neither is it desirable to have a lofty indifference to men. Our desire to win men to Christ is right. But to subordinate ourselves to their influence and favor is unworthy of us as Christians. There is probably no tendency in which we are more liable to indulge than this: the peril of adopting the will and pressure of men as our rule of life, to refer our conduct to men as the court of final appeal. Their sanctions control our motives and our conduct. This is a form of idolatry.

Pilate, rather than lose his place and standing with men, delivered the Lord Jesus Christ to be crucified. The extent of sins and denial of the truth to which the love of human favor and the worship of human idols lead men is enormous. Thousands of people who have been convicted of the truth are held back from accepting it because of what other people think. How many convictions by the Holy Spirit to obey the truth are thus silenced? How many minds are induced to resist the gospel and deny our Lord? He who seeks to please men rather than God submits to a multitude of lords, all sinful, weak mortals.

We must reckon it a small thing to be judged by man's judgment in comparison with God's judgment and His favor toward us.

# GO UP HIGHER

*When you receive an invitation, go and sit down in the lowest place, so that when your host comes he will say, "Come up higher, my friend." Luke 14:10, N.E.B.*

Jesus was speaking to men who eagerly grasped at the best places. Half the misery and anxiety in people's lives springs from the exaggerated importance they attach to themselves and continually cherish. These are people with a selfish temperament, who covet earnestly the best seats rather than the best gifts, status with men rather than standing with God.

Most of us proceed from the idea that we live in a society where self-defense is the first law of life, and the second is like unto it—self-assertion. It may just be that Christ's recommendation that we take the lowest place is worth trying.

About forty-five years ago in Oxford, England, there lived a brilliant young university professor, H. A. Hodges, an English don in Balliol College, Oxford's most illustrious school. He was passing through a period of doubt and skepticism. He had spent years arguing the fine points of the Christian religion. Then he experienced a complete change in his life. He himself tells the story. One evening he was walking down the main street of Oxford and happened to pass a bookseller's window. There among the books was a nineteenth-century print of Jesus washing the disciples' feet. His eyes were riveted to that scene. A ray of light from the Holy Spirit illumined his mind. It suddenly dawned on him what kind of person Jesus was. Hodges said he knew then that the God of heaven was his footman; all the truth about the Incarnation, the life and death of Christ, came into proper focus.

Do you know what a footman is? Hodges spoke as one familiar with the role of footmen in the great houses of England. The footman is the flunky. He does all the lowest menial duties. Hodges told himself, "If God is like that, He has my life. If God can descend from heaven and become the servant of mankind and give His life for men, I will commit my life to Him." He did just that.

Christ is saying to us, "The best way up is the way down." We are to humble ourselves, accept the low place of service in which our Lord Himself sat.

# NO SELF-DEFENSE NEEDED

*In quietness and in confidence shall be your strength.* Isa. 30:15.

The Christian has really matured when he no longer needs to defend himself, when he needs not to ask questions or push himself forward for the sake of acceptance and recognition, when his lips are neither opened in complaint nor in the importunity of men.

We are never more secure emotionally and spiritually than in those moments when, in a strength not our own, we are quiet before God and man. We need to resign anxieties about ourselves, the concern for what others think of us. We need to surrender the responsibility we feel for ourselves and let God carry it. The key factor that makes all this possible is God's love for us and His acceptance of us. When we are united to Christ we become one spirit with Him, just as in marriage, husband and wife become one. There follows a real sense of well-being.

We are to keep our hearts open to the free, rich, inspiring, and everlasting love of God. The fearful Christian is concerned with his own problems of life. We cannot hope to secure God's continued love and favor by a self-imposed pattern of staying by the rules. This kind of self-concern is ruled out by the unconditional love of God, for this very anxiety reveals a failure to trust in, and depend on, God. We need to let God love us and set us free.

Much of life makes great demands upon us. These are times when Christ must be everything. He is our shield and salvation. Moses said to the children of Israel when they were pursued by the Egyptian army and hemmed in before the Red Sea, "Fear ye not, stand still, and see the salvation of the Lord, which he will shew to you today. . . . The Lord shall fight for you, and ye shall hold your peace" (Ex. 14:13, 14).

If we were asked to point out the strong Christians, the successful ones, the impressive ones, we probably would select the self-reliant, the aggressive, the pushers, the bustling activist. In the Bible the great men of God neither strive nor cry. They quietly leave the problems of life to God. Their dependence and deep prayers are largely unspoken, and their service is devoid of display. Their lives are full of simple love and quiet confidence in God.

276

# CHARACTER THAT CANNOT BE HID

*A city that is set on a hill cannot be hid.* **Matt. 5:14.**

There is a certain type of religious experience that clamors for recognition, but the Christian faith is discredited by a desire for show. Christ abhorred any kind of religious parade. He was deaf to applause. He sought not honor from men. It was enough to have His Father's approval, His love, and approbation. Christ avoided publicity. He sought the solitude of the wilderness for prayer. When people wanted to make Him king He retired to a private place. What a rebuke to man's self-assertion, to the advertising of himself.

Genuineness of character, goodness, purity, are all self-revealing. This is true, in a large measure, of genius. A greatly gifted man needs not to proclaim his extraordinary abilities. They will proclaim themselves. If a man is a genuine Christian everyone having fellowship with him will know him to be such.

The hidden violets proclaim their presence in every passing breeze. The lark, hidden in the light of the sun, fills all the landscape with music. Christian character is all the more penetrating and convincing for its loveliness, all the more captivating for its humility, all the more renowned for its purity. The man who has Christ within cannot hide himself.

The apostle John was banished to the Isle of Patmos. But far from sinking from view in that solitary sea, he stands today before the world amid sublime prophecies in the book of Revelation. Enemies drove Martin Luther into Wartburg castle to hide; but there, in translating the Scriptures into German, he became the attraction of all eyes and minds. Bunyan's enemies consigned him to Bedford jail. There he began to write *Pilgrim's Progress* and became one of the foremost of the immortals of Christendom.

Men of surpassing Christian love and faith need not be concerned lest they should be overlooked or forgotten. They are the last to be ignored. The man of genuine goodness is the very last to be slighted. He who knows the deep things of God will be sought out far and wide. A man of genuine prayer will ever be sought for intercession with God.

# WILL TO DO HIS WILL

*If any man will do his will, he shall know of the doctrine, whether it be of God.* John 7:17.

I have always wanted to do justice to the will of man. I have always respected well-disciplined people who ordered their lives pretty much to the line. But many never seem to be able to break the chains of habit and make their decisions stick.

I have urged a lot of people in my time to make the right decision for God and for His character. When the pressure comes many simply do not want to be what they know they ought to be. Granted that a man should not be reckless or careless in his choices. There are times when a man must grant himself a delay in making some choices. But when confronted with Jesus Christ and the claims of His truth, we gain nothing by indecision.

There is always some risk to a man's choice. But if life in Christ is to have any reality at all, then one must move forward with a courage as did the Israelites at the Red Sea. The man who acts decidedly for Christ knows the power of God to save.

When we insist upon delay are we being really honest with ourselves? When we say we want more time is there not a tendency to trifle with the truth? Hesitation before the claims of Jesus Christ often reveals unwillingness to give up one's own way.

The more sincere and true we are in our devotion to truth, the more life will be settled for righteousness. The decision for Christ may involve changes; let us make them. There will be new adjustments. Let us make them. The longer we remain uncommitted and undecided, the fiercer becomes the conflict within us.

Our finest moments are those when we choose Christ. Our worst moods are those that seek to live apart from Him. God is sufficient for all our needs. A young woman who had strayed far from God came to see me during a Week of Religious Devotion. There was a new urgency in her manner, a committed tone in her voice. "I have determined to say Yes to Christ," she said. "I am prepared to give up all that comes between Christ and me. I have already told my friends." That commitment completely changed her life. She gained Christ. From then Christ took over as He always does.

# WHAT IS A CHRISTIAN?

*They marvelled; and they took knowledge of them, that they had been with Jesus.* **Acts 4:13.**

What is a Christian? How would you identify one? Of all the questions men and women ask of us, this one must be answered with clarity, certainty, and simplicity. As we read the account of the transformation of Peter, what comes clearly to our attention is that the power to live a genuine Christian life is realized once the presence of Christ actually comes into our life. A person without Christ is not a Christian.

A few weeks previously, Peter had shamefully denied his Lord. God found him, forgave him, and changed him. Now, in our text for today, we see the new Peter, empowered to witness and to live for Christ.

Just prior to Peter's denial, Christ said to him, "When thou art converted, strengthen thy brethren" (Luke 22:32). The first essential condition of being a Christian is that we must be genuine converts to Jesus Christ. This means that intellectually we are convinced that Jesus is the Son of God, that He died for our sins personally, that He lives for our restoration to the image in which He created us. Further, it means we have been morally and spiritually convicted of our need of Christ as Saviour and Lord, who alone has the answer to the sin problem in our own lives. Still further, it means we have yielded to His rulership; we now belong to Him. He has become the primary reality in our lives. Any religious activity that stops short of Christ stops short of being a Christian.

Becoming a Christian is an experience that cannot be bought, bribed, earned, or won. We can only accept Christ by faith. The word *believe* means that our whole life has been won over. In Christ we are new persons.

The Christian has the abundant life of Christ. We can be moving *in* a truth, *in* a religious body, and not really be *of* it. The church may enlist our services without our being a Christian. The outstanding quality of being converted to Christ is enduring allegiance as a follower, a willingness to bring our whole lives permanently into line with Him and with His Word. It involves unfailing love for God and man.

# REDISCOVERING JESUS CHRIST

*If from thence thou shalt seek the Lord thy God, thou shalt find him, if thou seek him with all thy heart. Deut. 4:29.*

The British journalist, Malcolm Muggeridge, wrote a book, *Jesus Rediscovered.* For most of his life he had been an unbeliever and a skeptic. He was interviewed on the television by a leading minister in the United States who asked him, "Why do you speak of rediscovering Jesus when He was never lost? He is better known than any other man who has ever lived." Muggeridge replied, "I do not mean that I had not heard of Jesus or read about Him. But for years Jesus Christ has been lost to my own understanding and experience. I now know Him as the answer to all my needs."

The unique power of Jesus Christ is His ability to reach men. We become a certain kind of people as a result of meeting Him, the kind of people He intended us all to be. We do not find Christ until we sense His claim upon our lives. We must take Him seriously. In a way it seems passing strange that when people get sick and in trouble, suddenly they feel a great need to trust God and experience His healing and delivering power. However, it is wonderful to realize that God has been there all the time.

The man who goes to church only when he gets sick and in need of help is saying, "God, You mean a little to me, but not much." The person who never goes to church to worship and to meet with God says, "God, You just do not mean a thing to me. I do not need You." The man who never prays is saying the same thing. When we study the Bible and pray, we say: "God, I need You. I trust You. I am dependent on You. I love You for what You are."

All this has to do with us as persons and a personal God. Nothing meets our needs or solves our problems without this relationship—God and I.

Service for God is a consequence of our knowing Him. This does not mean He is indifferent to our willingness to serve. But much religious programming is incidental. God wishes to share His love with us, for us to believe and accept that love. Then we want God at the heart of our lives. We have shifted our center from self to Christ.

# THE PEARL OF GREAT PRICE

*A merchant looking out for fine pearls found one of very special value; so he went and sold everything he had, and bought it.* **Matt. 13:45, 46, N.E.B.**

Christ, the Pearl of Great Price, is the one unique and supreme value in contrast with all the other treasures we have. The parable recognizes that we can have in this life many pearls of value: fine clothes, fine houses, fine food, fine positions. By nature many people desire the pearls in every area of life and are often satisfied with nothing less than the best.

But Christ is saying that there is one Supreme Pearl or Treasure that transcends everything that a man can have. Christ offers to us His stainless purity, His boundless love, His eternal sweetness and patience, His unbroken communion with our heavenly Father, His loftiness of mind, His wonderful peace, and His eternal righteousness. All this is the best answer to our hunger for life's values. If we are defeated it is by our failure to live by eternal values.

It is not the engrossment with the world but the grip of this Supreme Personality that sets our values straight. In Him alone can the world be put right. Christ gives to life a value and a wealth that saves and never destroys, that uplifts and never degrades.

Because we have found Christ we refuse to have materialism as a front for security. Take the gold of Fort Knox, strip men and women of all their pearls, take the gems of Asia's palaces, the rubies of the Orient; take everything of material value in the world—place on the scales of the Almighty all that men count treasure. Christ categorically affirms that one human being far outweighs it all in value. There is one Treasure, one Pearl, that outvalues them all.

Other things can be very desirable. But Christ outranks them all. When it comes to Jesus Christ, there really is no other treasure of importance. He stands unique in that every person in the world needs this Pearl.

# THE GAIN AND LOSS OF KNOWING CHRIST

*I count everything sheer loss, because all is far outweighed by the gain of knowing Christ Jesus my Lord, for whose sake I did in fact lose everything.* **Phil. 3:8, 9, N.E.B.**

Wealth, power, pleasure, popularity, fame, all can be legitimate desires. They are not necessarily wrong in themselves. The missiles that take men to the moon are filled with the most perfect and expensive machinery and equipment that men can create. But once superior equipment is invented, or a more excellent missile, then the old one must be scrapped. So with battleships and aircraft carriers.

These days so much depends upon our willingness to sacrifice excellence for those things that are even more excellent and efficient. The astronomer readily renounces his telescope lens for one more powerful. The art lover will give up all his second-rate pictures or paintings to acquire a masterpiece of Michelangelo or a Raphael. We all sacrifice the mediocre for the best.

Once we see the beauty and perfection of Christ, we must be willing to sacrifice every low standard, every questionable pleasure, friendship, and interest, if it means that to hold on to them denies Christ to us.

As far as the world as God made it is concerned, it cannot defile us. Except where man has been, it is a beautiful world and full of loveliness. Its fields are carpeted with flowers, its mountains are bathed in snow, its hills bright with green forests, its air loaded with the perfumes of flowers. The world of nature is full of God's handiwork. It was not the world in this sense that our Lord spoke of when He called Satan the prince of this world. The natural world to a great degree still shows evidence of Christ's power, not Satan's.

The Russian cosmonaut Nikolayev said he had not discovered God in the stratosphere. The American astronaut Gordon Cooper stated that he had seen many of the wonders that God created, that he had his heavenly Father with him when he was 150 miles above the earth as he did every day when he was on earth. Then Cooper added, "As for me, it is a tremendous assurance and strength to know that no matter where I am, I am in God's hands."

# UPON THIS FOUNDATION

*For other foundation can no man lay than that is laid, which is Jesus Christ.* **1 Cor. 3:11.**

Each of us is a builder, whether we purpose to be one or not. Every one of us determines whether to build on rock or on sand, whether to build with gold, silver, precious stones, or with wood, hay, and stubble. Building for eternity is not based on any mood of indifference to things as they are. A day of trial is just ahead of us that will test every man's work. Fire will purify the gold, the silver, and precious stones. It will consume the wood, hay, and stubble.

Noah was divinely commissioned to build an ark. In building, Noah followed divine directions. He used the finest plans, the hardest wood. He put forth the most diligent, persevering effort. He built to endure the Flood. He thereby saved his family and condemned the rest of the world who built with wood, hay, and stubble.

The day of the Lord is coming. That day will not be all sweetness and light. The time of trouble will shake everything that can be shaken. The final movements in our world's history will not take place in an attitude of careless contentment. There is no future for those who build their house upon that which will not stand the final test. It is a shame to fool young people with the idea that all you have to do with God is to "get by."

To build our lives on Christ is indeed the primary essential. Yet it is not enough to have the right foundation. The foundation alone does not spell out the finished work of God for our lives. Christ cannot be the living vine without branches and fruit. Neither can a foundation be laid in our lives without growing into a temple of the Lord.

What matters from here on is the quality of the edifice that is rising upon the foundation. It is possible to start out with the right foundation and yet not stand the test at the final day. What is the sum total of the material we are putting into our lives—the wood of inconsistent behavior, the hay and straw of an empty profession, the stubble of selfishness? Such a building will never hold together in a storm. The divine foundation calls for a corresponding superstructure. Daily we must build with Christ for now and for eternity.

# EVERY CHRISTIAN A BUILDER

*If any man's work abide which he hath built thereupon, he shall receive a reward. . . . Know ye not that ye are the temple of God, and that the Spirit of God dwelleth in you? 1 Cor. 3:14-16.*

Our great Architect intends that under His control and direction, we shall build a living temple which is manifest to all. We are not to take for granted that Christ will do everything and that we need do nothing. There is no hour in the day, no day in the week, no week in the year, when we are not to build our lives according to His purpose and by His power. We are to take Christ into all our pursuits: business, daily duties, into our homes and pleasures, honoring and serving the Lord at all times. Let us not think that even the finished work of Christ that He accomplished when on the earth is enough without our acceptance of His pardon and power to live the new life.

To claim to be safe and saved because we have accepted Christ as our foundation with no comparable building going up is a delusion. All we have then is a religious profession without vitality, theory without reality. Christ calls for the most solid work under the Spirit's control. We must rear an edifice of faith, love, purity, and righteousness by the power of God.

Once we have accepted Christ as our foundation, God does not expect us to go the rest of the way on our own. Christian building requires cooperation with Christ. Having Christ as our foundation is one half. The other half is equally important —building our lives into a temple of God. Paul makes clear the great risk involved in building our lives on wood, hay, and stubble. His concern means that all of life counts a good deal more than we sometimes may think.

Wrecking companies have their place. But I am not keen for the kind of landscape they provide in the home or in the church. We have time and energy only for that which builds up and does not pull down. Are we building with the riches of heaven? Do we build with all the commitment of our strength and time? There is little else that will endure when Christ comes. Let us begin this day and say, "Today I am building with Christ. I will put into my life only that which will make it true and beautiful. I will make everything count for God."

# WHAT IS YOUR LIFE?

*Your life, what is it? You are no more than a mist, seen for a little while and then dispersing.* **James 4:14, N.E.B.**

We may readily concede that life is like a "mist, seen for a little while." Life escapes us like the disappearing fog. We see it vanish before our eyes. Vapor, mist, fog, clouds, are very illusory. We cannot hold them in our hands and keep them. There is no way to put them in a safety deposit box.

At the same time the clouds and atmosphere can assume fascinating masterpieces of form and color. We have all looked up into the sky and seen them change into superb forms and pictures of grandeur that have called for the best in poetry and painting. Or again, we may be enshrouded by a mist, a dense cloud, or a forbidding fog that obscures the light and beauty of the sky. What makes the difference between beauty and gloom? It is the sun. It paints the clouds with color, illuminates them with brightness and shining rays, with shifting scenes of splendor.

Thus it is with life. It may be a thing of glory or a thing of gloom and sadness. What the sun is to the clouds and to the mist, God is to our lives. Life shines with joy and light, or saddens with darkness, according to our relationship to the Sun of Righteousness. At times we find life to be one of fear, gloom, and anxiety. All seems undesirable. Our lives lack beauty and dignity. The missing factor is Christ, the beauty of His life in ours. When God is in our thoughts, our affections, our desires, and our purposes, life is transformed.

Life in itself without Christ is indeed vapor, destitute of grandeur and soon to pass away. The life that has the Sun of Righteousness shining in the heart acquires the beauty of the rainbow. Our lives are nothing until they are lifted into the presence of Christ.

The mist of life may end in a gutter or in a rainbow. The American Indians have a legend that as the flowers fade in the forest and on the prairie, their lost beauty is gathered into the rainbow and glows again in richer colors than before. But it is no legend that promises us a life of moral and spiritual beauty with God. Then at last we shall find ourselves standing within the beauties of the rainbow about the eternal throne of God.

# THE DAYS OF MY PRIME

*If I could be as in the days of my prime, . . . while the Almighty was still there at my side.* **Job 29:4, N.E.B.**

Job was grieving over a past joy and early fellowship of the first years of his spiritual life. He could not quite comprehend the cause of his calamities or reconcile them with his idea of God. He could not believe he was making progress. He failed to realize that he was entering upon a nobler, purer, closer walk with God.

May it not be so with us? We look back to the dawn of our spiritual life, to our original dedication to God, to the joy that welled up within our hearts. But with the passing of time we conclude we are not so happy as we were then. We are not so holy and true and good. We do not love God as we once did.

But this is not necessarily true. The emotional flush and joy of early days have given place to loftier views of God, a deeper assurance and confidence in God which nothing can disturb. A garden in springtime is a thing of beauty and color. Yet it is when the precious fruits in red and gold are on the trees that we discover the real purpose of God in nature.

All of us know we have not done all we should have done. We have not been all we ought to have been. Our consciousness of weakness and imperfection is more vivid than ever. May not this awareness, this clearer sense of sin, indicate that we have grown more? Maybe we do not see ourselves as pure as we once were because the Holy Spirit has been opening our eyes, refining our tastes, heightening our spiritual sense. Our vision is clearer. Greater spiritual maturity more readily detects the deformities of the spirit. Our finer spiritual ear detects the discords that sin makes. Our deeper sense of sin has increased, not because evil has been gaining upon us, but because we are more in harmony with God.

We shall never understand the power and the folly of sin more than in the moment when the Holy Spirit has freed us from it. It is not the greatest sinner who senses the depths of sin, but the Christian who is closest to Christ. We can be growing spiritually, and at the same time feel more disturbed over the selfishness and sinfulness of which we become aware.

# DIVIDENDS FROM GOD

*And every one that hath forsaken houses, or brethren, or sisters, or fa-*
*ther, or mother, or wife, or children, or lands, for my name's sake, shall re-*
*ceive an hundredfold, and shall inherit everlasting life.* **Matt. 19:29.**

A king built a great temple, the most imposing structure in his realm. He lavished both wealth and effort in its construction. He hoped thereby to leave a monument to his own greatness. When the temple was completed, he was angry to find engraved on the foundation the name of an unknown woman instead of his own. As far as he knew she had contributed nothing, except that day after day she had taken pity on the laborers and on the oxen that pulled the wagons. For the love of God and man, she brought them water to drink in the hot sun and a little food to eat from her meager supply.

Christ is no one man's debtor. We are *all* in debt to Him. Whatever we invest with Him and in His kingdom will be returned again multiplied many times. In blessing His children, Christ uses a large measure, pressed down, running over.

To have much or little may be either an advantage or a disadvantage. It depends on how we use our possessions and what we gain from them in terms of human worth. If we use our wealth and possessions selfishly, then they are a disadvantage to us. We are that much poorer and worse off by having them. On the other hand, if they lead us to fulfill our lives, if they teach us to be unselfish, if they lead to a greater appreciation of God's goodness, then they are to our advantage.

To have the best and the most in life, we must use our possessions for what is more valuable and enduring. Christ makes us largehearted. He does not condemn the riches of the world. What matters is the use we make of them. God has given us all things, legitimate things to enjoy. But we do not enjoy them alone.

Wealth is the opportunity for our becoming a more loving, unselfish Christian. Christ's love within us is the guardian of all our wealth. We are secure against all the abuses of riches. In Christ, our possessions are not stumbling blocks but altar stairs, steps to God's throne and to people's lives.

# THE PLACE OF TEMPTATION

***Lead us not into temptation.* Luke 11:4.**

What can this statement mean? Certainly all of us would prefer to have temptation removed from us. It would make life much easier for us if we could pray to this effect and have our prayers answered. "Blessed is the man that endureth temptation: for when he is tried, he shall receive the crown of life" (James 1:12).

Temptation comes from two sources: the powers of evil outside of us and the power of the sinful nature inside of us. God tempts no man (see verses 13, 14). If we were not so weak and blind, temptations would lose their power. What does Christ mean when He teaches us to pray that God will not lead us into temptation? God has no pleasure in placing temptations in our pathway. However, God does bring His people, as He did Abraham, Joseph, Daniel, and even Jesus Himself, into circumstances both fitted and designed to test the strength of their faith and devotion.

We must face honestly those things that can be a real snare to us. We cannot prevent the world and the devil from tempting us. But God will strengthen us to meet those situations and circumstances that would otherwise overcome us in the areas of our weaknesses. Peter needed to ask God to do this, but he did not. Of his own accord he went into the hall of the high priest at the trial of Jesus. He was drawn into the atmosphere of temptation, turned coward, and denied his Lord. He should never have gone there.

A man with weak lungs, susceptible to lung disease, should not live in a cold, icy climate or engage in work that exaggerates his lung problem.

If you are greedy and have a serious weakness for money, you should stay clear of those "counting houses" where money is all-important. If you have exaggerated passions, then you should not go to those places or be found in that company that excites those passions. You should not read that kind of material or look at television programs that arouse the imagination. You should ask God to keep you from those positions that can only lead to your own destruction.

# "THIS ONE THING I DO"

*This one thing I do, . . . I press toward the mark for the prize of the high calling of God in Christ Jesus.* **Phil. 3:13, 14.**

The chisel strokes of the sculptor seem to mar the image on which he works. Yet in the end a glorious statue appears under his hand. So Christ our Supreme Artist perfects that which concerns us. The roughening ordeal is part of the polishing. We are humbled in what we consider our strong point, that our faults may be corrected. The trial of our temper, courage, patience, which seems to mar our characters, leads to a great sense of need that God's power may make us more triumphant. We find progress under seeming retrogression. We grow spiritually under seeming lapses. We discover lack of Christlikeness in the life in order to develop more of the beauty of Christ within us.

Under their first love, newlyweds express greater affection; vows of fidelity are more fervently affirmed. With the passing years there appear to be less passionate demonstrations, not because their love is less but because it is deeper. Thus it can be in our relation to God. Our love may not be so exciting and so ecstatic and joyful as at first. But it can be a love tested by sacrifice, prepared to suffer, ready to endure hardship and trial.

We love those to whom we pay ungrudging service. "If ye keep my commandments, ye shall abide in my love; even as I have kept my Father's commandments. . . . Ye are my friends, if ye do whatsoever I command you" (John 15:10-14). Does our love to God express itself in this way? Do we love the law and obey His will?

We may feel for various reasons that our faith does not seem as strong as it was at first. But what about our love for God? Does God have our confidence more now than ever? Are we prepared to say with Job, "Though he slay me, yet will I trust in him" (Job 13:15)? What about the early days in our Christian experience? Our faith may have risen to greater emotional expressions, yet it was easily discouraged. Now our confidence and trust are firm. We must not misrepresent the facts because our feelings are not the same. The essential thing is our allegiance to Christ, come what may.

# CHRISTIAN NOBILITY

*Teaching us that, denying ungodliness and worldly lusts, we should live soberly, righteously, and godly, in this present world. Titus 2:12.*

The Roman statesman, Pliny, wrote a letter describing the Christians. He governed the province of Asia Minor. As a result of Paul's great work of evangelism, the Christians were so numerous in his province that, as Pliny complained, the pagan temples stood empty and deserted. He knew little or nothing about Christian doctrine, but he knew that Christians worshiped Jesus Christ as divine. He said that they were just in their dealings, honest, chaste, truthful, and trustworthy. Just think of it: what struck these pagans was the pure, honest, true, and upright lives of the Christians.

God has commissioned us with the everlasting gospel to the world. We do well to believe that. It is not enough that we consent to the truth. We must embody God's truth in every part of our daily lives. The world needs lives, not just words; pure examples, not lengthy speculations; loving service, not a new theory of ethics. We are to produce the deepest impression on the people of this generation.

Any one of us who, by the power of the Holy Spirit, turns everyday life and work into an opportunity for diligence, integrity, purity, and love, will do more for the cause of God than if we spoke with the tongues of men and of angels. Daniel and his friends were both noble and good. When we consider the dangers and the temptations that come to young men in such high places, a genuinely godly man must be one of the most admirable of men and recognized as such.

There was food and wine of the richest sort; there was also the danger of displeasing the king and being cast into a dungeon. Would we have been surprised if Daniel had reasoned, "What does it matter? The notions and traditions of our fathers are out of date. Our policy is to please the king." If he had given in, his life would be unwritten and unsung. But he and his friends stood firm.

It is this kind of allegiance and integrity Christ needs today. The noblest of young men and women who walk the earth are needed at such a time. There seems to be so little of that type of Christian character.

# MAN'S ANXIETY AND CHRIST'S SERENITY

*Peace I leave with you, my peace I give unto you. . . . Let not your heart be troubled, neither let it be afraid. John 14:27.*

These are remarkable words to be spoken under such circumstances and at such a time. It was the night before Jesus was to die. He and His disciples were in the upper room in the city of Jerusalem. The city was crowded with pilgrims. Roman soldiers patrolled the streets to put down the first sign of rebellion. Unrest was in the atmosphere. At that moment the high priest was plotting Christ's death. Judas was with the high priest. He had sold his Lord for thirty pieces of silver. In a very short time Christ would go from that upper room to Gethsemane. All His disciples would forsake Him and flee. The soldiers would come to arrest Him; His trial and crucifixion would follow. But He says to His disciples, *"My peace* I give unto you. *My peace* I leave with you." How could He be at peace in view of all that was about to happen to Him? Yet He was. In Him was that almost incredible serenity and tranquillity of mind, born of His perfect harmony with, and trust in, His Father in heaven.

There is no anxiety in life quite so bad as seeing nothing beyond ourselves. The contradictions within are unsolvable by our own efforts. Frances Havergal, a radiant Christian and one of our great hymn writers, suffered from a pain-ridden body all her life. She said, "Everybody I meet is sorry for me except myself. I always see my pain in the light of Calvary." Many people develop basic anxieties owing to rejection they meet in life; others have a fixation upon worldly values, hoping to get meaning and satisfaction this way.

The serenity of Jesus came from His surrender to God, not from an escape from life's problems and responsibilities. Jesus does not give us peace by dulling the mind, but by lifting us into union with Himself. When we look into the sky at night we see the glorious majesty of a divine direction of the universe, free from haste, as though the stars were standing still. It is a measure of the serenity of God, who directs the stars in their distinctive paths. So it can be with us under His control and direction. One of the great privileges of the Christian is the gift of peace. This peace is not something apart from Christ. "The fruit of the Spirit is . . . peace."

# THE CHRISTIAN AND THE WORLD

*Love not the world, neither the things that are in the world.* **1 John 2:15.**

What is the true use of the world? The various non-Christian cultures have, for the most part, concentrated on the present world. "Enjoy life and the world. Do not renounce it." At the opposite end of the spectrum are those who renounce the world and seek to escape from it. Monks sometimes emptied themselves of riches, supposedly also of outward pride. They sought to prove their triumph over what the world most prizes. Often they lost sight of Christ's love for the world. This devotion to piety excites our admiration. But it leaves little hope for the rest of mankind.

How shall we use the world? We must be superior not only to its evils but to its earthly values. There is a life that triumphs over the world, the flesh, and the devil. No doubt many who devote themselves to prayer and to meditation are pleasing to God. But there is no such thing as winning favors from God by such procedures.

We are to be free from the dominance of all earthly things. We are to use all things to the glory of God. We are to be lord of all things, but slave to none. Whoever goes forth into life believing that salvation and righteousness will come by mere self-denial, giving up all natural things, will not find it. Christian sacrifice is always the service of love, love to Christ and to our fellow man. We deny ourselves and give ourselves for others as Christ did. Our true use of the world is not merely to rise above it, not chiefly to gain material wealth from it, but to love it as Christ did in order to save it.

We love the world of people because the Christian life is the only thing of real value. Leave out Christ, and there is no value, life, or future in the world. The meaning of life and the value of the world are expressed in Christ when He came to the earth.

Everything in the world was to be seen in its right relationship. Christ came to restore man to supreme value above things of earth. His ministry was one of reconciliation to God. We may amass great wealth. We may improve human conditions. All this is possible outside of Christ. But men are still lost. Christ loves the world in order to save it. That is our stand also.

# TO THE GLORY OF GOD

*He that glorieth, let him glory in the Lord.* **1 Cor. 1:31.**

The life of the apostle Paul is the story of a great man who lived to glorify God. He surrendered his private interests and personal reputation, and all chance of eminence in the Jewish hierarchy. His great desire to serve Christ and his fellow men rose above any desire to shine. "I count it so much garbage, for the sake of gaining Christ . . . , with no righteousness of my own, . . . but the righteousness which comes from faith in Christ" (Phil. 3:8, 9, N.E.B.).

This is a hard thing to do, especially if we have the ability to go to the top in almost anything we put our minds to. There are those who wish to exalt only Christ, and others who wish to shine and exalt themselves; those who seek to gain the attention of men and win their applause and favor, and those who humbly seek to reflect Christ and give glory to Him. There are on the one hand those who are ruled by ambition and on the other those who prefer to be used of God; those whose first aim is to be great and those whose first aim is to be Christlike; those who love fame and those who love people; those who covet honor from men and those who seek honor from God.

The sons of Zebedee, James and John, disciples of Christ, once sought great things for themselves, even the highest seats by the throne of God. Lucifer felt the same way.

Christ, however, "made himself of no reputation." He taught that the servant spirit fitted men for His service and His kingdom, that the only path to greatness was to live and work to the glory of God. The Jews believed they were the elect of God, and so they were. But the election was not to superiority or to salvation, but to service. Whoever wishes to rule must serve.

One of the major essentials of our time is to restore the servant spirit. If we are to live abundantly, we must become servants of the needy, a height to which no personal ambition, no love of fame, can ever lift us. The church can never in truth be the true church unless it takes seriously what it means to give glory to Him. Christ said of His life and work, "I have glorified thee on the earth: I have finished the work which thou gavest me to do" (John 17:4).

# SPIRITUAL BALANCE

**Be not righteous over much. Eccl. 7:16.**

This scripture does not mean that one can be too righteous or too committed to the cause of God. It warns against an overemphasis on the externals and the forms of religion as a substitute for the genuine thing.

In all religions extremists are to be found. Some are given to riding religious hobbies that usually do not deal with spiritual issues. We need to guard against religious crazes, where the mind is captivated by fanciful and extreme opinions and methods that project self into the center of religious controversy.

This is not to deny the value of new ideas and spiritual progress. But the basic truths of the Word of God do not stand in isolation. The real worth of the Christian faith does not lie in excess, in private and bizarre discoveries. Genuine faith in God and in His Word always makes for spiritual balance and maturity. To engage in religious fancies tends to deny our witness to Christ, to distract the attention of those who might be Christians from the fundamental truths of the Bible. In these crucial days we need all the energy of mind and heart directed to Christian growth and to an effective witness to Christ.

When people go off on tangents, religion is frittered away on things of little or no value. This type of religious profession feeds one's vanity but rarely exalts Christ or furthers the cause of God. It inevitably denies one's witness to the truth by isolating the individual.

A well-balanced and well-adjusted life is part of being a Christian. Christ lived that way, amid temptation and conflict. Believers need to apply the Christian faith at the point where life has meaning, where real temptations and conflicts arise that require spiritual power. One cannot move on to the fringes of religion without making mockery of the truth and withdrawing from the arena where the real battles of life are fought. A religion lived out on the fringes misrepresents a loving God and makes religion unattractive and undesirable. A life with Christ at the center is the most attractive religion in the world.

# UNASHAMED OF CHRIST

*Be not thou therefore ashamed of the testimony of our Lord . . . : but be thou partaker of the afflictions of the gospel according to the power of God.* **2 Tim. 1:8.**

In one of his sermons, Halford Luccock related the incident of a boy taken to church for the first time. The preacher entered the pulpit and made a terrible announcement. The boy felt it must have been important, because so many people had been called together to hear it. It was a rending tale of some brave and good man terribly hurt a long time ago. He suffered a dreadful pain because there was something that needed to be done for mankind that no one else could do. The boy wept beside his mother in the family pew, shrinking shamefacedly back into his corner. But the rest of the people seemed to be strangely tranquil. Later, when the boy questioned his mother, she only said that we must not take things too much to heart—people would think us odd and foolish if we did.

In all generations men have been both indifferent and ashamed of God's unspeakable gift of grace. This is man's folly: to turn to his land and to his estate, to his sports and his amusements, then count them as the principal things of which to be proud, the only things worthy of his time, energy, thought, and sacrifice.

We ought to listen to Jesus Christ with the utmost earnestness and seriousness. We ought to glory in Him who alone has the answers to all our questions. Let us take to heart God's supreme gift to us.

The peril of cowardice is best vanquished by an acknowledged appreciation of all that God is. The peril of being ashamed of Christ is most effectively overcome by one's response to the God-Man who gave His life for our redemption. The bane of religious boredom is banished as we contemplate the immortal love of God, who refused to surrender His children on earth to eternal loss. It is not enough to stand up within the walls of a church to sing praises to God. Before the callous indifference of an unbelieving world, we must witness courageously, unashamed of Christ, unashamed of His church, and of His last message to the world.

# THE KINGLY LIFE

*The kingdom of God is within you.* **Luke 17:21.**

The kingdom of God refers both to the sovereign rule of God that is yet to be established in the earth and also to the rule of Christ in our personal lives. The first speaks of the time when Christ's kingdom shall break in pieces all the kingdoms of the world.

God's purpose is to establish His kingdom, first in our hearts and then throughout the world. By His kingly rule in our lives He gives us a kingly nature. By God's grace and power we are to seek a kingly heart and mind, to accept from Christ a royal spirit, to live as sons and daughters of the King of kings.

We may set a diamond in lead, in copper, brass, silver, or gold. It is a diamond in any setting. We may put a Christian in almost any setting. He may be a common laborer or a prince. He may live in a southland villa or on the wrong side of the tracks. The kind of house we own is not as important as whether Christ lives in it. The King of kings resides in us as Christians. When Jesus is King, all the forces of our mind, soul, and body become His royal domain.

What constitutes the ruling devotion at the center of our lives? To develop a religious veneer is not enough. To be considered religious is not enough. We would not undervaluate these attributes, but they do not go deep enough. The kingdom of God within is opposed to a life that is simply a surface existence. There is no reason why we should be sad about legitimate activities and pleasures. But they are destructive without intelligence, thought, and high values. Much of the entertainment and pleasure of the world reveals the extreme frivolousness of the multitudes.

Jesus did not become incarnate in the interest of the superficial and the unreal. He did not die on the cross in the interest of make-believe. In His life and death and teachings He set beyond all doubt the worth of human nature and human destiny.

We should surely avoid a frothy mind and a sterile life. We ought to be grateful for anything that captures our lives for eternity, that drives us inward and upward to Christ.

# CHRISTIAN BOLDNESS

*In whom we have boldness and access with confidence by the faith of him.* **Eph. 3:12.**

The meaning of the word translated "boldness" includes unreserved communication, free and fearless confidence, cheerful courage—in this instance, in our relationship toward God. Steadfast confidence is one of the great needs of the Christian life. Many professed Christians run well for a time. But they lack steadfastness. They grow cold and leave the church. The crowning grace of confidence through Christ is missing. Such confidence makes us abound in hope, glory in tribulation; it makes us strong to resist and overcome temptation. No one can conquer without the spirit of a conqueror. Only when we have learned to be bold with God can we be bold to face the enemy. "Cast not away therefore your confidence, which hath great recompence of reward" (Heb. 10:35).

God urges us to "come boldly unto the throne of grace, that we may obtain mercy, and find grace to help in time of need" (chap. 4:16). We are to draw nigh to God without fear, without doubt, as a child speaking to his father. This steadfast confidence, this boldness, is the essence of a healthy Christian life. This is the God-given right of every child of God. We are not to live in fear, uncertain whether Christ has accepted us or not.

"Having therefore, brethren, boldness to enter into the holiest by the blood of Jesus, by a new and living way . . . ; let us draw near with a true heart in full assurance of faith" (chap. 10:19-22). By His own blood Christ rent the veil, giving us access to God. This is the measure of our boldness before the Father. The more we honor the sacrifice of Christ and see its worth, the stronger will be our confidence. The blood of Christ is the only currency that is acceptable to the Father. Bring this with you in faith as you approach Him. Believe that sinful and feeble as you are, you can draw nigh to God and enter into His presence. The proof that you have a living working faith is that it makes you to hold fast your confidence firm unto the end. Consequently, our religion never becomes a burden for us to carry.

*301*

# CAN WE FOLLOW CHRIST TODAY?

*He saw a man, named Matthew, sitting at the receipt of custom: and he saith unto him, Follow me. And he arose, and followed him. Matt. 9:9.*

Almost 2,000 years have passed since Jesus asked men for their unreserved commitment to Himself. He made it quite clear. They must be prepared to give up everything for His sake, leave family and friends if necessary. Can the same thing be done in our day? When Jesus was on earth, life was largely rural and very simple. Now life is highly complex, industrialized, sophisticated.

Jesus said, "I am the Truth." Is truth still the same? Can we count on it? The New Testament has two meanings for the word *truth*. First, truth means a logical consistency; it refers to clarity in our thinking, and believing what the Bible says. But there is much more to the meaning of truth than ideas, facts, words, that satisfy our need for a sound reasoning.

The second use of the word "truth" or "true" is to denote genuineness. Jesus is called the True Light, the True Bread. This has nothing to do with Christ's telling the truth. Truth here means that Jesus answers in His total person to that which is absolutely genuine. There is nothing about Him that is phony or false. The way Christ lived His life as a man and met every situation and every individual is the one genuine way.

Truth as genuineness can be known only when we ourselves become part of it and are thoroughly involved with it. We may study the facts and the evidence for Christ's resurrection and agree that the argument for it is logically sound. This is important, but it is not enough. We must share in the resurrection life of Christ to know the genuineness of it. It is of little use to cry, "The truth—we have the truth." We must face the issue of what a genuine Christian really is; what kind of person we actually are. Sin, lust, selfishness, hate, are such terrible realities. These are not empty words. They describe what we are from time to time. The only answer to these sinful realities is to experience the reality of Jesus Christ. Our trust and commitment is to be wholly genuine—oneness with Him as a power for love, not for hate; for humility, not pride; hope, not despair.

# THE PLACE OF OBEDIENCE

**To obey is better than sacrifice. 1 Sam. 15:22.**

I read once that some poisons such as arsenic can, under certain conditions, serve a medicinal function. But not so with disobedience. It has no virtue whatsoever. It takes the course of our lives entirely away from God.

Christians are to live a different kind of life than non-Christians. We ought not to allow the spirit of disobedience to stamp and mold our lives. We are to bear the stamp of Christ's likeness. We are to take seriously our right relationship to God and to His commandments. A will that is contrary to God's law can only destroy us at last.

The followers of Satan are termed "children of disobedience" (Eph. 2:2). The unconverted and unsanctified are geared to a warped idea of freedom from obedience to the will of God. The result is moral and spiritual deterioration. Men become less and less capable of seeing the truth and walking in it. They become full of hearing the Word of God. They find it increasingly difficult to clear the moral and spiritual air and return to the truth of God.

Christ strictly obeyed His heavenly Father and kept His commandments. The presence of Christ in our lives is always a power to obey and never to disobey. At the very heart of the gospel there lies not only the invitation to come to Christ but also a summons to obedience.

We choose the powers that make our lives. God has provided everything we need in the gospel, in His Son, and in His Word in order to live a life of obedience. God leaves us alone with our sinning, but He provides us with all the resources of heaven for righteous living. We are to set ourselves right down on God's side.

God does not allow us to tamper with truth in order to win our freedom. We do not beg God to make compromises and exceptions in our case because we are determined to go our own way. The God who still rules over our broken world waits longingly and earnestly for us to say Yes to Him. He has left us no other way.

303

# WANING SPIRITUALITY—1

*This is the Spirit that we have received from God, and not the spirit of the world.* 1 Cor. 2:12, N.E.B.

God's Holy Spirit is given to us that we may know, receive, and appreciate the things of God. The spiritual nature of the Christian gives us a position from which we are able to discern and choose that which belongs to God. We know the mind of Christ and we have that mind ourselves. This is to be the spiritual life of the Christian.

But there are perils along the way. We should be aware of signs of spiritual decline, of those things that cause our spirituality to wane. An early sign is a relaxed conscience. Whatever impairs the sensitiveness of our conscience, we should call into question. You may hear it said sometimes, "I am not as particular as I once was in matters of morality and conduct." Some people claim to enjoy more freedom from the particulars of religion. They claim freedom from all legalism and a rigidity that insists on a perfectionistic approach.

A spiritually mature Christian undoubtedly enjoys a larger freedom in spiritual things. But the relaxation of conscience is another matter. Any departure from the law of God is a sign of spiritual decay. The maturing Christian becomes more sensitive to sin. The great men of the Christian faith have had a conscience sensitive to sin in any form, coupled with a high courage to live up to their convictions.

It is not always easy to maintain a clear conscience. Sin impairs and sears both conscience and the sense of our responsibility to God and to His Word.

The world grows upon us with its interests, friendships, pleasures. So much of it tends to choke off the spiritual life. Those whose desires increase toward the world with its degrading practices will ultimately deny the faith. Let us hold positive convictions and a clear conscience before God.

Someone has observed that "of all the dust thrown in men's eyes none is more blinding than gold dust." One can say that about many things the world has to offer: fame, riches, pleasure, success. But Christ offers to us, free, all that is beautiful and noble. We truly live only when Christ's life flows into ours, when we become heirs of the inexhaustible riches of heaven.

# WANING SPIRITUALITY—2

*O Lord, how great are thy works! and thy thoughts are very deep. A brutish man knoweth not; neither doth a fool understand this. Ps. 92:5, 6.*

All men in the world face a serious crisis. It has to do with the state of their minds. "Be sober, be vigilant; because your adversary the devil, as a roaring lion, walketh about, seeking whom he may devour" (1 Peter 5:8). Time and again the Scriptures call upon us to exercise a sober mind. This does not mean a long face or a pessimistic outlook. It means a serious mind, a mind that is aware of the great issues. All too often superficiality and triviality describe the lives of men and women.

Christ calls on us to love God with all our minds. There is nothing more calamitous than the failure to think straight on the Word of God, or even not to think at all. People who fail to think straight will sooner or later fail to walk straight. Most of today's reading material and public entertainment is sheer trash. We are not really a thinking people any more. The whole cult of taking it easy and being entertained is unworthy of the mind God has given us.

How do we survive the final movements and crises when the powers of evil threaten to engulf the earth? One of the objectives of the remnant church is to develop mature Christians who can think straight, who can think for themselves. "Finishing the work" is a phrase that has come to be little more than a cliché. But the work of God cannot be finished by professed Christians who still wear the mental and spiritual garments of childhood. A church that is not able to produce mentally, emotionally, and spiritually mature members is in grave moral and spiritual danger.

We need to open our minds to receive all the truth God has for us, just as we open our windows to let in fresh air. But open windows need screens on them.

Let us nerve our minds on affirmatives from God's Word. We become invincible by virtue of our inner strength, by developing the mind of Christ. God pity us if we have only that which is frivolous and shallow to live by. Let us face the final conditions in our world with a poised, mature, and spiritual mind. The world will be no comfortable place to live in. The preparation time is now.

305

# LAMPS THAT FAIL

*Then all those virgins arose, and trimmed their lamps. And the foolish said unto the wise, Give us of your oil; for our lamps are gone out. Matt. 25:7, 8.*

The difference between the five wise and the five foolish virgins is significant. Consider the man whose religion is mainly a lamp without oil. He has polished the outside of the lamp. He is a church member. He believes the doctrines and the standards of the church. He is happy to associate with God-fearing men and women. But his piety stops right there. All this is not enough. The oil of the Holy Spirit is lacking. Christ must live within. The man's inner life must be in tune with God.

We can be morally good—at least, insofar as the world would judge—without God. We can praise justice and morality without God. But spiritual life is dependent upon supernatural power. Religion without commitment is a lamp without oil. Knowledge of God without obedience is also a lamp without oil. Of all the lamps kindled in the church, that which shows you Christ is the trustworthy one. This light lights up the dark places of life.

The foolish virgins' lamps burned brightly while the oil lasted, but they did not burn long enough. They ran out of constancy in their devotion and allegiance to God. They got tired of waiting for the bridegroom to come. They ceased to live their lives from that divine Center who gives life. Their trouble lay in loss of union with God. Christ was no longer present.

We can never do justice to the truth of God's Word until the Holy Spirit fulfills it in our hearts and lives. Religion can be mere lip service, without any real heart in it.

Nothing can be more serious than to be without life from God. By dependence on the Holy Spirit we share each day in Christ's life and His victory over sin. We do not shift our center to depend on ourselves. We are led continually by the Spirit.

The Holy Spirit symbolized by the oil will bring forth the fruit of the Spirit. Our concern is not with the shape or size of the lamp, its external appearance as such. It is the Holy Spirit within us that matters.

# CHRISTIAN GROWTH

*But grow in grace, and in the knowledge of our Lord and Saviour Jesus Christ.* **2 Peter 3:18.**

It is not enough that we become converted and enter the door to the Christian life. We must make progress. The attainment of the full stature of Christ is the greatest spiritual and moral adventure we can know. There is always the danger that, having taken the initial step into the Christian faith, we loiter by the roadside or we get sidetracked.

We cannot live from last month's meals. We are to read God's Word each day with delight, to feed on the preciousness of the truths found there. From time to time we feel distressed because we seem to get so little out of the Bible. We attend church regularly and believe that God is in this place, but we know it not as we ought to.

When I was a boy, I read in one of the schoolbooks the story of the measuring rod, a very remarkable instrument. The story was told as though the author had had a dream. In his dream, people were being called to account before God. As each name was called, the individual took his place beside the measuring rod. According to the moral and spiritual stature of his life on earth, he either grew or lessened in stature as he stood by the rod. The leader of the women's organization in the church seemed to have a lot going for her. She was busy in good works, but when she stood beside the rod she shrank to a small size. The old cobbler who never made much impression on people, a humble man given to love for others, grew to a great stature. A young man, good in sports, popular in school, voted the one most likely to succeed, did not rate very high. So it went. Finally the man relating the dream took his place beside the rod. He held an important position in the world but he felt himself shrinking in size. He cried out to the angel to give him one more chance to grow up into Christ, and according to the story it was given him.

Are we really persuaded of the urgency of the spiritual life? Do we give the best of our time, thoughts, and energy to permit Christ to grow upon us and into us? We who walk with Christ will assume the stature and image of our Lord. We grow if we really desire to grow.

# "NARROW IS THE WAY"

*Strait is the gate, and narrow is the way, which leadeth unto life, and few there be that find it. Matt. 7:14.*

It is because faith in Jesus Christ is so crucial to salvation that it requires so much of us in terms of our genuine response. One does not drift into the kingdom of God. One does not walk the narrow way by accident. There are no short cuts to eternal life. Paul wrote of fighting the "good fight of faith," of laying "hold on eternal life" (1 Tim. 6:12).

Most of our failures in life are usually in the direction of lukewarmness. Most of us have reason at times to be ashamed of our unwillingness to make sacrifices for God. We confess to dry and casual formalism in much of our worship.

The narrow way is both high and difficult. Few there be that stay on it. We easily descend to the broad road. It is more comfortable. Men are easily bored with religion. The grandeur of God's cause becomes tempered to our moods. We are content to accommodate the faith of our fathers to our indifference, and God's requirements to our weakness. It seems easy to go along with the crowd, as typified by the hobo. When asked how he decided which way to go, he replied, "I always go with the wind at my back."

True Christianity presupposes a total response to Jesus Christ and to His way of life. We must beware of lowering our moral and spiritual ideals. We need to behold again the glory of God's character, the beauty of His moral law that stands far above the ways and codes of men. Insight into the narrow way and courage to take that road are required at a time when the world is distinguished by its departure from it.

Let us seek enlightenment and power from God as the only true solution to the moral and spiritual problems of our time. Let us hunger and thirst for His righteousness. Let us ask God to give us an eye single to the glory of God, a braver and warmer heart and mind. It costs to develop a life of prayer and devotion. It costs time and effort to feed on the Word of God. Thus we become empowered with *might* by the Spirit of God. No more do we drag our feet in God's cause. The fire of the Spirit burns within the soul to stir us to accomplish great things for God.

# THERE IS A WAY THAT SEEMETH RIGHT

*There is a way which seemeth right unto a man, but the end thereof are the ways of death.* **Prov. 14:12.**

Some people have the false impression that one must go to the world to find happiness and personal fulfillment; that one can hardly be expected to find these things within the Christian faith. Where do people get the idea that riches, worldly success, and fame bring happiness and fulfillment? A man may spread his table with the finest foods and drinks, then develop ulcers and dyspepsia so that he cannot enjoy them. A man may build himself a mansion of marble, cover the walls with costly paintings, plant beautiful gardens, and then go blind. The only true condition of achieving fulfillment is that we be in a position to enjoy what life has to offer. A mean man cannot be happy. A selfish man cannot be a fulfilled man. An immoral man cannot experience inner freedom and peace. One must possess the right values.

> At the devil's booth are all things sold,
> Each ounce of dross costs its ounce of gold;
> For a cap and bells our lives we pay,
> Bubbles we buy with our whole soul's tasking.
> (Prelude to Lowell's "Vision of Sir Launfal.")

In life, if you want to buy hay and stubble, what does it cost? It costs money. That is the law. If you choose to be dishonest, you must give up the idea of being an honest man. If you choose to be impure, then you must give up the idea of being morally trustworthy. If you choose evil, you must surrender righteousness. "Each ounce of dross costs its ounce of gold."

Some years ago, a fire destroyed a famous night club. The newspaper told the story of a young woman who, with her friends, had left the night club in protest against a suggestive performance. She was hardly out of the building when it was turned into a blazing inferno.

Every man's work shall be tested as by fire. It is too bad when a person invested by God with a million-dollar capital does only a hundred-dollar-a-year business. Under God, the possibilities are incomparable and unlimited.

# THE POLES OF WISDOM AND FOLLY

*Then I saw that wisdom excelleth folly, as far as light excelleth darkness. The wise man's eyes are in his head; but the fool walketh in darkness. Eccl. 2:13, 14.*

We must educate the mind to see and hear. Unfortunately there are things that men do not want to see or hear. They are conveniently blind and deaf to the truth. It happens to all of us at times. God's voice and truth interfere with what we really want to do. We find it inconvenient to listen to God.

The rich fool in the Gospel of Luke who decided to build bigger barns to hold his produce was no fool as a farmer. He was a success. But he took an irresponsible attitude toward eternal values in favor of material things. No man ought to do that.

Nothing has real value until you enjoy it with Christ. Spiritual priorities alone are lasting. Without Christ, worldly pleasures and riches are phantoms. Stock market speculations exist only on paper. Lasting values and true meaning belong to him who loves Christ more than anything else. When it comes to serving Him, there are no "if's." All is eternally real. Christ offers no mocking crown, no shaky bank account. We share in the riches of our resurrected and glorified Lord, under whose feet all things are put in subjection.

The voice of God in His Word is clear and unmistakable. God makes the frequent charge against Israel: "You refused to obey my voice." Nothing more could be done. Not even Christ or the Holy Spirit can possess the mind and direct the life without our cooperation.

Scientific evidence has recently pointed out the relation of cigarette smoking to lung cancer. Thousands have broken the habit. But thousands more go on smoking in the face of the facts. Doubtless many of them will die of lung cancer. The truth on smoking as being the cause of cancer is not responsible for cancer. People have heard the truth. They are responsible. The verdict will agree with their choice.

The truth and claims of God are rationally sound, vital to life, eternally sure. The call is to live responsibly. But a man must make up his mind. There is no neutral ground.

# REJOICE GREATLY

*You are transported with a joy too great for words, while you reap the harvest of your faith, that is, salvation for your souls.* **1 Peter 1:8, 9, N.E.B.**

There is no place for a gloomy Christian. He is to be filled with delight. He bathes his mind and heart in the grandeur of God's love, in the beauties of the earth. Thereby he becomes oblivious to the petty cares of life and the pressure of duties.

However, the landscape of the Christian life does not always consist of fields of flowers and gentle rivers. There are gray days and great burdens to carry. In the midst of difficult times Paul cried out, "O the depth of the riches both of the wisdom and knowledge of God!" (Rom. 11:33). The apostle John, an exile sitting on a rock-bound coast, found his mind and life full of the glorious pageantry of the coming kingdom of God.

There is a triumphant buoyance of spirit in the life of the believers throughout the New Testament. A man is not much of a Christian who shows a long face for any length of time. Gloom and despondency are wrong. When the early Christians faced martyrdom, they gave themselves to it with songs. They were far too sure of Christ to wonder whether they would be able to make it. They had no time to bemoan their lot.

We are tied to the most triumphant life that ever walked the earth. He has this day thrust into our lives all that goes with triumph, victory, radiance, and holy gallantry. That is the inheritance He left us, with no trace of sadness in it. Because of this we are to face trouble and disaster with steady eyes, firmly poised against dreadful odds.

All this because Christ walks with us down every road and up every hill. He is our great and true Friend. He will never let go of us. He has given us love, joy, and peace. Christ is in our lives the divine music that knows no discord. He is for us the perfect character that has no blemish.

With all this, in Him we have found sublime things to live for. He has reserved for us the glories of an eternal kingdom. We are to lose our lives joyfully in the thrills of Christian service. We have been drawn into human need that is far greater than our own. We no longer live in a small world. The universe is within our grasp, and that for all eternity.

# SONS OF GOD

*Beloved, now are we the sons of God.* **1 John 3:2.**

The Christian is a son of God both by creation and by redemption, by the first birth and by the second. God is our heavenly Father. To say that only as we return to Him are we sons of God is not entirely correct. We may be rebel sons, disobedient sons. Our Father never relinquishes His claim upon us.

We have a Father who continually seeks to reveal His love to us, even though we may not always recognize or confess it. The unregenerate man does not cease to have a Father in heaven who loves him. At this point we must not confuse believers with unbelievers as though there were no difference between them. There is a great difference. The believer lives in Christ. God is his very life. Not so for the unbeliever. Christ died for all, but not all are being saved. One must believe that God is his Father. Forgiveness is ours. Righteousness is ours in Christ. Peace and love are ours. There is no change in the heart of God. But there must be a change in us.

Paul speaks of the unregenerate as "children of wrath" (Eph. 2:3). Our heavenly Father loves those who do not love Him. But Fatherhood is not the same to the unbeliever as it is to those who permit God to be their Father in truth. As bornagain Christians we are no longer children committed to the devil.

Christ made this clear in His dealing with the Pharisees who planned to kill Him. "Jesus said unto them, If God were your Father, ye would love me. . . . Ye are of your father the devil, and the lusts of your father ye will do" (John 8:42-44).

God is our true Father. The devil is not. But we may choose whom we will to be our father. God will not force us to live within His family. A man may refuse to belong to his true family, but the continual cry of God is, "My son, give me thine heart." Every day we need to explore how we can express our full sonship by letting God be to us what He truly is—our heavenly Father. Our heritage as Christians is to recognize that "now are we the sons of God," and to live that way.

# PEACE WITH ALL MEN

*If it be possible, as much as lieth in you, live peaceably with all men.*
**Rom. 12:18.**

Some people have the idea that Christians should be at peace with all men, that they are to never ruffle or cross anyone. This is not always possible. When tempted to compromise or sin, when called upon to stand for what we believe, conflict arises with other people. When a young man takes a stand to be firm for the right, honest, and clean, others who choose the wrong way may become antagonistic toward him. When Elijah took a firm stand against King Ahab, the king confronted him and said, "Art thou he that troubleth Israel?" (1 Kings 18:17).

A Christian witness sometimes stands in the way of other men's choices to do the unchristian thing. People do not like for us to "break up the party." So there may arise considerable ill feeling, even resentment. It is not easy for young people to stand alone in such circumstances. They do not wish to be rejected by their friends.

Although there are times when to stand alone brings admiration and applause, often it is the other way around. None of us can live the truth as it is in Jesus without disturbing some people. We cannot let that determine our course of action.

Our faith must issue in moral and spiritual commitments. A lot of belief never goes beyond thinking. We must be prepared to render a verdict in the spirit of Christ. We must say with love and firmness, "I will not act as if I am ashamed of Christ. I will stand up ready to be counted." In every age Christians have found it impossible to avoid conflict. It was said of the disciples, "These . . . [men] have turned the world upside down" (Acts 17:6).

Some people are afraid that the Christian will go to extremes. The cry is for compromise. It is easy to avoid conflict or reproach by keeping silent.

But our love for Christ must not lead us to subordinate the truth to popular opinion. Our faith is not one thing in doctrine and another in practice. Do not look bewildered if someone stands up for Christ. Every day God is on the lookout for people like this. He listens for voices that confess His name.

*313*

# THE DIGNITY OF THE CHRISTIAN FAITH

*Take my yoke upon you, and learn of me; for I am meek and lowly in heart: and ye shall find rest unto your souls. Matt. 11:29.*

The Christian faith begets in every believer a sense of greatness. But there is no struggle for self-supremacy, nothing that seeks attention. We live in an age of excitation and emotionalism, a time of frenzied eloquence, when the virtue of rebellion is extolled. Our text sets before us the quiet dignity that emulates Christ.

Our Lord gave no sanction to an artificially produced excitement in religion. He spoke and acted as a Man at harmony within Himself, with God, and with man. The eminence of His spiritual dignity in no way shattered the mind or overwhelmed the heart. Christ accepted the dignity of man made in the image of God. "A bruised reed shall he not break, and smoking flax shall he not quench." Because He knew of the sufferings and sins of men, He did not come with the shouts of the conqueror, the loud instruments of drum and trumpet, but with the gentleness of God, attracting little children.

Christ knew that to live the Christian life attractively, men must move quietly, with dignity, with the warmth of love. Someone has said that "real power is not measured by the noise men make." We are called to humility, not pride; to refinement, not coarseness; to peace, not to agitation.

Sensationalism places the emphasis upon the self. When men spend too much time seeking the ecstatic and the exciting, truth is subordinated to the exaltation of self. The individual is left with nothing to contemplate but the inflated feelings he claims to experience. A religious excitement that feeds upon itself is a parasite.

We live in a day of exaggerated advertising. There must be no self-advertisement in the true Christian. "The lack of true dignity and Christian refinement . . . is against us as a people, and makes the truth which we profess unsavory" *(Testimonies,* vol. 4, p. 358). One of the more insidious perils in religious life is the debasement of it by cheapening it through emotionalism. The antidote for emotionalism in religion is a close acquaintance with the sweetness of Jesus Christ. Here life reaches an eminence in divine quietness and loveliness that is irresistible.

# PEACE OF MIND

*The peace of God, which is beyond our utmost understanding, will keep guard over your hearts and your thoughts, in Christ Jesus.* **Phil. 4:7, N.E.B.**

Peace is one of those words we often use without knowing what it is all about. The dictionary calls it "calmness." We think of a tranquil sea after a storm. Or of freedom from war. Or of the entrance of the Sabbath after a week of hard work.

The peace that Christ gives us is not a static absence of all activity, such as comes when we do not need to think or to do anything. It is not the kind when you are alone, and the children have gone to school, and you have a few hours of undisturbed rest. This is not what Christ had in mind, at all.

Peace is the balance of a thousand forces in the human mind. Apart from trust in God, such a balance is quite unattainable; real peace is impossible. All men are full of endless striving, struggling, fightings within and anxieties without. In a world filled with sin there is no escape from discontent, except as we experience Christ in the life.

Peace is the effect of the presence of God in our lives, the balance between our tasks and tribulations and the power and ability to meet them. The peace of Christ in us means we can match ourselves with all that calls for the best in us. Jesus Christ came to restore the lost balance in our hearts. He brings our lives into harmony with God's will.

So much of life is disturbed by folly, stained by sinful indulgence, frustrated by inadequacy and vain pursuits, harassed by memories of guilty years. Often men try to free themselves of inner problems by denying them, or by indulging in worldly distractions and excitements. But inner discord can be successfully treated only from above. To try to deal with the conflicts of our nature by the superficial solutions offered by the world is simply a waste of time. If we truly desire peace we must let Christ deal with our motives, our emotional immaturities, our past sins. Only as we transcend our conflicts by God's love can we master them. We cannot live the past over again. We cannot atone for our sins and mistakes. Christ speaks peace and forgiveness to us. He gives us a new heart. The measure of our faith in our loving heavenly Father is the measure of our peace. We rest our minds on Him.

315

# GIRDED WITH GLADNESS

*Thou hast put off my sackcloth, and girded me with gladness.* **Ps. 30:11.**

In these times, the world is too much with us, clamoring loudly and insistently for our time and our energy. Our problem is that we talk too much with men and too little with God. We talk to men until we get weary of it, seeking to unload our burdens and our anxieties. We need to open our hearts in confidence to God, who knows everything about us. He can best sustain and comfort us.

All too often we are tempted to compare ourselves with others. We become unhappy because we seem not to have achieved what we desire or feel capable of. We strive to move up the ladder of status and achievement. One cannot remain in sackcloth and ashes while experiencing the abundant life in Christ.

God has wonderful ways to strengthen and deliver us from all that destroys our peace, our love, and our joy. Amid trying days and conflicts we should learn how to keep silent before men and trust simply to God. Fellowship with God avails. He has set us behind and before. This assurance raises one's sense of dignity and security, and helps him to be content with whatever lot he has.

By His love God breaks down the tyranny of fear and gloom. He turns our sorrows into joy, and for the spirit of heaviness He gives us the garment of praise. We need never despair. Whatever comes into our lives is sent or controlled by One who seeks only our happiness and spiritual growth. To be agitated by cares and tortured by problems is not part of the life with God.

There is in each of us a desire for going it alone, a will to plan our own lives, to shape our own course, to arrange our own circumstances. Let us believe that divine power and the resources of heaven are available for every duty, small and great. We are not bound to succeed in everything we undertake. We are bound to be true to the best we know.

How much gladness we lose by wrestling with problems apart from Christ. One is amazed at the spirit of gladness that can radiate from us when we come to believe that in waiting upon the Lord He will renew our spirits.

# A RELIGION OF CERTAINTY

*I know who it is in whom I have trusted, and am confident of his power to keep safe what he has put into my charge, until the great Day.* **2 Tim. 1:12, N.E.B.**

When Paul wrote these words, he was only a short time and distance from sudden death at the hands of the Romans. He speaks here of the certainty of his eternal destiny. We are to be overwhelmingly certain about our relationship with God, in the sure realization of what He has wrought in our lives. The question of certainty is quite a problem for many. Youth in particular want to be sure. Adults look for a strong staff to lean on.

God desires to produce in us an eminent Christian character. This is the day for the noblest and the best in life. Our faith is intended to produce in us a passion for purity, honesty, and Christlikeness. Everything noble in our lives springs from our identification with Him. He makes us strong to resist corruptions, sustains us to endure trials and sorrows, inspires us to make the greatest sacrifices in His service. "The people that do know their God shall be strong, and do exploits" (Dan. 11:32).

Commitment to Christ makes for a strong character, with certainty of life and purpose in the world. Weakness and sinfulness are the characteristics of uncertain men. Certainty in Christ makes us brave and obedient unto death, with a constancy and valor greater than all the armies of the world.

At Pentecost the timid, weak, uncertain fishermen and tax collector became the majestic apostles, whose mighty witness and work began to change the face of the world and to establish the Christian church. Ever since that time there have been sure and certain Christians.

When Christ walks beside us and His life lives within us, we are men and women with a plus. Christ compels us to be more than we have ever been before. We are committed to be more in life and work and witness than we knew was possible before we met Him. Christ puts divine certainty into our hearts. We have more of the love of Christ in our hearts than before. We can go the second mile and more. We are sure that Christ makes all the difference in the life we live.

# THE HOME THAT UNDERGIRDS LIFE

*Honour thy father and mother; which is the first commandment with promise; that it may be well with thee, and thou mayest live long on the earth. Eph. 6:2, 3.*

What makes the present home situation difficult is loss of respect and love, failure to honor the parents and each member of the family. The prevalence of divorce and the betrayal of children are the dire consequences. There are few issues today that seem more vital to us all.

God offers us the turning of the "heart of the fathers to the children, and the heart of the children to their fathers" (Mal. 4:6). Our Lord is big enough and loving enough to cope with all the home problems. It is almost impossible to overstate the vital necessity of a truly Christian home. Whether we participate in the final triumph of the church of God will depend to a great extent on the condition of our homes. What an indestructible and indispensable value is the home that asserts the supremacy of Christ's morality, never letting that go, regardless of what happens elsewhere.

One consistent Christian home, holding out for what God originally had in mind when He created us, is of untold worth to the church, the school, and to all society—where life is no longer thought of as cheap, where family members discover the inspiration and limitless possibilities of a love that is master over all the sinful forces in the world.

A Christian home is not a luxury, it is a necessity. It is a home that issues a challenge to our conscience to be true to each other, that nourishes a righteous love in our hearts, and shines like a light set on a hill.

We need to make Christ the head of the household where members enjoy the presence of the divine: All the hurry, strife, and struggle that is met outside may be countered by the stability of a Christian home. After venturing out, we return home each day to enrich ourselves emotionally, morally, and spiritually. When a young person turns his back on a home where shines the light of love, the love of God slowly dies within him.

The Christian home does something for us that nothing else can do. It meets our basic needs. It satisfies us.

# HEZEKIAH'S HOME

*What have they seen in thine house?* **2 Kings 20:15.**

This question was asked of King Hezekiah more than 2,600 years ago. The Scripture says of him that "he did that which was right in the sight of the Lord." None of the kings of Israel experienced greater demonstrations of God's care and power. When King Sennacherib of Assyria invaded Judah and laid siege to Jerusalem, Hezekiah placed his trust in God. The Assyrian army was overthrown in one of the most remarkable miracles found in the Bible. When Hezekiah lay sick unto death, God healed him miraculously and added another fifteen years to his life. Other countries and leaders heard of what God had done to and for him. They marveled at the reports of these miracles.

The king of Babylon was so impressed that he sent ambassadors and gifts to Hezekiah. Now came the great test. Hezekiah was flattered that the great empire of Babylon should send representatives to his little kingdom. Just what did Hezekiah do? He "showed them all the house of his precious things, the silver, and the gold" (2 Kings 20:13). He failed to bear witness to the love and mercy God had shown him. He neglected to speak of God's marvelous grace and healing power.

So Isaiah asked, What have they seen in thy house—the fear of God or the greatness of man? Proof of divine love or of human folly? The love of luxury or love of the Lord? The greatness of God or the pride of men? Just what have they seen in thy house?

This question has lost none of its significance. Let us answer it honestly relative to our own home and situation. What testimony do we bear in our homes? The church can never be any stronger than the moral and spiritual stature of its families.

Jesus Christ has no beatitude for the clever or the rich. He has no objection to our having nice homes and gardens, but these are not the highest things. A home where the righteous love of God abounds, where He is worshiped and revered; a home that fears God, drinks deeply of the Water of Life. These things are fundamental.

319

# WHEN GOODNESS COMES NATURALLY

**The Prince of this world approaches. He has no rights over me. John 14: 30, N.E.B.**

We are secure in the perfect righteousness of Christ. He gives us victory over evil, not by increasing demands but by giving us His mind and life—the love of that which is true, righteous, and elevating. This makes it impossible for us to desire and enjoy the defiling ways of the world, the flesh, and the devil.

We are like a musician who has perfect pitch. He steps into a room filled with musicians. Automatically he detects out-of-tune notes and reacts against them. We Christians need to develop the same delicate spiritual sense. We become invulnerable to evil in proportion to our degree of spiritual life and health.

The Christian life is not a sheltered, isolated life. We do not live in a cloister. There is no way we can withdraw physically from the world. We walk where sin is. It invades our homes on television. It is shed abroad in the drivel and slush of filthy literature. We can eliminate the television set and refuse the literature, but there will be other temptations and dangers. But we have the Holy Spirit as a wall of fire in our minds, and the love of righteousness in our hearts. In the midst of a world of sin, we abound in love for Christ and His righteousness.

We will not willfully expose ourselves to the ways of sin. We are not to gamble with our spiritual lives by leaving the light and walking in the darkness of the enemy. We are to keep our garments unspotted from the world. We are to fill our minds with truth, our imagination with beauty, our hearts with love, our hands and time with the work of God. We are to renew our strength daily by waiting upon God.

We are to set our affections on things above and not on the earth. We delight ourselves in the Lord and in His service. We are privileged to walk on the high places of the earth. The Lord has promised this to us. God's way is to fill our hearts and minds with goodness. Let us trust in Him whom our spiritual fathers trusted, who so often proved the power of Christ's righteousness over all unrighteousness.

320

# OVERCOME EVIL WITH GOOD

*Be not overcome of evil, but overcome evil with good.* **Rom. 12:21.**

Christian maturity is not achieved by a so-called goodness that holds badness merely in check. The Christian life is not badness stamped out, but crowded out. Error is overcome by truth. Darkness is overcome by the light. Hate is dispelled by love.

Conflict in the Christian life is a problem for many. Some try forcing the will. But the will cannot be flogged into submission. We do not conquer our personal problems and our sins by concentrating on them. A life redeemed from failure is not the result of pulling up the tares, but of developing the wheat. Continual brooding over the defects of our lives and the sins of the past is most likely to lead to discouragement.

Unfortunately, many sincere people form the undesirable habit of letting the mind revolve around those things that are painful, ugly, and undesirable. It is in the presence of Christ that we overcome evil. In the power of His overflowing love and purity we make evil impossible. Self cannot overcome self. Hate will never turn into love. The Christian must not settle for less than what Christ is. In vain will humanity be redeemed by anyone less than the perfect man, Christ Jesus. Sin will not be overcome by the pressure of rules and regulations. The belief that all that is needed is another rule properly administered, is naive and deceiving. The law can make a man pay his income tax, but it cannot make him generous. The law can make a man conform to rules of the road, but it cannot make him courteous. The law can make a man conform to a moral code, but it cannot make him honest. The law may hold evil in check, but it will not make a man righteous.

It does not help to fulminate about the sins and mistakes of people. Granted it is easier to do this than to redeem people by love and understanding. It is far better to light a candle than to curse the darkness. It is far wiser and profitable as Christians to look continually to Christ than to contemplate the array of people's sins. The secret of victory is to look away from self and others to the only perfectly victorious, most loving Person who ever lived among us.

11

# THE BLESSING OF GOD—1

*The Lord bless thee . . . : the Lord make his face shine upon thee. . . .*
*The Lord lift up his countenance upon thee, and give thee peace.* Num.
6:24-26.

This blessing upon God's people has three parts, each of which begins with the name of the Lord. It is believed by many that the three parts correspond to the three Persons of the Godhead in their work of redemption. The blessing is remarkable in its beauty and desire for the fulfillment and happiness of God's children.

"The Lord bless thee"—how important it is to have this. God loves us, cares for us, watches over us, orders and directs our lives, so that whatever befalls us here, we know "that all things work together for good to them that love God" (Rom. 8:28). God's blessing comes first because it gives meaning and fulfillment to the whole of life.

The blessings of the world are deceptive and illusory. God can never be superseded or excelled because He is infinite and everlasting in His love, wisdom, truth, and goodness. We cannot rest happy with what the world offers. The blessing of God alone is sufficient.

Let us make sure that we have God's blessing on all we are and do. This means we are to have God's favor, that, living close to God, we might discover and realize the fulfillment of our capacities here and now. What God blesses is bound to succeed. What He curses is bound to fail. How important it is to have God's blessing upon our marriage, home, children, work, business.

The blessing of God causes us to triumph in life. He puts no straightjacket upon us. He represses no possibility and potentiality we have. There is something great about the man who is blessed of God. We begin and continue with God's favor if we are to do anything in life that is truly worthwhile.

The blessing of God is guaranteed to make a difference in our everyday living. Some people have the idea that sin is exciting. They are quite mistaken. To step out every morning knowing that God has blessed us for this day is something to get enthusiastic about.

# THE BLESSING OF GOD—2

*The Lord is thy keeper: the Lord is thy shade upon thy right hand.*
**Ps. 121:5.**

We are talking about God's hold on us, the grip of His heart and hand. "The Lord is my shepherd; I shall not want. He maketh me to lie down in green pastures: he leadeth me beside the still waters. He restoreth my soul: he leadeth me in the paths of righteousness for his name's sake" (Ps. 23:1-3).

These words were written by David, whose life record fell far short of the will of God. Yet finally he came to say this, because it had happened to him. God had really done something for him. He had gone a long way down and come a long way back. God never gave up on David. He will never give up on us. It is one thing to stand before our sins in despair. It is an entirely different thing to stand before our Lord with His hand upon our shoulder, gripped by a love that gives us back life and a future that has a triumphant song in it all the way.

"The Lord make his face shine upon thee." What a difference it makes when the sun shines. When God's face shines upon us, we walk in brightest sunshine. But let God veil His face and we are troubled. "Thou didst hide thy face, and I was troubled" (Ps. 30:7). There is no sunshine if we keep the mind shut up to ourselves. Money, success, or fame cannot bring the smile of Christ into our lives.

Let us allow God's face to shine upon us each day. "The Lord, The Lord God, merciful and gracious, longsuffering, and abundant in goodness and truth" (Ex. 34:6). Christ is slow to mark our sins and mistakes. He is always ready to accept us. He has never yet turned away one sincere, repentant, believing soul. His face is always toward us in love.

"The Lord lift up his countenance upon thee, and give thee peace." The figure is that of a king when his subjects seek an audience with him. He lifts up his face and they feel esteemed. They are invited to come close to him in private audience. He holds out his scepter of acceptance.

Our God lets us freely into His presence. We find favor with Him as did Esther when she went in to see the king. God's love and grace know no bounds. We live in the light of His countenance of love.

# JESUS WILL RECEIVE YOU

*The man who comes to me I will never turn away.* John 6:37, N.E.B.

The monarchs of the world have, for the most part, affected great seclusion. They have surrounded themselves with impassable barriers of state. Remember Queen Esther. Though the monarch was her husband, she went with her life in her hands when she ventured to present herself before the king.

This is not so with the King of kings. His courts are far more splendid, His person is far more worshipful, yet we are invited to draw near unto Him at all times. On occasion when Christ was on earth, the disciples were inclined to restrict access to their Lord. Christ always corrected this idea and welcomed all those who wished to see Him. The door of His house of mercy is set wide open. Over the lintel of His palace gate is written, "Come unto me, all ye that labour and are heavy laden, and I will give you rest" (Matt. 11:28).

We may come to Christ without any righteousness of our own. He has in Himself all the righteousness that we need and is ready to impute it to us. When Moses descended from Mt. Sinai, he stood before the people with such a flaming countenance that they asked him to wear a veil. But if Christ should come to us in His earthly form, there would be no closed eyes, no covering of the face, no alarm, no anxiety.

Not one sincere seeker after Christ has ever been turned away. If there had been we should have known of it by now. Satan would have told it. The devil will tell us that God is a hard taskmaster, for he is the father of lies. But God is love and that love embraces all who come to Him.

Luke tells us that "there is joy in the presence of the angels of God over one sinner that repenteth" (Luke 15:10). When God created this world and man, the Bible tells us that "the morning stars sang together, and all the sons of God shouted for joy" (Job 38:7). When man sins, the whole universe suffers. When he repents, the universe awakens to music; the whole creation is stirred to the acclamations of praise to God.

When we think of sin and its degradation, we cannot understand how a sinner can be saved. When we think of our heavenly Father and His beloved Son, we cannot understand how any man can be lost.

324

# THE HONOR OF THE SAINTS

*This honour have all his saints. Praise ye the Lord.* **Ps. 149:9.**

The Christian church is a divine aristocracy. Every member has the same high standing and privileged calling before God. Therefore we must not rest content with an inferior sense of self-worth. We are to claim the fullness of the blessing of the gospel of Christ.

We all have that great honor of equal access to our heavenly Father. "In whom we have boldness and access with confidence by the faith of him" (Eph. 3:12). If Christ received only perfect people into His fellowship, He would sit alone. But He receives us, whatever may be our faults. He waits to give freely and richly to us all. "For the same Lord over all is rich unto all that call upon him" (Rom. 10:12). We may come to God with the confidence of Moses, with the triumphant spirit of Daniel, even with the undefeatable spirit of the apostle Paul. We are to live our lives like princes of God, sons and daughters of the King of kings.

God is no respecter of persons. Let us make the great commitment. The cold Christian can be stirred to new life. The hardest characters can become musical instruments in the hands of God. The coarse, rough personality can become a polished shaft. The vessels of clay can be transformed into urns of alabaster. Measureless treasures have been made available to us all.

One of the saddest stories in the Old Testament tells of when "Absalom dwelt two full years in Jerusalem, and saw not the king's face" (2 Sam. 14:28). It is easy to imagine the misery of men situated like the disgraced son of King David. They witness the joys and pleasures in which they cannot share. They are close to power without any sense of security. They live in the shadow of the king's palace with the feelings of a captive. Absalom grew desperate to see his father's face. He finally obtained reconciliation.

God is not like that. We have not so learned Christ. We are not to remain in suspense and sadness outside the pale. We believe in God's acceptance of us to forgive us for every sin.

# HONOR FROM GOD OR FROM MAN

*How can you have faith so long as you receive honour from one another, and care nothing for the honour that comes from him who alone is God?* John 5:44, N.E.B.

In Paul's day men in the Corinthian church gave their loyalty and honor to men. "I am of Paul." "I am of Apollos." "I am of Peter." It is always a serious problem when professed Christians are more attracted to men than they are to Christ, when they are divided in their loyalties, when they engage in competition for the honor and praise of men. Then they prefer the words of men to those of the Bible, and are loyal to a particular church rather than to the truth of Scripture.

The god of this world so easily blinds the eyes of men to the eternal God. Granted that we need all the culture and the learning we can develop. The power of thought, the ability to go to the root of great questions, the mastery of words—we can welcome them all. Above all these is the wisdom of God, fully revealed in Christ. In becoming His disciples we honor and give glory to God rather than to men.

Speaking of the Pharisees Christ said, "For they loved the praise of men more than the praise of God" (John 12:43). They preferred the favor of men to the favor of God. Love of recognition runs competition with obedience to Christ when man is the measure of all things. Desire for human favor is not necessarily wrong—it is part of our basic need for acceptance. We are not to be indifferent to personal approval. But it is to be subordinated to the honor of God. To make our object in life to please men and secure their favor rather than to please God is unworthy of us as Christians and is a fatal preference.

The temptation to seek honor from men is close enough to all of us to merit careful consideration. If we are going to be able to live genuine Christian lives we have to come to grips with this question of self-esteem. We all crave approval and shrink from men's poor opinion of us. But of all the factors that determine our standing as Christians, what people say about us is the least important. God's estimate of us is what really matters.

# FOLLOW CHRIST, NOT SELF

**Jesus then said to his disciples, "If anyone wishes to be a follower of mine, he must leave self behind." Matt. 16:24, N.E.B.**

To this call of Christ for our lives, the passion for worldly honor and distinction is directly opposed. If we do homage to wealth, to beauty, to brilliance, we shall not seek first the kingdom of God and His righteousness.

We should guard against seeking glory from men because it leads away from the moral and spiritual standards we claim to believe in. If we listen to men of repute who consider serious and complete obedience to God too far out, then we will easily join them in following the latest pleasures and sports with a diligence that derides and denies the claims of Christ.

Pilate sold his sense of justice. He ordered the crucifixion of Christ because he considered the favor of the Jewish leaders, the enemies of Christ, essential if he were to continue to hold his position in the Roman State. The sin to which the love of human favor leads me is the denial of Christ.

There are tens of thousands of people who, because of their desire to stand well with unbelievers, turn from obeying the fourth commandment. Thousands, especially among young people, are held back in giving priority to the claims of Christ. How many personal convictions of truth and resolutions of obedience to God are silenced by submission to men?

Bias against religion is the worst kind. Impressions and opposition have taken the place of facts. When this is the case the disapproval of others is a compliment to us.

There is a strong tendency in human nature to modify or change our thinking and conduct in proportion to the approval or disapproval of men, especially if they are our superiors. Bit by bit the moral and spiritual stature of our Christian experience begins to crumble. For us the appraisal of men should not be the motivating concern of our lives.

When we come to the cross and look into the face of Jesus Christ, we should be able to see ourselves correctly and not think more highly of ourselves than we ought to think. We must reckon it a very small thing to be judged of man's judgment, in comparison with the final sentence of approval from Christ, who will fix our destiny for eternity.

# THE CHRISTIAN LIFE

*And the disciples were called Christians first in Antioch.* **Acts 11:26.**

What is the Christian life? The answer is simple enough: it is a life lived with Christ, a life abiding in Christ (John 15:4), a life rooted and built up in Him (Col. 2:7). It is a life lived in the love of God (Jude 21), a life lived by the Holy Spirit (Gal. 5:16, 25), a life led by the Spirit (verse 18). Tens of thousands of Christians will tell you that it is a changed life, a life of love, joy, peace, and power to which previously they had been complete strangers. It is a life regenerated, a life made new by the power of God.

Undoubtedly we are all conscious of past failure and, quite often, of present defeat. We all have a life that we live alone; a life of thoughts that never find expression; of ambitions and resolutions that are never realized. We even have thoughts about people: envious, hostile feelings; evil imaginations cherished and gloated over; self-indulgence. God knows and sees it all. All this is our true condition before God.

To open our lives to God is basic. Otherwise we become self-deceived. Dishonesty with ourselves, a refusal to face the truth about ourselves, is tantamount to closing our life to God. It is saying to Him, "I do not want these matters included in our life together. I want them kept separate. Here I intend to be on my own. I want it kept that way." Such an attitude empties our relationship with Christ of any vital meaning.

We do not make this kind of division or separation when we get married, not if we are really sincere about it. Neither should we do it with God. Furthermore, it is no use praying to God, "Keep me from sin and self today," if we insist on keeping Him out of some particular aspect of our lives.

Life with Christ means that we banish forever from our minds all reservations. He saves us to the uttermost. The uttermost goes only as far as we invite Him. This "uttermost" means that we do not have to fail. The want of unreserved openness, of trust and dependence upon Him, makes life full of failure. Let us not blame God. We limit Him.

A life of sin and self cannot be part of a life with Christ. He came to save us from our sins. To experience this, daily surrender, consecration, and commitment are necessary.

## JOY IN THE LIVING GOD

*My heart and my flesh give a shout of joy for the living God.* **Ps. 84:2, Goodspeed.**

We usually reserve thrills for the ball game, or for other forms of sport and entertainment. Usually the church does not mind a little joy, providing it is well dressed and behaves itself; but thrills in religion? Hardly that. People get the idea that when we become Christians, this is the end of joy and thrills.

Christ's constant word to us is, "Be of good cheer." When we see the disasters and the ominous signs of the end of the world descending upon us, God's Word to us is clear: "When these things come to pass, lift up your heads, look up. All is well." This reigning buoyancy and elevation of spirit is recorded from Matthew's Gospel to the book of Revelation, from Rome's arena to the Middle Ages, from the days of the Inquisition to the Reformation, and from then until now. We cannot be Christians and wear a long face.

The religion of Jesus Christ is equal to any emergency. If your soul and mind are not full of good cheer from God, then going away for a vacation will not help much. You have to take yourself with you. If your mind is sick with worry and anxiety, there is little profit in getting behind the wheel of your car and burning the wind.

Have you ever discovered the joy that comes from the power of one single promise that God meant just for you? "O taste and see that the Lord is good" (Ps. 34:8).

The reason why people are so much harassed with care is that they are too concerned with themselves. When the love of God in our hearts reaches out to people, when we are possessed by God's great cause, the joy of God will triumph over all that brings discontent, anxiety, and misery. We enjoy people for what they are and can become in Christ.

> If Christ be in the mind,
> The wildest winter storm is full of solemn beauty;
> The midnight flash but shows the path of duty.
> Each living creature tells some new and joyous story;
> The very trees and stones all catch a ray of glory,
> If Christ be in the mind.

*—Author Unknown*

# REDEMPTIVE CHASTISEMENT

*For whom the Lord loveth he chasteneth.* Heb. 12:6.

The classic example of paternal chastisement or discipline by our heavenly Father is the experience of Job. Such discipline appears outwardly severe, but it is intended in love to work the fruits of righteousness and cause the character of a man to shine forth with greater luster. Such discipline is a mark of love, not rejection by God. Ours is a world of sin and suffering, but for God's children it provides the environment and the opportunity for the development of character with a view to eternal life.

God's discipline is tempered by love and mercy. He determines exactly the measure of our trials and tribulations. He permits nothing more than the perfecting of our characters. God sifts like wheat. He does not mar or destroy us. He does not go beyond the moral and spiritual correction we need.

Sin has brought disorder and suffering to the whole world. "By one man sin entered into the world, and death by sin; so death passed upon all men, for that all have sinned" (Rom. 5:12). When this happened God did not execute upon us judgment to the uttermost. He could have registered His displeasure and opposition to sin by total destruction.

One of the great truths of redemption by the Son of God bears witness to the tempering mercy and long-suffering of God. The whole world rests in the shadow of Him who stands between us and eternal death, the wages of sin. Because of God's intervention in His Son for our salvation, we behold divine compassion moderating the agonies and penalties of sin. The artist Rubens pictured Golgotha, the place of a skull, where Christ was crucified, as though it were a garden; a viewer can scarcely see the skull for the flowers. This is symbolic of our sinful world. The sins and agonies of men are half-hidden by the flowers of God's love and mercy. God knows our end from the beginning. God uses His foreknowledge on our behalf. When we have passed through the trials, the redemptive guidance of God stands revealed.

As night brings out the stars, so times of adversity provide God with the opportunity to extend His grace and sustaining love that the image of God might be restored in us.

# "PERFECT THROUGH SUFFERING"

*Shall we not much rather be in subjection unto the Father of spirits, and live? . . . That we might be partakers of his holiness.* **Heb. 12:9, 10.**

On the side of unbelievers is a darkened world. On the side of Christ is an enlightened world. When the darkness of trial comes upon us, God illuminates our minds. He becomes our strength in the midst of weakness. All this He does to an extraordinary degree when we turn to Him and trust Him.

For the most part we are anxious for increased good health, the reduction of life's cares and anxieties, escape from loss, grief, and tribulation. We want God to temper life by making it less difficult. But this is not usually God's way. He does not lessen the trials and difficulties so much as He lifts and strengthens the heart and mind within us. "Most gladly therefore will I rather glory in my infirmities, that the power of Christ may rest upon me" (2 Cor. 12:9).

We must be as desirous for more Christian character as we are for fewer thorns. God's love is never more revealed than when He strengthens us to live triumphantly and radiantly in the face of trial. We must praise God more for what He makes of us than for what He gives us in the way of earthly blessings. If sickness has taken hold upon you, God will make sure it will rob you of nothing. If you have been reduced to poverty, the richness of your heart in Christ shall be the measure of your crown and treasure in heaven. If some thorn in the flesh has appeared to impoverish your ability and service, God shall enrich you an hundredfold in His kingdom. God's redemptive work will be done in you.

We believe in the love, the unselfishness, the righteousness, and the sacrifice that we see in Christ. We plan to put on the robe of Christ's righteousness and the character that goes with it. But this is more than a pious exercise, more than a religious routine.

Are we willing to pay the price to be made like Jesus? Christ said it was going to cost us something to follow Him. He means business. Do we? Let us go forth with renewed faith and courage. It is said of the righteous, "He shall not be afraid of evil tidings: his heart is fixed, trusting in the Lord. His heart is established, he shall not be afraid" (Ps. 112:7, 8).

# THE WORLD FADES—GOD REMAINS

*Buyers must not count on keeping what they buy, nor those who use the world's wealth on using it to the full. For the whole frame of this world is passing away.* **1 Cor. 7:31, N.E.B.**

This text states that the "frame" or the "fashion," the whole outward aspect, the external side of life, is fading away. Hence the importance of not fixing our affections on shifting forms but on eternal realities. What would happen if you no longer could believe in your doctor, your banker, your employer, your government? Or if you lost all your money and property, the things that you count essential to life? The moment we are threatened with the loss of them, our security tends to collapse.

The sweep of change is rapid. Much of what we live by is in perpetual flux. This creates anxiety and uncertainty for many. What do you think will happen to us when there is no value to the money we have, and little or nothing to buy?

Paul urges us not to count on keeping what we can buy, or to set our affections on such things, or to consider them indispensable for our happiness and peace of mind. We can count on God, His truth, His righteousness, His love. We are to use the world as long as we can. But let the uncertain nature of the things of the world teach us that they cannot possibly satisfy us and meet the needs of the soul. Do not try to live your life on wealth that has wings, on pleasures that are here today and gone tomorrow, on worldly achievements that are as clouds in the sky. Learn that all the world offers us—its art, beauty, science, labor—serves only to prove the vanity and frailty of them all. Invest your life in fellowship with God and in service to man.

Businessmen thank God they are not unskilled. Doctors thank God they will always be needed and never out of a job. Lawyers thank God they are not politicians running for election. Professional men thank God they are not running a store. Yet even the professions do not offer ultimate security. To Christ alone we owe the way, the truth, the life that never changes and never passes away. We have eternal life from Him who is our life, a divine possession that is beyond all rank, wealth, culture, profession.

# THE PATH TO GREATNESS

*Even as the Son of man came not to be ministered unto, but to minister, and to give his life a ransom for many. Matt. 20:28.*

Christians who live by the principle of service are easily recognized. They seek not great things for themselves. They do not pander to their own egos. They love and serve people for their real and enduring worth before God. To make men submissive to our wants and desires is to taint the work we do with selfishness and pride. We are not to serve others for our own good, but for their good. We are to let our reputation take care of itself.

We may have great eminence as scholars or artists and may be distinguished by gifts and attainments before men, yet we are to have the servant spirit. All Christians are to possess this. We are to be useful rather than conspicuous.

"By faith Moses, when he was come to years, refused to be called the son of Pharaoh's daughter; choosing rather to suffer affliction with the people of God, than to enjoy the pleasures of sin for a season; esteeming the reproach of Christ greater riches than the treasures in Egypt: for he had respect unto the recompence of the reward" (Heb. 11:24-26).

The closer we come to Christ, the more we rejoice that He has called us and made us His servants. To live to the glory of God and for the salvation of men is of ourselves quite beyond our reach. Without the Holy Spirit within us selfishness, the craving for self-exaltation, and self-esteem will motivate us. Ultimately God will call us great because we sought not great things for ourselves but lived to serve.

Christ organizes our lives around some other motive than personal gain and profit. As Christians, what kind of a contribution are we making to human life and human need? "Inasmuch as ye have done it unto one of the least of these . . . , ye have done it unto me" (Matt. 25:40). Christ will examine us for this, not for how we did socially, economically, or politically. Christ's idea of happiness and success is to be useful, to be servants to our neighbors. Happiness is the inevitable result of a certain kind of life—the servant life. The proof of this comes from the Man of Nazareth.

# THE RELIGION YOUTH NEED MOST

*I am come that they might have life, and . . . have it more abundantly.*
**John 10:10.**

Youth want a religion that offers life to the fullest. To them such religion is vital. As breathing is vital to physical life, so Jesus Christ is vital to the Christian religion. How young people regard the life, death, and mission of Jesus determines whether or not Christianity is vital for them.

Christ said, "Ye will not come to me, that ye might have life" (John 5:40). We must not argue indifferently about God and life. God is not known by aimless forums, debates, and dialogs. Jesus is no legalistic code. He is the restorer of life, the regenerator of us all.

We need genuine freedom, not blind conformity or slavery. Youth are confronted with the responsibility to ask for the truth that really matters and that sets men free. No freedom exists where there is self-complacency about truth. Freedom comes with the development of the inner life that makes it impossible to desire the cheap, the ugly, the unclean, and the dishonorable.

Indifference to the truth from God makes genuine religion impossible. Too many do not care to live by the truth. They live with a mixture of truth and error. Jesus is the truth, not because the church's teachings are true but because He changes and transforms us and leads to the complete fulfillment of our lives.

True freedom is part of the Christian faith. Life is not going to turn out right unless we experience that freedom. There is no use claiming to be free while leaving Christ out of our lives. Bondage to self or to sin is an utterly futile program for any life. It simply will not work. There has to be a fundamental change in our lives. Only Christ guarantees the kind of program we can live by. The springs of our lives must be clean if we want freedom. Then our life forces of body and mind flow like a river, boundless and free.

God created us with a marvelous potential and unlimited capacities. "Let us make man in our image, after our likeness" (Gen. 1:26). Jesus Christ seeks to make that design a reality in our lives.

*334*

# THE LOVE YOUTH NEED MOST

*May you be strong to grasp . . . what is the breadth and length and height and depth of the love of Christ.* **Eph. 3:19, N.E.B.**

This time is called the age of Aquarius. Aquarius is the eleventh sign of the Zodiac, the water carrier, unstable, unpredictable, eccentric. Youth born under this sign are said to advocate a philosophy of free love, an uninhibited life-style. Emancipation is the key word. It is almost unbelievable that so many young people should choose a life that rejects material things.

The religion youth need is a religion of love, a love that can be trusted. The religion of God's love is not merely a hunger that needs to be filled, but a fullness that spills over and gives away the best and the highest. It means pouring oneself out to others regardless of what others do to you. Then nothing people say to you can hurt you.

Genuine Christian love will not let you continue through life on the fringe of friendship and fellowship. It will not play emotional tricks on people. It will not victimize people emotionally or physically. It will not allow you to overlay your heart and mind with a veneer of religious and moral platitudes, labels, and easy recipes. The world offers you love without purity and without integrity. Christ offers love with integrity, a capacity to love that fulfills to the uttermost.

What do you really want out of life? What counts most with you? Christ gives us the capacity to love and to receive love; love without jealousy, without hostility, envy, or selfishness; a love that preserves our serenity of mind and spirit.

The righteous love of God is the only thing under heaven that takes all the inner inconsistencies, the conflicting elements in life, the twisted emotions, and heals and binds them together to make you a loving person.

You do not need to be told how easily a young person can lose his capacity to love truly. The very conditions that prevail in the world have dragged love down to the level of the physical, causing people to live fragmentary lives. Christ makes you whole. He will not let you love with less than the best that is in you. He would have you know His own love, that "ye might be filled with all the fulness of God" (Eph. 3:19).

# THANKS BE TO GOD—1

*Being enriched in every thing to all bountifulness, which causeth through us thanksgiving to God. 2 Cor. 9:11.*

The key words in this verse—enriched, bountifulness, thanksgiving unto God—constitute one of the basic moods of the Christian spirit. The possessor of a vibrant, buoyant, grateful faith does not need to be pressured into telling about it. A living experience with Christ invariably becomes articulate in one way or another. Gratitude to God is natural for the true Christian.

At the heart of our gratitude is the fact that God loves us to the point of giving His Son to live and die for us. For the most part selfish people are not grateful. Preoccupation with oneself leaves nothing to thank other people for. Doctors tell us that cancer kills more people than almost any other disease. But selfishness is far more fatal. Christ fills the heart with gratitude and sweetness. But selfishness sours the life, freezes the better qualities that make for mental and physical health.

Christ sweetens the life by giving us a new perspective and a new sense of meaning. He releases in our hearts and minds the joy of His own presence. A glad gratitude is a good test of mental and spiritual health. The religion of some people is depressing. However, to be a true Christian is to be like a bird taken out of its cage and let loose to fly through the air. It means to have a life freed from the prison house of sin and guilt.

In training children and young people it is important to love them into obedience without malign feelings and rejection for their failures. It is possible to be disagreeable in our efforts to bring them into line. One can be so rigid in his religion that there is little or no attractiveness about the way he lives. The quality of our life is the ultimate thing. Unlovely lives may believe intellectually the right doctrines. Christ came to make us lovable Christians.

When Jesus walked the earth, little children ran to Him. Sinners were invited to righteousness by His presence. The unclean were purified by His love and acceptance. The Christian spirit is to be like that. Then it can only increase the happiness and gratitude in other people.

# THANKS BE TO GOD—2

*Were there not ten cleansed? but where are the nine? There are not found that returned to give glory to God, save this stranger.* **Luke 17:17, 18.**

Someone made the observation that there are two kinds of people—those who are unhappy about what life has done for them or denied them, and those who are grateful for what it has done for them. The outward circumstances in both cases may be pretty much the same. The kind of response has little to do with how much of this world's goods one has. While self-pity is not unique among the poor and the sick, gratitude does not flourish automatically in an atmosphere of comfort and ease. The idea that thankfulness in life is spontaneously evoked by outward circumstances, dependent upon the fortunes of life, is false. Nothing could be further from the truth.

The story of the ten lepers portrays these two kinds of people. All of them were miraculously healed by our Lord. Nine of them took it for granted. What kind of people were they? The one leper returned to give thanks and praise to God. Jesus did not need the man's gratitude. He was not injured or upset by the failure of the nine to respond. But gratitude and praise to God reveal a certain quality of spirit. In actual fact, only the one man who turned back to God was completely healed in both body and mind.

We can be apparently well in body but far from healthy in mind. We should never feel sorry for ourselves, believing that life has been too hard on us. William Booth, founder of the Salvation Army, in one of his poems enters heaven with Christ. He describes himself with his motley crew of homeless, ragged, hungry, and deprived. They have gathered in the square of the heavenly city to hold a Salvation Army service. Down the street they come, those who have come from the dregs of society, women who have fallen, men who have gambled their lives away, all of them trophies of the grace of Christ. They halt at the square for prayer and praise.

What is your song today? What is the note from your heart? What tune will you sound in the home, at school, or at work? Some light and jazzy music from the modern library of music? Or some great hymn from Calvary's page? What better thanks can you give than to make your life a praise to God?

# ASSURANCE

*For our gospel came not unto you in word only, but also in power, and in the Holy Ghost, and in much assurance.* **1 Thess. 1:5.**

Personal assurance goes hand in hand with experiencing Christ. To deny assurance is to deny that we are sure of Christ. Our assurance is real because God who is for us is mightier than all those who are against us. We have assurance because God "spared not his own Son, but delivered him up for us all," and with Him will "freely give us all things" (Rom. 8:32). We have assurance because "there is therefore now no condemnation to them which are in Christ Jesus" (verse 1). We have assurance because nothing can "separate us from the love of God" (verse 39). We have assurance because Christ is with us always, "even unto the end of the world" (Matt. 28:20).

The kingdom of God is joy in the Holy Spirit. God forbid we should have no assurance of salvation. Christ offers us newness of life. This new life is full of certainty and assurance. Paul was sure of God. He had no doubts about the future. Assurance is something to be experienced and enjoyed so long as our lives are hid with Christ in God. We are not whistling in the dark. While we are conscious of our weaknesses and our shortcomings, we are very sure of Christ as our Lord and Saviour. We do not belong to ourselves. We are Christ's.

Furthermore, our witness must be with that same assurance, otherwise people will not believe us. This is no complacency. We must spread the good news with a courageous, assured heart that we know redemption in Christ to be true. For we have ourselves experienced the truth of it. We know that God has forgiven us. We are messengers of certainty. In the name of Jesus Christ we offer all those we meet a chance to live the same life of assurance.

In the midst of all the agony on the cross, Christ was concerned to save a criminal. He gave him that assurance before He died.

We may never give another person exactly the same experience we have, but we can make him hungry for what we have. We can lead him to Christ and from Him receive true assurance. "Let us draw near with a true heart in full assurance of faith" (Heb. 10:22).

# THE DEATH AND RESURRECTION OF MOSES

*And Moses was an hundred and twenty years old when he died: his eye was not dim, nor his natural force abated. . . . And there arose not a prophet since in Israel like unto Moses.* **Deut. 34:7-10.**

Moses had notified the children of Israel of his coming departure. When the day came, all Israel assembled, weeping, to bid him farewell. They followed him until he signaled he would go on alone. From the top of Mt. Nebo God showed him the Promised Land. Then he died and was buried.

A man grows old and his powers of mind and body grow faint. Finally he dies with, we hope, dignity. We thank God and know that all is well. With Moses it was different. He was in the full strength of manhood. He could have led Israel into the Promised Land. Israel needed him more than ever. Surely one display of anger should not have shut him out. He had turned away from becoming a Pharaoh. He had rejected the pleasures of the kingdom of Egypt for the sake of leading Israel out of bondage into the Promised Land. He had made untold sacrifices to follow God. At the last moment the greatest man of God in the Old Testament was denied entrance to Canaan.

Yet at the same time his death was not a defeat, but a triumph. His plea and prayer that he might go over into the Promised Land was not really denied him. He did not get to earthly Canaan, but to the heavenly Canaan. His prayer was answered in a larger sense than he had conceived of.

This story shows us that, on the one hand, sin brings death, but forgiveness and love bring life eternal. Sin impoverishes our lives. It is now almost four millenniums since Moses was buried in the grave which no man knew. Yet he is now alive, active, at work. He is an assistant to Christ, who still leads the children of God into the heavenly Canaan.

But Moses' experience can be ours. The voice of God speaks to us through the living Moses who lives and serves God in a greater capacity. Here we live and here our destiny is decided. God has strange ways of rewarding and leading His children. But the sentence of death that reminds us of our sins, also tells us that in Christ we shall have life to the full for an eternity with Him.

# GOOD SUCCESS

*This book of the law shall not depart out of thy mouth; . . . that thou mayest observe to do according to all that is written therein: . . . then thou shalt have good success. Joshua 1:8.*

I admire those who succeed in life. But what do we mean by "success"? We can hardly apply the word in a spiritual sense to a man who is good on the trapeze, or to a skilled car driver, or to one who knows the right clothes to wear. We would not want to apply the word to men with low ideals. As the Bible uses it, one needs to get behind the scenes into the secret chambers of a man's life. For it is possible that here one may find nothing but failure.

Men rarely apply the word "success" to Jesus Christ. He met few of the objectives men usually admire. He was despised and rejected of men. There was no beauty in Him that man should desire Him. Yet no man has so affected the destiny of mankind for good and for eternity. All that the artists have painted through the centuries cannot begin to communicate His grandeur. In Him is the sum of all that God intended man to be: in purity, in love, in kindness, in justice, in courage, in wisdom, in humility, and in unselfishness.

For the Christian, what is a successful life? It is a life approved of God, a life that endures into eternity, where the character of a man is greater than the deterioration of his body and the passing of time. Success is the triumph of the spiritual and moral character in one's life.

A friend brings a bouquet of roses to the house. The fragrance is unmistakable. We walk through a field of newly cut hay and the odor is distinct and attractive. We drive among the pine trees, and their fragrance fills the air. We come into the presence of a man who is a loving and lovable Christian. The influence and warmth of that man are unmistakable. Paul speaks of the Corinthian believers as "living epistles."

A man who opens his life fully to Christ cannot possibly be a failure. You can't make a failure out of that kind of man simply because he loses money or position or worldly status or even health. Age, with gray hairs and wrinkles on the face, does not change him. You cannot seduce him. You cannot "imprison" a man who walks with Christ.

340

# WHAT PRICE FAME AND GLORY?

*Whosoever will be chief among you, let him be your servant.* **Matt. 20:27.**

Great exploits in the world are no guarantee of lasting fame. Do you remember the name of the man who made the first flight in an airplane across the English Channel? At the time it was a world-shattering record. Few remember him now. He was a Frenchman named Bleriot.

Do you know the name of the rich young ruler who came to Christ? Do you know the name of the leader of the charge of the Light Brigade in the Crimean War? Scarcely one of that cavalry regiment is known. One person is remembered from that war: Florence Nightingale.

In Africa, India, China, who are the men with lasting fame? Not those who enslaved the black man. Not those who exploited the nations to gain wealth and power. But men like David Livingstone and Stanley, Hudson Taylor of China, William Carey of India—these are the unforgettable heroes.

If you wish everlasting fame, glory, and honor, the best way to get it is in the service of God. The fundamental principle is this: it is most surely obtained by loving deeds and not by great exploits.

Which would you rather be called today—a Pharisee or a Samaritan? In his day the respected and respectable Pharisee looked upon the other as "a dog of a Samaritan" until the event on the Jericho Road when the Samaritan did what the Pharisee refused to do—go to the help of a stricken man. Whom would you want to emulate? Whose record would you want as yours in the books of heaven? Jesus "came not to be ministered unto, but to minister" (Matt. 20:28). He left heaven and the throne of God because people mattered more to Him than anything else. The great men of the Bible are called "servants" of the living God. That was their fame.

If the people around us are no better for our having lived, for our influence, then they are poorer for our having been here. Every worthwhile life is one of unselfish service, of inspiration to others. God made every living thing in the world that way. The trees, the blossoms, the flowers, add sweetness to life. Live to love and to serve. You shall find every day happier than you can imagine.

# TOLERANCE

*Woe unto you, scribes and Pharisees . . . ! for ye shut up the kingdom of heaven against men.* **Matt. 23:13.**

There is a Christian intolerance which is not narrow and dogmatic. None of us who love the truth should feel lenient toward the evil and the corruption that mark so much of life today. A capacity for high resentment against that which destroys people is essential. No man really loves truth who does not hate untruth. No man really loves righteousness who does not feel within him something of the opposition of God against unrighteousness.

Unfortunately, tolerance of sin is often recommended. In truth it entails a neutrality on moral issues that leads to the spread of evil and the poisoning of life itself. Many hold an easy accommodation toward sin under the impression that there is something Christian about such an attitude. Not for a moment can we regard the highest good of our children and our friends as open to question.

We must maintain truth and oppose untruth. We must do this with love. Anything that exalts Christ should be proclaimed. Anything that ignores Christ and shuts Him out should be opposed. Abhorrence of impurity is indispensable to purity.

The more one loves good music, the more distasteful to him is cheap music. The more one loves art, the more abhorrent are the crude and almost pornographic paintings and prints that pass under the name of art, and the more indignant he is against that which ministers to immorality and lust.

I am not in the least disposed to belittle tolerance of other people's views on religion or their right to differ with me. But we must be convinced that we have found the truth, that we have been led by the Spirit into truth.

People often use the word "dogmatic" when speaking of those whose stand on Bible truth is unshakable and whose advocating of it is unbending. But if tolerance means that one is never certain of anything, then this is one of the most discouraging obstacles to winning others to Christ. We need to be divinely empowered to offer the truth of God's Word with clear, searching force.

# THE DRAWING POWER OF EVIL

*But every man is tempted, when he is drawn away of his own lust, and enticed.* James 1:14.

Life is constantly drawing us nearer to Christ as our life center, or drawing us farther away. Most of those who lose their way, do not actually reject Christ. They simply say No to Him in a part of their lives.

Often we are tempted, like the prodigal, to take our portion of goods and enjoy them apart from the Father. Material prosperity and worldly pleasures may make a man forget his God. The fascinations of the world and the flesh may make us insensitive to our daily fellowship with Christ.

Things which lead men astray may be considered trivial. We tolerate things contrary to the Spirit of the Lord. Rarely do men make some radical departure from truth and uprightness. We speak of men falling into sin. More commonly they slide into it. There are hosts of satanic subtleties by which people are led away from the truth. There are half-way houses to denial of Christ. There are dubious entertainments and engagements whose questionableness sap the clear convictions once held and which, like a thief in the night, drain men of the fruit of the Spirit.

Prayer is not abandoned. One simply can get along without it most of the time. One still goes to church. Insidiously, life with God is reduced.

Who of us can detect one's slow departure from God and the truth? A mountain climber explained the birth of a crevasse in a glacier. At first the break in the ice is almost imperceptible. Later one can barely step across it, and finally the fissure becomes an impassable chasm.

Adam and Eve had no intention of departing from the Garden and from God. Gehazi had no thought of leprosy when he lied. Judas Iscariot anticipated no suicide when he betrayed the Son of God. One may drift into sin in many ways without any intention to deny God. Departure from truth in any form is always perilous. It may not take us out of the church. But it may take us away from God. It is always to our spiritual and moral advantage to maintain strict fidelity to the truth as God has given it to us.

343

# BE YE ALSO READY

*Therefore be ye also ready: for in such an hour as ye think not the Son of man cometh. Matt. 24:44.*

This insight into the times has always been a matter of urgency with God. There were multitudes of people in Noah's day, in Abraham's day, and throughout the times of Israel who did not or would not see the approaching day of God's visitation.

It is a poor sort of mountain guide who cannot tell whether there is danger of an avalanche, or if the ice over a crevasse is about to give way. It is a poor sort of ship pilot who fails to know the cut of the channels and the run of the currents. It is a poor sort of lifeguard who sees a swimmer being carried away in the grip of a current and does not try to save him from being swept out to sea. It is a poor sort of Christian who does not read aright and with insight as to the world and church conditions in such a time as this.

It is nighttime for the world. This is the darkest of all the dark ages. We are to be a light to the world. It is unpardonable to lack insight as to the drift of millions who are going down into perdition. Someone suggested that the seven deadly sins of modern life are politics without principles, wealth without work, pleasure without conscience, knowledge without character, industry without morality, science without humanity, and worship without sacrifice.

"Nevertheless when the Son of man cometh, shall he find faith on the earth?" (Luke 18:8). Unbelief is a way of life where we seek to achieve our personal fulfillment through some motivating interest other than trust in God and in the blessed hope of His soon return. One of the more difficult problems for us all—and often the most unwelcome—is the development of the mind of Christ in us, because we find life according to the world more interesting.

Our future is with Christ in the new earth. Some hope that Christ's coming can be delayed for a while at least. Life here has so much to offer. That is the surest recipe for losing everything. All man's blueprints for a better world have been torn to shreds. As stewards of the gospel of the grace of God, we must take as many people with us as we can when Christ returns.

# MORE THAN CONQUERORS

*If God is on our side, who is against us? . . . Overwhelming victory is ours through him who loved us.* **Rom. 8:31-37, N.E.B.**

Did you ever take time, in looking over your old school annuals, to find out what happened to those you went to school with? Some of them have taken the escalator going up in life. Others have taken it going down. The Bible records the same thing about men of old—Pharaoh, Belshazzar, Judas Iscariot— all spiraled down to the dust. Abraham, Joseph, Moses, Daniel, Paul, the other apostles—all took the narrow road leading up to God.

Our Lord has promised and planned for us to be conquerors. As we look to Him and turn away from self and sin we share His own confidence and assurance through His victory on our behalf. When Christ sent forth His disciples commissioned and empowered, "the seventy returned again with joy, saying, Lord, even the devils are subject unto us through thy name." For us today the same victory is possible. God is leading us to triumph in truth and righteousness over the powers of evil.

How little of this appears to the natural eye. We often become fainthearted because we see so little evidence of the triumph of Christ. Let us stand firm on Christ's victory. Let us share in His confidence. Since Christ is so sure about our victory, let us identify ourselves with it. His victorious love inspires us into immortal goodness and beauty of character. He not only gives us right truth but makes truth to prevail in our lives.

God-reliance is our need. Self-reliance fails us. We are not victorious by some unknown magic. Christ draws our hearts and minds unto Himself. He is our impregnable defense, our refuge and our fortress. Beside us walk shining squadrons of angels who bear us up in their hands.

We become victorious not by the restraint of fear, but by the love of God, who is our strength. To look to Christ is to look away from evil. To discern the beauty of Christ is to exclude the devil. To satisfy the mind with the inexhaustible riches of God is to remain unmoved by the false glitter of earthly things. The Lord we trust is the omnipotent God. Through Him we fight to conquer.

# DESTINED FOR GREATNESS

*You may know what is the hope to which he calls you, what the wealth and glory of the share he offers you among his people in their heritage, and how vast the resources of his power open to us who trust in him.* **Eph. 1:18, 19, N.E.B.**

The Christian is a person of divine destiny. All the circumstances that come to us conspire in our favor. In the heart of God we are destined to be like Christ. God provides us with an eternal calling and opportunity so magnificent as to make all other offers undesirable by comparison. He has made us partners in His everlasting enterprise. He arranges all the forces on our side.

Consider God's ultimate purpose for our lives. An artist sees the picture in his mind before he begins it. Michelangelo, before he sculptured his masterpiece, David, looked at that block of marble and saw there the image that he wished to produce.

God looks at us and sees the Christlikeness into which our lives can be shaped. This is God's supreme purpose for us. We can see the finished picture in Jesus. We see what we ought to be. We have no need to invent such a picture; it is already revealed to us. Our eternal destiny is in Christ. Christ is the archetypal man, the man God intends to produce in us.

Describing his conversion and commitment to Christ, Martin Luther wrote, "I feel as if I had been wafted through the gates of Paradise." We who live with Christ in view remind ourselves of the sublime purpose for which we live now. Our life is not a haphazard thing, lived from hand to mouth, at random, disjointed and fragmentary.

The painter does not go on aimlessly smudging the canvas, adding one blotch of color to another, and yet turn out a worthy picture. The sculptor does not chip the marble at random and produce a David such as Michelangelo's, or a Christ such as Thorvaldsen's. What is our purpose in life? One cries wealth; another, position or fame; another, worldly greatness and honor. These are intoxicating words breathed often from the impassioned lips of those who are captured by such things. We have an image greater than all these, more splendid, more enduring—the restoration of the image of Christ in us.

# "A GLORIOUS CHURCH"

*A glorious church . . . holy and without blemish.* **Eph. 5:27.**

We belong to the church of the living God because we believe it is more in harmony with God and His Word than any other. We hold fast those truths from Him, to confess, without scruple or disguise, our attachment to them, our preference for them; to do all in our power to maintain them and extend their influence as far as possible. We are to excel in honesty, integrity, purity, and the righteousness of Christ. We accept and strive after the most exalted ideal and Person who ever lived.

The true church is God's chosen institution. By it His truth is upheld, lived, and made known through all the earth. Without the true church the truth, unproclaimed, would perish from the earth. The church fears nothing. She recognizes the changes taking place in the world. She senses that the end is near. She does not exhaust herself on petty issues and legalistic moralizations. She is valiant for the truth.

To avoid the charge of sectarianism, the church refuses to abandon her stand on the whole Word of God. In order to exemplify the character of Christ and love everybody, she refuses to surrender her allegiance to Bible truth.

Because we belong to the church of the living God, she ought to be dearer to us than any other. We ought to take a deeper interest in her support and enlargement, to be more willing to labor and sacrifice. To allow personal pique, or injustice from another, to separate us from the church that we claim to love and to prefer, is a tragic mistake of judgment.

Bear in mind that, should you quarrel with another church member, you have no quarrel with your Saviour. The church of the living God is His sanctuary; it does not belong to the one who offended you. The fact that you find a professed church member untruthful does not mean that you should be ready to deny the truth, or leave the church.

Let us hold to the truth in love. The church is commissioned to proclaim and teach the whole truth from God. You and I are part of that. We need the church, and the church needs us.

# "UNTO YOU, YOUNG MEN"

*I have written unto you, young men, because ye are strong, and the word of God abideth in you, and ye have overcome the wicked one. 1 John 2:14.*

The rich young ruler who came to Christ seeking eternal life had just about everything. We do not know how he looked, how tall he was. He had brains, personality, education, and probably was attractive. He may have had all the makings of a good athlete. He asked the right questions. He had a good moral character. He had everything, but he was not ready to give it away for that which was supremely worthwhile, the one indispensable qualification for success, the willingness and ability to commit himself to the cause of God.

The present generation of young people are the most competent we have ever seen and also the most criticized. Many are ready to commit their lives to some worthy cause. They do not ask, "Is it hard?" but "Is it worthwhile?" The Christian faith has something heroic that can capture young people. It requires total involvement.

It is easy to say that all that young people need is a right relationship to God, then all other things will be taken care of; but youth problems and desires are not solved by clichés.

The name of Jesus must become more than a catchword, more than a sentimental phrase. Being a Christian carries with it the clear conviction that loyalty to our God and obedience to the Word of God precedes all else.

Allegiance to God and His Son means conflict with the world. There is no way we can reconcile ourselves as Christians to the paganism of our day. Christ has redeemed us to a life that is true, free, bold, daring, compassionate. He offers no soft and easy road into the kingdom of God. The challenge is to sacrifice and suffering. There must be no turning back.

Within the institution of religion we must avoid that mental attitude that insists on the privilege to rule, rather than to serve. This is no time for an easy adherence to a program. We must go beyond that. All churches are not alike. We must believe in the uniqueness of the remnant church to which we belong and in the divine commission given to us. We must hear and answer the call of God to join the drive that will prepare the way for the coming of Christ.

# THE CHURCH OF THE LIVING GOD

*The house of God, which is the church of the living God, the pillar and ground of the truth.* **1 Tim. 3:15.**

In every generation there have been churches whose members have felt that theirs would become the church glorious to usher in the return of Christ. You and I believe that we belong to that kind of church, the remnant church. On what basis do we have the right to make this claim?

First, the triumphant church must have a triumphant mission. We must contend earnestly for the faith once given to the saints. Conscientious people are not inclined to join a church unless she calls upon them to do for God and man that which is beyond what other religions call upon them to do, and what is beyond what they already have. Therefore we live, we speak, we witness, we commit ourselves.

Second, the triumphant church is to be "the pillar and ground of the truth." One possible peril is the loss of faith in the Bible as the charter of truth. Men today are ever seeking to modify the Word of God. The overwhelming tendency is to corrupt the truth of God. The true church is to be the pillar of the truth. So are the church members. We are entrusted with the responsibility to hold the truth, to teach the truth, to maintain the truth, to defend it, and to proclaim it.

The church is the ground of the truth. Trust rests in a church that is stable, firm, and unshaken as to the Word of God. It is exceedingly important that we believe what we seek to proclaim. We are to keep alive the knowledge of God's truth.

Third, the church triumphant is the house of God. This means that God is present in the church and in us. Here the blessed presence and power of God is felt and experienced. We present a high moral and spiritual life before the world.

Always the danger presents itself that we might become a sleeping church. Sabbath worship becomes a matter of convenience. A sleeping church is unconcerned. She is indifferent to those outside of Christ. An awakened church is never the result of an accident, but of earnest prayer, of settled purpose, and of a supreme desire toward Christ. The Son of man goes forth to war and to victory. The church is to triumph with Him.

# CAN LAODICEA GIVE GLORY TO GOD?

*Not unto us, O Lord, not unto us, but unto thy name give glory.* Ps. 115:1.

The Laodicean church fails in understanding her true relation to God. She attaches glory to herself. "I am rich, and increased with goods, and have need of nothing" (Rev. 3:17). She has the delusive idea that she is self-sufficient, self-contained. Consequently, there is much dependence on herself and too little on God.

The truth about Laodicea seems so obvious. It was the sin of ancient Israel who insisted on fighting under her own power too many times. The most serious problem of modern Laodicea is rooted in confidence in our own power and ability to do it ourselves. We stumble over our religious status and accomplishments. Consequently, we assume an impossible independence from God and the Holy Spirit. We are lifted up above our need for Jesus Christ and His righteousness, since we have now achieved so much of our own. Spiritual decline starts with the belief that we can center life in ourselves and succeed. To the degree that we magnify ourselves, we do not give glory to God.

Christ shows us the way. He is meek and lowly in heart. He did nothing of Himself. He lived in complete dependence on His Father. This is the life Christ came to communicate to us. The very essence of salvation is living by Christ alone. Our religion must not be directed toward our own exaltation and self-sufficiency.

This problem of Laodicea tends to visit especially those of us who come to occupy positions of respect, leadership, status, ability. Sure of our own superiority, we fail to see how adversely this affects our dependence on the Holy Spirit.

Our confidence is to be entirely in Christ. Whatever value we place upon each other is because we know that God has redeemed us.

Unless Christ lives His life in us we will never survive spiritually or even morally in the end. Waiting upon God means the end of self-esteem and self-serving. "The loftiness of man shall be bowed down . . . the Lord alone shall be exalted in that day" (Isa. 2:17). God has given us one truth to live by: the absolute insufficiency of ourselves, the absolute sufficiency of God.

# A SURE FOUNDATION

*The foundation of God standeth sure.* **2 Tim. 2:19.**

We do not build a sixty-story skyscraper on a one-story foundation. It takes a sure foundation to support our lives as Christians, to build a character that will endure unto eternity. In planning our lives, the first responsibility is to build on that which is eternally true. Joseph, who faced a moral battle in the house of Potiphar, had built his life on God. Daniel, who met the temptation to compromise his principles in Babylon, stood firm on God. Moses, with the glories of an ancient empire offered to him, had built his life on Christ. So had Paul, when he stood before Nero. So have all loyal Christians. No human structure ever collapsed until the individual moved away from Christ.

As a teacher, I have always wanted young people to make sure their lives were founded on Christ and on His Word. I have known many cases where young men and women developed a strong moral character. They stood firm under the most severe temptations. I have known others who were not that careful. They meant well, but they daily went their own way and relied on themselves. It was never enough. Their intentions seemed good enough, but their moral performance, their endurance and loyalty to that which is true, proved to be very mediocre.

Moral and spiritual failure is always a serious problem. What happens when a man has nothing more to depend on than himself? People try by the force of will to overcome some bad habit, a bad temper, a craving for questionable things. There is a continual inner conflict. In the end, the defects in character show up and win out. To build on our own power is quite useless. Said Christ, "Without me ye can do nothing" (John 15:5).

Much of religious teaching and preaching takes the form of moralizing—we ought to do this or we ought not to do that. People get tired of religious lectures. We must find meaning to what we believe. Christian faith moves deeper and deeper in certainty as to what Christ is to us. In every life decision we cast our deciding vote on His side. Faith in Christ is the only way to victorious power.

*351*

# NOT BOWED THE KNEES TO BAAL

*Yet I have left me seven thousand in Israel, all the knees which have not bowed unto Baal.* **1 Kings 19:18.**

Elisha the Tishbite was a remarkable person, one of the greatest men in Old Testament times. He was a man of unusual vigor and force of character. He lived in difficult times when almost all Israel, led by King Ahab and Queen Jezebel, had gone over to a deadly idolatry. By and through this one man, Elijah, God combated the evil and restored the true worship of God.

Jezebel took an oath to effect the prophet's death. Elijah fled for his life and hid in a cave. He declared himself before God as the only one left who worshiped Jehovah. In reply God told him that He had seven thousand who had remained true to Him.

In our day there is left a large number about whom the same could be said—those who maintain their integrity before God. There are hosts of young people who count not their lives dear unto themselves in order that they might "testify [to] the gospel of the grace of God" (Acts 20:24).

When the hosts of Midian came up to destroy Israel, Gideon had 32,000 men. God quickly reduced these to 300. God knew these few men would never quit. They would never compromise. They would never retreat. They would go forward under God. With these few He overthrew the hosts of Midian. That is how God has always done it. God does not stress numbers. He calls for people who are prepared to stand regardless of what is happening around them.

Everywhere today people bow the knee to "Baal." Are we prepared to stand? God needs to know that. He needs to know whether we have joined the church with one foot in and one foot out. We cannot improve and advance the cause of God any faster than we can improve ourselves under God.

There are thousands of Christians today whose relationship to God is a dynamic force in the life. They speak boldly for Christ. They do not stand remote in ivory towers making formal pronouncements about the truth. They are real people prepared to witness anywhere for Christ.

# TRIUMPH OF THE STILL SMALL VOICE

*And, behold, there came a voice unto him, and said, What doest thou here, Elijah?* **1 Kings 19:13.**

The truth implied in God's dealing with Elijah is significant. God is not in the sensational and the loud. The gentle pressure of God is its own announcement and its mightiest power. The truth is so contrary to the shouting, the trumpet-blowing and loud advertising.

Nothing can reach our hearts but the "still small voice." It is well that we have less faith in noise and more faith in a quiet godly character; that our lives are more potent than our words. To be filled with the Spirit is not to be filled with religious riot.

We might remind ourselves that the power of the "still small voice" is greater than the indulgence of religious intoxication. "Thy gentleness hath made me great" (2 Sam. 22:36). In expressing our faith to others, the mightiest influence is love.

The quiet, persistent, undiscouraged power of the kindness and love of God should possess our hearts and minds. This is no easy optimism, no passing fancy that all is well. The "still small voice" is a sober, deep conviction by the Spirit that leads us into a life of peace, assurance, modesty, meekness, and patient endurance in the ways of the Lord.

Behind all the true accomplishments for God are spiritual forces that have taken possession of our lives. This is especially true of Christian character. Our great abilities are not the wisest part of us. The men of God have ever realized most clearly the direct action of the Holy Spirit upon their hearts. The voice of God has called them out of false paths into the way everlasting.

The heroic constancy of the glorious army of martyrs, the myriads of humble souls who have triumphed over adverse circumstances, shine like stars. The Spirit of the Lord changes us from glory to glory.

By the still small voice of the Holy Spirit, God draws near to us. He is not in the earthquake of some shattering excitement. He is not in the whirlwind of emotional frenzy or fanaticism, but in the sanity and serenity of the soul. The Holy Spirit resolves all our inner discords.

12

# "A GREAT DOOR . . . IS OPENED UNTO ME"

*For a great door and effectual is opened unto me, and there are many adversaries. 1 Cor. 16:9.*

The apostle Paul is writing of the opportunity opened to him for service in God's work. The call of God rings through the rooms of his soul, so that necessity is laid upon him. His choice is not a preference among other alternatives. All other possibilities fall into the background. He has one clear open door from God. God both opens doors and closes them. Everywhere as Christians we are confronted with opportunities and open doors.

"And there are many adversaries." The conjunction that joins these two sentences is worthy of note. Paul does not use the word *but*. He might have said "a great door is opened unto me, but," indicating that these adversaries made a difference whether or not he should go through that door or stop because of the adversaries.

He has taken into consideration all these adversaries. They make no difference. They cannot change his mind and purpose. Mind you, for all of us who choose Christ, there are big iniquities, frowning like dark clouds. There is much that could make us afraid if we gave in to it. We face a world sick with fear. But there is an open door to service for God. Living the Christian life is no charmed circle. There is many a temptation, many a challenge that does not spell ease and comfort, but strife and peril. It looks difficult. It is going to cost you a lot of sacrifice and discomfort. You are called to break loose from all the material comforts of life. Take a good look at this door opened unto you. You are being called in question, not on your orthodoxy, but on your personal faith and courage.

We must direct our attention to this high calling to us from God. "The word of the Lord came unto Jonah." God had opened the door to the great city of Nineveh. One man was God's chosen instrument. Jonah arose to flee. Ultimately he was delivered miraculously from the belly of the whale. God still needed him to take His word to Nineveh. The hour had struck for its destruction. God had one man. This was Nineveh's last chance. The door was open. The adversaries were legion. But Nineveh was saved.

# VALIANT FOR TRUTH

*Stand therefore, having your loins girt about with truth.* **Eph. 6:14.**

One of the characters in Bunyan's *Pilgrim's Progress* is Mr. Valiant for Truth. Said Valiant for Truth, "Let a man have one of these blades, with a hand to wield it and skill to use it, and he may venture upon an angel with it." Who is this Valiant for Truth? And what is this sword that is so effective in the Christian fight. "The sword of the Spirit, which is the word of God" (Eph. 6:17).

Valiant for Truth means that the truth is in our heart. That we are basically pure, honest, upright in heart. The Holy Spirit has brought the truth into our lives. This is the kind of character we are to have. We love the truth. We are prepared to stand for it at any cost to ourselves. Let us remember that by the Spirit the Word of God acts directly upon our minds and lives, setting in motion God's eternal principles of truth. The Spirit speaks directly to us, inspires us, leads us. At this point doubts are dissolved. We naturally obey from the heart those truths and standards whose moral and spiritual beauty long tantalized us from afar. Instead of being weary of trying, we live with exhaustless energy from God. Every truth-led Christian is assured of this fact when the Holy Spirit draws nigh to us, and our lives are stirred and captured for God. All that is evil and sinful is overcome.

Let us not impede the transforming power of God's truth in our lives by unbelief, worldliness, and unfaithfulness of life. We must not neglect the royal power of God's Word by the Spirit, but avail ourselves of it to master all evil, to transform, uplift, and renew us in Christ's image.

Have we joined the remnant church today with the clear understanding that God has commissioned us with a special message to the world? I know of no conception of our life that so dignifies and inspires us as the realization that God has called us and chosen us to carry His last message to the world. I cannot imagine our coming to God and saying, "Lord, why did You call me to be a Seventh-day Adventist?" and then hearing God say, "Well, I really had nothing specific in mind at all." We too are Valiant for Truth. By firsthand experience we will discharge all the duties of Christ's ambassadors.

# AN UNSHAKABLE CHARACTER
# IN A SHAKEN WORLD

*I will make a man more precious than fine gold; even a man than the golden wedge of Ophir. Therefore I will shake the heavens, and the earth shall remove out of her place. Isa. 13:12, 13.*

We all know people who cannot be shaken out of the Christian faith. We have known others who have been shaken out. In our faith and position as Christians, we like to believe that we have within us the quality of the imperishable, the unshakable. The last days are to be the crucial test in a man's life. Everything that can be shaken will be shaken.

Just what do you think will happen to you then? When do we become unshakable? We cannot live by the position and opinions of men. Some positions will change. Some will never change. With the first, we must be willing to test everything by the Word of God. The Word of God stands on its own divine origin. That makes it unshakable. Because God always keeps His word, the promises and prophecies of the Bible are true. To establish us in the faith, the Holy Spirit works by and with the Word of God. He produces in our lives an experience that cannot be explained unless the Bible be the Word of God.

When we take Jesus Christ and His Word seriously, we must face the issue of becoming personally involved. What Jesus said, did, and taught, now becomes a personal matter. There is always the temptation to remain distant. The Holy Spirit creates a sense of urgency about salvation, righteousness, and obedience that makes it undesirable that we keep hesitating, waiting, and arguing for a more convenient time, and until we have solved every difficulty and every question is answered.

If we keep on raising questions and doubts we will escape the necessity to become personally involved. Be sure that your discussion of truth is not a cover-up for the lack of spiritual reality, a refusal to face the truth about yourself. The knowledge of truth does not become saving truth until it leads us to personal commitment. Without that commitment deterioration sets in until we rest satisfied with discussing without commitment. We are to let the Spirit search our lives; we are to seek to do God's will, and obey it the moment the Spirit convicts us.

# ON GOD'S SIDE

**With my whole heart have I sought thee: O let me not wander from thy commandments. Ps. 119:10.**

The first thing to consider when faced with the claim of God upon us is to make up our mind just how far we intend to go; to sit down and count the cost. This is the difference between a child and a man. The child thinks only of his immediate gratification. The finest type of Christian men and women fix their minds on Christ. They are prepared to make sacrifices now to realize the supreme purpose of God for their lives. No Christian life can be true or successful that is lived from hand to mouth, at random, indifferently. We must settle for this alone: our total allegiance to Christ and to His Word. Then we are not afraid of anything.

The safe side for living the Christian life is always on the side of God and His Word. Our feelings may be elated or they may be despondent. The perilous way is to let feelings decide. We must carry with us the conviction to do what God says, not what our feelings would dictate to us. Where two courses are before us, take the one that is in harmony with God. Do not set up expediency against principle.

"I have set the Lord always before me" (Ps. 16:8). This is the key to life. Our loyalty cannot be partial if our eye is fixed on Christ. Let not anything divert us from this prize of our high calling: to be Christ's, to be fully awake each day to the life we are to live. It is impossible to fail when we are wholly on God's side. Everything about us will be caught up into a grander life, a transformed life.

Let not this wholeheartedness be adjourned to old age. Youth often say, "Let us have our way now. Let us have some enjoyment now. There is time enough to serve God when we get past 30, 40, 50, or 60." The best guarantee for standing with Christ when He comes or when we are old is to be wholly on God's side now. Then when we reach old age or when Christ comes we shall find His purity, His beauty, His truth in our lives unshakable and ourselves immovable. We are to put our whole life in God's hands now. He will direct and manage our life with eternal security. With God everything is dependable and trustworthy. God has the last word.

*357*

# CHRIST OUR HOPE

*Looking for that blessed hope, and the glorious appearing of . . . our Saviour Jesus Christ.* Titus 2:13.

To have Christ as our hope means to believe in a different kind of life where exists every possible perfection. Then we shall be as we were meant to be. The law of heaven will then be the law of the new earth. We who confess Christ acknowledge that He will do right by us. He will restore us to that state in which He originally created us. In eternity we shall have neither guilt within us nor enemies about us nor death before us.

Only the work of Christ in our lives will remain, and nothing of sin. The things and glories of this world lack the quality of eternity. Christ's coming will cause joy on the one hand and sorrow on the other. For the saved, Christ's coming will be the realization of all their hopes. We shall have none but good company, and they will be better than they are now. With delightful surprise we shall experience what God has in store for us. It will excel all that we have had down here.

We live by hope. What patience this hope engenders! What strength we have to sustain our hopes! What resignation to the shortness of life, knowing that we have an eternal future with Christ! What occasions for Christian witness and what heroism this hope inspires! What faith to keep on through weary years inspires us to be true to God. We know the devil can make life difficult on this earth. He causes men to destroy the earth and pollute that which God originally made beautiful. But he cannot take the faith, the love, the joy, and the beauty out of our hearts and lives.

With our hope centered in Christ, we must learn to live bravely and truly without much thought of earthly consequences. I pity the people who are continually looking for more things to make life smoother and more secure. We cannot spend our days doing that. In a few years life will all be washed up, finished on this earth. We stand on the perilous edge of eternity. We live now as God's people. That puts every unworthy, selfish purpose in its proper place. The blessed hope shines in our hearts and on our faces.

# HOPE REALIZED

*But we long for every one of you to show the same eager concern, until your hope is finally realized.* **Heb. 6:11, N.E.B.**

We are quite sure that the future holds more for us than anything we have in the present. We refuse to sacrifice future eternal realities for temporary advantages and pleasures. The value of transitory things in the light of eternity is soon dissipated.

Christ is the second Adam, the head of the race. There can be no error as to the certainty of His imminent return. Sinful man has proved his complete incapacity and inability to save civilization, to bring about the reign of truth and righteousness. The coming reign of Jesus Christ is not based on anything man can do.

We who are truly converted to Christ reject any possible reign of sinful man on the earth and any human solution to the sin problem. The promises of Christ to return to earth to resurrect His followers and translate us into the kingdom of glory inspire us with hope, wonder, and delight. There is an unbridgeable gulf between man's promises and God's. We shall live forever because we know Him, because He has already given to us eternal life. He will never abandon us. In the Word of God we find promise and prophecy of immortality to come.

Several years ago one of the universities of this country established a crypt of civilization in which the evidences of this generation were locked and sealed and protected against decay, hopefully until the year A.D. 8113, when it is to be opened. The only people who will see the year A.D. 8113 are those who belong to Christ now, who put their hope in Christ now.

The end of life on this planet is but the true beginning for us. We do not live and die as followers of Christ only to have some gravedigger shovel dust upon us and let that be it. "For we are saved by hope: but hope that is seen is not hope: for what a man seeth, why doth he yet hope for? But if we hope for that we see not, then do we with patience wait for it" (Rom. 8:24, 25). There is bound to be a triumphant sequel to the history of our world. We can all make up our minds to hope and to work for it, and to hasten that day.

# DESTINATION: THE KINGDOM OF GOD

**But seek ye first the kingdom of God, and his righteousness; and all these things shall be added unto you. Matt. 6:33.**

In 1934 I was a student at a university. In those days money was not very plentiful. I earned my way waiting table in a fraternity. Most of the fellows were the sons of rich men. The most serious student there was a Communist. One day he took me along to a meeting. It was exciting, not because of what was said, but because of the spirit. The hall was small, the place crowded. This particular young man was one of the leaders. He had a real sense of mission.

On the way back to the fraternity I asked him, "What about your future? What do you intend to do?" He replied, "I have security, not because I am rich, but because I know where I am going. I belong to a movement that will ultimately conquer the world."

I said to him, "You are mistaken. Communism has no future. I am a Christian. I too know where I am going. I also know what is coming. This world is not to be a Communist kingdom, but the kingdom of God. I have a future that reaches into eternity." He was in pursuit of an earthly kingdom for his own interests. The supreme thing was the glory of man. For me it was God, His kingdom, and the rule of His righteousness. His philosophy was self-centered. Mine was Christ-centered.

We have come to the hour when we are lodged, as it were, between two worlds: the world we know and live in, and the new earth yet to be born. The first is visible. Potentially it is dead. It has no future. There is no solution to the world's fatal sickness within the present historical process. The world we belong to is invisible.

We call for a devotion greater than that of any other philosophy or earthly system. Christ alone has the power to subdue all things unto Himself. There never was a more fateful experiment than when God created our world, which He knew would rebel against Him. He knew that His holy love must triumph before the universe. We live with an awareness of how much is at stake in this matter. All members of the Godhead staked everything on the person and work of Jesus Christ on earth, and won.

# OUR MANY MANSIONS

*In my Father's house are many mansions. . . . I go to prepare a place for you.* John 14:2.

There is a heaven for the people of God. Christ was sure about that. The everlasting gospel requires such a glorious consummation. Salvation does not stop at the grave. Christ brought life and immortality to light, a deliverance that reaches far beyond this present sinful world.

Without the fulfillment of Christ's promise to us of many heavenly mansions, we can look only for disappointment and death. "If in this life only we have hope in Christ, we are of all men most miserable" (1 Cor. 15:19). The promise is based on the truth of the resurrection. The triumphant resurrection of Jesus will be gloriously realized in His people. Enoch and Elijah ascended to heaven without seeing death. Moses was resurrected and taken to heaven. Both Elijah and Moses stood in their robes of light with Christ on the Mount of Transfiguration. At the close of His ministry Christ Himself was caught up from the Mount of Olives in a cloud of glory and returned to His heavenly Father. So it will be with us.

We need a faith that rises beyond the sin and death of this life to the certainty of our future home in heaven. John describes life there with no night, no sorrow, no sighing, no tears, nor any more pain or death. There is no possibility of our being disappointed. Jesus Christ will return. He will resurrect His children to everlasting life. He will accompany us back to our Father's house where there are many mansions.

These heavenly dwelling places are not temporary like the houses we have on earth. They are permanent residences, incorruptible, that fade not away. We shall experience the fullness of all that is good and true.

We shall bear His image and likeness for all eternity. We shall be restored to perfect capacity of body, mind, and heart! What range of knowledge will be ours! What research into God's works! Our minds will be immensely enlarged, faculties refined and glorified, so that all the truth of God will be opened to our view. We shall witness to millions of other beings on other worlds, and enjoy fellowship with all the members of God's heavenly family.

# WHEN CHRIST RETURNS

*Nevertheless when the Son of man cometh, shall he find faith on the earth?* **Luke 18:8.**

Two points of truth are stated in this text. First, "When the Son of man cometh"; there we have the certainty of God. Second, "Shall he find faith on the earth?" There we have the uncertainty of man.

The text does not read, "If the Son of man comes," but "when." "I will come again," Christ promised. We are guaranteed the return of Christ. One day the world as we know it will come to a full stop. This we can count on. Christ Himself will usher in the end of the world as we know it. This event will not be accomplished by the nuclear wars of men or the collapse of civilization. "When the Son of man cometh." "Even so, come, Lord Jesus." This is the certainty of God.

"Shall he find faith on the earth?" There is always an amazing contrast in the Bible between the certainty of God and the uncertainty of man. Concerning God, the Bible is always sure. Concerning man, there are serious questions. Faith will be hard to find. Nothing is abiding in life except as it is rooted in Christ and in His Word. Christ never fails us, though we often fail Him. Are we sure about our relationship to God?

Imagine an angel guest knocking on our door. Christ said He is standing at the door of our hearts. But here is a man so busy counting his gold that he cannot hear, or planning his pleasures so that he is indifferent; or the scholar so intent upon his books that he cannot be bothered; or the youth so captured by sports that he has no other interest.

Those for whom the end will be this sinful world, will be those who live worldly lives. Those who find the end is an empty blank will be those who have lived empty lives. Those for whom the end is destruction will be those who have lived sinful lives. Those for whom the end is Jesus Christ will be those who have lived in fellowship with Him.

The man who is without Christ's righteousness cannot afford to meet the Son of man whose life is one of perfect sinlessness. The man who has followed Christ here and now, will welcome Him when He returns. The Christ we live with now will be the same Christ we will live with for eternity.

# MAN'S DOMINION OVER THE EARTH—1

*So God created man in his own image . . . and said to them, "Be fruitful and increase, fill the earth and subdue it, rule over . . . every living thing."* Gen. 1:27, 28, N.E.B.

"The serpent said, 'Of course you will not die! God knows that as soon as you eat it, your eyes will be opened and you will be like gods knowing both good and evil' " (Gen. 3:4, 5, N.E.B.).

Here are two offers from two very important persons. Which one would you accept if you did not know about Satan's opposition to God? Both offers in themselves look attractive. Satan promises you just about as much as God does— world dominion, to be like God.

When God created man and placed him on this little planet he was a minority among the various species of animals. With his fall he exercised only limited dominion. There is little or no evidence that man did extend his dominion over the earth.

But now in the twentieth century all has changed. Up to the eighteenth century the earth population did not exceed 300 million so far as we are able to tell. During the nineteenth century the population reached one billion; by 1930, two billion; by 1962, three billion. By the end of the century, the earth will be twice as crowded as it is now.

Had not sin entered, man would have fulfilled God's purpose, replenished the earth and held sacred dominion over it. Apart from the rule of God, man's dominion has effected only pollution of the atmosphere and the seas, has desecrated the earth and squandered the treasures in the earth placed there for man's creative genius and development. Under God man would not have been in this position.

There is now no place to go. Sinful man has developed a world-destructive power of which no previous generation had any idea—nuclear energy. Nuclear energy is not a strange thing. It is not a human invention. It is the natural energy of the universe. All the galaxies of stars, billions of suns, use this nuclear energy. It can be a great blessing. But it can be a terrible curse. We are face to face with the terrible possibility inherent in sinful man's dominion over the earth. The fundamental question is: Does man have control over himself under the Lordship of Christ, or is he under Satan's dominion?

# MAN'S DOMINION OVER THE EARTH—2

*What is man that thou shouldst remember him, mortal man that thou shouldst care for him? Yet thou hast made him little less than a god, crowning him with glory and honour. Ps. 8:4, 5, N.E.B.*

We on this planet have been on a long journey through space for six thousand years. This is a time of great foreboding. How do we adjust ourselves mentally, emotionally, morally, and spiritually, where world dominion is in the hands of sinful men?

We are still confronted with the offer of world dominion, either under God or under Satan. The issue is decisive. Satan has gained dominion over man. He offers man open eyes to everything—science without God, morality without God, art and education without God. What will sinful man do with nuclear power a few years from now? Within twenty-five years, it is expected that more than thirty nations will have harnessed this energy.

All our pollution and destruction are from ourselves and the dominion of sin and Satan. All our salvation is from God. All man's slavery to sin is from Satan. Redemption is from Jesus Christ. All death comes from sin and Satan. Life alone is from God.

Think of our sun, more than eight hundred times greater than all of the planets put together. Think of all that energy burned every day. God has been exploding more hydrogen bombs on the sun than man will ever do on earth. What does God do with all this power in His hands? Under the control of our heavenly Father nuclear energy is nothing to be afraid of. It is no burden to the flowers in the field. It does not crush the lily, or the rose, or the blossoms on the trees. All are indebted to the sun's energy for the continuance of life. It makes them grow. It infuses them with fragrance and beauty. It paints them as no painter on earth can do. It brings them to maturity to bless man and satisfy his needs. The Lord is that kind of God.

The world needs the dominion of Christ, for He alone can save it. Christ wants and loves the world, for He has redeemed it. Who now has dominion over our hearts, Christ or Satan?

# THE JUSTICE OF GOD

**Shall not the Judge of all the earth do right? Gen. 18:25.**

This statement was made in connection with God's announced plan to destroy the cities of the plain. God is not only a God of love and mercy but a God of righteous judgment. Abraham found it difficult to believe that in these two cities there were not to be found some righteous people. How could God destroy them, if there were such people? God must do justly. Abraham's statement is a declaration of his trust in and reliance on God's character. He would not distrust or doubt God. He knew that God would do the right thing.

We are to trust God not only in good times but in difficult times. To live this way is a mark of spiritual stability and maturity. For us who live in the time of the end, Christ made it clear there would be difficult days, very difficult; that we would have nothing much to go on but faith in Him. His forecast of world conditions in our time should lead us to expect that, before it is all over, we will lose everything we own; that "only our bread and water will be sure."

Beyond that our future is certain. The only forecast that makes life worth living is what we get from Christ. If we are to triumph, we must be strong in faith as Abraham was, knowing that Christ will do the righteous thing. "Without any weakening of faith he [Abraham] contemplated his own body, as good as dead . . . and the deadness of Sarah's womb, and never doubted God's promise . . . , but, strong in faith, gave honour to God, in the firm conviction of his power to do what he had promised" (Rom. 4:19-21, N.E.B.).

As surely as God destroyed the cities of the plain, so is the coming end of our world. The world is not going to be the easiest place to live in. We are to look for a better country. We should invest the utmost and the best we have in the new earth, asking for no rewards here but only to belong to Him, to serve Him with all our hearts and lives. God will do the right thing. Let us venture to live our lives and fashion our conduct in this world as did the Man of Galilee, loving everyone in it to the end that we will join company with all those who look for new heavens and a new earth, wherein dwells righteousness.

# KNOWING AND DOING

*If any man will do his will, he shall know of the doctrine, whether it be of God, or whether I speak of myself. John 7:17.*

The only way personally to know with certainty the truth of God's Word requires our willingness to do His will. When confronted with the claims of Christ we must be willing to surrender to those claims. Then we experience the reality and the certainty of what the Bible teaches as truth. To have an enlightened mind, we must bring our whole life to the light. Not to do so means we will remain in darkness regardless of how much religious information we may have. "If ye know these things, happy are ye if ye do them" (John 13:17).

This text does not say, "Happy are ye if ye know them intellectually." Knowledge without deeds and practice is worth nothing. We need both. Do you want to know the truth? Then walk in it. What makes people turn from the truth is not lack of information, but lack of willingness to do God's will and to obey His Word.

We may memorize the books of the Bible, and still it may profit us nothing. We may gather knowledge about all the great men of the Bible. We may count the number of verses in every chapter, and it will get us nowhere. We must set our minds and hearts to obey God. We must bring an attitude of willingness to do God's will. With diligence and sincerity we must ask the question "Lord, what will you have me to do?" God is not giving us theological lectures in the Bible. He is giving Himself. He is revealing His will and purpose for our lives. He is inviting us to walk the narrow way with Him.

The Christian faith is a very practical thing. God speaks to us in His Word. We must come to hear God speak. It is open for our understanding, acceptance, and obedience. The Word of God changes our lives. Nothing is to shake our faith.

If we read the Bible as a mere form we shall find many other books more entertaining. If we read it simply for information we may find other books more instructive. But if we read it to know and to do God's will we will hear God's voice. Every page will be a lantern to our feet and a light to our path.

# CONFESS CHRIST

*Whosoever therefore shall confess me before men, him will I confess also before my Father which is in heaven.* **Matt. 10:32.**

This verse is part of Christ's counsel to His disciples by way of encouragement in face of persecutions they will be called upon to endure. The confession involves our coming out as Christ's followers under all circumstances and in face of all hazards. It includes every kind of confession involving the whole course of one's life.

We are not to let other men influence us to the contrary, not even members of our own household. To please men rather than God is to submit to a multitude of lords, all sinful, weak mortals. It is a small thing to be judged by man's judgment in comparison with the judgment Christ will render before His Father in heaven. Let us not fear the opposition of those who are aroused by the Christian stand we take. If we are going to triumph with the truth, we can find no better time than now. Many a Christian young man drafted into the Army has been called upon to stand alone, to suffer ridicule and disdain, even court martial, because of his firm position of obedience to the Commandments.

Let us not become apologetic about what we believe. The Christian faith is not a frail thing. We are to enter courageously into a personal witness to Christ, to do it with the firm belief that there are those who listen to us who will take us seriously and desire to know the truth. It is not as difficult or as unacceptable to others as we sometimes think. Let us not make our religion an exclusive thing, but the guiding and the main thing in life. Increasingly we are to set Christ before us. "In all thy ways acknowledge him."

When Christ has become an experience we are bound to let others know it one way or another. This cannot be kept secret. The more we are partakers of Christ's righteousness, purity, integrity, beauty of character, the more we are enabled to witness to it. What a crucial issue it is—whether Jesus will confess or deny us before the Father and before the angels in heaven!

# "UNTO US A SON IS GIVEN"

*For unto us a child is born, unto us a son is given . . . and his name shall be called Wonderful, Counsellor, The mighty God, The everlasting Father, The Prince of Peace. Isa. 9:6.*

Every Christmas there comes to us down through the corridors of time, the news that a Child is born unto us that is the Son of God. Bethlehem is the watershed of history. Two thousand years ago God invaded this world in human form: lived, walked, talked with men. This priceless gift is "Emmanuel . . . God with us," in all of life; in trials, temptations, and disappointments. We are not alone. God has thrust into our lives a divine presence so glorious and powerful that no sin can hold us, no fear can destroy us, no unhappiness can possess us.

Happy are we if we can boast that the Son of God has come into our lives. Humble and grateful in ourselves, we are conscious of divine royalty in Him at whose feet we lay our lives. Happy are we when we can boast of our Lord and Saviour Jesus Christ, proud of His righteousness and His love.

Happy are we when we can glory in His church because we belong to a band of Christian disciples whose hearts God has captured; that by the indwelling Spirit we reflect so much of the likeness of the Son of God. Happy are we because of the priceless value God has placed upon us. What indescribable grandeur for eternity is offered to us, that we should be made the sons of God. Happy are we because the Son of God will soon return, eternally to be God with us; no longer a babe, but King of kings and Lord of lords. What glory is already ours!

Illustrious Christians shine without egotism, and the humble serve without shame. All eternal values are gifts to us from God. Our cup is full. We envy no Christian for the size of his cup that overflows with love in the fellowship of God. Christ has made us alive to beauty and to righteousness beyond our utmost expectation.

We are well born when twice born—that change of nature which purges us from selfishness into a life of love and purity, excelling in eternal life with Christ. Christmas is no burning out like light bulbs on a tree, but joy in the coming of our Lord that marches on forever.

## "NOW IS THE JUDGMENT"—1

*Now is the judgment of this world: now shall the prince of this world be cast out. John 12:31.*

This chapter tells of the Greeks who came and asked to see Jesus. They desired a private interview. Christ told them of His mission to the world, that His hour had come. This was the crisis of the world. One main idea dominates the discussion: death is the inescapable condition of life.

The cross is both the salvation and the judgment of the world. "Father, glorify thy name. Then came there a voice from heaven. . . . The people therefore, that stood by, and heard it, said that it thundered: others said, An angel spake to him. Jesus answered and said, This voice came not because of me, but for your sakes. Now is the judgment" (John 12:28-31).

God's voice from heaven made clear that Christ's death involved the whole world. Christ saw in the coming of the Greeks, and His being lifted up on the cross, the destiny of all men.

The cross of Christ puts us all on trial, not to condemn, but to provide us with the one crucial choice for life or death. We are confronted with the full revelation of God's love for us. God is made visible to our eyes, calling on us to be reconciled to Him. If we turn from the uplifted Christ, what more can God do for us? By what means now can we be persuaded, convinced, won over, and saved?

When confronted with a decisive choice like this, there is no place else to go. "For we must all appear before the judgment seat of Christ" (2 Cor. 5:10). What we think of Christ and our relationship to Him is all-important.

If we acknowledge Him, then the judgment will be in our favor. But if we merely tolerate Him, admire Him as simply a good man, then we are self-judged. If we are not right with Christ, then nothing can be right. If we refuse Christ as Lord, then Satan is our master.

Christ's life and death is the most divine act ever done in our world. How foolish to live as though Christ is not our Saviour, Lord, and Judge! It is terribly important that we make it possible for Christ to be on our side in the final judgment. We decide that here and now.

# "NOW IS THE JUDGMENT"—2

*And this is the condemnation, that light is come into the world, and men loved darkness rather than light.* John 3:19.

God Himself will finally agree with the judgment we make in our confrontation with Jesus. The importance of this cannot be overstressed. Judas Iscariot did not really sell Christ for thirty pieces of silver. He sold himself. The price he set on himself was thirty pieces of silver. In His ultimate judgment, God will agree with the value Judas put on himself.

Never let it be said that God is harsh in His judgments, that He has kept us out of heaven. When Christ met Zacchaeus the crucial moment of the publican's life had come. He knew he was a crook, that he ought not to take money dishonestly, that he ought to set things straight. He must either accept Christ and all He stood for or he must go on selling his soul for money. He chose Christ. God in the final judgment will agree with the choice he made.

Light has been presented on cigarette smoking linking it with cancer. Multitudes of people continue smoking. For those who die of lung cancer, it is preposterous to believe that the revelation causes the penalty of death. People pass judgment on themselves. The laws of health and life corroborate the death sentence.

Men who declare they will not have Jesus Christ to rule over them will find themselves exactly in this situation. One grows a little weary of people who want to talk and smile destiny away, regardless of how they live. Christ was no Pollyanna Saviour, lightly talking away the seriousness of making the right choice.

It matters little what kind of excuse a man wants to make. He can argue that he has been led into the pursuit of wealth and self-indulgence by others. He may tell himself that other people turned him off, that his responsibilities were so great and so all-engaging that he never had any time for Christ. Nevertheless, whatever our choice is, whatever the pattern set, God will agree with it in the judgment. He will not call hate love, dishonesty honesty, disobedience obedience. Whatever category our lives fit into, Christ will agree with it. Now is the time of our visitation.

# SOWING AND REAPING

*Be not deceived; God is not mocked: for whatsoever a man soweth, that shall he also reap. Gal. 6:7.*

Christ came to destroy the works of the devil and defeated him. We are indeed redeemed. Satan no longer has the right to be our master.

Is it too late for you? It is never too late. Every coming of Christ to you, every conviction from the Holy Spirit, is the crucial moment for decision. In Christ we have a guarantee of the expulsion of sin, the enthronement of love and righteousness. It is all there. God has given us everything.

As we hunger and thirst after righteousness here, in the earth made new Christ will satisfy us with just that. If we love the truth of God, in the new earth God will provide for us to live by it for all eternity. People may live now like the apostle Paul or like the emperor Nero; they will be judged accordingly. There will be a different judgment and destiny for the apostle John, who was Jesus' friend, than for Judas Iscariot, who was His betrayer. This very separation is in harmony with the choices these men have made.

All men will reap what they have sown. Christ's compassion does not propose a different standard of conduct for believers and unbelievers. The lifting up of Christ does not reduce the moral order to an anarchy of so-called love, where, regardless of how men live, God will pass it by.

By the revelation of the character of God in Christ, God will have the right to destroy sin and rebellious sinners and save those who have chosen redemption by Him. We ought to acclimatize our minds and lives to the need for making the right decisions and for our own personal responsibility in light of what Christ has done. Every hour bears witness to what we are.

Who will rescue us at last from the wages of sin and eternal death? We are sure that Christ will. Who at last will establish righteousness in the earth for all the universe to see and understand? Who but Jesus Christ? Who but the one who carried a cross, who prayed for His enemies, and who will create a new earth wherein dwells righteousness? Who but Christ will stand up for us and proclaim us eternally secure?

# ALL THE TIME IN THE WORLD

*As for man, his days are as grass. . . . But the mercy of the Lord is from everlasting to everlasting.* Ps. 103:15-17.

So little time—yet time to wait upon the Lord and renew our strength. So little time, but enough to live courageously for Christ. So little time, but enough to sit at the feet of truth. So little time, but enough to keep company with the mighty men of God in the Bible. So little time, but enough to know Jesus Christ. So little time, but enough to prepare ourselves for eternity.

How do we measure time? The psalmist said that the days of our age are "three score years and ten." That can be a liberal estimate. Suppose you live until you are 70. At that rate you who are 20 years of age have 18,250 days left; you of 25 have 16,425; you of 30, 14,600 days. You of 40, 10,950 days. That is your capital to which you cannot add. It draws no interest. You live on the principal. If you had $20,000 you might think it a goodly sum, but if you could add nothing to it and must live on the principal, it would not last long.

"Rejoice, O young man, in thy youth . . . but know thou, that for all these things God will bring thee into judgment" (Eccl. 11:9). Youth is the foundation of manhood. It will never come back to us. We can never be in this world what we might have been if we have wasted our youthful energy.

God's purpose for every young man and woman is to "rejoice in thy youth." To be able to do this you need, first, a healthy body. One of the great blessings God gives us is health and the way to keep it. Whatever helps to make you clean in body, temperate in habits, orderly in life, rejoice in it.

The second essential is a happy home. When Christian love and goodness prevail in the home, every member is strengthened to face the battles and temptations he meets in the world outside. One does not easily betray the love found in a Christian home. The third essential is a heart right with God, trusting in His merits, sanctified by His grace, fulfilled by His love.

We all have time enough for these things. Rejoice in the work of God. Rejoice that we live for Christ and our fellow men. Rejoice in the truth that makes us free. Rejoice in the love of Christ, in the love of all others who bear His image.

# SO LITTLE TIME

*Remember now thy Creator in the days of thy youth.* **Eccl. 12:1.**

I learned recently of a film strip, the first picture of which showed a small boy playing with a sailboat and a train. The caption read, "Too small to think about God." Next picture: the boy is larger now, and engaged in sports. Caption: "Too occupied to think about God." Next picture: He is still a young man making his way in the world. Caption: "Too self-sufficient to think about God." Next picture: with his arm about his girl friend he is "too happy to think about God." Later, with the responsibilities of home and family, he is "too busy to think about God." We catch a glimpse of him in bed, "Too tired to think about God." Then as an executive with many responsibilities, he is "too worried to think about God." Worn out with age and work he has become "too old to think about God." Written on his grave marker, standing among the weeds that almost hide it: "Too late to think about God."

All time belongs to God. We have time only as a stewardship. God may require an accounting of us at any moment. People say they can do what they want with their own time. They forget that the sequel to life is God's.

We keep the seventh-day Sabbath according to the commandment. It is the Lord's day. God is the Lord of time as He is the Lord of the Sabbath. The same is true with the wealth we have. Neither exists outside of God. We give up both when we die. We have time enough to spend it with God. We have money enough to spend it for God. God has given us so much time and so much money.

Each Sabbath we meet to worship God. Thereby we say, "Thank You, Lord, for time to worship You." We are resolved to have Christ as the Lord of all the time we have. We want no time apart from Him. To keep the Sabbath means that we have no desire to do with our time anything we want. Eternity with God is just ahead. Only then will time maintain its eternal youth and freshness.

Time without God makes a difference. It offers no future of an eternal Sabbath with God. To deny that time belongs to God is to reject His purpose for our lives. We are to redeem the time, to live responsibly to God.

# NUMBERING OUR DAYS

*So teach us to number our days, that we may apply our hearts unto wisdom.* **Ps. 90:12.**

One of the great questions of life is concerned with the race against the calendar and the passing years. The year comes to a close, and it has passed like a breeze.

A young man once said to me after deciding against Christ in favor of the world, "Look, I have lots of time. I want my fill of the world and its pleasures. I will think about being a Christian later in life." But it is not that simple. This habit of not making up our minds is disastrous. We may not make up our minds, but we cannot stop making up our lives. Not to decide is to decide. Every time we make a decision our life is made up one way or another.

We are creatures of time. We cannot call the years back and begin over again. We can turn the clock back, but not our birthdays. What looks like plenty of time is only an illusion. There is only one time for crucial decisions: Now. Recently a newspaper employed a young reporter. Before long he received his first big assignment to write a news story of prime importance. The young man could hardly write fast enough, he was so excited. The editor, seeing his concern, came over to him and said: "Take your time, son, you still have two minutes." Now is the day of salvation. Take your time, son, you still have two minutes.

The pressing question remains as to how best we may number our days and our decisions. Only as we experience divine forgiveness and cleansing of the sin that destroys the soul; only as we experience the working in us of His might, the indwelling of the Holy Spirit; only as Christ pilots our lives into the years beyond, in fellowship with Him who is our constant refuge and delight, lies the secret of life.

The idea that survival is all that counts—enough food to live on, a little plot of land far away from the agonies of men, and a running stream—is unrealistic. That kind of role for Adventists is played out. Jesus Christ is directing our world and our lives. Our job is to keep in step with Him with all the time we have.